# JOURNAL FOR THE STUDY OF THE OLD TESTAMENT SUPPLEMENT SERIES
## 304

Sheffield Academic Press

# Zemah and Zerubbabel

## Messianic Expectations in the Early Postexilic Period

## Wolter H. Rose

Journal for the Study of the Old Testament
Supplement Series 304

To my parents
Henk Rose
and
Siny Rose (née Borger)

Copyright © 2000 Sheffield Academic Press

Published by Sheffield Academic Press Ltd
Mansion House
19 Kingfield Road
Sheffield S11 9AS
England

Typeset by Sheffield Academic Press
and
Printed on acid-free paper in Great Britain
by Bookcraft Ltd
Midsomer Norton, Bath

British Library Cataloguing in Publication Data

A catalogue record for this book is available
from the British Library

ISBN 1-84127-074-1

# CONTENTS

ACKNOWLEDGMENTS

This volume is a revision of a DPhil thesis completed in 1997 at Oxford University, under the supervision of Professor H.G.M. Williamson. It was a great privilege to work under his supervision, and for whatever is good in this work I am much indebted to him for his knowledge, encouragement and criticism.

I realise that the case I argue in this book constitutes in many ways a radical departure from the established interpretation of the passages under discussion. However, I am convinced that a combination of grammatical, semantic and literary-critical considerations clearly points in this direction.

I want to thank the following bodies for their generous financial support: Stichting Afbouw, Kampen; Erica de Blocq Weduwe van Franckenaleen, Leeuwarden; Stichting Dr Hendrik Muller's Vaderlandsch Fonds, 's-Gravenhage; and Pusey & Ellerton Fund, Oxford. The Theology Faculty of Oxford awarded me a Denyer and Johnson Studentship 1994–95. The most substantial donation to help cover the costs of nine terms in Oxford was made by someone who preferred to stay anonymous.

I want to thank the staff of the following libraries for their help. In Oxford, the Ashmolean Library, Bodleian Library, Oriental Institute, Theology Faculty. In the Netherlands, the Theologische Universiteit van de Gereformeerde Kerken in Nederland, Broederweg, Kampen; Theologische Universiteit van de Gereformeerde Kerken in Nederland, Oudestraat, Kampen; Rijksuniversiteit, Leiden. Tyndale House, Cambridge, with its excellent facilities provided a stimulating atmosphere to work on the final stages of the thesis and on this revision.

My years in Oxford have been very happy, thanks to the friendship and love of so many people. They are too many to mention here. I hope they will not be offended if I mention just a few names: Iain and Barbara Duguid and all the people at Redeemer Presbyterian Church, and Michael Pollitt and all the friends at Commonwealth House. Many thanks!

I pay tribute to Guus Borger, whom I consider my respected friend and academic mentor and much more. His coaching skills, friendship, keen interest and the many conversations we have had over the last ten years have proved to be an invaluable source of challenge and direction.

The book is dedicated to my parents, in grateful appreciation of raising me in a Christian home, and unwaveringly supporting me through my long years of study. They have looked forward to seeing this book finished as much as I have.

Most of all I delight in thanking God. With the apostle Paul I say, τί δὲ ἔχεις ὃ οὐκ ἔλαβες.

And with David I say:

תודיעני ארח חיים שֹבע שֹמחות את־פניך נעמות בימינך נצח

Wolter Rose
Theologische Universiteit van de Gereformeerde Kerken in Nederland
Broederweg, Kampen

2000

# ABBREVIATIONS

| | |
|---|---|
| AB | Anchor Bible |
| *ABD* | David Noel Freedman (ed.), *The Anchor Bible Dictionary* (New York: Doubleday, 1992) |
| ABL | R.F. Harper (ed.), *Assyrian and Babylonian Letters* (Chicago: The University of Chicago Press, 1892–1914) |
| *AfO* | *Archiv für Orientforschung* |
| AGJU | Arbeiten zur Geschichte des antiken Judentums und des Urchristentums |
| AHW | Wolfram von soden, *Akkadisches Handwörterbuch* (Wiesbaden: Otto Harassowitz, 1965–1981) |
| ALASP | Abhandlungen zur Literatur Alt-Syrien-Palästinas |
| *ANET* | James B. Pritchard (ed.), *Ancient Near Eastern Texts Relating to the Old Testament* (Princeton: Princeton University Press, 3rd edn, with supplement, 1969) |
| AOAT | Alter Orient und Altes Testament |
| AOS | American Oriental Series |
| *ARAB* | Daniel David Luckenbill (ed.), *Ancient Records of Assyria and Babylonia* (Chicago: University of Chicago Press, 1927) |
| *AS* | *Anatolian Studies. Journal of the British Institute of Archaeology at Ankara* |
| ASOR | American Schools of Oriental Research |
| ASORDS | ASOR Dissertation Series |
| AT | Arbeiten zur Theologie |
| ATANT | Abhandlungen zur Theologie des Alten und Neuen Testaments |
| ATD | Alte Testament Deutsch |
| ATSAT | Arbeiten zu Text und Sprache im Alten Testament |
| *AuOr* | *Aula orientalis* |
| AuOrSup | *AuOr*, Supplementa |
| *AUSS* | *Andrews University Seminary Studies* |
| *BA* | *Biblical Archaeologist* |
| *BBR* | *Bulletin for Biblical Research* |
| BDB | Francis Brown, S.R. Driver and Charles A. Briggs, *A Hebrew and English Lexicon of the Old Testament* (Oxford: Clarendon Press, 1907) |

| | |
|---|---|
| BEATAJ | Beiträge zur Erforschung des Alten Testaments und des Antiken Judentums |
| BETL | Bibliotheca ephemeridum theologicarum lovaniensium |
| *BHS* | *Biblia hebraica stuttgartensia* |
| BHT | Beiträge zur historischen Theologie |
| *Bib* | *Biblica* |
| BibOr | Biblica et orientalia |
| *BibRes* | *Biblical Research* |
| BJS | Biblical and Judaic Studies from the University of California, San Diego |
| BKAT | Biblischer Kommentar: Altes Testament |
| BL | Hans Bauer and Pontus Leander, *Historische Grammatik der hebräischen Sprache des Alten Testamentes* (Halle: Max Niemeyer, 1922) |
| BLA | Hans Bauer and Pontus Leander, *Grammatik des Biblisch-Aramaeischen* (Halle: Max Niemeyer, 1927) |
| *BN* | *Biblische Notizen* |
| *BRL²* | Kurt Galling, *Biblisches Reallexikon* (HAT; Reihe 1.1; Tübingen: Mohr, 2nd edn, 1977) |
| BS | Biblische Studien |
| BTS | Beiruter Texte und Studien |
| BWANT | Beiträge zur Wissenschaft vom Alten und Neuen Testament |
| *BZ* | *Biblische Zeitschrift* |
| BZAW | Beihefte zur *ZAW* |
| *CAD* | Ignace I. Gelb *et al.* (eds.), *The Assyrian Dictionary of the Oriental Institute of the University of Chicago* (Chicago: Oriental Institute, 1964–) |
| CAH | Cambridge Ancient History |
| CAT | Commentaire de l'Ancient Testament |
| CB | Century Bible |
| CBC | Cambridge Bible Commentary |
| *CBQ* | *Catholic Biblical Quarterly* |
| CBQMS | *CBQ*, Monograph Series |
| CBSC | Cambridge Bible for Schools & Colleges |
| CJAS | Christianity and Judaism in Antiquity Series |
| ConBOT | Coniectanea biblica, Old Testament |
| COT | Commentaar op het Oude Testament |
| *CR:BS* | *Currents in Research: Biblical Studies* |
| CTA | A. Herdner (ed.), *Corpus des tablettes en cunéiformes alphabétiques découvertes à Ras Shamra–Ugarit de 1929 à 1939* (Paris: Imprimerie nationale Geuthner, 1963) |
| DB | Darius's Bisitun Inscription |
| *DCH* | David J.A. Clines (ed.), *Dictionary of Classical Hebrew*. (Sheffield: Sheffield Academic Press, 1993–) |

| | |
|---|---|
| *DCPP* | *Dictionnaire de la civilisation Phénicienne et Punique* (Turnhout: Brepols, 1992) |
| *DBSup* | *Dictionnaire de la Bible Supplément* |
| *DNWSI* | Jacob Hoftijzer and Karel Jongeling, *Dictionary of the North-West Semitic Inscriptions* (HdO; I, 21; Leiden: E.J. Brill, 1995) |
| DSB | Daily Study Bible |
| EBib | Etudes bibliques |
| *EI* | *Eretz Israel* |
| *EstBíb* | *Estudios bíblicos* |
| *ETL* | *Ephemerides theologicae lovanienses* |
| EÜ | Einheitsübersetzung |
| *ExpTim* | *Expository Times* |
| FRLANT | Forschungen zur Religion und Literatur des Alten und Neuen Testaments |
| FTS | Freiburger theologische Studien |
| GB | Wilhelm Gesenius' *Hebräisches und aramäisches Handwörterbuch über das Alte Testament* (H. Zimmern, W. Max Mueller, O.Weber and Frants Buhl; Leipzig: Vogel, 17th edn, 1921) |
| GKB | Wilhelm Gesenius, E. Kautzsch and Gotthelf Bergsträsser, *Hebräische Grammatik* (Hildesheim: G. Olms, 28th edn, 1962); ET *Gesenius' Hebrew Grammar* (ed. E. Kautzch, revised and trans. A.E. Cowley; Oxford: Clarendon Press, 2nd edn, 1910) |
| HA | Handbuch der Altertumswissenschaft |
| *HAH* | Wilhelm Gesenius, *Hebräisches und aramäisches Handwörterbuch über das Alte Testament* (Heidelberg: Springer, 18th edn, 1987–) |
| *HALAT* | Ludwig Koehler *et al.* (eds.), *Hebräisches und aramäisches Lexikon zum Alten Testament* (5 vols.; Leiden: E.J. Brill, 1967-1995) |
| HAT | Handbuch zum Alten Testament |
| HdO | Handbuch der Orientalistik |
| *HeyJ* | *Heythrop Journal* |
| HKAT | Handkommentar zum Alten Testament |
| HSAO | Heidelberger Studien zum Alten Orient |
| HSAT | Heilige Schrift des Alten Testaments |
| HSM | Harvard Semitic Monographs |
| HSS | Harvard Semitic Series |
| *HUCA* | *Hebrew Union College Annual* |
| ICC | International Critical Commentary |
| *IEJ* | *Israel Exploration Journal* |
| *IR* | *Iliff Review* |
| *JAOS* | *Journal of the American Oriental Society* |

| | |
|---|---|
| JB | *Jerusalem Bible* |
| *JBL* | *Journal of Biblical Literature* |
| JBTh | Jahrbuch für Biblische Theologie |
| *JEA* | *Journal of Egyptian Archaeology* |
| *JETS* | *Journal of the Evangelical Theological Society* |
| *JJS* | *Journal of Jewish Studies* |
| *JNES* | *Journal of Near Eastern Studies* |
| *JNSL* | *Journal of Northwest Semitic Languages* |
| *JSOT* | *Journal for the Study of the Old Testament* |
| JSOTSup | *JSOT*, Supplement Series |
| *JSS* | *Journal of Semitic Studies* |
| JSSMS | *JSS*, Monograph Series |
| JSSSup | *JSS*, Supplement Series |
| KAI | the number of a text in the edition of *KAI* |
| *KAI* | H. Donner and W. Röllig, *Kanaanäische und aramäische Inschriften* (3 vols.; Wiesbaden: Harrassowitz, 1962–64) |
| KAT | Kommentar zum Alten Testament |
| KEHAT | Kurzgefasstes exegetisches Handbuch zum Alten Testament |
| KHAT | Kurzer Hand-Kommentar zum Alten Testament |
| KTU | the number of a text in the edition of *KTU*; unless indicated otherwise, reference is made to the second edition (*KTU/CAT*) |
| *KTU* | Manfried Dietrich, Oswald Loretz and Joaquín Sanmartín, *Die keilalphabetischen Texte aus Ugarit; Einschliesslich der keilalphabetischen Texte ausserhalb Ugarits* (AOAT, 24; Kevelaer: Butzon & Bercker; Neukirchen–Vluyn: Neukirchener Verlag, 1976) |
| *KTU/CAT* | Manfried Dietrich, Oswald Loretz and Joaquín Sanmartín, *The Cuneiform Alphabetic Texts from Ugarit, Ras Ibn Hani and Other Places* (*KTU*; second, enlarged edition; Münster: Ugarit-Verlag, 1995) |
| KV | Korte Verklaring der Heilige Schrift |
| *Leš* | *Lešonénu* |
| LH | *Lexicon hebraicum Veteris Testamenti* (quod aliis collaborantibus ed. Franciscus Zorell [ad finem perduxit Ludovicus Semkowski; ind. addidit Petrus Boccaccio]; Rome: Pontifico Instituto Biblico, 1940–1984) |
| LOS | London Oriental Series |
| LSJ | H.G. Liddell, Robert Scott and H. Stuart Jones, *Greek– English Lexicon* (Oxford: Clarendon Press, 9th edn, 1968) |
| MT | Masoretic Text |
| *NAWG* | *Nachrichten der Akademie der Wissenschaften in Göttingen* |
| NCB | New Century Bible |
| NEB | New English Bible |
| NICOT | New International Commentary on the Old Testament |

| | |
|---|---|
| NJPS | *Tanakh: The Holy Scriptures. The New JPS Translation According to the Traditional Hebrew Text* (Philadelphia: Jewish Publication Society of America, 1988) |
| OBO | Orbis biblicus et orientalis |
| *OED* | *Oxford English Dictionary* |
| OPNE | Occasional Papers on the Near East |
| OTG | Old Testament Guides |
| OTL | Old Testament Library |
| *OTS* | *Oudtestamentische Studiën* |
| POT | Prediking van het Oude Testament |
| PN | personal name |
| *PTR* | *Princeton Theological Review* |
| *RA* | *Revue d'assyriologie et d'archéologie orientale* |
| *RAO* | *Recueil d'archéologie orientale* |
| *RB* | *Revue biblique* |
| REB | Revised English Bible |
| *RHPR* | *Revue d'histoire et de philosophie religieuse* |
| *RLA* | *Reallexikon der Assyriologie und Vorderasiatischen Archäologie* |
| RSV | Revised Standard Version |
| SAA | State Archives of Assyria |
| SB | Sources bibliques |
| SBA | Stuttgarter Biblische Aufsatzbände |
| SBL | Society for Biblical Literature |
| SBLDS | SBL Dissertation Series |
| SBLEJL | SBL Early Judaism and its Literature |
| SBLSCS | SBL Septuagint and Cognate Studies |
| SBLMS | SBL Monograph Series |
| SBS | Stuttgarter Bibelstudien |
| *SEÅ* | *Svensk exegetisk årsbok* |
| *SEL* | *Studii epigrafici e linguistici* |
| SH | Scripta Hierosolymitana |
| SJLA | Studies in Judaism in Late Antiquity |
| SP | Studia Phoenicia |
| SSN | Studia Semitica Neerlandica |
| SSS | Semitic Study Series |
| STDJ | Studies on the Texts of the Desert of Judah |
| *TG* | *Tijdschrift voor Geschiedenis* |
| *THAT* | Ernst Jenni and Claus Westermann (eds.), *Theologisches Handwörterbuch zum Alten Testament* (Munich: Chr. Kaiserer Verlag, 1971–76) |
| *TLZ* | *Theologische Literaturzeitung* |
| TOB | Traduction oecuménique de la Bible |
| TOTC | Tyndale Old Testament Commentaries |
| *TQ* | *Theologische Quartalschrift* |

| | |
|---|---|
| *Trans* | *Transeuphratène: Etudes sur la Syrie-Palestine et Chypre à l'epoque Perse* |
| *TSK* | *Theologische Studien und Kritiken* |
| TTS | Trierer Theologische Studien |
| *TUAT* | *Texte aus der Umwelt des Alten Testaments* |
| *TynBul* | *Tyndale Bulletin* |
| *ThWAT* | G.J. Botterweck and H. Ringgren (eds.), *Theologisches Handwörterbuch zum Alten Testament* (Stuttgart: W. Kohlhammer, 1970–) |
| *TZ* | *Theologische Zeitschrift* |
| UB | L'universe de la Bible (Turnhout: Brepols, 1984) |
| *UF* | *Ugarit-Forschungen* |
| *USQR* | *Union Seminary Quarterly Review* |
| UT | Urban-Taschenbücher |
| *VT* | *Vetus Testamentum* |
| VTSup | *VT*, Supplements |
| *VuF* | *Verkündigung und Forschung* |
| WBC | Word Biblical Commentary |
| WMANT | Wissenschaftliche Monographien zum Alten und Neuen Testament |
| *ZA* | *Zeitschrift für Assyriologie* |
| *ZAW* | *Zeitschrift für die alttestamentliche Wissenschaft* |
| ZBAT | Zürcher Bibelkommentare Alte Testament |
| *ZDMG* | *Zeitschrift der deutschen morgenländischen Gesellschaft* |
| *ZDPV* | *Zeitschrift des deutschen Palästina-Vereins* |
| *ZKT* | *Zeitschrift für katholische Theologie* |

## Chapter 1

## INTRODUCTION—NO KING IN YEHUD

The first two decades of the sixth century BCE saw the final collapse of the nation-state of Judah. The kingdom lost its independent political status, the territory was incorporated into the Babylonian empire, the capital Jerusalem and the temple of YHWH in it were destroyed, and the king was one of the many to be deported to Babylon.

Things were never the same again, not even when in the second half of that same century the empire which had brought their ruin was now taken over by another empire, run by the Persians, who gave permission for deported people to return to their home countries. A number of people deported from Judah, but not all, returned in stages to the territory which in the past had enjoyed political independence but now was a small province (for which I will use the name 'Yehud'[1]) of the immense Persian empire. Funded by the Persian government, they made a start (or maybe two) with the rebuilding of the temple.

On the impact of these changes, Mason writes:[2]

> It is difficult to exaggerate the profundity and far-reaching consequences of the change from a pre-exilic Yahwism which was the mortar binding the nation-state, so inextricably bound up with the Davidic dynasty and the city of Jerusalem, to a post-exilic religion of a small, non-monarchic and remote province of a foreign world empire. Questions of continuity, identity and authenticity must have been immense.

Chief among such 'questions of continuity, identity and authenticity'

---

1. Yehud was the Aramaic name of the territory known as Judah (then a kingdom) before the exile, as the name *yhwd* in passages in Ezra (5.1, 7; 7.14) and Daniel (2.25; 5.13; 6.14) and on seals dating to the Persian period indicates.

2. R. Mason, *Preaching the Tradition: Homily and Hermeneutics after the Exile Based on the 'Addresses' in Chronicles, the Speeches in the Books of Ezra and Nehemiah and the Postexilic Prophetic Books* (Cambridge: Cambridge University Press, 1990), p. 131.

would have been those dealing with what McConville has called the
'three pillars' of the worldview of the people of Judah: the king, the
temple and the land:[3]

> In 587 BCE the heart of the belief system of Judah was taken out. If a
> Judahite had been asked, in the time of Josiah, what were the main pil-
> lars of his or her faith (or of the covenant), he or she would have iden-
> tified three things: the king, the temple and the land... For the Judahite,
> these three things quite simply represented the substance of the people's
> relationship with Yahweh...
>
> But now these three pillars had fallen. The Davidic dynasty was
> brought once and for all to an end. The temple lay in ruins. And the
> majority, or at least the élite, of the people had been removed by force
> from their land. It is hard to think of a greater trauma for a people.

## 1. *What the Book Is About*

In this book I will deal with questions related to the 'pillar' of kingship.
The main interest of this book will be with what happened to the 'pillar'
of kingship after the first waves of exiles had returned to Yehud. Of the
two prophets active in this early postexilic period, at least one uses
language that relates unmistakably to this issue. This prophet, Zechariah, introduces a person about whom he states that he 'shall bear royal
honour, and shall sit and rule upon his throne' (Zech. 6.13). In the
Hebrew text the name of this person is צמח. This name is usually translated 'Branch'. For reasons which I will discuss later, I will use a transcription of this name, Zemah,[4] rather than a translation, which is the
usual practice in studies of these matters. This figure Zemah will be the
main focus of this study. A great number of scholars believe that the
other of the two prophets, Haggai, also deals with the issue of kingship
when he delivers an oracle in which YHWH says about Zerubbabel, the
governor of Yehud: 'I will take you, O Zerubbabel my servant, the son
of Shealtiel, says the LORD, and make you like a signet ring; for I have
chosen you' (Hag. 2.23).

---

3.    G. McConville, *Old Testament* (Teach Yourself Books—World Faiths; London: Hodder & Stoughton, 1996), pp. 57-58. Perhaps McConville is a bit optimistic
about the belief system of the average Judahite, but the points he mentions were
certainly true for the devoted worshipers of YHWH.

4.    This is my attempt to reconstruct how an English language translation of the
Bible would have transcribed Hebrew צמח. A more precise transcription would be
*Ṣemaḥ*.

a. *Survey*

The identification of the figure called 'Zemah' and the precise nature of the expectations of Haggai and Zechariah with respect to either a restoration of the monarchy or the coming of an eschatological messianic figure are issues on which scholars have come to opposing conclusions.

*Zemah to Be Identified with Zerubbabel.* A great number of scholars believe that Zechariah identified Zemah with Zerubbabel, the governor of Yehud, and that he expected a restoration of the monarchy (I will call this the ZZ view). According to this view, Haggai's expectations with respect to the restoration of the monarchy would have been similar to those of Zechariah. In a brief survey (not intended to be exhaustive), I will mention a selection of representatives of this view.

(1) In his study *He that Cometh* Mowinckel rejects 'the common interpretation that Haggai and Zechariah virtually lay on Zerubbabel's shoulders the mantle prepared for the Messiah, and announce, "Now Messiah has come"'. He interprets the prophecies of Haggai and Zechariah concerning Zerubbabel as saying in effect, 'In this man the house of David will be restored in its ancient glory. Once again we shall have a king who will fulfil the ancient ideal of kingship'. These prophets 'regard the new historical situation as its restoration by Yahweh, and as already in process of being realized. The new ideal king of the ancient line is already present'.[5]

In 1972, the German scholar Beyse published his monograph *Serubbabel und die Königserwartungen der Propheten Haggai und Sacharja* ('Zerubbabel and the Royal Expectations of the Prophets Haggai and Zechariah'). As the title indicates (but note the word *Königserwartungen*), the subject of this monograph is close to the one of this book. The questions which Beyse wants to investigate are how after a complete collapse of the Jewish state both Haggai and Zechariah were able to present Zerubbabel as the future king, and what came of their expectations.[6] That these two prophets presented Zerubbabel as a king is not the conclusion of the book, but its assumption, for example 'It

---

5. S. Mowinckel, *He that Cometh* (trans. G.W. Anderson; Oxford: Basil Blackwell, 1956), pp. 119-120; cf. pp. 19-20.

6. K.-M. Beyse, *Serubbabel und die Königserwartungen der Propheten Haggai und Sacharja: Eine historische und traditionsgeschichtliche Untersuchung* (AT 1.48; Stuttgart: Calwer Verlag, 1972), pp. 9-10.

should be kept in mind once again, that Haggai and Zechariah—each in his own way—saw in Zerubbabel the king for the imminent era of salvation, though they ascribed the bringing about of this future to Yahweh only'.[7]

Carroll in *When Prophecy Failed* notes that the two central elements in the prophecies of Haggai and Zechariah are 'a concern with the building of the temple and the support of Zerubbabel's claim to be the rightful occupant of the Davidic throne'. The two prophets 'obviously believed in Zerubbabel's royal status, his role in completing the building of the new temple and his designation as bearer of the prophetic title "branch"...he would occupy the royal throne'.[8]

In a recent essay, called 'The Old Testament's Contribution to Messianic Expectations', by Roberts, one finds this line of scholarship summarized in the following way. With respect to Haggai, Roberts writes about the oracle about Zerubbabel in Hag. 2.20-23, 'Given the context of God's promise to overturn other kingdoms, such an oracle clearly implied the elevation of Zerubbabel to the Davidic throne of his ancestors'.[9] On the צמח oracles in Zech. 3.8 and 6.12, he states that '[t]here can be little doubt that Zechariah identified Zerubbabel as the one who would restore the Davidic dynasty'.[10]

(2) The most radical forms of this theory were developed by Waterman and by Bickerman. Waterman adopts the phrase 'three messianic conspirators' to refer to the prophets Haggai and Zechariah and to Zerubbabel. The latter, in Waterman's view, became the victim of the political propaganda of the two prophets: '...two devoted prophets and a worthy governor of the royal line of David who unwittingly and solely because of inefficient means of communication were thus pilloried

---

7.    'Es verdient noch einmal festgehalten zu werden, daß Haggai und Sacharja tatsächlich—jeder in seiner Weise—in Serubbabel den König für die unmittelbar bevorstehende Heilszeit gesehen, aber das Heraufführen dieser Zukunft allein Jahwe zugeschrieben haben' (*Serubbabel*, p. 40; compare p. 37): in spite of voices to the contrary one has to maintain 'daß sich für Haggai in Serubbabel die davidische Dynastie fortsetzt und Serubbabel der erste königliche Herrscher in der von Jahwe herbeigeführten Heilszeit sein soll'.

8.    R.P. Carroll, *When Prophecy Failed* (London: SCM Press, 1979), pp. 159-164.

9.    J.J.M. Roberts, 'The Old Testament's Contribution to Messianic Expectations', in J.H. Charlesworth (ed.), *The Messiah: Developments in Earliest Judaism and Christianity* (Minneapolis: Fortress Press 1992), pp. 39-51 (49).

10.   Roberts, 'Messianic Expectations', p. 50.

before the larger world and liquidated as craven conspirators'.[11]

More recently, Bickerman has argued that Zerubbabel was sent to Jerusalem by Bardiya-Gaumata, a rival of Darius, during the eventful months in which Darius had to fight for his succession of Cambyses on the throne of the Persian empire, and that Zerubbabel was subsequently killed by Darius as a usurper.[12]

(3) A new element is added to the mainline view by a group of mainly Italian scholars,[13] who argue that Zerubbabel (like Sheshbazzar) was actually a vassal king of Judah under the Persians. In this scenario, the prophets Haggai and Zechariah when proclaiming that Zerubbabel would be king,[14] were not revolutionaries, but simply backing a vassal kingdom sponsored by the Persian government.

*Zemah a Future Figure.* A small number of scholars have objected to the ZZ identification and have argued that Zechariah did not mean to identify Zemah and Zerubbabel: Zemah should be identified with a future figure.[15] I will call this the FF view.

11. L. Waterman, 'The Camouflaged Purge of the Three Messianic Conspirators', *JNES* 13 (1954), pp. 73-78 (78); cf. A.T. Olmstead, *History of the Persian Empire* (Chicago: University of Chicago Press, 1959), pp. 138-39, 142. For another conspiracy view, see M. Smith, *Palestinian Parties and Politics that Shaped the Old Testament* (London: SCM Press, 2nd edn, 1987), pp. 87-88.

12. E.J. Bickerman, 'En marge de l'écriture. I. Le comput des annés de règne des Achéménides; II. La seconde année de Darius', *RB* 88 (1981), pp. 19-28 (27-28); reprinted in E.J. Bickerman, *Studies in Jewish and Christian History*, III (AGJU, 9; Leiden: E.J. Brill, 1986), pp. 335-36.

13. F. Bianchi, 'Le rôle de Zorobabel et de la dynastie davidique en Judée du VIe siècle au IIe siècle av. J.-C.', *Trans* 7 (1994), pp. 153-65. The thesis is adopted by scholars like J.A. Soggin, *An Introduction to the History of Israel and Judah* (London: SCM Press, 1993), p. 284; G. Garbini, 'Hebrew Literature in the Persian Period', in T.C. Eskenazi and Kent H. Richards (eds.), *Second Temple Studies. II. Temple Community in the Persian Period* (JSOTSup, 175; Sheffield: JSOT Press, 1994), pp. 180-88 (182).

14. In another context, Bickerman ('Marge', p. 24 n. 18; *Studies*, p. 332 n. 18) notes that Theodore of Mopsuestia (350–428 CE) believed that Zerubbabel had become king (in Aggeum, 1.1; *PG*, 66.477) κατὰ τὰς ἐπαγγελίας τὰς θείας ἐβασίλευε τότε τοῦ λαοῦ; similarly Cyrille of Alexandria (*PG*, 71.10); on Theodore of Mopsuestia and his interpretation of Zechariah, see D.Z. Zaharopoulos, *Theodore of Mopsuestia on the Bible: A Study of his Old Testament Exegesis* (Theological Inquiries; New York: Paulist Press, 1989), pp. 164-65.

15. Most recently, H.G. Reventlow, *Die Propheten Haggai, Sacharja und*

Rudolph has argued[16] that originally Zechariah set his hopes on Zerubbabel, but did not identify him with the 'Sprout' (*Sproß*). Only after the expectations had failed to materialise did Zechariah (himself) set his messianic expectations on the 'Sprout'.[17] Haggai, on the other hand, did point to Zerubbabel as the Messiah: 'he is the Messiah, even when the name is not mentioned explicitly'.[18]

Van der Woude disagrees with Rudolph's view that Zechariah changed his mind and thus relocated his messianic expectations from Zerubbabel to the 'Sprout': 'Already in the night visions of the year 519 Zechariah set his hopes on the emergence of two future saviour figures and he did not change these since'.[19] Like Rudolph, Van der Woude finds also a difference between the views of Haggai and Zerubbabel: Haggai 'welcomed Zerubbabel as the servant of Yahweh and as royal signet ring, cf. Hag. 2.23. In contrast to Zechariah, Haggai does not know the diarchy of the future leadership of the community of the era of salvation'.

In her recent book *Tradition and Innovation in Haggai and Zechariah 1–8*, Tollington concludes her study of Haggai and his oracle concerning Zerubbabel:

> Haggai's inclusion of the Davidic patronym and the use of traditional motifs in relation to him stress his royal lineage and suggest that the

*Maleachi* (ATD, 25.2; Göttingen: Vandenhoeck & Ruprecht, rev. edn, 1993), p. 55; R. Murmela, *Prophets in Dialogue: Inner-Biblical Allusions in Zech 1–8 and 9–14* (Åbo: Åbo Akademi University, 1996), p. 65.

16. W. Rudolph, *Haggai, Sacharja 1–8, Sacharja 9–14, Maleachi* (KAT, 13.4; Gütersloh: Gerd Mohn, 1976), pp. 100, 108, 130-31.

17. This appears to mean that Zechariah himself replaced a reference to Zerubbabel in 6.12 by a reference to the 'Sprout' (Rudolph, *Haggai, Sacharja*, p. 100): 'Die Exegese von 6,9-14 wird zeigen, daß die Ersetzung Serubbabels durch den »Sproß« schon auf Sacharja selbst zurückgeht'. Cf. p. 130 'hier [haben] nicht spätere Hände eingegriffen...sondern Sacharja selbst redet'.

18. 'Er ist der Messias, auch wenn der Name nicht ausdrücklich genannt wird' (Rudolph, *Haggai, Sacharja*, p. 54; cf. p. 108).

19. 'Sacharja [hat] schon in den Nachtgesichten des Jahres 519 seine Hoffnung auf das Erscheinen zweier künftiger Heilsgestalten gesetzt und diese seitdem nicht geändert'. 'Hatte Serubbabel als Knecht Jahwes und als königlichen Siegelring begrüßt, vgl. Hag. 2,23. Im Gegensatz zu Sacharja kennt Haggai nicht die Dyarchie des künftigen Führerschaft der Gemeinde der Heilszeit'. From the conclusion of A.S. van der Woude, 'Serubbabel und die messianischen Erwartungen des Propheten Sacharja', in O. Kaiser (ed.), *Lebendige Forschung im Alten Testament* (BZAW 100; Berlin: W. de Gruyter, 1988), pp. 138-56 (155).

prophet was anticipating some form of restored monarchy for the community of the new age, centring on Zerubbabel.[20]

After a study of Zechariah 1–8 she concludes that Zechariah developed
both a short-term vision and a longer-term vision on the issue of the
leadership of the community. Zechariah's understanding of the role of
Zerubbabel in the short-term vision is substantially different from that
of Haggai: given the absence of any indication 'whether Zerubbabel's
authority to perform this important task derives from his role as civil
governor, or because he is of Davidic lineage and proleptic king', she
concludes that 'Zechariah was not an ardent proponent of the restoration of the monarchy, though it would be unwise to claim that he was
totally against it in the early stages of his ministry'.[21]

In the longer-term vision, the hopes were set on the Branch, 'a new
ruler who would be an idealized David'. However, 'Zechariah did not
believe that any contemporary figure fulfilled the criteria for this
position of supreme leadership'. The advent of the Branch was pro-
jected into the future, and so Zechariah also considered the matter of an
interim rule, 'which he envisaged as a diarchy between Joshua and
Zerubbabel'. Zechariah 'probably believed that the Branch would come
during the lifetime of these two men'.[22]

b. *Outline*
In this book I will argue that the ZZ view is wrong in almost every one
of its aspects, and that the FF view is an improvement, but still qualifies
for refinement on several points. The outline of the book will be like
this. In Chapter 2 I will discuss the importance of the fact that the צמח
oracles are embedded in oracles addressed to members of the priesthood. In Chapter 3 I will study the precise meaning of the Hebrew noun
צמח. All this prepares for the discussion in Chapter 4, where I deal with
the portrait which Zechariah draws of Zemah, and with the issue of
identification. In Chapter 5 I will deal with literary-critical questions
concerning the צמח oracles in Zechariah 1–6. In Chapter 6 I will study
Zech. 4.14, a passage that has been closely linked with the צמח

20. *Tradition and Innovation in Haggai and Zechariah 1–8* (JSOTSup, 150;
Sheffield: JSOT Press, 1993), pp. 143-44.

21. *Tradition*, p. 179. Cf. S.L. Cook, *Prophecy and Apocalypticism: The Postexilic Social Setting* (Minneapolis: Fortress Press, 1995), p. 132 n. 35.

22. *Tradition*, p. 179.

oracles.[23] In Chapter 7 I will examine the relationship between the royal or messianic expectations of Zechariah and those of Haggai, whose prophetic ministry preceded and partly overlapped that of Zechariah. Haggai did not speak about Zemah, but in the final oracle of the collection in the book named after him he spoke about Zerubbabel, in an oracle which has strong political overtones and has usually been interpreted as pointing to the restoration of the monarchy with Zerubbabel as the new king.

The nature of the book is exegetical, and many broader issues (e.g. apocalypticism)[24] will not be dealt with or only touched upon. In some cases there is reason to go back to basics, and I hope to show that the subject of this book is such a case.

*Note on the Use of the Term 'Messianic Expectations'.* The word 'messianic' has been used in different ways. Some scholars propose a strict definition, for example De Jonge, who in order to avoid confusion adopts this convention in his survey of 'Messiah' in the Old Testament, early Judaism and later Jewish writing: 'we should employ the words "anointed" and "Messiah" only where the sources use the corresponding word in their own language. Similarly, "messianic expectation" should only denote the expectation of a redeemer who is actually called "Messiah"'.[25]

The Hebrew word משיח is not used in any of the texts which I will study in this book. So if I were to follow De Jonge's definition, I would not be able to use the phrase 'messianic expectation' at all. However, many scholars use the word in a looser definition,[26] and that is the

---

23.  Since the main focus of this study is on the figure called Zemah, there will be no separate treatment of Zech. 4.6-10. This passage mentions Zerubbabel but does not go beyond the horizons of his role in the temple building project. It subsequently plays a minor role in the discussion of the identity of Zemah and the nature of the expectations set on him (cf. Van der Woude, 'Serubbabel', p. 147; K.E. Pomykala, *The Davidic Dynasty Tradition in Early Judaism: Its History and Significance for Messianism* [SBLEJL, 7; Atlanta, Scholars Press, 1995], pp. 56-57).

24.  See the recent study of Cook (*Prophecy*), which points in some new directions. On a number of points I found myself in agreement with Cook's treatment of Zechariah, though not on all.

25.  M. de Jonge, 'Messiah', *ABD*, IV, pp. 777-88 (778).

26.  E.g. J. Barton, 'The Messiah in Old Testament Theology', in J. Day (ed.), *King and Messiah in Israel and the Ancient Near East: Proceedings of the Oxford Old Testament Seminar* (JSOTSup, 270; Sheffield: Sheffield Academic Press, 1998),

practice which I will follow here. I will use 'messianic expectation' to refer to expectations focusing on a future royal figure sent by God who will bring salvation to God's people and the world and establish a kingdom characterised by features like peace and justice.

## 2. *The Historical Background*

The passages in Zechariah and Haggai which will occupy us in this book are precisely dated to the year 520, that is, approximately 20 years after the Jews were granted permission to return to the land where they had been deported from. In the second part of this Chapter, I will first present a broad outline of the history of the early postexilic period, and then discuss in some more detail three historical issues which are relevant to the subject of the book.

### a. *The Early Persian Period: An Historical Outline.*
The part of the postexilic period in which the prophets Haggai and Zechariah were active is known as the Persian Period. The beginning of the Persian Period is usually dated to the year 539, when Cyrus II the Great captured Babylon. The victory over the Neo-Babylonian empire also meant that its holdings in Syria-Palestine now became part of the Persian Empire. The Persian or Achaemenid Empire would last for more than two hundred years[27] until Alexander the Great triumphed over it in 332.

pp. 365-79 (373-74), who refers to Neusner's definition in J. Neusner, W.S. Green and E.S. Frerichs (eds.), *Judaisms and their Messiahs at the Turn of the Christian Era* (Cambridge: Cambridge University Press, 1987), p. ix: 'A Messiah in a Judaism is a man who at the end of history, at the eschaton, will bring salvation to the Israel conceived by the social group addressed by the way of life and world view of that Judaism'. For a collection of 26 definitions of messianism, see H. Cazelles, *Le Messie de la Bible: Christologie de l'Ancien Testament* (Collection 'Jésus et Jésus-Christ', 7; Paris: Desclée de Brouwer, 1978), pp. 217-24; for the discussion about terminology see, M. Sæbø, 'Zum Verhältnis von "Messianismus" und "Eschatologie" im Alten Testament: Ein Versuch terminologischer und sachlicher Klärung', in E. Dassmann and G. Stemberger (eds.), *Der Messias* (JBTh, 8; Neukirchen–Vluyn: Neukirchener Verlag, 1993), pp. 25-56.

27. For a general survey of the history of the Persian empire, see J.M. Cook, *The Persian Empire* (London: Dent & Sons, 1983); R.N. Frye, *The History of Ancient Iran* (HA, 3.7; Munich: Beck, 1984); M.A. Dandamaev and V.G. Lukonin (eds.), *The Culture and Social Institutions of Ancient Iran* (Cambridge: Cambridge University Press, 1989); M.A. Dandamaev, *A Political History of the Achaemenid*

Cyrus was succeeded by his son Cambyses (530–522). In 525 Cambyses went on campaign in Egypt, which kept him there for several years. During this stay in Egypt he received the news about the revolt of a man called Gaumata (the revolt is dated to 11 March 522). Cambyses immediately headed for Persia but he died[28] on his way back (July 522). After the killing of Gaumata by Darius[29] and his fellow conspirators (29 Sep 522) Darius became king (522–486). He was confronted by many uprisings in different parts of the empire, which kept him busy for a whole year. At the end of his first year the order in the empire was restored.[30]

Cyrus had issued a decree in 539 in which he allowed the Jews to return to their home land and to rebuild the Temple.[31] A number of

---

*Empire* (Leiden: E.J. Brill, 1989); A. Kuhrt, *The Ancient Near East. c. 3000–330 BC* (Routledge History of the Ancient World; London: Routledge, 1995), pp. 647-701; P. Briant, *Histoire de l'empire Perse: De Cyrus à Alexandre* (Paris: Fayard, 1996).

28. It is not fully clear what caused the death of Cambyses. Darius' Bisitun Inscription (DB) §11 has been interpreted to suggest that Cambyses committed suicide, but according to R. Borger and W. Hinz, 'Die Behistun-Inschrift Darius' der Grossen', in *TUAT*, I (1984), pp. 419-50 (426-27, comment f [ad §11]), the word translated 'he died his own death' refers to a natural death. Hinz argues ('Kambyses', *RLA*, V, pp. 328-30 [329]) that Cambyses died as a result of blood poisoning, after he had accidentally wounded himself with his Median sword.

29. Darius was from the same family as Cambyses, but from a different branch: he was a great-grandson of Ariaramnes, the brother of Cyrus I (c. 640–600), the great-grandfather of Cambyses (II), the predecessor of Darius; see the genealogical table, 'Kings of the Achaemenid Empire', in J.M. Balcer, *Herodotus and Bisitun: Problems in Ancient Persian Historiography* (Historia Einzelschriften, 49; Stuttgart: Steiner, 1987), table 6.

30. For a thorough discussion of the chronological problems related to Darius's Bisitun Inscription, see R. Borger, 'Die Chronologie des Darius-Denkmals am Behistun-Felsen', *NAWG*, I. *Philologisch-historische Klasse*, 3 (1982), pp. 105-31. Darius's claim to have defeated all his opponents 'in one and the same year' can be accepted as true: the year was a leap year, with an extra 13th month (p. 21).

31. Cf. Ezra 1.2-4 and 6.3-5, and the Cyrus Cylinder (*ANET*, pp. 315-16; *TUAT*, I, pp. 407-10; Kuhrt, *Ancient Near East*, pp. 601-602). The policy of Cyrus is often contrasted with that of his predecessors of the Assyrian and the Babylonian empire as being very mild. There has been a tendency 'to oversimplify the changes' (Ackroyd, *Israel under Babylon and Persia* [Oxford: Oxford University Press, 1970], p. 163) between these empires. A. Kuhrt ('The Cyrus Cylinder and Achaemenid Imperial Policy', *JSOT* 25 [1983], pp. 83-97) and R.J. van der Spek ('Cyrus de Pers in Assyrisch perspectief', *TG* 96 [1983], pp. 1-27) put Persian policy in a historical

Jews returned in several 'waves' (probably a small one in Cyrus's time, and larger ones in the early years of Darius, and around 458 BCE) to Yehud,[32] now a province[33] of the at that time still undivided Babylonia and Beyond-the-River satrapy. The book of Ezra dates Zerubbabel's return to the time of Cyrus (2.1-2), and mentions him in connection with the first attempts at rebuilding the temple (3.1-6). Apparently, these first efforts did not amount to much, and another start was made during the reign of Darius.[34]

perspective and show that as to religious tolerance and the treatment of submitted nations Cyrus and his successors were not unique.

32. For a description of the territory of the province in the Persian period, see H.G.M. Williamson, 'Persian Administration', *ABD*, V, pp. 81-86 (84); C.E. Carter, 'The Province of Yehud in the Postexilic Period', in Eskenazi and Richards (eds.), *Second Temple*, pp. 106-45 (114-20); A. Lemaire, 'Histoire et administration de la Palestine à l'époque perse', in E.-M. Laperrousaz and A. Lemaire (eds.), *La Palestine à l'époque perse* (Paris: Cerf, 1994), pp. 11-53 (20-21).

33. J. Elayi and J. Sapin, *Nouveaux regards sur la Transeuphratène* (Turnhout: Brepols, 1991), p. 11; ET *Beyond the River: New Perspectives on Transeuphratene* (trans. J. Edward Crowley; JSOTSup, 250; Sheffield: Sheffield Academic Press, 1998), p. 15, define 'province' as 'une subdivision territoriale de la satrapie, correspondant souvent à une entité géographique, ethnique et linguistique, avec des structures politiques parfois héritées des Empires précédents' ('a territorial subdivision of a satrapy, often corresponding to a geographical, ethnic and linguistic entity, with political structures often inherited from preceding Empires...'); compare E. Lipiński, 'Géographie linguistique de la Transeuphratène à l'époque achéménide', *Trans* 3 (1990), pp. 95-107 (97).

34. Briant, *Empire Perse*, pp. 57, 913; B.E. Beyer, 'Zerubbabel', *ABD*, VI, pp. 1084-86 (1085). The date of the return of Zerubbabel and the nature of his involvement in the first stage of the rebuilding of the temple (in the time of Cyrus) are much debated by scholars. A number of scholars date Zerubbabel's return to the time of Darius, and deny any involvement of him in rebuilding efforts at the time of Cyrus (if there were such efforts). E.g. J.L. Berquist, *Judaism in Persia's Shadow: A Social and Historical Approach* (Minneapolis: Fortress Press, 1995), p. 57; see, for discussion, S. Japhet, 'The Temple in the Restoration Period: Reality and Ideology', *USQR* 34 (1991), pp. 195-251 (201-24); *idem*, 'Composition and Chronology in the Book of Ezra–Nehemiah', in Eskenazi and Richards (eds.), *Second Temple*, pp. 189-216 (201-208); H.G.M. Williamson, *Ezra, Nehemiah* (WBC, 16; Waco, TX: Word Books, 1985), pp. 32-33, 43-46, 79-80. For a survey of the debate, see P.R. Ackroyd, *Exile and Restoration: A Study of Hebrew Thought of the Sixth Century BC* (London: SCM Press, 1968), pp. 143-48; P.R. Bedford, 'Discerning the Time: Haggai, Zechariah and the "Delay" in the Rebuilding of the Temple', in S W. Holloway and L.K. Handy (eds.), *The Pitcher is Broken: Memorial Essays*

This brings us to the time in which the prophets Haggai and Zechariah were active. I will now discuss in more detail three issues. First, I will look into the question how one can connect the dates in Haggai and Zechariah to an absolute chronology. Next, I will discuss the political status of Yehud in this early part of the Persian period. Finally, I will consider the problem of what happened to Zerubbabel.

b. *The Dates in Haggai and Zechariah*
In Haggai and Zechariah 1–8 one can witness an interesting development in the increasing number of oracles that have a precise date attached to them.[35] Scholars in general accept the authenticity of these dates.[36] Ackroyd is more hesitant about accepting the reliability of the dates. He admits that there 'is no obviously discernible significance in the dates as such, which makes arguments for their being invented less persuasive'. Yet on the basis of 'the example of Esther, and the fact that it is of the nature of fictional material to offer precision', he wants to reckon with 'the possibility that here too we may be dealing with a construction'.[37]

Kessler points out[38] that Ackroyd's position (referring to earlier statements of Ackroyd)[39] is implausible. He points to the question

*for Gösta W. Ahlström* (JSOTSup, 190; Sheffield: Sheffield Academic Press), pp. 71-94 (86-92).

35. D.L. Petersen, *Haggai and Zechariah 1–8* (OTL; London: SCM Press, 1984), p. 33; S. Amsler, *Aggée; Zacharie 1–8* (CAT, 11c; Geneva: Labor et Fides, 2nd edn, 1988), p. 9.

36. E.g. Beyse, *Serubbabel*, p. 11; Chr. Jeremias, *Die Nachtgesichte des Sacharja: Untersuchungen zu ihrer Stellung im Zusammenhang der Visionsberichte im Alten Testament und zu ihrem Bildmaterial* (FRLANT, 117; Göttingen: Vandenhoeck & Ruprecht, 1977), p. 18; Rudolph, *Haggai, Sacharja*, p. 74; Petersen, *Haggai and Zechariah*, pp. 33, 43-44; Reventlow, *Haggai, Sacharja*, p. 10. Reventlow summarizes the consensus thus (p. 2): 'Obwohl die Daten redaktionell sind, ist ihre Zuverlässigkeit allgemein anerkannt'. A recent exception to this consensus would be A. Sérandour, 'Les récits bibliques de la construction du second temple: leurs enjeux', *Trans* 11 (1996), pp. 9-32 (18), who considers Hag. 2.20-23 to be a secondary addition.

37. P.R. Ackroyd, *The Chronicler in his Age* (JSOTSup, 101; Sheffield: JSOT Press, 1991), pp. 115-16.

38. J.A. Kessler, 'The Second Year of Darius and the Prophet Haggai', *Trans* 5 (1992), pp. 63-86 (64-66).

39. P.R. Ackroyd 'Two Old Testament Historical Problems of the Early Persian Period', *JNES* 17 (1958), pp. 13-27 (22).

raised by Ackroyd himself as to the difficulty of finding the reasons for inventing the dates. He further shows the problem with Ackroyd's suggestion for the function of the dates as demonstrating that the prophets' words came true, in that the fulfilment of the words of the prophets in the completion of the temple and its reconsecration is not recorded in Haggai and Zechariah.

If one accepts the reliability of the dates in Haggai and Zechariah, the following chronology can be reconstructed:[40]

Figure 1. *The Dates in Haggai and Zechariah.*

| | |
|---|---|
| 29 Aug 520 | (first?) public appearance of Haggai (Hag. 1.1) |
| Oct/Nov 520 | (first?) public appearance of Zechariah (Zech. 1.1) |
| 18 Dec 520 | start rebuilding of the temple (Hag. 2.10, 18) |
| 18 Dec 520 | the oracle in Hag. 2.20-23 |
| 15 Feb 519 | Zechariah's visions (Zech. 1.7) |

*Bickerman's Second Year.* This is how most scholars would reconstruct the chronology relating to the prophecies of Haggai and Zechariah. Bickerman has challenged this view,[41] and has dated Darius's second year to 521–520, rather than the usual 520–519, which would move all dates one year earlier. To discuss Bickerman's views, I will begin by giving a brief sketch of the international political developments.[42]

In order to find out what was the exact chronological relationship between the events in the early years of Darius and the prophetic ministry of Haggai and Zechariah we need to know what year Haggai's 'second year of Darius' refers to. In the ancient Near East several calendar systems[43] were used. The years a king reigned could be counted

40. For a more detailed table, see C.L. Meyers and E.M. Meyers, *Haggai, Zechariah 1–8* (AB, 25B; Garden City, NY: Doubleday, 1987), p. xlvi Chart 2.

41. Bickerman, 'Marge'; *Studies*, pp. 327-36.

42. For a general survey of the history of the Persian empire in the 520s, see W. Schottroff, 'Zur Sozialgeschichte Israels in der Perserzeit', *VuF* 27 (1982), pp. 46-68 (51-53); Cook, *Persian Empire*, pp. 46-57; Frye, *Ancient Iran*, pp. 96-102; A. Kuhrt, 'Babylonia from Cyrus to Xerxes', CAH, IV, pp. 112-38 (127-30); Dandamaev and Lukonin, *Ancient Iran*, pp. 91-95. Much more detailed is the treatment in Dandamaev, *Achaemenid Empire*, pp. 70-135.

43. On the calendar systems in the ancient Near East, see E.R. Thiele, *The Mysterious Numbers of the Hebrew Kings* (Chicago: University of Chicago Press, 3rd edn, 1985), pp. 67-78; J. Hughes, *Secrets of the Times: Myth and History in*

in different ways, depending how the months between the accession
and the first day of the New Year (the first of Nisan) after the accession
were counted. One way, called 'accession year dating' or 'postdating',
was to count these months as an accession year, in which case the first
year of the king was the first full Nisan year after the accession. Another
way, called 'non-accession year dating' or 'antedating', was to count
the months preceding the first day of the New (Nisan) Year as the first
year of the king.

If postdating was used by Darius, his second year would have lasted
from 3 April 520 to 22 March 519. Haggai's oracles would then all
have been proclaimed after Darius had beaten his nine opponents and
established his throne (Fig. 2). But the use of antedating would make
Darius second year last from 14 April 521 to 3 April 520 *and* locate
Haggai's oracles in the time when Darius was still fighting his opponents (Fig. 3).

Figure 2. *The Second Year of Darius, Postdating*

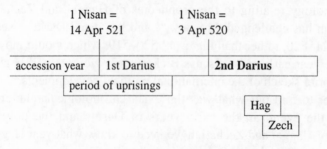

Figure 3. *The Second Year of Darius, Antedating*

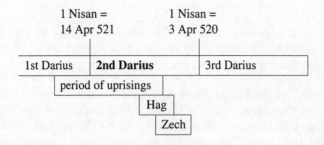

*Biblical Chronology* (JSOTSup, 66; Sheffield: JSOT Press, 1990), pp. 159-60; and
Kessler, 'Second Year', pp. 69-71, 79-80.

How do we know which dating system was used by Darius, or Haggai? While most scholars think Darius used postdating, some scholars argue that he used antedating. The latter base their view either[44] on the use of non-accession year dating in Nehemiah 1–2,[45] or[46] on the claim that Darius antedated the beginning of his reign to make it coincide with the death of Cambyses and so to deny any legitimacy to Gaumata (a similar practice was adopted by Cambyses after his conquest of Egypt, eliminating the reign of Psammeticus III).

However, the question is whether one should use this evidence to solve the problem, when more direct evidence from Darius himself points in another direction. In contrast to what Cambyses did in Egypt (apparently adapting a local practice for some reason), the evidence of Darius's Bisitun Inscription[47] (DB) makes clear[48] that Darius did not try to eliminate the reign of Gaumata from the records of history, and did not count the period before 1 Nisan 521 as his first year. In DB explicit mention is made of the reign of Gaumata (DB §11-12) and his assas-

44. Waterman, 'Messianic Conspirators', p. 77; for a critical discussion of Waterman's views, see Ackroyd, 'Early Persian Period', pp. 15-19).

45. It is possible that non-accession year dating was used in Neh. 1–2. Here (we are talking now about the court in Susa in the fifth century) one may want to follow Bickerman who suggests ('Marge', pp. 19-23; reprinted in *Studies*, pp. 327-31) that in these chapters another dating system is used: the years of the king were calculated from the day of his accession, so without direct reference to the calendar year. The Persians took this practice over from the Elamites. With Kessler one may call this third system 'royal dating' ('Second Year', p. 75).

46. Bickerman, 'Marge', p. 25; *Studies*, p. 333.

47. A transliteration and translation of the Old Persian text of Darius's Bisitun Inscription (DB) can be found in R.G. Kent, *Old Persian: Grammar, Texts, Lexicon* (AOS, 33; New Haven: American Oriental Society, 1953), pp. 107-108, 116-35; for the Babylonian version, see E.N. Von Voigtlander, *The Bisitun Inscription of Darius the Great: Babylonian Version* (Corpus Inscriptionum Iranicarum: Part 1, Inscriptions of Ancient Iran. II. The Babylonian Versions of the Achaemenian Inscriptions; Texts 1; London: Lund Humphries, 1978); but notice the critical remark about this edition by Borger, 'Chronologie', p. 106: 'in Bezug auf Editionstechnik nicht gerade eine Glanzleistung'; for the Aramaic version, see J.C. Greenfield and B. Porten (eds.), *The Bisitun Inscription of Darius the Great: Aramaic Version* (text, translation and commentary; Corpus Inscriptionum Iranicarum; Part 1, Inscriptions of Ancient Iran; V. The Aramaic Versions of the Achaemenian Inscriptions, etc.; Texts 1; London: Lund Humphries, 1982); for more recent bibliographical information, see Borger, 'Chronologie', and Borger and Hinz, 'Behistun-Inschrift', p. 420.

48. Kessler, 'Second Year', p. 80.

sination (DB §13), and Darius counts his accession from the date of Gaumata's death (DB §13). Even if Darius had wanted to eliminate Gaumata it is doubtful whether he would have counted the months preceding 1 Nisan 521 as his first year, since they were part of what was counted as Cambyses' eighth year.[49] So the source most close to Darius shows that he used postdating.[50]

If this evidence justifies the position that in the Persian Empire in the late sixth century BCE postdating was used, we may assume that the Persians inherited this postdating from the Babylonians (the Persians also borrowed the Babylonian calendrical system[51]). The use of postdating by Darius in DB, combined with the fact that the Babylonian system of postdating had been the practice in Judah at least since the late seventh century[52] leaves no reason to suggest (as Bickerman does) that Haggai would have used another system, that is, antedating.

To sum up, there is no evidence that antedating was used for the calculation of the reign of Darius, either by Darius himself, or by the prophet Haggai. The second year of Darius (Hag. 1.1) was most likely from 3 April 520 to 22 March 519.

c. *The Political Status of Yehud*
The precise nature of the political status of Yehud during the period under examination in this study has become a matter of dispute. In 1934 Alt wrote an essay[53] in which he argued that from the destruction of

49. H.W. Wolff, *Dodekapropheton. VI. Haggai* (BKAT, 14.6; Neukirchen–Vluyn: Neukirchener Verlag, 1986), p. 56.

50. Dandamaev and Lukonin (*Ancient Iran*, p. 291) and Kessler ('Second Year', p. 78) refer to an Aramaic papyrus from Elephantine dated 'the 21st year [of Xerxes], the year of the accession of Artaxerxes to the throne' (= 464), and an Aramaic document from Samaria dated 'the 20th day of Adar of the 2nd year [of Arses], the accession year of Darius [III]' (= 335), which suggests that there is evidence for postdating up until the second half of the fourth century.

51. Dandamaev and Lukonin, *Ancient Iran*, p. 290. The Persians introduced their own names for the months. Borger and Hinz ('Behistun-Inschrift', p. 421) produce a convenient list of the correspondences between the Persian and Babylonian month names (as used in DB).

52. Hughes, *Biblical Chronology*, p. 181. Cf. Kessler, 'Second Year', p. 79.

53. A. Alt, 'Die Rolle Samarias bei der Entstehung des Judentums', in A. Alt, Friedrich Baumgärtel *et al.* (eds.), *Festschrift Otto Procksch zum 60. Geburtstag* (Leipzig: Deichert and Hinrichs, 1934), pp. 5-28 (reprinted in A. Alt, *Kleine Schriften zur Geschichte des Volkes Israel*, II [Munich: Beck, 1953], pp. 316-37); for a summary of Alt's views, see K.G. Hoglund, *Achaemenid Imperial Administra-*

Jerusalem to the appointment of Nehemiah Yehud was considered a part of the province of Samaria and that Yehud became a province of its own only in the days of Nehemiah. This view has for a long time been a consensus, and it still has a number of adherents.[54]

A growing number of scholars has abandoned this view, however, and has adopted a view of Yehud as a separate administrative unit.[55] The reasons for the adoption of this view are the following. There is evidence from biblical texts which suggests that from the first years of the return Judah had its own governors. This evidence includes:[56] (a) the fact that both Sheshbazzar (Ezra 5.14) and Zerubbabel (Hag. 1.1, 14; 2.2, 21) are called פחה[57] 'governor'; (b) the statement in Neh. 5.15 about governors preceding Nehemiah, which only makes sense if like is compared with like (that is, the governors were governors of Judah); and (c) the official inquiries in Ezra 4–5 in which not the governor of

*tion in Syria-Palestine and the Missions of Ezra and Nehemiah* (SBLDS, 125; Atlanta, Scholars Press, 1992), pp. 69-71.

54. E.g. Rudolph, *Haggai, Sacharja*, p. 31; S.E. McEvenue, 'The Political Structure in Judah from Cyrus to Nehemiah', *CBQ* 43 (1981), pp. 353-64 (364); Petersen, *Haggai and Zechariah*, pp. 26-27; P.L. Redditt, 'Nehemiah's First Mission and the Date of Zechariah 9–14', *CBQ* 56 (1994), pp. 664-78 (671-72); *idem, Haggai, Zechariah, Malachi* (NCB; London: Marshall Pickering; Grand Rapids: Eerdmans, 1995), pp. 5-8.

55. See, e.g., G. Widengren, 'The Persian Period', in J.H. Hayes and J.M. Miller (eds.), *Israelite and Judaean History* (OTL; London: SCM Press, 1977), pp. 489-538 (509-11); S. Japhet, 'Sheshbazzar and Zerubbabel: Against the Background of the Historical and Religious Tendencies of Ezra–Nehemiah', *ZAW* 94 (1982), pp. 66-98 (80-86); A.S. van der Woude, *Haggai–Maleachi* (POT; Nijkerk: Callenbach, 1982), p. 22; I. Eph'al, 'Syria-Palestine under Achaemenid Rule', CAH, IV, pp. 139-64 (160-61); *idem*, 'Serubbabel', p. 139 n. 2; H.G.M. Williamson, 'The Governors of Judah under the Persians', *TynBul* 39, pp. 59-82; E.-M. Laperrousaz, 'Jérusalem à l'époque Perse (étendue et statut)', *Trans* 1 (1989), pp. 55-65 (60-63); A. Lemaire, 'Populations et territoires de la Palestine à l'époque Perse', *Trans* 3 (1990), pp. 31-73 (32-36); Élayi and Sapin, *Nouveaux regards*, p. 179-81; ET *Beyond the River*, pp. 150-52; Hoglund, *Administration*, pp. 22, 23, 69-86; Williamson, 'Persian Administration', *ABD*, V, pp. 81-86 (83-84); Lemaire, 'Histoire', pp. 11-53 (16-19); Briant, *Empire Perse*, pp. 503-504, 913, 976.

56. Williamson, 'Governors', pp. 76-77; Lemaire, 'Histoire', pp. 16-18.

57. On the use of this term for different functions in different settings, see T. Petit, 'L'Evolution sémantique des termes Hébreux et Araméens *PḤH* et *SGN* et Accadiens *PĀḪATU* et *ŠAKNU*', *JBL* 107 (1988), pp. 53-67; Lipiński, 'Géographie linguistique', pp. 96-97; and Hoglund, *Administration*, pp. 78-81.

Samaria but the Jews are called to account, which presupposes Judah's relative autonomy.

This interpretation of the biblical material can be supported by the find of a hoard of bullae and seals with what are probably the name and title of a governor of Judah, published by Avigad.[58] The dating of this material is somewhat problematic, however. The archaeological context of the finds is unknown, and so dating can only be done on the basis of palaeography. Avigad dates the script to the sixth century.[59] There might be a confirmation of this date if the woman called Shelomith (a rare name, both in biblical genealogy and on seals) on one of the seals[60] can be identified with the Shelomith of 1 Chron. 3.19, a daughter of Zerubbabel.[61] While not all problems concerning this epigraphic evidence have been resolved, a number of scholars have accepted the contribution it makes to the thesis of the position of Yehud as a separate province.[62] This would imply that on the basis of the biblical and the archaeological material the presence of governors can be established from the second half of the sixth century BCE to the late fourth century BCE (though not always with equal certainty).

If a succession of governors can be established in this way, one should also take a fresh look at the position of the high priest during this period. For a long time it was believed that from an early time after the exile, the secular powers of the high priest were increasing. Such a

58. N. Avigad, *Bullae and Seals from a Postexilic Judean Archive* (Qedem, 4; Jerusalem: The Institute of Archaeology, The Hebrew University, 1976).

59. *Bullae and Seals*, p. 17.

60. See the discussion in N. Avigad, *Corpus of West Semitic Stamp Seals* (revised and completed by Benjamin Sass; Jerusalem: Hebrew University, 1997), pp. 31 and 33-34 n. 45.

61. So, e.g., Williamson, 'Governors', p. 75; Lemaire, 'Populations', pp. 34-35.

62. E.g. H.G.M. Williamson, *Ezra, Nehemiah* (WBC, 16; Waco, TX: Word Books, 1985), p. 243, and the extensive discussion in 'Governors', pp. 74-77; Meyers and Meyers, *Haggai, Zechariah*, pp. 12-16; Eph'al, 'Syria-Palestine', pp. 160-61; Lemaire, 'Populations', pp. 34-35; Élayi and Sapin, *Nouveaux regards*, pp. 179-81 (ET *Beyond the River*, pp. 150-52); Hoglund, *Administration*, pp. 81-82; Kessler, 'Second Year', pp. 73-74; Lemaire, 'Zorobabel et la Judé à la lumière de l'épigraphie (fin du VIe s. av. J.-C.)', *RB* 103 (1996), pp. 48-57 (54-55). Ackroyd finds the evidence of palaeography and the identification of Shelomith unsatisfying ('Persian Period', pp. 97-98). Avigad's dating is rejected by E. Stern (*Material Culture of the Land of the Bible in the Persian Period 538–332 B.C.* [Warminster: Aris & Phillips; Jerusalem: Israel Exploration Society, 1982], p. 206); but see the comment of Williamson, 'Governors', p. 64.

view of the early rise of a hierocracy in Yehud becomes problematic if at that time there were actually governors who led the administration of Yehud. The presence of governors down to the late fourth century BCE would therefore push the date for the emergence of a hierocracy down to a much later period, perhaps—as Laperrousaz has argued—to the beginning of the Hellenistic period.[63]

### d. *Whatever Happened to Zerubbabel?*
The main role in this study is given to Zemah, but Zerubbabel comes in a good second place. While Zemah is only a visionary character, Zerubbabel is also a historical figure. Yet we know far less about him than one would wish. Through the patronymic 'son of Shealtiel'[64] we are able to trace his ancestry back to the line of David,[65] the title פחה indicates his office,[66] but many other things are unclear. For example, when precisely did he come to Jerusalem, and what happened to him?

The first issue is only of secondary relevance to the subject of this book. The precise date of Zerubbabel's arrival in Yehud is difficult to

---

63. E.-M. Laperrousaz, 'Le régime théocratique juif a-t-il commencé à l'époque perse, ou seulement à l'époque hellénistique?', *Semitica* 32 (1982), pp. 93-96, and 'Jérusalem', pp. 61-63; Eph'al, 'Syria-Palestine', p. 152; Williamson, 'Persian Administration', p. 85; Soggin, *History*, pp. 284, 294 (but note his hesitations concerning the bullae and seals, p. 285). Laperrousaz also notes ('Régime théocratique', p. 96) that such a date would have implications for the dating of texts and passages in the Bible which reflect such a hierocracy in Jerusalem. D.W. Rooke, 'The Role and Development of the High Priesthood with Particular Reference to the Postexilic Period' (DPhil thesis, Oxford University, 1996), has argued that the high priest as such never assumed civil power, but in the Hellenistic period some civil leaders also became high priest.

64. Hag. 1.1; 2.23; Ezra 3.2, 8; 5.2; Neh. 12.1.

65. See the genealogy in 1 Chron. 3.17. In 1 Chron. 3.17 Pedaiah is mentioned as the father of Zerubbabel; the usual solution of this problem is the assumption that Shealtiel died childless, and that Zerubbabel was born to Pedaiah who had married Shealtiel's widow in a levirate marriage. E.g. W. Rudolph, *Chronikbücher* (HAT, 21; Tübingen: J.C.B. Mohr [Paul Siebeck], 1955), p. 29; H.G.M. Williamson, *1 and 2 Chronicles* [NCB; Grand Rapids: Eerdmans; London: Marshall, Morgan & Scott, 1982), p. 57 (he points out that '[s]ince our list, which is to be dated later, puts him in an apparently less exalted position, it is likely to rest on sound tradition'). This levirate marriage solution has been accepted by a great number of scholars, though not by all. See, e.g., J.M. Miller and J.H. Hayes, *A History of Ancient Israel and Judah* (London: SCM Press, 1986), p. 456; Berquist, *Judaism*, p. 63 and p. 84 n. 54.

66. See the discussion of the political status of Yehud, above.

establish due to a lack of conclusive evidence. Opinions differ between an arrival soon after 538 BCE on the one hand and any moment between 538 and 520 BCE on the other.[67]

The second requires more discussion. The problems surrounding the question as to what happened to Zerubbabel are a result of the fact that the sources in which he is mentioned at a certain stage fail to mention him any more. In Ezra 3 and 5 one can find Zerubbabel together with the high priest Joshua involved in the project to rebuild the temple, but neither is mentioned in the narrative of the completion and dedication of the temple (Ezra 6.14-18). A number of scholars have concluded that Zerubbabel disappeared from the political stage or was removed from his office.[68] Others are more cautious and leave what happened to Zerubbabel open, even allowing for the possibility that he was present at the dedication of the temple, but for one reason or another was not mentioned.

The second view seems to be more plausible. In the first place one should realise that the phenomenon of a narrative falling silent on a certain person is, in the words of Ackroyd, 'not uncharacteristic of biblical narrative'. He points to 'numerous instances of "disappearance" which simply mark the narrative as having other concerns'. In this particular case, Ackroyd maintains, the 'status of Zerubbabel and his activity are more important than what subsequently happened; and there is no indication in the narrative that action against him could have been taken by the Persians'.[69]

Secondly, the sources fall silent not only on Zerubbabel, but also on Joshua, but the removal hypothesis, as Japhet points out, 'may explain the silence concerning Zerubbabel but not of [sic] the silence concerning Joshua'.[70] Thirdly, Ackroyd already mentioned the absence of evi-

---

67. See the discussion in Ackroyd, *Exile*, pp. 146-48 (Ackroyd prefers a date during the time of Cambyses [530–522 BCE]); and Williamson, *Ezra, Nehemiah*, pp. 44-45 (Williamson favours an early dating soon after Cyrus's decree [538]).

68. That is the way the silence is interpreted by, e.g., Waterman, 'Messianic Conspirators', p. 78. This also applies to the view that Zerubbabel was 'removed from the throne by the priestly class led by Joshua' (Garbini, 'Hebrew Literature', p. 182).

69. Ackroyd, *Chronicler*, p. 106; other examples he mentions are Nehemiah and Ezra.

70. Japhet, 'Temple', p. 248 n. 60; the same point is made by Van der Woude, 'Serubbabel', p. 140.

dence in the narrative to support the removal hypothesis.[71] To this it should be added that on the other hand there is evidence which makes the idea that he was removed from office by the Persians because of a messianic conspiracy (either one in which he was the leader, or one in which he was a sort of victim) highly unlikely.

Scholars have pointed to the following data.[72] (a) If there had been some rebellious activity at this time it is difficult to explain why the 'adversaries of Judah and Benjamin' would have waited until the reign of Artaxerxes to accuse Jerusalem and its inhabitants of being 'rebellious and wicked' (Ezra 4). (b) There is no indication of any interruption in the rebuilding of the temple, or of an intervention or change of policy towards the Jews on the side of the Persians. In reaction to an investigation by Tattenai and his colleagues, Darius was willing to confirm the permission for 'the governor of the Jews and the elders' to rebuild the temple (Ezra 6.7). The document itself does not identify 'the governor' as Zerubbabel, but this identification can be inferred from the context (cf. Ezra 5.1-5).[73]

We have to conclude that we simply do not know for what reason we

71. Cf. G. Wallis, 'Erwägungen zu Sach 6, 9-15', in *Congress Volume Uppsala 1971* (VTSup, 22; Leiden: E.J. Brill, 1972), pp. 232-37 (233); Van der Woude, 'Serubbabel', p. 140.

72. For these points, see Ackroyd, *Exile*, p. 165; and H.G.M. Williamson, 'Eschatology in Chronicles', *TynBul* 28 (1977), pp. 115-54 (128). For a critique of the conspiracy and removal idea, see also A. Bentzen, 'Quelques remarques sur le mouvement messianique parmi les juifs aux environs de l'an 520 avant Jésus-Christ', *RHPR* 10 (1930), pp. 493-503; K. Galling, 'Serubbabel und die Wiederaufbau des Tempels in Jerusalem', in A. Kuschke (ed), *Verbannung und Heimkehr; Beiträge zur Geschichte und Theologie Israels im 6. und 5. Jahrhundert v. Chr.* (Festschrift W. Rudolph; Tübingen: J.C.B. Mohr, 1961), pp. 67-96 (94-96); K. Galling, *Studien zur Geschichte Israels im persischen Zeitalter* (Tübingen: J.C.B. Mohr [Paul Siebeck], 1964), pp. 147-48; Ackroyd, *Exile*, p. 165; Beyse, *Serubbabel*, p. 45; Williamson, 'Eschatology', p. 128; Japhet, 'Zerubbabel', pp. 78-79.

73. For a discussion of the questions concerning Ezra 6.7, see Williamson, *Ezra, Nehemiah*, pp. 72, 81-82. There is a growing consensus concerning the authenticity of the Aramaic documents in Ezra 1–6. See the literature mentioned in B.T. Arnold, 'The Use of Aramaic in the Hebrew Bible: Another Look at Bilingualism in Ezra and Daniel', *JNSL* 22.2 (1996), pp. 1-16 (p. 4 n. 11). For recent challenges to this consensus, see L.L. Grabbe, 'Reconstructing History from the Book of Ezra', in P.R. Davies (ed.), *Second Temple Studies. I. Persian Period* (JSOTSup, 117; Sheffield: JSOT Press, 1991), pp. 98-106, and J. Briend, 'L'édit de Cyrus et sa valeur historique', *Trans* 11 (1996), pp. 33-44.

suddenly stop hearing about Zerubbabel,[74] but that the evidence that is there speaks against a removal hypothesis.

## 3. *Matters of Redaction*

a. *The Redaction of Haggai and Zechariah 1–8*

While the dates of the oracles have found acceptance among a broad spectrum of scholars, no unanimity has been reached about the nature of the redaction of Haggai and Zechariah 1–8. Usually the redaction process of both Haggai and Zechariah 1–8 is seen as closely linked. Some scholars argue for an early date of the redaction, not a long time after 520,[75] while others allow for a period of one hundred years or more between the moment the oracles and the visions were originally received and the final redaction,[76] which then creates space and time for

74. There is no evidence to tell whether he was present at the consecration ceremony and died soon after it (so Beyse, *Serubbabel*, pp. 48-49) or retired around 510 (so Reventlow, *Haggai, Sacharja*, p. 55), as other scholars have argued.

75. E.g. O. Eissfeldt, *Einleitung in das Alte Testament unter Einschluss der Apokryphen und Pseudepigraphen sowie der apokryphen- und pseudepigraphen-artigen Qumran-Schriften: Entstehungsgeschichte des Alten Testaments* (Neue theologische Grundrisse; Tübingen: J.C.B. Mohr, 3rd edn, 1964), p. 579 (with respect to Haggai); ET *The Old Testament: An Introduction, Including the Apocrypha and Pseudepigrapha, and also the Works of Similar Type from Qumran. The History of the Formation of the Old Testament* (Oxford: Basil Blackwell, 1965), pp. 428-29; Rudolph, *Haggai, Sacharja*, pp. 22-23, 39, 63; Meyers and Meyers, *Haggai, Zechariah*, p. xlv; Kessler, 'Second Year', p. 66; Reventlow, *Haggai, Sacharja*, pp. 5, 33; Redditt, *Haggai, Zechariah*, pp. 12, 42, 80. Meyers and Meyers and Reventlow conclude from the absence of a mention of the completion of the temple that the redaction must have happened before 515 BCE. Given the centrality of the theme of the temple, this is an attractive suggestion, yet it remains an *argumentum e silentio*.

76. W.A.M. Beuken, *Haggai–Sacharja 1–8: Studien zur Überlieferungs-geschichte der frühnachexilischen Prophetie* (SSN, 10; Assen: Van Gorcum, 1967), *passim*, summary on pp. 331-36, distinguishes between an early pre-Chronistic edition and a final redaction in a Chronistic milieu some one hundred years later. R. Mason, 'The Purpose of the "Editorial Framework" of the Book of Haggai', *VT* 27 (1977), pp. 413-21 (415, 418, 420-21), 'Prophets', p. 145, and Williamson, *1 and 2 Chronicles*, p. 101, have criticized the location of the redaction in a Chronistic milieu. For a critique of the usual approach of treating the narrative framework in Haggai as a secondary addition, see M.H. Floyd, 'The Nature of the Narrative and the Evidence of Redaction in Haggai', *VT* 45.4 (1995), pp. 470-90.

a more complex redaction process.[77] The great interest in the rebuilding of the temple and the leadership of the community around 520, found in these books, seems most plausibly understood on the assumption of an early date for the redaction of Haggai and Zechariah 1–8.[78]

Two issues require more discussion: the position of Zechariah 3 in the vision cycle, and the position of some of the oracular material in the vision reports in Zechariah 1–6.

### b. *The Origin of Zechariah 3*

It has been argued that Zechariah 3, the chapter as a whole, is a secondary addition, adding another vision to an original sequence. Two reasons are given for this opinion: (a) the unique formal features in the vision report in Zechariah 3, and (b) the disruption of the symmetry of a sequence of originally seven visions.

*Formal Features*. The formal features which are said to be unique in Zechariah 3 are:[79] instead of the usual ואשא את־עיני וארא והנה one finds here the introductory formula ויראני. The Interpreting Angel (המלאך הדבר בי) is absent, instead one finds מלאך יהוה. Zechariah is only a witness to the action, he does not ask questions which are then answered by the Interpreting Angel, as in the other visions. The oracle is addressed not to the prophet, but to a historical person, Joshua, the high priest.

---

77. K. Seybold, *Bilder zum Tempelbau: Die Visionen des Propheten Sacharja* (SBS, 70; Stuttgart: KBW Verlag, 1974), pp. 22-23 (4 stages in Zechariah 1–8); L.A. Sinclair, 'Redaction of Zechariah 1–8', *BibRes* 20 (1975), pp. 36-47 (37-47; 4 stages in Zechariah 1–8); H.-G. Schöttler, *Gott inmitten seines Volkes: Die Neuordnung des Gottesvolkes nach Sacharja 1–6* (TTS, 43; Trier: Paulinus Verlag, 1987), pp. 164-68, 287-448; 5 stages in Zechariah 1–6).

78. Cf. Redditt, *Haggai, Zechariah*, p. 80 (Redditt distinguishes between an original edition, sent back to the exiles in Babylon, and a second edition, in which 4.6-10, 6.11b-13 and 3.1-10 were added; concerning this second edition he states, 'The night visions, however, would have lost much of their impact after the completion of the temple... While a later date for these chapters cannot be disproved, it would seem best to date the final edition of Zechariah 1–8 (with Haggai placed before it) between November of 518 and April of 516'.

79. Jeremias, *Nachtgesichte*, pp. 201-202; Seybold, *Bilder*, pp. 17, 57; P.L. Redditt, 'Zerubbabel, Joshua, and the Night Visions of Zechariah', *CBQ* 54 (1992), pp. 249-59 (253-54); Cook, *Prophecy*, p. 136 n. 49; Redditt, *Haggai, Zechariah*, pp. 40, 42.

For these arguments to work, there needs to be a significant level of uniformity in the presentation of the visions. However, when one looks at the vision reports in Zechariah 1–6, one finds that there is a great deal of diversity.[80] In the opinion of Niditch, such liberty of experimenting with the form of visions is characteristic for this period: 'In the late 6th century B.C., the time of the restoration, the form undergoes growth and change'.[81]

This diversity can easily be shown when one looks at the introductory formulas.[82] I have collected all the introductory formulas to be found in the vision reports in Figure 4.

Figure 4. *Introductory formula in Zechariah 1–6*

| | |
|---|---|
| 1.8 | ראיתי הלילה והנה |
| 2.1* | ואשא את־עיני וארא והנה |
| 2.3 | ויארני |
| 2.5* | ואשא את־עיני וארא והנה |
| 3.1 | ויראני יהוה |
| 4.1 | וישב המלאך הדבר בי |
| | ויעירני כאיש אשר־יעור משנתו |
| | ויאמר אלי ... |
| | ואמר ראיתי והנה |
| 5.1⁽*⁾ | ואשוב ואשא עיני וארא והנה |

80. F. Horst, *Die zwölf kleinen Propheten: Nahum bis Maleachi* (HAT, 14; Tübingen: J.C.B. Mohr [Paul Siebeck], 1964), p. 210; compare also M. Butterworth, *Structure and the Book of Zechariah* (JSOTSup, 130; Sheffield: JSOT Press, 1992), p. 67. Interestingly, J.W. Rothstein, *Die Nachtgesichte des Sacharja: Studien zur Sacharjaprophetie und zur jüdischen Geschichte im ersten nachexilischen Jahrhundert* (BWANT, 8; Leipzig: J.C. Hinrichs, 1910), turned the whole argument upside down by arguing that the presence of unique formal features in Zechariah 3 strongly supports the authenticity of the chapter: he considers the uniqueness of the formal features in Zechariah 3 (p. 102) 'ein besonders bedeutsames Zeugnis dafür, daß wir hier wirklich der eigenen Aufzeichnung Sacharjas gegenüberstehen. Schwerlich wäre eine fremde Hand so sehr aus der Rolle gefallen'.

81. S. Niditch, *The Symbolic Vision in Biblical Tradition* (HSM, 30; Chico, CA: Scholars Press, 1980), p. 73; cf. Butterworth, *Structure*, p. 67 (on the unusual formal features in Zech. 3.1-7), 'These points do not conclusively prove the work of another hand, since it is not possible to predict the range of variations that a particular writer might employ—certainly not on the basis of the sample of Zechariah's work available to us'.

82. See Tollington, *Tradition*, pp. 34-35.

Figure 4. (cont.)

| 5.5[*] | ויצא המלאך הדבר בי |
| | ויאמר אלי שא נא עיניך וראה |
| 5.9* | ואשא את־עיני וארא והנה |
| 6.1[*] | ואשב ואשא עיני וארא והנה |

What is called the usual introductory formula, ואשא את־עיני וארא והנה, is found unmodified three times (marked with '*'), and more or less modified three more times (marked with '[*]'). Apart from the unusual formula at the beginning of Zechariah 3, one can count three more unusual formulae. In my view such diversity makes the force of taking the presence of one of the unusual formulas as an indication of the secondary nature of a specific vision report rather weak.

I will now turn to the absence of the Interpreting Angel and the absence of a dialogue in which details of the vision are explained. Again, one can exaggerate the uniformity in the other vision reports on this point. In the vision report in 2.5-17, the prophet interacts with a figure introduced as איש ובידו חבל מדה, but not about the explanation of objects seen in the vision. There is no interaction between the prophet and the Interpreting Angel, who does figure in the vision. The absence of the Interpreting Angel in 3.1-10 can also be explained from the fact that there was nothing in the vision which he needed to clarify.[83] His absence seems also to be presupposed by the remark about his return in 4.1: ...וישב המלאך הדבר בי.

Finally, let us look at the feature that the oracle is addressed not to the prophet, but to a historical person, Joshua, the high priest. This is indeed a distinctive mark of this vision report (but perhaps less distinctive for those who accept Zech. 4.6-10 with its mention of Zerubbabel as original to the vision report in Zechariah 4 [on the relationship between visions and oracles, see Chapter 5]). How one assesses this unique feature depends on how much creativity one allows for Zechariah.

*Symmetry.* The second reason why scholars consider the vision report in Zechariah 3 a secondary addition is the disruption of the symmetry of a

---

83. Rothstein, *Nachtgesichte*, p. 102; Beuken, *Haggai–Sacharja 1–8*, p. 283; Rudolph, *Haggai, Sacharja*, p. 93; L. Bauer, *Zeit des zweiten Tempels—Zeit der Gerechtigkeit: Zur sozio-ökonomischen Konzeption im Haggai–Sacharja–Maleachi-Korpus* (BEATAJ, 31; Frankfurt: Lang, 1991), p. 236.

sequence of originally seven visions which it causes.[84] Not only does the number of visions which scholars find in Zechariah 1–6 differ (options vary from seven, eight, to ten visions; see Fig. 5), but those who take the vision report in Zechariah 3 as original also are able to find symmetry in the vision reports.[85]

Figure 5. *The Number of Visions in Zechariah 1–6*

| chapter | 1 | 2 | | | 3 | 4 | 5 | | | 6 | |
|---|---|---|---|---|---|---|---|---|---|---|---|
| verse | 8— | 1-2 | 3-4 | 5— | 1— | 1— | 1-4 | 5-8 | 9-11 | 1— | 9— |
| 7 [86] | I | II | | III | | IV | V | VI | | VII | |
| 7+ [87] | I | II | | III | + | IV | V | VI | | VII | |
| 8 [88] | I | II | | III | IV | V | VI | VI | | VIII | |
| 9 [89] | I | II | | III | IV | V | VI | VI | | VIII | IX |
| 10 [90] | I | II | III | IV | V | VI | VII | VIII | IX | X | |

This makes it difficult to exclude one of the vision reports because it allegedly disrupts the symmetry of the cycle.

*Conclusion.* Two reasons have been given for considering Zechariah 3 as a vision report which originally did not belong to the cycle. The first one, the presence of unique formal features, has been shown to assume too high a level of uniformity. The second reason, the disruption of symmetry within the visions cycle is a very subjective matter: one can find symmetry in a vision cycle with Zechariah 3 included and in one without that chapter.

One can, therefore, still consider Zechariah 3 as an original part of the visions cycle.[91] More or less in the middle of the vision reports one

84. Jeremias, *Nachtgesichte*, p. 202; E.J.C. Tigchelaar, 'L'Ange qui parlait à Zacharie, est-il un personnage apocalyptique?', *EstBíb* 45 (1987), pp. 347-60 (349-50 n. 8); Van der Woude, 'Serubbabel', p. 147.

85. Beuken, *Haggai–Sacharja 1–8*, p. 282; J.G. Baldwin, *Haggai, Zechariah Malachi* (TOTC; London: Tyndale Press, 1972), p. 113.

86. Meyers and Meyers, *Haggai, Zechariah*.

87. Seybold, *Bilder*; Jeremias, *Nachtgesichte*; Amsler, *Aggée; Zacharie 1–8*; Redditt, *Haggai, Zechariah*.

88. Beuken, *Haggai–Sacharja 1–8*; L. Rignell, *Die Nachtgesichte des Sacharja* (Lund: C.W.K. Gleerup, 1950); Baldwin, *Haggai, Zechariah*.

89. M.-J. Lagrange, 'Notes sur les prophéties messianiques des derniers prophètes', *RB* NS 3 (1906), pp. 67-83.

90. Bauer, *Zeit*.

91. With R. Siebeneck, 'The Messianism of Aggeus and Proto-Zacharias', *CBQ*

would thus find two visions in which the two leaders of the temple building project each are addressed, Joshua in Zechariah 3, and Zerubbabel in Zechariah 4. Each has their own unique position and role, and each has their own unique needs to be provided for.[92]

### c. *Visions and Oracles*

Since the beginning of the twentieth century a consensus has emerged which holds that part of the oracle material in Zechariah 1–6 does not originally belong to the visions, but was inserted at a later stage, either by the prophet himself, or by a later redactor. The material that is generally considered to be secondary is 1.16-17, 2.10-17, 3.8-10, 4.6b-10a and 6.9-15 (see Fig. 6).

Figure 6. *Original and Secondary Oracles*

|         | original | secondary |
|---------|----------|-----------|
| 1.14-17 | 14-15    | 16-17     |
| 2.10-17 |          | 10-17     |
| 3.6-10  | 6-7      | 8-10      |
| 4.6-10  |          | 6-10      |
| 6.9-15  |          | 9-15      |

It is perhaps worth stressing that usually not all the oracle material in the vision reports is considered as secondary, but only part of it.[93] So,

19, pp. 312-28 (319-20); Beuken, *Haggai–Sacharja 1–8*, pp. 282-83; Baldwin, *Haggai, Zechariah*, p. 113; Rudolph, *Haggai, Sacharja*, pp. 63, 93-94; B. Halpern, 'The Ritual Background of Zechariah's Temple Song', *CBQ* 40 (1978), pp. 167-90 (170); W. Harrelson, 'The Trial of the High Priest Joshua: Zechariah 3', *Eretz Israel* 16 (H.M. Orlinksy Volume; 1982), pp. 116*-24* (118*); Petersen, *Haggai and Zechariah*, p. 112; R.L. Smith, *Micah–Malachi* (WBC, 32; Waco, TX: Word Books, 1984), pp. 198-99.

92. Cf. Baldwin, *Haggai, Zechariah*, p. 93.

93. Petersen, *Haggai and Zechariah*, pp. 120-21, is as far as I know the only one who argues that all the oracle material (1.14-17; 2.10-17; 3.6-10; 4.6-10; 6.10-14) in 1.7–6.15 is secondary. In D.J. Clark's analysis ('Vision and Oracle in Zechariah 1–6', in R.D. Bergen [ed.], *Biblical Hebrew and Discourse Linguistics* [Winona Lake, IN: Eisenbrauns, 1994], pp. 529-60 [553-54]), with respect to the whole of 1.14-17 and 3.6-10 'there is no real ground for separating the material from its traditional context in the vision', but 2.10-17, 4.6-10a and 6.9-15 are taken as secondary in their position in the vision reports. Redditt, 'Night Visions', pp. 254-59, considers 1.16-17 and 2.10-17 as original, and 3.1-7, 9, 4.6b-10a and 6.11b-13 as secondary; 3.8, 10 was added in another later stage.

for example, in the first chapter vv. 14-17 comprise the oracle material which the Interpreting Angel tells the prophet to proclaim (קְרָא לֵאמֹר), but the secondary material is said to be present only in part of vv. 14-17, that is in vv. 16-17. In Zechariah 3 the oracle material stretches from vv. 6-10, but only vv. 8-10 are seen as secondary. But, as the figure shows, both צמח oracles (3.8 and 6.9-15) would fall into the category of secondary oracles.

In the last fifteen years or so several scholars have abandoned such a separation between original and secondary in the oracles in Zechariah 1–6, arguing that all the oracle material said to be secondary should be seen as integral to the vision reports.[94] It seems almost impossible to discuss this issue without falling into some form of circular reasoning, whether one deals with it before one starts examining the text, or after one has finished studying the text. Yet it is difficult to make up one's mind over this issue before one has at least some understanding of what the visions and the oracles are about.

For example, Redditt writes, 'Some scholars routinely eliminate the oracles and exhortations as additions, but visions frequently include oracles…and later apocalyptic literature characteristically combined visions with exhortations'. He then offers a criterion for distinguishing between original and secondary: 'The real issue is whether all the material in the second section is self-consistent'.[95] When Redditt proposes to leave a routine approach behind and to use the issue 'whether all the material in the second section is self-consistent' as a criterion (which leads him to conclude that Zechariah 3, 4.6b-10a and 6.11b-13 are secondary), one needs to have a thorough understanding of what the text says in order to be able to evaluate the use of such a criterion.

---

94. See in particular Van der Woude, 'Serubbabel', pp. 141-46; cf. Halpern, 'Ritual Background', pp. 168-70 (however, Halpern relocates 4.6-10 to be read after 3.8); Van der Woude, *Zacharia* (POT; Nijkerk: Callenbach, 1984), p. 30; Harrelson, 'Trial', p. 119; Tigchelaar, 'Ange', p. 352 and n. 13; R. Hanhart, *Dodekapropheton*. VII. *Sacharja 1–8* (BKAT, 14.7; Neukirchen–Vluyn: Neukirchener Verlag, 1998), p. 46.

95. Redditt, *Haggai, Zechariah*, p. 39; a similar criticism is found in M.H. Floyd, 'Cosmos and History in Zechariah's View of the Restoration (Zechariah 1:7-6:15)', in H.T.C. Sun, Keith L. Eades, *et al.* (eds.), *Problems in Biblical Theology: Essays in Honor of Rolf Knierim* (Grand Rapids: Eerdmans, 1997), pp. 125-44 (126 n. 5), where he calls the excision of the oracular materials in Zech. 1.14-17, 3.8-10 and 4.6aβ-10 from the vision reports 'purely arbitrary and unwarranted'.

Therefore, the strategy I will adopt is the following. I will first study the text as we have it now and then in a separate chapter (Chapter 5) return to the question of the relationship between visions and oracles, where I will deal with the question whether the present text which I have sought to explain is really the original text of the vision reports.

Chapter 2

ZEMAH AND THE PRIEST(S)

When one reads the צמח oracles, one finds that there are a number of
connections between Zemah and priests. (a) The oracles which announce the coming of Zemah are both addressed to Joshua, the high
priest; in the first case he is accompanied by his colleagues (3.8), in the
second he appears on his own (6.11-12). (b) The second oracle is
attached to a symbolic act in which Zechariah is told to set a crown on
the head of Joshua the high priest (6.11). (c) In the course of the second
oracle an unidentified priest figures (6.13).

These various connections between Zemah and different members of
the priesthood are the subject of this Chapter. I will first discuss the fact
that both oracles are addressed to priests. Secondly, I will study the
symbolic action in which Zechariah is told to set a crown on the head of
Joshua the high priest. Thirdly, I will look at the position of the priest
who figures in the צמח oracle in 6.12-15. Finally, I will look at the
position of Joshua, the high priest, in Zech. 3.7. (I will discuss the
supposed presence of a priest in Zech. 4.14 in Chapter 6.)

1. *Priests as the Addressees of the Oracles Concerning* צמח

a. *The Priests 'Men of Omen'*
The first oracle in which the coming of Zemah is announced is
addressed to 'Joshua the high priest, you and your friends' (Zech. 3.8).
Here Joshua and his colleagues are addressed as אנשי מופת 'men of
good omen'.

The same word מופת is used for the prophet Isaiah and his children
(Isaiah 8.18 [מופת complements אות]; 20.1-5). While Isa. 8.18 does not
make explicit in what sense Isaiah and his children are 'signs and
portents', in Isaiah 20 Isaiah's going naked and barefoot for three years
is 'a sign and a portent against Egypt and Ethiopia'. The prophet
Ezekiel is also a מופת, when he packs his bag to leave for exile (Ezek.

12.6-7, 11), when he does not mourn when his wife has died (Ezek. 24.16-17, 24), and when he is able to speak again after YHWH has taken away the pride and glory of Jerusalem (Ezek. 24.27). These examples show what the מופת אנשי in Zech. 3.8 have in common with other people who are called to be מופת: they are a portent to others. The examples also show what is unique about the use of מופת in Zech. 3.8: here it is not the prophet (or his family), but other people (priests) who are the אנשי מופת.[1]

In his study of prophetic drama in the Old Testament, Stacey describes the difference between אות and מופת, the two words often used for sign or portent, in the following way:

> *môpēt* is used to describe people and events only, whereas *'ôt* is used for objects as well...*môpēt* usually means something extraordinary and *'ôt* can often mean something mundane... Occasionally *môpēt* implies the ominous, whereas, in this respect, *'ôt* is neutral.[2]

Eichrodt describes the function of a מופת as[3] a 'sign to accompany a miracle and revelation of God', which amplifies an oracle of Yahweh and shows that it is true.

Most scholars interpret the function of מופת in Zech. 3.8 as providing a guarantee that the oracle about the coming of צמח will be fulfilled. So, Ackroyd considers the existence of the priestly order as 'a divine sign of the favour which God is about to show to his people'. Joshua and the priests 'are themselves, by their very presence, signs of something which is to take place... The presence of Joshua and his associates foreshadows the appointment of this royal figure...'[4]

---

1. F. Hitzig, *Die zwölf kleinen Propheten erklärt* (KEHAT; Leipzig: Hirzel, 1881), p. 345. Cf. Meyers and Meyers, *Haggai, Zechariah*, p. 200.

2. W.D. Stacey, *Prophetic Drama in the Old Testament* (London: Epworth Press, 1990), pp. 17-18. Cf. Meyers and Meyers, *Haggai, Zechariah*, pp. 199-200.

3. 'Ein «Wunder- und Offenbarungszeichen Gottes», das eine Weissagung Jahves bekräftigt und als wahr erweist' (W. Eichrodt, 'Vom Symbol zum Typos: Ein Beitrag zur Sacharja-Exegese', *TZ* 13 [1957], pp. 509-22 [511]).

4. Ackroyd, *Exile*, p. 189-90. Cf. Lagrange, 'Prophéties', pp. 70-71; M. Bič, *Das Buch Sacharja* (Berlin: Evangelische Verlagsanstalt, 1962), p. 50; Baldwin, *Haggai, Zechariah*, p. 116; K. Elliger, *Die Propheten Nahum, Habakuk, Zephanja, Haggai, Sacharja, Maleachi* (ATD, 25.2; Göttingen: Vandenhoeck & Ruprecht, 6th edn, 1967), p. 124; Amsler, *Aggée; Zacharie 1–8*, p. 83; Hanhart, *Sacharja*, p. 194; Mason, *Preaching*, p. 211; Reventlow, *Haggai, Sacharja*, p. 55. Others use language somewhat stronger than 'sign', e.g. T. Chary, *Aggée, Zacharie, Malachie* (SB; Paris: J. Gabalda, 1969), p. 81, 'Ils sont plus qu'un simple signe: leur présence

I will argue that this is also the direction in which the answer to the
question why the crown was set on the head of Joshua the high priest
must be sought. As a member of the priesthood he was an איש מופת
(Zech. 3.8). As the most prominent member of the priesthood he was
the most obvious one to be singled out to participate in the symbolic
action which introduced the second, and much more specific, oracle
concerning the arrival of צמח, the future ruler. The precise nature of
this symbolic action is the subject of the next section.

## 2. A Crown to Be Set on the Head of Joshua the High Priest

The second oracle in which the coming of Zemah is announced is
embedded in a symbolic action which the prophet is commanded to
perform on the high priest. Zechariah is commanded to make a crown
from silver and gold which he is to receive, and set it on the head of the
high priest, and then to deliver an oracle from the LORD concerning the
coming of צמח (Zech. 6.9-15).

In this section I will discuss the command to set the crown upon the
head of Joshua, the son of Jehozadak, the high priest. Both the presence
of a crown, interpreted as a 'royal crown', and the act of setting this
crown on the head of the high priest, interpreted as a coronation, have
caused a considerable amount of puzzlement on the part of scholars,
and these two elements have become some of the reasons for altering
the text to make the head of Zerubbabel the destination of the crown
(see my discussion in Chapter 5). However, the case for identifying the
crown as a royal crown and the act as a coronation is not as clear as has
often been assumed.

### a. How Many Crowns?
The first thing to establish is the precise number of crowns. In Zech.
6.9-15 one finds two different forms of the Hebrew noun עטרה. In the
first (v. 11) instance the form is עֲטָרֹות, in the second instance (v. 14),
עֲטָרֹת. At first sight these forms look like plural forms, and in dictio-

---

en ce lieu, leur existence dans les conditions actuelles constitue une garantie, on
pourrait risquer le terme de "sacrement" de la venue de "Germe"'; compare J. Wellhausen, *Die kleinen Propheten übersetzt und erklärt* (Berlin: Reimer, 3rd edn,
1898), p. 181, 'Bürgschaft'; S.R. Driver, *The Minor Prophets. Nahum, Habakkuk,
Zephaniah, Haggai, Zechariah, Malachi* (CB; Edinburgh: Jack, 1906), p. 197,
'pledge'; Beuken, *Haggai–Sacharja 1–8*, p. 275, 'Garantie'.

naries one finds that the usual form for 'crown' (singular) is עֲטָרָה. Is it really one crown, then, or are there more?

Scholars take three positions: (a) In both cases the noun is singular, and only one crown is intended.[5] (b) The noun is plural in both v. 11 and v. 14.[6] (c) In v. 11 עטרות is plural and refers to two crowns, one of which is commented upon in v. 11, the other of which appears in v. 14 where עטרת is to be taken as singular.[7]

The problem with finding two crowns in this passage is that there is no unmistakable evidence in the text to support it. Meyers and Meyers, for example, have to resort to an artificial reading of the text, which adds elements in the translation that are absent in the Hebrew: ועשׂית עטרות ושׂמת בראשׁ יהושׁע is translated 'make crowns. You will place [one] on the head of Joshua', and ...והעטרת תהיה לזכרון becomes 'The [other] crown will be...as a reminder'.

The only element in the text itself which could be taken as indicating that there were crowns (plural) is the form of the word used for crown: עֲטָרוֹת in v. 11, and עֲטָרֹת in v. 14. However, עטר(ו)ת can also be explained as a form with a singular (!) feminine ending -ōt.[8] This would not be the only occasion where a word ending in -ōt is a singular form: I discuss a number of cases in an excursus at the end of this Chapter (Excursus 1). If one interprets both forms as singular feminine, there is no need to alter the vocalisation in v. 14 to read עֲטֶרֶת,[9] an operation which would solve one problem and create a new one: the proposed form עֲטֶרֶת with final -t is never attested as a form in the absolute state,

5. Rignell, *Nachtgesichte*, p. 223; Beuken, *Haggai–Sacharja 1–8*, p. 275; E. Lipiński, 'Recherches sur le livre de Zacharie', *VT* 20 (1970), pp. 25-55 (34-35); Rudolph, *Haggai, Sacharja*, p. 128; Schöttler, *Gottesvolk*, p. 147; Mason, *Preaching*, p. 210; Reventlow, *Haggai, Sacharja*, p. 72.

6. Beyse, *Serubbabel*, p. 38; G. Wallis, 'Erwägungen', pp. 235-36; Petersen, *Haggai and Zechariah*, p. 275; Redditt, *Haggai, Zechariah*, pp. 40, 77.

7. Meyers and Meyers, *Haggai, Zechariah*, p. 336, 350-52, 363.

8. Rudolph, *Haggai, Sacharja*, p. 128; Beuken, *Haggai–Sacharja 1–8*, p. 275 n. 1; Hanhart, *Sacharja*, p. 408; Reventlow, *Haggai, Sacharja*, p. 72.

9. An alteration made by, e.g., K. Marti, *Das Dodekapropheton* (KHC, 13; Tübingen: J.C.B. Mohr, 1904), p. 420; W. Nowack, *Die kleinen Propheten* (HKAT, 3.4; Göttingen: Vandenhoeck & Ruprecht, 3rd edn, 1922), p. 353; H.G. Mitchell, *A Critical and Exegetical Commentary on Haggai and Zechariah* (ICC; Edinburgh: T. & T. Clark, 1912), p. 189; Elliger in *BHS*; Horst, *Propheten*, p. 236; Amsler, *Aggée; Zacharie 1–8*, p. 105 n. 4; Meyers and Meyers, *Haggai, Zechariah*, pp. 349-51.

only in the construct state;[10] the form in the absolute state is עֲטָרָה.

Two other observations confirm the correctness of the idea that just one crown was intended. (a) 'The crown' (singular) leads to the most straightforward way of interpreting the singular form of the verb in v. 14 (תהיה), even though the presence of a verb in the singular is not an absolute proof that the subject of the verb is singular (not only when the order is Verb–Subject, but even when the order is Subject–Verb).[11] (b) Zechariah has been quite precise in counting objects on other occasions: 'four horns' and 'four smiths' in 1.18, 20; 'seven facets' on the stone in 3.9; the 'seven lamps' of the lamp stand in 4.2; 'two olive trees', 'two sons of oil' in 4.14; 'two women' in 5.9; 'four chariots... from between two mountains' in 6.1; and peaceful understanding 'between them both' in 6.13. The absence of the numeral 'two' in 6.12-14 is another element which makes the idea of two crowns unlikely, 'in which case one would also expect שתי עטרות (cf. 4.14; 6.13bβ)', as Schöttler remarks.[12]

To sum up: translating 'make a crown' in v. 11, rather than 'make crowns' (that is, two crowns), is the simplest way to account for the absence of a numeral to indicate that more than one crown was meant, and also for the singular verbal form תהיה in v. 14. The feminine ending *-ōt* can be explained as singular, as it occasionally is in biblical Hebrew.

### b. *The Crown to Be 'Set on the Head'*
Some scholars have questioned the correctness of the translation 'set upon the head', and as a result have denied that the destination of the crown is the head of the high priest. They suggest interpreting the

10. Cf. *HALAT*, s.v.; A. Petitjean, *Les oracles du Proto-Zacharie: Un programme du restoration pour la communauté juive après l'exil* (Paris: Gabalda; Louvain: Éditions Imprimerie Orientaliste, 1969), p. 280; Rudolph, *Haggai, Sacharja*, p. 128; contra Meyers and Meyers, *Haggai, Zechariah*, pp. 349-51, 361. The only place Meyers and Meyers mention in support of their thesis that עטרת is an absolute state is Isa. 62.3, but there עטרת is most likely not an absolute state, but a construct state: והיית עֲטֶרֶת תפארת ביד־יהוה 'You shall be a crown of beauty in the hand of the LORD'.

11. See F.E. König, *Historisch-kritisches Lehrgebäude der Hebräischen Sprache*, III (Leipzig: J.C. Hinrichs, 1897), §348q; P. Joüon and T. Muraoka, *A Grammar of Biblical Hebrew* (SB, 14; Rome: Pontificio Istituto Biblico, 1991), §150g; cf. Redditt, *Haggai, Zechariah*, p. 77.

12. 'Dann wäre auch שתי עטרות (vgl. 4,14; 6,13bβ) zu erwarten' (Schöttler, *Gottesvolk*, p. 153).

phrase שׂים בראשׁ as meaning 'set before', either by altering בראשׁ into לפני (cf. נתן לפני in 3.9),[13] or by taking שׂים בראשׁ (to be distinguished from the usual שׂים על ראשׁ for 'set on the head') as an idiomatic expression for 'put at someone's disposal, entrust' (like the Akkadian *šakānu ina rēši*).[14]

Both proposals fail to convince. The suggestion of Van Hoonacker to alter בראשׁ into לפני involves an emendation of the text, which should only be considered if there is no way to make sense of MT (but there is, as I hope to show below). The alternative proposal of Van der Woude to translate 'entrust it [the crown] to Joshua' is problematic for two reasons. In the first place, there are problems with Van der Woude's remark about the distribution of the two phrases שׂים בראשׁ and שׂים על ראשׁ. Van der Woude states, in Biblical Hebrew 'set on the head' is usually not *śîm beroʾš* (so Zech. 6.11b), but *śîm ʿal roʾš*, cf. Zech. 3.5; Gen. 48.18; Exod. 29.6 etc'. [15]

But this is not a satisfactory presentation of the evidence. In Figure 7 I have set out the instances where שׂים + [prep] + ראשׁ is used for 'set on the head of X' (and X is a person). I have also included the synonymous נתן + [prep] + ראשׁ (Van der Woude rightly points to this synonymy).

Figure 7. *The Distribution of* בראשׁ *and* על ראשׁ

|  | על | | ב | |
|---|---|---|---|---|
|  | שׂים | נתן | שׂים | נתן |
| head dress | Exod. 29.6; Lev. 8.9; Zech. 3.5 | 1 Sam. 17.38 | 1 Kgs 20.31; Est. 2.17 | Est. 6.8; Ezek. 16.12 |
| hand | Gen. 48.18; 2 Sam. 3.19 |  |  |  |
| oil |  | Lev. 14.18, 29 |  |  |
| (requite) sin |  |  |  | 1 Kgs 8.32 = 2 Chron. 6.23; Ezek. 17.19 |

13. A. Van Hoonacker, *Les Douze Petits Prophètes traduits et commentés* (EBib; Paris: Gabalda, 1908), p. 632.

14. Van der Woude, 'Serubbabel', pp. 149-50.

15. 'Dennoch heißt ›setzen aufs Haupt‹ im Bibelhebräischen in der Regel nicht *śîm beroʾš* (so Sach 6,11b), sondern *śîm ʿal roʾš*, vgl. Sach 3,5; Gen. 48,18; Exod. 29,6 usw' ('Serubbabel', p. 149).

The first thing to be noticed is the low frequency of each of the phrases, which should lead to caution concerning any generalizing statement. But it seems fair to say that the evidence (note particularly the more or less equal distribution of cases where the verb is used with a headdress as object) does not support Van der Woude's suggestion that על ראש שים is the more usual phrase for 'set on the head'. This conclusion would make the choice of שים בראש in Zech. 6.11 far less significant than it is in Van der Woude's analysis, and therefore the presence of this phrase does not contribute to a justification for his alternative translation.

In the second place, Van der Woude's case is seriously weakened by the fact that he is not able to refer to a single passage in the Old Testament where the Hebrew phrase שים בראש is used in a way similar to the Akkadian *šakānu ina rēši* 'put at someone's disposal, entrust'. In sum: both forms of the proposal to translate שים בראש as 'set before' do not satisfy, which means that the crown is indeed to be 'set on the head of Joshua'.

### c. *A Crown on the Head of a High Priest*
The problems which scholars find in having the head of the high priest as the destination of the crown are summarised by Rudolph in the following words:[16] 'The crown was a symbol of royal dignity, while the high priest would wear a turban… This is the reason why so many interpreters replace "Joshua" in v. 11 with "Zerubbabel"'.

---

16. 'Die Kröne war doch Symbol der Königswürde, während der Hohepriester den Turban trug […] Das ist der Grund, weshalb so viele Exegeten in V. 11 Josua durch Serubbabel ersetzen' (Rudolph, *Haggai, Sacharja*, p. 130, and also p. 132). Others find the problem not so much in the reference to setting a crown on the head of the high priest as such, but in its early occurrence just after the exile. Beuken writes (*Haggai–Sacharja 1–8*, p. 275), 'Ein Ritual, in welchem dem Hohenpriester die Königskrone aufs Haupt gesetzt wird, ist so früh nach dem Exil gewiß eine höchst unwahrscheinliche Sache'. Schöttler argues along the same lines: he thinks (*Gottesvolk*, p. 381; see also pp. 387, 398, 448) it is improbable 'daß in dieser Zeit konsolidierter persischer Herrschaft ein "Hantieren mit Königskronen" oder gar eine solche (stellvertretende oder vorläufige) Krönung gefahrlos möglich waren'. He takes v. 12 to be secondary and therefore interprets the crown on the head of the high priest Joshua as a sign of *his* ruler position. For him, the presence of the idea of a royal crown destined for the head of the high priest is one of the reasons to date the insertion of this episode to the end of the fifth or somewhere in the fourth century BCE.

Such an observation seems to be based on at least the following two assumptions: (a) the crown should be identified as a royal crown,[17] and (b) the action the prophet is commanded to perform should be seen as a coronation.[18] Both assumptions require a closer investigation. I will first look at the semantics of עטרה, the word for 'crown' used in Zech. 6.9-15, and then discuss in the next section ('The Action not a Coronation') the question whether the concept of 'coronation' is an appropriate description of the action which Zechariah is told to perform.

*The Semantics of* עטרה. For a proper understanding of the meaning of עטרה, and the associations this word may convey, a detailed discussion of the use of this word in the Old Testament is essential. The noun עטרה is used to refer to a number of different crowns in different contexts, of which I will provide a brief survey.

עטרה is very popular in the vocabulary of the prophets. Isaiah denounces 'the proud crown of the drunkards of Ephraim' (Isa. 28.1, 3). In an oracle spoken by the prophet Ezekiel, God speaks tenderly about 'the beautiful crown' which he put on the head of Jerusalem, personified as a young woman (Ezek. 16.12). Ezekiel summons the wicked prince (נשיא) of Israel to 'remove the turban, and take off the crown' (Ezek. 21.31[26]); the same prophet describes the men who committed adultery with Oholibah as those who 'put bracelets upon the hands of the women, and beautiful crowns upon their heads' (Ezek. 23.42). In prophetic literature עטרה is used metaphorically of God:

> In that day the LORD of hosts will be a crown [עטרת] of glory, and a diadem [צפירת] of beauty, to the remnant of his people (Isa. 28.5).

and of Zion/Jerusalem:

> You shall be a crown of beauty [עטרת] in the hand of the LORD, and a royal diadem [צניף מלוכה Q] in the hand of your God (Isa. 62.3).

The shattered community after the destruction of Jerusalem laments

---

17. Rudolph, *Haggai, Sacharja*, p. 130, and also p. 132; cf. Beuken, *Haggai–Sacharja 1–8*, p. 275, 'die Königskrone'; Amsler, *Aggée; Zacharie 1–8*, p. 107, 'la couronne est l'insigne d'un roi'; Meyers and Meyers, *Haggai, Zechariah*, p. 353-54, 'the crown which, to a certain extent, is a royal insignia of office'; Schöttler, *Gottesvolk*, p. 382, cf. p. 387, 'Zeichen königlicher Herrschaft und Würde'.

18. A great majority of scholars; for references, see section d. 'The Action not a Coronation' below.

(Lam. 5.16), 'The crown has fallen from our head; woe to us, for we have sinned!'

עטרה is also found in wisdom literature. In Proverbs the son/student is told not to forsake wisdom, because she 'will place on your head a fair garland [לוית־חן]; she will bestow on you a beautiful crown [עטרת]' (Prov. 4.9). עטרה is used metaphorically of a good wife (Prov. 12.4), of grandchildren (Prov. 17.6), of wisdom (Prov. 14.24) and of grey hair (Prov. 16.31). Job blames God because he 'has stripped from me my glory, and taken the crown from my head' (Job 19.9). Job looks forward to receiving the indictment written by his adversary, 'Surely I would carry it on my shoulder; I would bind it on me as a crown' (Job 31.36).

In a number of passages עטרה is associated with kings. In such passages it is most often (but not always) used for the crown which a king wears. The occasions are various: the daughters of Zion are invited to (Song 3.11) 'behold King Solomon, with the crown with which his mother crowned him [עטרה שעטרה־לו] on the day of his wedding, on the day of the gladness of his heart'. God sets a crown on the head of the king as a token of his favour (Ps. 21.4);[19] the crown of a defeated enemy king is taken from his head and set on David's head (2 Sam. 12.30 [= 1 Chron. 20.2])[20]. The loss of the crown is also the fate of a king and a queen mother in Judah in one of the oracles of Jeremiah, 'Take a lowly seat, for your beautiful crown has come down from your head' (Jer. 13.18).

עטרה is once used for the crown which a king gives to one of his loyal subjects: on the day when Haman's plot to annihilate the Jews folded and Haman himself was impaled, Mordecai presented himself before king Ahasuerus, was given the king's (signet) ring, which once belonged to Haman, and eventually Mordecai 'went out from the presence of the king in royal robes of blue and white, with a great golden crown and a mantle of fine linen and purple' (Est. 8.15).

Such a broad range of contexts in which the noun עטרה may be found would justify a conclusion drawn by Kellermann[21] that עטרה is a

---

19. On the interpretation of the setting of Ps. 21.4, see Excursus 2 at the end of the Chapter.

20. In a similar episode, this time dealing with the crown of king Saul, not עטרה but נזר is used (2 Sam. 1.10).

21. D. Kellermann, 'עטר', *ThWAT*, VI, cols. 21-31 (24).

more general term and that it functions as a superordinate[22] term (*Überbegriff*) in its lexical field, which includes words like לֹוְיָה 'wreath, garland', מִצְנֶפֶת 'turban', נֵזֶר 'crown', צָנִיף 'turban', and צְפִירָה 'diadem' (see the diagram, Fig. 8).

Figure 8. עֲטָרָה *in its Lexical Field*

Does this evidence concerning the use of עטרה support the assumption made by many that the עטרה in Zechariah 6 is a 'royal crown'? In my opinion, this depends on what is meant by the phrase 'royal crown'. From the nature of the discussion of the phrase and its meaning in the context of the צמח oracle, one gets the impression that 'royal crown' is often taken to imply 'coronation crown'.[23] It may be useful to define more precisely the terms used here. A 'coronation' I will define as 'setting a crown on someone's head as an action (or part of a sequence of actions) which serves to install that person in a particular office, for example that of king'. I will use the word 'crowning' to refer to 'setting a crown on someone's head'.

As the survey has shown, עטרה is used in a variety of contexts for crowns associated with kings, and in that sense it can be said to be a royal crown. That not every royal crown is also a coronation crown can be shown when one takes a closer look at the passages where we find crowns (עטרה, but also other words) which are in one way or another associated with kings. Only in a limited number of cases are the crowns identified as 'royal', for example כתר מלכות.[24] Yet in most cases it can be said that there is something royal about the crown and there is no problem in considering them to be 'royal crowns' in a more general

---

22. J. Lyons, *Introduction to Theoretical Linguistics* (Cambridge: Cambridge University Press, 1968), pp. 454-55, illustrates the use of the term 'superordinate' with the following example: 'We will say that *scarlet, crimson, vermilion*, etc., are co-hyponyms of *red*, and *tulip, violet, rose*, etc. co-hyponyms of *flower*. Conversely, we will say that *red* is *superordinate* with respect to its hyponyms'.

23. E.g. the discussion in Meyers and Meyers, *Haggai, Zechariah*, pp. 352-54.

24. Est. 1.11; 2.17; 6.8.

sense. As the passages make clear, there may be various occasions
when a king wears a crown: a coronation ceremony (נזר),[25] a royal wedding (עטרה),[26] defeat of an enemy king (נזר and עטרה),[27] the occasion
of the bestowal of divine favour (עטרה).[28] Then there are occasions
where not a king but someone else wears a crown, presented to him by
or on behalf of the king, a crown either identified as 'royal' (כתר
מלכות),[29] or without such an identification (עטרה).[30]

This latter case might be one where the correctness of the label 'royal
crown' might be disputed. The crown given to Mordecai (Est. 8.15) is
obviously not *the* royal crown which the king wears; on the other hand,
the phrase לבוש מלכות indicates that a piece of clothing not worn by
the king can be described as 'royal' (and compare the כתר מלכות in an
identical case in Est. 6.8). Another case where one may want to dispute
the qualifier 'royal' for a crown is the crown presented to king Solomon
on the day of his wedding (Song 3.11). Such objections do not create
problems for my position.

But I find it problematic to label all these crowns as 'coronation
crowns'. At least two of the crowns mentioned in the passages quoted
above are unquestionably not the same as the coronation crown: the
crown given at the occasion of the wedding (Song 3.11), and the crown
taken from the defeated enemy king and set upon the head of his victor
(2 Sam. 12.30 [= 1 Chron. 20.2]). To these one might want to add the
crown presented by the king to a benefactor (Est. 8.15), if one does not
object to seeing this as a royal crown in a more general sense. Here we
have royal crowns which clearly are not coronation crowns.

*Words for Crowns Used in Coronations.* In my view, such evidence
gives reason to question the identification of the royal crown in Zech.
6.11, 14 as a coronation crown. It would go too far to state that the use
of the more general word עטרה excludes such an identification, yet it
remains fair to say that there is nothing in the use of עטרה that requires

---

25.  2 Kgs 11.12 (= 2 Chron. 23.11).
26.  Song 3.11.
27.  2 Sam. 1.10; 2 Sam. 12.30 (= 1 Chron. 20.2).
28.  Ps. 21.4.
29.  Est. 6.8.
30.  Est. 8.15. Though it is not stated explicitly that the king was the one who
gave the crown to Mordecai, it seems natural to assume that the crown was given to
him by the king or on behalf of the king.

this identification, and that—more significantly—עטרה is not the most obvious choice for a word for a crown used in a coronation. Out of all these passages which mention crowns associated with kings there is only one with regard to which someone might want to argue that עטרה is used in a context dealing with a coronation. The interpretation of that passage, Ps. 21.4, is somewhat controversial, but in my view this passage does not deal with a coronation, as I will argue in Excursus 2.

On the other hand, in the two accounts in the Old Testament which describe a coronation (or something which comes very close to a coronation, in the case of Esther) the noun used is *not* עטרה, but either נזר or כתר:

> Then he brought out the king's son, and put the crown upon him [ויתן עליו את־הנזר], and gave him the testimony; and they proclaimed him king, and anointed him; and they clapped their hands, and said, "Long live the king!" (2 Kgs 11.12 [= 2 Chron. 23.11]).

> the king loved Esther more than all the women, and she found grace and favour in his sight more than all the virgins, so that he set the royal crown on her head [וישם כתר־מלכות בראשה] and made her queen instead of Vashti (Est. 2.17).

*Conclusion.* I conclude that עטרה is a rather general word for 'crown', used for the headdress worn by all sorts of people,[31] including kings,

31. Cf. Redditt, 'Night Visions', p. 252, 'Petersen is correct that the crown(s) need not have been royal'; Tollington, *Tradition*, p. 166, 'In the Old Testament the word עטרה (crown) is sometimes associated with royalty although it occurs more often in a figurative sense symbolizing honour or status'. In my view it is difficult to find in the materials from which the crown in Zechariah 6 is made (silver and gold) a clue concerning the precise nature of the crown. Our information about the material from which a royal crown is usually made is extremely limited. Meyers and Meyers state (*Haggai, Zechariah*, p. 354) that 'traditional royal (and priestly) crowns...were made of gold according to the biblical sources and according to the evidence of archaeological and iconographic sources'. They do not specify what archaeological and iconographic sources present this evidence (nor how they can tell the material of a crown from an iconographic source). The biblical sources they refer to (pp. 348-49) are Exod. 28.36-37 and Ps. 21.4. The reference to Exod. 28.36-37 is of limited relevance, since it deals with the 'plate of pure gold' belonging to the headdress of the priest. That leaves us with the reference to Ps. 21.4, which is problematic because one cannot be sure whether the crown is a coronation crown, a royal crown, or just a crown. Meyers and Meyers also mention a 'late Hellenistic (?) Phoenician text' (p. 363; *KAI* 60) where the lines '...to crown with a

but—as far as the evidence allows us to tell—not priests.[32] As far as the evidence goes, it is not used for the crown worn on the occasion of a royal coronation: in the two accounts of such a coronation one finds נזר and כתר. In other words, עטרה may be labelled a 'royal crown' in specific contexts (and Zech. 6.12-15 would be one of those, as the continuation of the passage suggests), but the word is not an especially likely candidate for a 'coronation crown'.

### d. *The Action not a Coronation*
So far I have argued that the crown in Zechariah 6 is not necessarily a 'coronation crown'. Now I want to explore this issue further by asking the question concerning the precise nature of the action which Zechariah is commanded to perform.

*A Coronation?* A great number of scholars refer to the action the prophet is commanded to perform as a coronation. They either use a word like 'coronation' to describe the act,[33] or they use language which describes a state of affairs which is the result of a coronation, phrases

---

wreath son of Magon / whom the community appointed over the temple...a golden wreath ['*ṭrt*] weighing fully 20 dareikens' are said to provide 'unexpected support for our proposal that the true monarchic crown was crafted in gold'. Unfortunately, they do not discuss how one can derive information about the material of which a 'true monarchic crown' is made from a passage dealing with someone 'appointed over the temple'.

32.    The usual headdress of the priest is either a נזר 'crown' or a מצנפת 'turban' (e.g. Exod. 28–29; Lev. 8.9; 21.12; the cognate צניף is used in Zech. 3 for the turban on the head of Joshua the high priest). One finds a priest wearing a crown in texts outside the Hebrew canon of the Old Testament. E.g. עטרה in Sir. 45.12, and στέφανος in 1 Macc. 10.20 and *T. Levi* 8.1-10 (see the discussion in Schöttler, *Gottesvolk*, pp. 382-86). In the light of this, Redditt's conclusion at the end of his brief survey of the use of עטרה in Zech. 6.11, 14 (*Haggai, Zechariah*, p. 77, 'the crowns could have been intended for anyone') needs a minor qualification: anyone, apart from the priest. Compare also *BRL*[2], p. 288 'Nach dem Zeugnis des ATs trugen verschiedene Personen bei unterschiedlichen Anlässen Diademe (hebr. "*ʿṭārā*)'.

33.    Others use the word ritual: Beuken, *Haggai–Sacharja 1–8*, p. 275, 'Ritual'; H.G. May, 'A Key to the Interpretation of Zechariah's Visions', *JBL* 57.2 (1938), pp. 173-84 (p. 175 n. 14), 'ordination ritual' (it seems that his use of the word 'ordination' overlaps with my definition of 'coronation'). Mowinckel seems to argue along similar lines (*He that Cometh*, p. 121), if his remark about 'reflections of the ritual of the enthronement of the king' in the visions refers to this passage.

like Joshua having received a 'position of a ruler'.[34] Petersen is one of a small number of scholars who—in my view appropriately—question the belief that what we are dealing with in Zech. 6.9-15 is a coronation. He argues that setting a crown on someone's head in ancient Israel was not by itself performative, 'the act of placing a crown on someone's head did not in itself signify the actual conferral of kingship or high priesthood'.[35]

In my discussion of the semantics of עטרה I have produced evidence that supports this line of interpretation. In the Old Testament one finds various instances of a crowning that is not a coronation, occasions like a wedding (Song 3.11; cf. Ezek. 16.12), a victory over an enemy king (2 Sam. 12.30 [= 1 Chron. 20.2]), and the bestowal of approval (Ps. 21.4; cf. Est. 8.15).

As we have seen, whereas one finds the word עטרה used on all these occasions, it is not used in the two cases where we are actually dealing with a coronation (here one finds הנזר in the context of the Jerusalem court, and כתר־מלכות for the Persian court). Along the lines of Petersen, I would suggest that the act Zechariah was commanded to perform on Joshua was a crowning, not a coronation (or ordination).

The most important implication of this line of interpretation is the following. One cannot deduce from the fact that a crown is set on the head of the high priest Joshua that he is now granted authority to rule. The action does not change anything in his political status or authority.[36]

---

34. Schöttler, *Gottesvolk*, p. 381: Joshua wears the crown 'als Zeichen *seiner* herrscherlichen Stellung' (emphasis original); pp. 395-96: the high priest 'ist an der Stelle des Königs getreten'; Meyers and Meyers, *Haggai, Zechariah*, p. 353-54, 'the power that accrues to the high priest by virtue of his wearing the crown which, to a certain extent, is a royal insignia of office'; Mason, *Preaching*, p. 212, 'the continuing priestly line rules over the theocracy'.

35. Petersen, *Haggai and Zechariah*, p. 275; see also Rignell, *Nachtgesichte*, p. 224: Joshua is 'nicht gekrönt...um ein Amt zu bekleiden'; Wallis, 'Erwägungen', p. 234, 'Daß damit irgendein Inthronisationsritus gemeint ist, sagt der Text nicht aus'.

36. Compare Reventlow, *Haggai, Sacharja*, p. 72: Joshua 'wird nicht selbst in eine königliche Position erhoben'. Tollington opts for an interpretation of the 'coronation' as having 'symbolic or proleptic significance' (*Tradition*, p. 168), but she admits (p. 167), 'it is possible for Joshua to have been crowned to signify the honour accorded him as senior priest without it implying monarchic aspirations focusing on him'.

*A Dramatic Action*. The command to set a crown on the head of the
high priest should be interpreted in the light of Zech. 3.8, where the
high priest and his colleagues are said to be אנשי מופת. At that stage
the precise nature of the מופת was left unspecified. Now in 6.11-15 it
becomes more clear in what way the high priest and his men are אנשי
מופת. The high priest, the head of the college of priests has a crown set
on his head, in a symbolic action[37] which makes the presence of the
priesthood a sign guaranteeing that the promise concerning the rule of
Zemah will certainly be fulfilled.[38]

   This is different from seeing the high priest as a precursor type of the
rule of Zemah,[39] that is someone who for the time being takes the
position or office which Zemah one day will occupy. The crown is a
sign of the rule of Zemah ('he shall rule…'), not of the rule of Joshua,
which is not mentioned at all.[40] The priest(hood) will function as a
guarantee that God will one day fulfil his promise concerning the coming of צמח, the future ruler.

### e. Conclusion

In this part of the Chapter I have discussed the interpretation of the
command given to Zerubbabel to 'set a crown on the head of Joshua,
the son of Jehozadak, the high priest'. The interpretation of עטרות in
v. 11 and עטרת in v. 14 as both singular forms seems the most attractive way to make sense of these forms in their context. A noun form

---

37.   Cf. R.D. Nelson, *Raising up a Faithful Priest: Community and Priesthood
in Biblical Theology* (Louisville, KY: Westminster/John Knox Press, 1993), who
considers the act of crowning which Zechariah performs (p. 123) 'as a symbolic act
typical of prophets. The crown itself was dedicated as a memorial in the temple
rather than becoming part of the high priest's permanent wardrobe. Such a crown
would be a symbol of high honor but not necessarily an indication of royalty'.

38.   E.g. R. Mason, 'The Prophets of the Restoration', in R. Coggins, A. Phillips and M. Knibb (eds.), *Israel's Prophetic Tradition: Essays in Honour of Peter S.
Ackroyd* (Cambridge: Cambridge University Press, 1982), pp. 137-54 (148).

39.   So Eichrodt, 'Typos', p. 518; cf. K. Seybold, 'Die Königserwartung bei den
Propheten Haggai und Sacharja', *Judaica* 28 (1972), pp. 69-78 (76-77) (reprinted in
U. Struppe [ed.], *Studien zum Messiasbild im Alten Testament* [SBA, 6; Stuttgart:
Verlag Katholisches Bibelwerk, 1989], pp. 243-52). Amsler (*Aggée; Zacharie 1–8*,
p. 108) and Van der Woude ('Serubbabel', p. 148) rightly object to such an inter-
pretation.

40.   For a refutation of the view that Zemah should be identified with Joshua,
see Chapter 4, section entitled 'The View that Zemah and Zerubbabel Are One and
the Same Person'.

ending in -*ōt* is unusual for a singular feminine noun, but similar forms can be found elsewhere in the Old Testament. Attempts to interpret the phrase וְשָׂמֹת בְרֹאשׁ יְהוֹשֻׁעַ בֶן־יְהוֹצָדָק הַכֹּהֵן הַגָּדוֹל in Zech. 6.11 in such a way that it does not refer to setting a crown on the head of the high priest have been shown to be misguided. The word used for 'crown' is a rather general one, עֲטָרָה, and not one of the words found elsewhere in contexts dealing with the coronation of a king. This opens the possibility of interpreting the action not as a coronation but as a crowning for a different purpose (again, not unique in the Old Testament), in this case as a sign providing the guarantee for the fulfilment of the promise concerning the coming rule of the figure called Zemah.

## 3. *The Relationship between Royal Figure and Priest in Zechariah 6.13*

In this part of the Chapter I will examine the nature of the relationship between Zemah and the priest at his throne mentioned in Zech. 6.13. The phrase וְהָיָה כֹהֵן עַל־כִּסְאוֹ is in many ways enigmatic. It is tempting to fill in details which the text does not provide,[41] but in my view one should be very cautious in doing so.

The translation of RSV, 'And there shall be a priest by his throne', suggests that royal figure and priest are two separate persons. Some commentators translate something like, 'and he [the royal figure] shall be priest', and argue that royal figure and priest are one and the same person.[42] This idea would not be completely novel in the Old Testament

41. The process of filling in details has its beginning already in the ancient versions: LXX adds the article, while the Targum reads כֹהֵן רַב 'a high priest'.
42. J.D. Davis, 'The Reclothing and Coronation of Joshua: Zechariah iii and vi', *PTR* 18 (1920), pp. 256-68 (260, 268); B. Holwerda, '...*Begonnen hebbende van Mozes ...*' (Terneuzen: Littooij, 1953), p. 67; Bič, *Sacharja*, p. 85; J.G. Baldwin, '*Ṣemaḥ* as a Technical Term in the Prophets', *VT* 14 (1964), pp. 93-97 (96-97), 'the Shoot...will combine both offices'; J. Ridderbos, *De kleine Profeten. III. Haggai, Zacharia, Maleachi* (Kampen: Kok, 3rd edn, 1968), pp. 103-104; M. Barker, 'The Two Figures in Zechariah', *HeyJ* 18 (1977), pp. 38-46 (44); M.G. Kline, 'The Structure of the Book of Zechariah', *JETS* 34 (1991), pp. 179-93 (182); M.J. Selman, 'Messianic Mysteries', in P.E. Satterthwaite, R.S. Hess and G.J. Wenham (eds.), *The Lord's Anointed: Interpretation of Old Testament Messianic Texts* (Tyndale House Studies; Carlisle: Paternoster Press; Grand Rapids: Baker, 1995), pp. 281-302 (295-96). Baldwin's position in her later commentary is not fully clear: she speaks (*Haggai, Zechariah*, pp. 136-37) both of 'a priest by his throne', which seems to suggest a person different from the royal figure, and of the symbolic

(cf. Ps. 110.4), but there are two reasons why the interpretation of this passage in this way is improbable. (a) Mention is made of 'peaceful understanding between them both' (שְׁנֵיהֶם 'the two of them'), which clearly suggests the presence of two persons.[43] (b) The second reason is less compelling, but it remains striking that the personal pronoun הוּא, which has been repeated two times in the preceding phrases, is not found here, while its presence would have avoided any potential misunderstanding.

### a. *The Lack of Specificity in the Description of the Priest*

What makes the reference to the priest remarkable is what one can call the lack of specificity in the description of the priest. (a) He is referred to as simply כֹהֵן '*a* priest'. There is no article which would have allowed for the possibility of identifying him as '*the* priest', a phrase which in the Old Testament is sometimes used to refer to the high priest. He is not called (ה)כֹהֵן (ה)גָדוֹל either, the title for 'high priest' which Zechariah uses in the rest of his book (3.1, 8; 6.11). He could be any priest.

The absence of the article should make us suspicious of a simple identification of the figure called כֹהֵן with Joshua, the high priest. A great number of scholars make such an identification. However, specific clues for such an identification are completely absent,[44] whereas in an earlier oracle Joshua is explicitly addressed as יְהוֹשֻׁעַ הַכֹהֵן הַגָדוֹל (Zech. 3.8).

(b) A comparison of the description of the royal figure and his functions and that of the priest and his functions presents a striking difference (Fig. 9). One finds an itemized description of the royal figure and his role, and a mere mentioning of the presence of the priest.[45] This

coronation and the enigmatic term 'Branch' as referring to 'a future leader, who would fulfil to perfection the offices of priest and king' and of 'the priestly and royal offices...unified'.

43. Cf. Marti, *Dodekapropheton*, pp. 420-21. Nowack, *Propheten*, p. 366; Cook, *Prophecy*, p. 135.

44. Cf. Meyers and Meyers, *Haggai, Zechariah*, p. 360, 'The MT...has no article before priest. The identity of the priestly official is thus rather indefinite. Such a situation is appropriate to the unspecified future time indicated in this oracle'.

45. This difference is also noticed by Meyers and Meyers, *Haggai, Zechariah*, p. 361, though I find their phrase referring to the priest as 'sitting on his throne' problematic.

vagueness may have been deliberate, as Schöttler has argued,[46] and the likelihood increases when one takes into account the significance of the use of the verb היה.

Figure 9. *The Description of Royal Figure and Priest in Zech. 6.12-13*

| צמח | כהן |
|---|---|
| הנה־איש צמח שמו ומתחתיו יצמח | והיה כהן על־כסאו |
| ובנה את־היכל יהוה | |
| והוא יבנה את־היכל יהוה | |
| והוא־ישא הוד | |
| וישב ומשל על־כסאו | |

| | |
|---|---|
| ועצת שלום תהיה בין שניהם | |

(c) The presence of the prepositional phrase על כסא as a complement to the verb היה is unique in the Old Testament. In the more than 50 cases where על כסא complements a verb, the verb is almost always[47] ישב.[48] But here in 6.14, the priest just 'will be present': neither are we

46. According to Schöttler, the function of the priest is (*Gottesvolk*, p. 159) 'nicht mehr mit ישב, sondern bewußt unbestimmt mit והיה כהן beschrieben und das Verb משל [ist] gar nicht mehr aufgenommen'. Van der Woude leaves it open ('Serubbabel', p. 152), 'zugestanden werden muß, daß der überlieferte Text die Sache (absichtlich?) in der Schwebe läßt'.

47. There seem to be just a few exceptions: כרת מעל כסא and נתן על כסא. However, it could be argued that the two cases where מעל כסא is found with the verb כרת ni. are in fact elliptical for a phrase which includes ישב (G participle). The construction is found in one of two forms:

| | | | |
|---|---|---|---|
| מעל כסא | איש | לא־יכרת ל | 1 Kgs 2.4; 9.5 |
| על כסא | ישב איש | לא־יכרת ל | 1 Kgs 8.25 (= 2 Chron. 6.1); Jer. 33.17 |

It is difficult to find any difference in meaning between the two forms of the phrase. The same is true for the phrase נתן...על כסא (four times), which also can be said to be elliptical for a phrase which includes ישב (G participle).

| | | |
|---|---|---|
| על כסא | נתן | 1 Kgs 5.19; 10.9; 2 Chron. 9.8 [שים for נתן in 2 Kgs 10.3] |
| נתן ישב על כסא | | 1 Kgs 1.48; 3.6 |

If this analysis is correct we are left with just one more case where the phrase על כסא does not complement ישב, but a different verb, viz. מלך: 'so that he shall not have a son to reign on his throne' (Jer. 33.21).

48. Cf. Beuken, *Haggai–Sacharja 1–8*, p. 277.

told that he will be 'sitting' (יֹשֵׁב) on a throne, nor that he will be 'standing' (עֹמֵד) by the throne.

This observation may seem trivial, but I think it is not. 'Sitting' or 'standing' are words to describe the posture of being in office. For a king in office the posture is to 'sit': יֹשֵׁב.[49] The posture typical[50] for a priest in office is to stand: the phrases in Hebrew to describe a priest in office are עֹמֵד לִפְנֵי יהוה,[51] עֹמֵד לְשָׁרֵת,[52] or a combination of both.[53] Here none of these phrases is used. The conclusion of this must be that we are not told that the priest will be in office as priest. This does not necessarily mean that the priest is not in office, but the thing to observe is that the oracle does not make much of it. Neither should one as interpreter of the oracle. After the reference to the royal figure building the temple, one would not be surprised to be told of the role of the priest in that temple, but the passage does not address the issue.[54] Furthermore, the observation should also be made that Zechariah does not use language which would indicate that the priest has a position as one of the officials of the royal figure, for example something like וְעָמַד עָלָיו כֹּהֵן.[55]

---

49.    Expressions identical to the Hebrew יֹשֵׁב עַל־כִּסֵּא are found in other Semitic languages; see T. Ishida, *The Royal Dynasties in Ancient Israel: A Study on the Formation and Development of Royal-Dynastic Ideology* (BZAW, 142; Berlin: W. de Gruyter, 1977), p. 104.

50.    I am not saying that one never finds a priest sitting, because one does. Twice one reads that Eli (the priest) 'was sitting on the seat [יֹשֵׁב עַל־הַכִּסֵּא]' (1 Sam. 1.9; 4.13). For a refutation of the view that this makes Eli a royal figure (so R. Polzin, *Samuel and the Deuteronomist: A Literary Study of the Deuteronomistic History*. II. *1 Samuel* [Indiana Studies in Biblical Literature; Bloomington: Indiana University Press, 1989], pp. 23, 64), see F.A. Spina, 'Eli's Seat: The Transition from Priest to Prophet in 1 Samuel 1–4', *JSOT* 62 (1994), pp. 67-75 (67-70). But what I am saying is that this is not the posture typical for a priest exercising his office.

51.    Deut. 18.7; Judg. 20.28.

52.    Deut. 17.12; 18.5; 1 Kgs 8.11.

53.    Deut. 10.8; 2 Chron. 29.11; Ezek. 44.15.

54.    In my view there is therefore no justification for Dommershausen's conclusion, 'ein Davidide wird König sein und den Tempel herrlich vollenden, ein Hoherpriester wird einträchtig neben ihm amtieren' (W. Dommershausen, 'Der "Spross" als Messias-Vorstellung bei Jeremia und Sacharja', *TQ* 148 [1968], pp. 321-41 [330]). Such a statement makes explicit what remains unmentioned in the passage. One may question whether this procedure is correct.

55.    For עֹמֵד עַל as a phrase for the position of an official at the royal court, see the discussion of Zech. 4.14 in Chapter 6. As such, Petersen is right when he writes

(d) It is extremely difficult to decide what the phrase עַל־כִּסְאוֹ[56] in the clause וְהָיָה כֹהֵן עַל־כִּסְאוֹ refers to:[57] is this still the throne of the royal figure (so RSV: 'And there shall be a priest by his throne'),[58] or does the priest have a throne of his own ('and there shall be a priest at his throne')[59]? The presence of a more specific verb would have helped to settle the issue: יָשַׁב would have made the idea of a throne of the priest himself more plausible, עָמַד would have resolved the issue in favour of the throne still being that of the royal figure. The lack of specificity of the verb הָיָה defies any certain solution of the dilemma.

כִּסֵּא does not necessarily have to mean (royal) 'throne', it may refer to just a 'seat' of any official,[60] or to a 'chair'.[61] In the case that this is a

---

(*Haggai and Zechariah*, p. 277), 'The image of someone standing over or by the throne is clearly that of an attendant or someone of importance, though of lesser status'. However, in the oracle we are not told that the priest is standing (עָמַד), he is just present (הָיָה).

56. LXX translates the phrase עַל־כִּסְאוֹ with ἐκ δεξιῶν. On the basis of this a number of scholars suggest alteration of MT to read עַל־יְמִינוֹ (e.g. Wellhausen, *Propheten*, p. 185; Beuken, *Haggai–Sacharja 1–8*, p. 278; Chary, *Aggée, Zacharie*, p. 114; Wallis, 'Erwägungen', p. 235; R. Mason, *The Books of Haggai, Zechariah and Malachi* [CBC; Cambridge: Cambridge University Press, 1977], p. 61; Smith, *Parties*, p. 188 n. 46). The attraction of this proposal is that it resolves the problem of the identity of the person to whom the suffix -ō refers. But it is in my view questionable whether LXX suggests a different Hebrew *Vorlage*. The significance of the difference between the phrases עַל־יְמִינוֹ and עַל־כִּסְאוֹ can be easily exaggerated. So I would agree with Rudolph's judgment that the reading of LXX is 'sachlich richtig, führt aber auf keinen anderen Text' (Rudolph, *Haggai, Sacharja*, p. 128) and with Meyers and Meyers, 'the LXX cannot be cited as evidence for a different text' (*Haggai, Zechariah*, p. 361). Others explain the LXX rendering as an early interpretation of the words we have in the MT. E.g. Rignell, *Nachtgesichte*, p. 231; B.A. Mastin, 'A Note on Zechariah vi 13', *VT* 26 (1976), pp. 113-16 (115).

57. According to Kline, the 'majestic priest...shall sit and rule upon his [Yahweh's] throne ('l-ks'w) and shall be priest upon his [Yahweh's] throne ('l-ks'w)' ('Structure', p. 182, borrowing the idea from 1 Chron. 29). This view has to be rejected, because a 'throne of Yahweh' is not mentioned at all in this context (cf. Ridderbos, *Profeten*, p. 103 and n. 1; Rudolph, *Haggai, Sacharja*, p. 128).

58. So Lagrange, 'Prophéties', p. 71; A. Jepsen, 'Kleine Beiträge zum Zwölf-prophetenbuch III', *ZAW* 61 (1945–48), pp. 95-114 (108); Rudolph, *Haggai, Sacharja*, p. 131; Petersen, *Haggai and Zechariah*, p. 277; Van der Woude, *Zacharia*, p. 117.

59. So Ackroyd, *Exile*, pp. 198-99; Meyers and Meyers, *Haggai, Zechariah*, pp. 361-62; Schöttler, *Gottesvolk*, p. 159; Hanhart, *Sacharja*, p. 410.

60. 1 Sam. 1.8; 4.13, 18; Neh. 3.7; Jer. 1.15.

reference to a seat for the priest, we would then have a sudden change of meaning within a verse, something which would not be unique: in 1 Kgs 2.19 (within one and the same verse) the word כסא is used to refer to the throne of the king first and then to the seat brought for the king's mother.

Perhaps it can be said that as a reference to another throne, a throne of the priest, the phrase על־כסאו seems to be somewhat too casual. A throne is not an object that one would directly associate with a priest. A king will be found sitting on his throne, but for a priest it would be less usual. Something of an explanation would have been called for if this was a second throne, namely, that of the priest. 1 Kgs 2.19, the passage already mentioned, shows some lexical overlap with Zech. 6.13: here one finds an explanation how a כסא for someone other than the king came to be there (1 Kgs 2.19):

| | |
|---|---|
| ותבא בת־שבע אל־המלך שלמה | So Bathsheba went to King Solomon, |
| לדבר־לו על־אדניהו | to speak to him on behalf of Adonijah. |
| ויקם המלך לקראתה | And the king rose to meet her, |
| וישתחו לה | and bowed down to her; |
| וישב על־כסאו | then he sat on his throne, |
| וישם כסא לאם המלך | and had a seat brought for the king's mother; |
| ותשב לימינו | and she sat on his right. |

When one compares the two passages one notices two differences: (a) the identification of the כסא as different from the one the king is sitting on, and (b) the explicit statement of the fact that the king's mother is sitting.

To sum up: acknowledging that it is impossible to say anything with great certainty concerning the identity of the throne in the second occurrence of the phrase על־כסאו, there seem to be two factors which would favour the idea that in this particular case it is still the same throne[62] (that of the royal figure): the casual nature of the reference to the throne, and the absence of any explanation of the throne to which the priest is in some way linked. As I will discuss below, the choice one makes on this issue is not crucial to the interpretation of the passage as a whole.

---

61.  2 Kgs 4.10, as part of the basic furniture of a guest room.

62.  If this interpretation is correct, then the preposition על changes its meaning between the first phrase על־כסאו ('at') and the second ('by').

b. *The Role of the Priest*

The ambiguous reference to 'a priest' does not provide much information concerning what exactly he is doing there. The only clue to the actual role and position of the priest is found in the words that follow the brief reference to his presence: 'and peaceful understanding [עצה] shall be between them both'. This is the only explicit statement about the role of the priest. If the phrase refers to an official position of the priest it suggests that the most one can say about the role of the priest is that it is something like that of the counsellor of the king.[63]

The history of the kings of Judah and Israel indicates the crucial role a counsellor (יועץ; note that the word is not used in Zechariah 6, but the cognate עצה is) may play in the fortunes of king and nation. While in the past history of the kingdom of Judah counsellors more than once had changed the fate of king and nation for the worse,[64] the result of the counsel of royal figure and priest will be very different: no rebellion, no tragedy, but peace.

As has been pointed out by several scholars[65] שלום in the phrase עצת שלום does not just describe the relationship between royal figure and priest, but rather the result of their planning together (cf. 'the chastisement that made us whole' מוסר שלומנו in Isa. 53.5).[66] The counsel of royal figure and priest will bring peace, well being to the community.

63. So also Petersen, *Haggai and Zechariah*, p. 278 n. 7. On the 'counsellor', see P.A.H. de Boer, 'The Counsellor', in M. Noth and D. Winton Thomas (eds.), *Wisdom in Israel and in the Ancient Near East* (VTSup, 3; Leiden: E.J. Brill, 1955), pp. 42-71 (56-57).

64. E.g. the counsellors of Solomon's son Rehoboam who helped him lose most of the kingdom to Jeroboam (1 Kgs 12); or King Ahaziah of Judah, whose 'mother was his counsellor [היתה יועצתו] in doing wickedly [להרשיע]', and who also had the house of Ahab, 'as his counsellors [היו־לו יועצים], to his undoing [למשחית]' (2 Chron. 22.3-4). More references to failing counsellors can be found in Isa. 19.11; Ezek. 11.2. The prophet Isaiah announces a time when God 'will restore your judges as at the first, and your counsellors as at the beginning' (Isa. 1.26).

65. See, e.g., Ackroyd, *Exile*, p. 199; Van der Woude, *Zacharia*, p. 117.

66. See the discussion of the 'genitive of effect' in B. Waltke and M. O'Connor, *An Introduction to Biblical Hebrew Syntax* (Winona Lake, IN: Eisenbrauns, 1990) §9.5.2c; cf. GKB §128q. So עצת שלום cannot be taken as evidence for a rivalry between Zerubbabel and Joshua or king and priest (with Rignell, *Nachtgesichte*, pp. 230-32; Ackroyd, *Exile*, p. 199; Beyse, *Serubbabel*, pp. 83-84, 99; contra Wellhausen, *Propheten*, p. 185; Marti, *Dodekapropheton*, p. 421; Smith, *Parties*, p. 188 n. 46).

## c. *Equal Status, Supremacy, or Submission?*

Perhaps the enigmatic character of the reference to the priest explains why scholars have come to conflicting views on the relative status of the royal figure and the priest. I will now discuss the three options which scholars have defended.

(a) Those who argue that originally the destination of the crown was the head of Zerubbabel argue that the purpose of the reworking of the original oracle into the text as we have it now was to adapt the oracle to a situation in which the high priest was the supreme ruler.[67]

(b) Others say that royal figure and priest have equal status—they rule together. This is by far the most popular view, as Pomykala observes, 'amid all uncertainty about the precise interpretation of these verses, one aspect is clear: a dyarchic leadership is envisioned. There will be two figures at the head of Israel, a priestly figure and the צמח, whether understood as Zerubbabel or a future royal messiah'.[68] One regularly finds words like 'diarchy' in the description of the political organization found in this passage.[69]

---

67.  See Chapter 5.

68.  Pomykala, *Dynasty Tradition*, p. 59. Rignell, *Nachtgesichte*, p. 230, states that Joshua and the Messiah have a similar position (*ähnliche Stellung*) with neither being dominant. According to Petitjean, *Oracles*, p. 293, prince and priest share the responsibilities and the prestige of power, in a diarchical form of government (*autorité bicéphale*). Ackroyd, *Exile*, pp. 198-99, comments, 'Each sits on his own throne, and together they carry out the rule of the community'. See further Chary, *Aggée, Zacharie*, p. 115; Butterworth, *Structure*, p. 263; Nelson, *Priest*, pp. 122-23; Tollington, *Tradition*, pp. 175, 178.

69.  Seybold, 'Königserwartung', p. 75, 'Israel wird zur *Dyarchie*; zwei Gesalbte stehen an der Spitze'; Van der Woude, 'Serubbabel', p. 152, 'Jedenfalls wird eine Dyarchie des künftigen Königs und Hohenpriesters in Aussicht gestellt'. Schöttler uses the phrase 'diarchic system' ('Es handelt sich jetzt um ein dyarchisches System der Herrschaft (König und Priester)', *Gottesvolkes*, p. 158), yet at the same time maintains that it is only צמח who does the ruling (p. 159). Meyers and Meyers use the phrase 'dyarchic pattern' (*Haggai, Zechariah*, p. 373; see also pp. 361, 362), 'king and priest together will rule in perfect harmony. The dyarchic pattern of leadership that is later reflected in the Dead Sea community at Qumran is hereby elevated to a position of legitimacy in Zechariah as a consequence of postexilic events and circumstances'. T. Lescow, 'Sacharja 1–8: Verkündigung und Komposition', *BN* 68 (1992), pp. 75-99 (86), finds in 6.13 'ein bikephales Herrschaftsmodell, das schon in der Vision von den beiden Ölbäumen = "Ölsöhnen" im vierten Nachtgesicht angedeutet ist...'

(c) Finally there are those who have argued for a lower status for the priest. Interpreting the position of the priest 'standing over or by the throne' as that of an 'attendant or someone of importance, though of lesser status', Petersen concludes, 'The high priest is, therefore, implicitly given a status lower than that of the Davidide'.[70]

*Discussion.* What are we to make of these diverging proposals? As I have argued above (section entitled 'The Role of the Priest'), the highest position one can give to the priest is that of a counsellor. But the position of a counsellor does not give a status equal to that of the royal figure, or create a political situation that can be rightly called 'diarchy'. In this respect it does not make a difference whether the priest sits on a throne of his own, or stands by the throne of the royal figure. Similarly, the mere mention of occupying a throne, even in the immediate presence of a king and his throne, does not imply that the person rules in the same capacity as that king, or that this is a case of a diarchy. No one argues for a diarchy of Solomon and the king's mother Bathsheba, though she is said to sit at the right hand of the king, on a throne of her own (1 Kgs 2.19). No one argues that there was a diarchy of king Ahasuerus and Haman, even though the king 'advanced him and set his seat above all the princes who were with him' (Est. 3.1). Only when one is prepared to fill in details which are left unspecified in the passage can one find support for the 'equal status' view.

The same arguments disqualify the view which gives the priest supremacy over the royal figure. The view that the priest will have a lower status than the royal figure is the most plausible one. Such an interpretation can be supported by both the elusiveness of the description and the nature of the role of a counsellor.

---

70.   Petersen, *Haggai and Zechariah*, p. 277; see also p. 278 n. 7. Cf. J. Becker, *Messiaserwartung im Alten Testament* (SBS, 83; Stuttgart: Verlag Katholisches Bibelwerk, 1977), p. 61 (ET *Messianic Expectation in the Old Testament* [Edinburgh: T. & T. Clark, 1980], p. 66), 'Der "Sproß" wird bevorzugt behandelt'; A. Laato, *Josiah and David Redivivus: The Historical Josiah and the Messianic Expectations of Exilic and Postexilic Times* (ConBOT, 33; Stockholm: Almqvist & Wiksell, 1992), p. 250 n. 171: 'the royal figure has a more dominant role'; J.M. Ward, *Thus Says the Lord: The Message of the Prophets* (Nashville: Abingdon Press, 1991), p. 266, 'the civil leader, in the person of Zerubbabel ("The Branch"), has precedence over the priest, who stands beside the other's throne. This superior status for Zerubbabel, descendant of the Davidides...'

### d. *Conclusion*

Compared with the description of the royal figure, the portrait of the priest at the throne of the royal figure is very vague. Only his presence is mentioned. The reference to 'peaceful counsel' between royal figure and priest suggests a role for the priest as a counsellor. These two features indicate that his position is of lower status than that of the royal figure, and evidence for a diarchy, so often found in this passage, is lacking.

### 4. *The Position of Joshua, the High Priest, in Zechariah 3.7*

Having discussed the role of the priest in the portrait of Zemah in Zech. 6.12-13, it makes sense to look also at the role and position of the high priest in another passage in the vision reports, Zech. 3.7. There, the angel of the LORD addresses the high priest directly, without the mediation of the prophet Zechariah. Joshua is given this charge:

> Thus says the LORD of hosts: If you will walk in my ways and keep my charge, then you shall rule my house and have charge of my courts, and I will give you the right of access among those who are standing here.

### a. *Preliminary Observation: Protasis and Apodosis in v. 7*

The charge is conveyed in a conditional clause. The problem with this particular conditional clause is that it appears extremely difficult to decide where the protasis ends and the apodosis begins. Some[71] have argued that the protasis begins with the phrase וגם־אתה. This interpretation is reflected in the translation of the RSV:

[P] If you will walk in my ways and keep my charge,
[A] then you shall rule my house and have charge of my courts, and I will give you the right of access among those who are standing here.

Others find the beginning of the apodosis in the phrase ונתתי.[72] Staying close to the RSV, one could then translate:

---

71. E.g. C.F. Keil, *Die zwölf kleinen Propheten* (Leipzig: Dörflin und Franke, 3rd edn, 1888), p. 556; Marti, *Dodekapropheton*, p. 410; Driver, *Prophets*, p. 196; Van Hoonacker, *Prophètes*, p. 609; Mitchell, *Haggai and Zechariah*, p. 154; Elliger, *Propheten*, p. 120; Ackroyd, *Exile*, pp. 186-87; Rudolph, *Haggai, Sacharja*, pp. 92-93; Hanhart, *Sacharja*, p. 167; J.C. VanderKam, 'Joshua the High Priest and the Interpretation of Zechariah 3', *CBQ* 53 (1991), pp. 553-70 (558).

72. E.g. Bič, *Sacharja*, pp. 42, 48; Beuken, *Haggai–Sacharja 1–8*, pp. 292-93;

[P]   If you will walk in my ways and keep my charge,
      and if you shall rule my house and have charge of my courts,
[A]   then I will give you the right of access among those who are standing
      here.

From a syntactical point of view, the following features could be taken to support the case for the apodosis beginning at וגם־אתה. (a) The particle אם is used only with the first two verbs (אם...תלך ואם תשמר...), not with any of the other verbs. (b) The subject of the first four verbs is the same: they are all second person singular forms. Therefore the presence of the personal pronoun with the third verb in the verse cannot be explained as indicating change of subject. In that case, the personal pronoun either indicates emphasis, or as part of the phrase וגם־אתה it indicates the beginning of the apodosis. Vander-Kam[73] also points to a change in sentence structure: the verbal forms are in final position in clauses 1-2 (word order: OV), and in front position in clauses 3-5 (VO).

Syntactical features which would favour the apodosis beginning at ונתתי are the following. (a) The change of subject from second person singular in the first four verbs to first person singular in the form ונתתי can be argued to be a mark of the beginning of the apodosis. (b) There is no personal pronoun with the verb in first person singular, which, someone could suggest, would have been natural after the personal pronoun אתה, if that clause was already part of the apodosis.

It is very difficult to decide in this matter. My preference is for the second option: the reason that there is no אם with the verbs תדין and תשמר may be related to the presence of גם, which particle could be interpreted as indicating the continuation of the protasis and the accumulation of conditions.[74] One could then translate וגם 'and what is more',[75] or 'and moreover if'.[76] The repetition of the personal pronoun

Rignell, *Nachtgesichte*, pp. 119, 122-23; Chary, *Aggée, Zacharie*, p. 78; Petersen, *Haggai and Zechariah*, pp. 206-207; Van der Woude, *Zacharia*, pp. 68-69; Schöttler, *Gottesvolk*, p. 335 (n. 145); Reventlow, *Haggai, Sacharja*, p. 54.

73. VanderKam, 'Joshua', p. 558.

74. Cf. Beuken, *Haggai–Sacharja 1–8*, pp. 292-93; Petersen, *Haggai and Zechariah*, p. 206.

75. Cf. Moberly's comments (R.W.L. Moberly, *The Old Testament of the Old Testament: Patriarchal Narratives and Mosaic Yahwism* [Overtures to Biblical Theology; Philadelphia: Fortress Press, 1992], p. 29 n. 29) on וגם in Exod. 6.4-5.

76. Tollington, *Tradition*, pp. 158, 160.

may indicate that there is something special about the conditions
וגם־אתה תדין את־ביתי וגם תשמר את־חצרי. It is difficult in this interpretation to explain the change in sentence structure with regard to the
position of the verbal forms, but perhaps this change is not meant to be
significant.

In the end, the resolution of this problem does not affect the following discussion in a serious way. The actions expressed in the third and
fourth verbal form are either conditions or rewards to be granted when
certain conditions are met.

### b. *'Judge' or 'Govern'?*

One of the more controversial elements in this passage is the precise
meaning of the clauses וגם־אתה תדין את־ביתי וגם תשמר את־חצרי.
The problem is the meaning of the verb דין. Scholarly opinion is divided whether the use of the verb דין here indicates jurisdiction or not.
דין is elsewhere always used for 'to render judgment' or 'to provide
justice', and so a number of scholars argue that the semantic feature of
jurisdiction is also present in Zech. 3.7 and translate 'to judge'.[77]

*Jurisdiction.* On this view the passage is said to indicate that the high
priest after the exile replaced the king as chief judicial officer and that
the temple precinct rather than the palace became the seat of justice.[78]
Petersen finds in Zech. 3.7 a situation which differs from the one in
Ezekiel 44: responsibility for judging at the temple is now concentrated[79] 'not on a class of priests (the Levitical priests), but rather on the
high priest himself'. According to Hanhart,[80] in the new political structure of Israel after the exile jurisdiction is concentrated on the high
priestly representative; apart from the priesthood there is no judicial
authority.

*'My House' as the Object of* דין. The problem with this view is the
nature of the object of the verb in Zech. 3.7: 'you will דין *my house'*.
Usually, when used for 'to exercise judgment' or 'to provide justice',

---

77. E.g. Mason, 'Prophets', p. 147; Meyers and Meyers, *Haggai, Zechariah*,
p. 195; Z. Rokay, 'Vom Stadttor zu den Vorhöfen: Ps 82—Sach 1–8 (ein Vergleich)', *ZKT* 116 (1994), pp. 457-63 (462).

78. Meyers and Meyers, *Haggai, Zechariah*, p. 195.

79. Petersen, *Haggai and Zechariah*, p. 205.

80. Hanhart, *Sacharja*, pp. 189-91.

the verb דין has a person or group of persons as object.[81] The person is
the one to whom justice is restored, for example:

> He judged the cause of the poor and the needy
> ['He upheld the rights of the poor and the needy' NJPS] (Jer. 22.16).

When a group is mentioned as the object, דין is used in a description
either of the fact, or of the nature of judgment, for example:

> he judges the peoples with equity (Ps. 9.9).

What is unusual in Zech. 3.7 is that the object is not a person or a group
of persons, but something inanimate, a building: ביתי.[82] It seems that
Meyers and Meyers have felt the problem, and tried to solve it by
translating תדין את־ביתי as 'render judgment in my House',[83] apparently in complete defiance of Hebrew syntax (ביתי is preceded by את,
to indicate that the noun is the object of the verb דין). Petersen seems to
make a similar shift from ביתי as the object of judgment to ביתי as the
locus of judgment. He discusses several passages in the Old Testament
where judging by Levitical priests is done 'at the temple', and then
states that the claim in 3.7 'concentrates responsibility for judging at the

---

81. 1 Sam. 2.10 seems to be the only exception to this rule: 'The LORD will
judge the ends of the earth'. Here דין is used to indicate the extent of God's right of
judgment.

82. As Jeremias (*Nachtgesichte*, p. 214 n. 48) observes, בית in Zechariah only
refers to people when specified by יהודה or ישראל (8.13, 15, 19); otherwise it refers
to a house (5.4; 6.10), or to the temple (1.16; 4.9; 5.11; 7.3; 8.9). That the word בית
must refer to the temple building is also clear from the parallel 'courts' in the
following clause (A. Köhler, *Der Weissagungen Sacharjas erste Hälfte, Cap. 1–8*
[Die Nachexilischen Propheten Erklärt, 2; Leipzig: Deichert, 1861], p. 118; Van
Hoonacker, *Prophètes*, p. 609; Rudolph, *Haggai, Sacharja*, p. 93; Jeremias, *Nachtgesichte*, p. 214; Petersen, *Haggai and Zechariah*, p. 205; Hanhart, *Sacharja*,
p. 190). The house–courts parallelism makes the interpretation of ביתי as referring
to the Jewish community implausible. Such a community interpretation has been
proposed by Hitzig, *Propheten*, pp. 344-45; Rignell, *Nachtgesichte*, p. 120; and
recently P. Marinkovic, 'What Does Zechariah 1–8 Tell us about the Second
Temple?', in Eskenazi and Richards (eds.), *Second Temple*, pp. 88-103 (99-100): he
takes the חצרים to refer to the 'open and unfortified settlements that surrounded
Jerusalem', and offers the following translation of the clause in v. 7 (p. 100): 'You
will judge my community and be in charge of my farmsteads'. חצרים can indeed be
used to refer to such settlements (Marinkovic mentions Neh. 12.29), but the context
of Zechariah makes this interpretation unlikely.

83. Meyers and Meyers, *Haggai, Zechariah*, p. 178.

temple...on the high priest...' Hanhart interprets the first clause of v. 7b
as a promise of jurisdiction over (or for) the house of the YHWH, which
implies that the jurisdiction (*Rechtsprechung*) and the ordering of the
cult are now laid in the hands of the high priest. The priesthood now
has not only the authority to teach the law, but also the authority to
judge.[84]

Such an extension of jurisdiction beyond matters of temple and cult is
certainly the implication of the interpretation of Meyers and Meyers
(and possibly of Petersen). But when one reads את־ביתי in the only way
which Hebrew syntax allows, that is, as the object, not the locus of דין,
such an extension becomes problematic. If one wants to keep the
semantic feature of jurisdiction of דין, and interpret ביתי as the temple,
the only appropriate way to read this clause is as indicating jurisdiction
over matters of temple and cult.

*Government and Administration.* A number of scholars, however, doubt
that the semantic feature of jurisdiction is articulated here in 3.7, and
argue that the interpretation of דין should be connected with that of the
verb שמר in the parallel clause which follows: the use of the verb שמר
in a sense 'colours' the meaning of דין. On this basis they translate דין
in 3.7 in the broader sense of 'to govern', 'to rule', or 'to administer'.[85]
Evidence that the root דין allows such a broader sense may be found in
the noun מדינה 'province', the meaning of which developed from

---

84. It seems that for Hanhart this authority to judge goes further than matters of
temple and cult, but his argument lacks clarity at this point. I base my reading of
Hanhart on his repeated remark that the priesthood is left as the only institution of
judgment, and on phrases like 'eine innere Zuordnung von kultischem und
profanem Recht' (*Sacharja*, p. 190).

85. Keil, *Propheten*, p. 557; Wellhausen, *Propheten*, p. 181; Marti, *Dodekapropheton*, p. 410; Van Hoonacker, *Prophètes*, p. 609; Rothstein, *Nachtgesichte*,
p. 101; Mitchell, *Haggai and Zechariah*, p. 154; Nowack, *Propheten*, p. 341;
Ackroyd, *Exile*, pp. 186-87; Chary, *Aggée, Zacharie*, p. 81; Baldwin, *Haggai, Zechariah*, p. 115 (she interprets v. 7b as indicating 'sole authority in the Temple and its
courts', but the verb דין 'suggests the exercise of judicial functions...as well as
governing the ritual'); G.J. Botterweck, and V. Hamp, 'דין', *ThWAT*, II, cols. 200-
207 (203; the context indicates that here דין 'nicht ausschließlich richterliche
Tätigkeit meint, sondern auch im weiteren Sinn die Leitung und Verwaltung am
Tempel'); Rudolph, *Haggai, Sacharja*, pp. 92, 97; Mason, pp. 49, 51; Elliger, *Propheten*, pp. 120-21; Amsler, *Aggée; Zacharie 1–8*, p. 78; Reventlow, *Haggai, Sacharja*, p. 54.

'judicial district' to 'governmental district', as Schöttler observes.[86] A similar change from 'to judge' to 'to govern, rule' can be noticed in a verb which is used in a way often parallel to דין, the verb שפט.[87] Zechariah 3.7 may be an indication that such a shift also occurred in the meaning of the verb דין. That no other examples of this usage of דין can be found may be a matter of statistical coincidence: דין is used far less frequently (54 times) than שפט (229 times).

If one accepts the interpretation of דין as 'govern' (and both the object of the verb and the parallel שמר favour this interpretation), then the clause וגם־אתה תדין את־ביתי would indicate that the high priest is now given the power of government and administration of the temple.

c. *Joshua and the Council of Yhwh in Zechariah 3.7*
The final clause of Zech. 3.7 reads in RSV:

---

86. This reconstruction seems to be preferable to the one suggested by Van der Woude (*Zacharia*, pp. 69-70), according to whom דין in Zech. 3.7 may be a form of a second root דון/דין, related to the Akkadian *zanānum*. *CAD* gives the meaning 'to provide food, to provide an institution (temple or city) with means of support'. It is interesting to notice that several occurrences of this verb, listed in *CAD*, are found in a context where mention is made of rebuilding a sanctuary, e.g., 'I rebuilt the sanctuaries of Babylon and Borsippa and provided [*aznun*] for them...' Van der Woude finds the same root used in Job 36.31, where a form of the verb דין is used with נתן־אכל in the parallel clause. RSV translates, 'For by these he judges peoples; he gives food in abundance'. However, the element of judgment is present in the immediate context of the verse (God is 'jealous with anger against iniquity', v. 33), so perhaps this is not a directly convincing parallel.

87. G. Liedke, *Gestalt und Bezeichnung alttestamentlicher Rechtssätze: Eine formgeschichtlich-terminologische Studie* (WMANT, 39; Neukirchen–Vluyn: Neukirchener Verlag, 1971), concludes his study of the meaning of שפט by stating that the verb refers to the action to restore the disrupted order (שלום) of a community. When used for a continuing activity, the meaning of שפט shifts to 'to rule, govern' (pp. 62-72; esp. pp. 70-72). Such a shift can be noticed, for instance, when one compares 1 Kgs 3.9-11 and 2 Chron. 1.10-11. In the first passage the notion of judgment is clearly present (cf. the phrase 'discern between good and evil' in v. 9, and the episode of the case of the two harlots in vv. 16-28 ['all Israel heard of the judgment which the king had rendered...[T]hey perceived that the wisdom of God was in him, to render judgment', v. 28]). In the 2 Chronicles passage the notion of judgment is absent, and the verb שפט (the same verb as in the 1 Kings passage) is now used for 'to govern, rule' (see S. Japhet, *I and II Chronicles: A Commentary* [OTL; London: SCM Press, 1993], p. 531).

and I will give you the right of access among those who are standing here.

The key to the understanding of this last clause of v. 7 is the meaning of the word מהלכים. The form has long puzzled commentators. The early versions unanimously interpret it as a verbal form meaning 'those who go/walk' (ἀναστρεφομένους in the LXX; *ambulantes* in the Vulgate; and cf. רגלין מהלכן in the Targum). Modern interpreters (almost) similarly unanimously[88] take the form as a plural of the noun מהלך, and translate it as 'access'. However, there are several problems with this later interpretation.[89]

(a) In the Hebrew Bible a noun מַהֲלָךְ 'journey; passage(way)' is attested. It is used four times, always in the singular.[90] In all four cases מהלך is something which is or can be quantified (in time [days], or in cubits). The plural of this form is not attested. The problem is that the word מהלך is never used for 'entrance', or 'access'.

The Hebrew language has other words to express these concepts. For 'entrance' one finds most often either the noun פתח or a form of the root בוא,[91] while on one occasion the noun איתון is used. For the idea of 'access' or admission to a place or building one finds again (a phrase with) a form of the root בוא:

---

88. Köhler, *Sacharja*, pp. 120-21; Keil, *Propheten*, p. 557; Wellhausen, *Propheten*, p. 181; Van Hoonacker, p. 609; Marti, *Dodekapropheton*, p. 410; Driver, *Prophets*, p. 197; Nowack, *Propheten*, p. 341; Bič, *Sacharja*, p. 42; Chary, *Aggé, Zacharie*, p. 78; Baldwin, *Haggai, Zechariah*, p. 115; Rudolph, *Haggai, Sacharja*, p. 93; Petersen, *Haggai and Zechariah*, p. 207; Smith, *Micah-Malachi*, pp. 198, 200; Meyers and Meyers, *Haggai, Zechariah*, p. 196; Amsler, *Aggée; Zacharie 1–8*, pp. 78, 82; Hanhart, *Sacharja*, p. 173; Reventlow, *Haggai, Sacharja*, p. 54; Nelson, *Priest*, p. 121; Tollington, *Tradition*, p. 160.

89. For these problems, see P.A.H. de Boer, *De voorbede in het Oude Testament* (OTS, 3; Leiden: E.J. Brill, 1943), pp. 101-102; Schöttler, *Gottesvolk*, pp. 337-39.

90. Neh. 2.6, 'How long will you be gone [מהלכך; KJV: 'For how long shall thy journey be?'], and when will you return?'; Ezek. 42.4, 'And before the chambers was a passage inward [מהלך], ten cubits wide and a hundred cubits long, and their doors were on the north'; Jon. 3.3-4, 'Nineveh was an exceedingly great city, three days' journey [מהלך] in breadth. Jonah began to go into the city, going a day's journey [מהלך]'.

91. Either a noun (usually מבוא, once מובא, and once באה), or a form of the verb (מלבוא, עד לבוא, or עד־באכה לבוא).

mark well those who may be admitted to the temple [מבוא; RSV mg: 'Heb *the entrance of*'] and all those who are to be excluded from the sanctuary. (Ezek. 44.5; cf. 44.7 'in admitting [בוא hi.] foreigners, uncircumcised in heart and flesh, to be in my sanctuary').

Again, it is a form of the verb בוא which is used in phrases expressing 'allow to enter',[92] and 'forbid to enter'.[93] In 1 Kgs 15.17 (= 2 Chron. 16.1) one finds a phrase with יצא ובוא:

> that he might permit no one to go out or come in to [לבלתי תת יצא ובא ל] Asa king of Judah.

In this case,[94] one is not dealing with entry into a building, but access to a person (cf. Dillard's translation of 2 Chron. 16.1:[95] 'to cut off all access to King Asa of Judah'). A phrase like this seems to come closest to what scholars want to find in Zech. 3.7.

Both verbs יצא and בוא are found in Zechariah, once in the combination יצא ובוא.[96] What we find in 3.7, however, is not a form of בוא, but of הלך. Rudolph claims[97] that the verb הלך may mean 'to enter', but he fails to produce conclusive evidence. The only place which he mentions to prove his claim is Gen. 12.1:

> Go [לך-לך] from [מן] your country and your kindred and your father's house to [אל] the land that I will show you.

However, here הלך is used to describe not the entrance of the land, but the whole journey from Ur to Canaan. It is instructive to see the use of both בוא and הלך a few verses later, in 12.5:

> and they set forth to go to the land of Canaan [ויצאו ללכת ארצה כנען]. When they had come to the land of Canaan [ויבאו ארצה כנען] ...

So, in order to find the desired meaning '(right to) access' here, scholars have to make two unsubstantiated assumptions: first, that מהלך can mean something like 'entrance' (for which there is no evidence whatso-

---

92. נתן לבוא, Exod. 12.23; Josh. 10.19; Judg. 15.1; 2 Chron. 20.10.

93. צויתה לא-יבאו, 'thou didst forbid to enter', Lam. 1.10.

94. Cf. Josh. 6.1, 'Now Jericho was shut up from within and from without because of the people of Israel; none went out, and none came in [אין יוצא ואין בא']'.

95. R. Dillard, *2 Chronicles* (WBC, 15; Waco, TX: Word Books, 1987), p. 113.

96. Zech. 8.10, 'safety from the foe for him who went out or came in [ליוצא ולבא; TOB '[p]our qui allait et venait...']'

97. Rudolph, *Haggai, Sacharja*, p. 93.

ever), and then that in this concrete meaning the word can be used for
the abstract idea of '(right to) access'.[98]

(b) Another problem is that this interpretation is not able to give a
satisfactory explanation of the plural of the form מהלכים.[99] It is of
course always possible to find a convenient label for the plural, like
'plural of extension',[100] or plural to express repetition,[101] but suggestions like these are more a matter of naming the problem, and not of
really dealing with it.

*A Verbal Form.* It seems better to follow the ancient versions, who
unanimously have interpreted מהלכים as a verbal form. At first sight,
the form מהלכים may look like a participle of the hiphil, but this
analysis seems impossible, since the hiphil forms of הלך always have
/ō/ in the first syllable.[102] Zechariah adheres to this pattern, as the form
מוֹלִכוֹת (hiphil participle feminine) in 5.10 shows.

However, few scholars seem to have paid proper attention to the idea
that מהלכים in Zech. 3.7 may be a participle of the piel of הלך. The
possibility is mentioned in passing (but not adopted) by Hitzig.[103]
*HALAT* (s.v. מהלך) suggests this interpretation when it proposes to see
the word as a variant of מהלכים, referring to two passages in the book
of Daniel, where the Aramaic מהלכין seems to stand for מהלכים, the
participle of the piel.[104] Schöttler is the only one to be unequivocal: he

98. Others derive the meaning 'access' from an interpretation of the word as
'goings' (BDB, their approach is adopted by Meyers and Meyers, *Haggai, Zechariah*, p. 196, cf. *Gänge* in Marti, *Dodekapropheton*, p. 410; Nowack, *Propheten*,
p. 341), but how this leads to the specific meaning 'access' is left unexplained.

99. Besides De Boer and Schöttler at this point König should be mentioned
(F.E. König, *Historisch-kritisches Lehrgebäude der Hebräischen Sprache: Erste
Hälfte: Lehre von der Schrift, der Aussprache, dem Pronomen und dem Verbum*
[Leipzig: J.C. Hinrichs, 1881], p. 416), '...dagegen, dass die Form Substantiv sei,
spricht mir hauptsächlich die Pluralform; dann auch die zu grosse Dunkelheit des
Ausdrückes für den Gedanken, welchen Köhler in der Stelle findet "Ich werde dir
mit deinen Bitten freien Zutritt zu meinen Thron gewähren"'. Cf. Rothstein,
*Nachtgesichte*, p. 100, 'Der Pluralis läßt sich begreiflich nicht gut rechtfertigen'; he
then suggests the possibility of a scribal error, and takes the interpretation 'access'.

100. Hanhart, *Sacharja*, p. 173.

101. Rudolph, *Haggai, Sacharja*, p. 95.

102. Cf. Köhler, *Sacharja*, p. 119.

103. Hitzig, *Propheten*, p. 345, 'die Punct. hatte offenbar das Partic. Pihel (für
מְהַלְּכִים) im Auge'.

104. Dan. 3.25, 'I see four men loose, walking [מַהְלְכִין] in the midst of the fire';

identifies the form as 'unequivocally…a piel participle…'[105]

The piel participle of הלך is attested in both the singular and the plural. In the singular it is found in Ps. 104.3:

who ridest [הַמְהַלֵּךְ] on the wings of the wind

and in Prov. 6.11:

poverty will come upon you like a vagabond [כִּמְהַלֵּךְ]

The plural is found in Eccl. 4.15

I saw all the living who move about [הַמְהַלְּכִים, piel participle plural] under the sun [תַּחַת הַשֶּׁמֶשׁ], as well as [עִם] that youth, who was to stand [יַעֲמֹד] in his place [תַּחְתָּיו]

NJPS translates this verse:

[However,] I reflected about ᵍ⁻all the living who walk under the sun with⁻ᵍ that youthful successor that steps into his place.
(note in the margin: ᵍ⁻ᵍ 'I.e., "the contemporaries of"')

With the preposition בֵּין the verb הלך piel is found in Ps. 104.10:

…springs…they flow [יְהַלֵּכוּן] between the hills

In all these examples of the piel participle of הלך the doubling is maintained, and that is the difference with מַהְלְכִים, for which one would have expected מְהַלְּכִים. I discuss this unusual vocalisation in Excursus 3 at the end of this Chapter. Even if we are not able to explain the present form as it is vocalised by the Masoretes in a completely satisfactorily way, this is a minor problem compared to the number of problems with the 'access' interpretation.[106]

---

and 4.34[37], 'those who walk [מַהְלְכִין] in pride he is able to abase'. Baumgartner (editor of the text of Daniel in *BHS*) proposes in a note in the apparatus to read מְהַלְכִין, with a Cairo Genizah fragment and Vˢ (a variant reading in H.L. Strack, *Grammatik des Biblisch-Aramäischen, mit den nach Handschriften berichtigten Texten und einem Wörterbuch* [Clavis Linguarum Semiticarum, 4; Munich: Beck, 6th edn, 1921]). Cf. for a similar suggestion F. Rosenthal, *A Grammar of Biblical Aramaic* (Porta Linguarum Orientalium, 5; Wiesbaden: Harrassowitz, 1983), p. 54 §169. This suggestion would accord well with the use of the piel participle in Dan. 4.26[29], 'he was walking [מְהַלֵּךְ] on the roof of the royal palace of Babylon'. Note also that there are no forms of the hiphil of (Aramaic) הלך attested, but that may just be a coincidence, given the low frequency of the presence of the verb in the Aramaic of Daniel.

105. 'Windeutig…ein Partizip Piel Plural…' (Schöttler, *Gottesvolk*, p. 338).

106. There are also problems with the Masoretic vocalization of the form when

*'I will give you ...'* If we find a participle in the form מְהַלְכִים, the construction of the clause as a whole would give נתן + לְ + object-in-participle. The next question is, does Hebrew syntax allow a construction like that? There is at least one[107] example of the same construction in Isa. 36.8 (= 2 Kgs 18.23):

> I will give you two thousand horses, if you are able to set riders upon them [לתת לך רכבים עליהם, 'if you can produce riders to mount them', NJPS].

The whole clause in Zech. 3.7 could then be translated as

> then I will provide for you persons who go between these attendants.

The promise is not so much one of direct access, but more of figures who serve as mediators between the council of YHWH and the high priest. A few modern commentators suggest interpreting מְהַלְכִים along these lines. Beuken translates, 'men who go [from among those who are staying here]'.[108] Similarly Schöttler provides the translation, 'and I give to you those who go...'[109] VanderKam does not offer a translation, but according to him it 'is quite well possible...that the promise to Joshua is more indirect: he will be given individuals who have direct access to the divine presence...'[110]

To sum up: the usual translation '(right of) access' for the word מהלכים in Zech. 3.7 is problematic for reasons of semantics. It is preferable to take the form as a verb, a piel participle, meaning 'those who

---

it is interpreted as a plural of a noun מהלך. The plural of such a *ma/iqtal* form would be מַהֲלָכִים, which is different from the form which is found in the MT. To solve this problem one has either to alter the vocalisation in order to read the proper plural form of the word מַהֲלָךְ (e.g. Marti, *Dodekapropheton*, p. 410; Nowack, *Propheten*, p. 341; Chary, *Aggée, Zacharie*, p. 78; Amsler, *Aggée; Zacharie 1–8*, p. 78 n. 7) or to postulate a different word, מַהֲלָךְ (Köhler, *Sacharja*, p. 121; Keil, *Propheten*, p. 557; Rudolph, *Haggai, Sacharja*, p. 93), a noun which, however, is not attested in the Hebrew Bible.

107. The clause 'the LORD set an ambush against the men of [נתן יהוה מארבים עַל־בְּנֵי] Ammon, Moab, and Mount Seir...' in 2 Chron. 20.22 may be of a similar construction (cf. the same construction but with a form of the verb שִׂים in Judg. 9.25, 'And the men of Shechem put men in ambush against him [וישימו לו בעלי שכם מארבים]').

108. 'Männer die gehen [unter denen, die hier stehen]' (Beuken, *Haggai–Sacharja 1–8*, pp. 293-96).

109. 'Und ich gebe dir welche, die gehen...' (Schöttler, *Gottesvolk*, pp. 337-39).

110. 'Joshua', p. 560.

go'. The implication of this is that there is no evidence left to support the view that Joshua was given the privilege of access to the heavenly court, a privilege which prophets enjoyed.[111] Whatever the changes in the position of the high priest introduced in Zech. 3.7, access to the heavenly court does not belong to them.

*What Are the Intermediaries Doing?* When it comes to a more concrete interpretation of what the final clause of v. 7 interpreted as mediating beings refers to, different positions are taken. They can be labelled 'revelation' and 'intercession'. For Beuken[112] the keyword is 'revelation'. He sees the mediation as a movement from heaven to earth: angels communicating God's decrees to Joshua. The passage assumes a situation in which prophecy has died out and the high priest has taken over from the prophet the task of mediating the word of YHWH. Mediation through angels has become an ordinary form of revelation, ascribed not to the prophet, but to the high priest.

For Schöttler[113] the keyword is 'intercession'. He sees the mediation as a movement from earth to heaven. Zechariah 3.7 has to be understood against the background of 1.8-12, where the angel of YHWH communicates the disappointing result of the patrol of the horsemen in the form of a lament (as indicated by עַד־מָתַי) to YHWH. The מַהְלְכִים are to be identified as angels of YHWH who connect heaven and earth by carrying the requests and prayers of the high priest before YHWH.

The problem in making a decision between these proposals is that the context is extremely vague about the nature of the mediation between priest and heavenly council. As so often in the vision reports in Zechariah 1–6, things are only mentioned, but not made specific. An important question to consider is this: who in general are the persons who can participate in the heavenly court? One category of course would be heavenly beings. But what about human beings, do they participate in the heavenly court, and if so, any human being, or only a particular category? Most scholars would state that participation in the heavenly court was a privilege of prophets,[114] but while some say that

---

111. Contra, e.g., Tollington, *Tradition*, p. 160. See Chapter 6 of this book for a discussion of the question which categories of human beings enjoyed the privilege of access to the heavenly council.

112. Beuken, *Haggai–Sacharja 1–8*, p. 296.

113. Schöttler, *Gottesvolk*, pp. 339-40.

114. E.g. P.D. Hanson, *The People Called: The Growth of Community in the*

this was the prophets' privilege exclusively,[115] others say that it was a privilege of kings as well.[116]

Two passages are referred to in order to support the case that the king also was a participant in the heavenly court: Isa. 9.5 and Jer. 30.21. In my view the case fails to convince. Isa. 9.5 mentions פלא יועץ ('Wonderful Counselor' in the RSV) as one of the names of the child born to be king, but Jeremias fails to show in what way this relates to the heavenly court, and what this prophetic oracle tells us about actual Israelite kings. In Jer. 30.21 none of the language specific to heavenly court settings is present. The verbs one finds used in that verse are קרב hiphil 'making someone draw near', and נגשׁ niphal 'approaching' God, which is language related to the priestly cult.[117] I conclude that these passages fail to produce the evidence for human beings other than prophets as participants in the heavenly court, so that—at least in the rest of the Old Testament—participation in the heavenly court is a privilege of prophets exclusively.[118]

Perhaps one could argue that the lack of detail in Zech. 3.7 favours the revelation mode suggested by Beuken, because revelation or

*Bible* (San Francisco: Harper & Row, 1986), p. 265; C.A. Newsom, 'Angels', *ABD*, I, pp. 248-53 (249).

115. E.T. Mullen, Jr, *The Divine Council in Canaanite and Early Hebrew Literature* (HSM, 24; Chico, CA: Scholars Press, 1980), pp. 215, 219, 'This position belongs to the prophet alone; it is not a position that can be attained by an ordinary man'; cf. Meyers and Meyers, *Haggai, Zechariah*, p. 197; VanderKam, 'Joshua', p. 560, 'a prerogative that once belonged to the prophet'.

116. Reventlow, *Haggai, Sacharja*, p. 54, 'ein königliches…oder prophetisches Privileg'. In Jeremias's view it was not so much a privilege of the king, but of the anointed one (*Gesalbte*), see Jeremias, *Nachtgesichte*, p. 218. Mason seems to hold to the same notion of participation in the heavenly court as a royal prerogative when he states that (Mason, *Haggai, Zechariah*, p. 51) 'the privileges granted to Joshua [in Zech. 3.7], namely administration of the temple and its precincts and the role of intermediary between God and the community, all belonged to the king before the exile'.

117. See W.L. Holladay, *Jeremiah 1: A Commentary on the Book of the Prophet Jeremiah Chapters 1–25* (Hermeneia; Philadelphia: Fortress Press, 1986), p. 179; J.A. Thompson, *Jeremiah* (NICOT; Grand Rapids: Eerdmans, 1980), p. 562.

118. I do not think one can appeal to Psalm 110 either: the first verse positions the king (who is also a priest) at the right hand of God, but a suggestion that this should be located specifically in a heavenly court setting is lacking (compare H.-J. Kraus, *Psalmen*. I. *Psalmen 1–59*. II. *Psalmen 60–150* [BKAT, 15.1-2; Neukirchen–Vluyn: Neukirchener Verlag, 5th edn, 1978], pp. 757-58).

prophecy seems a more obvious connection between heavenly council and earth than intercession. Prophets do make intercession but nowhere else in the Old Testament is that part of their ministry connected specifically with the heavenly council. The problem with Beuken's specific proposal is his suggestion to consider this clause as belonging to a situation in which prophecy has died out, which assumes a specific view on a late redaction of the book and which makes it difficult to understand how the clause ever ended up precisely here.

Within the context of v. 7, one may relate the gift of intermediaries between priests and heavenly council with the extension of the authority of the high priest over the temple and its cult. I have discussed above that this implies that the high priest took over prerogatives which once belonged to the king. The מהלכים may fit into that picture.

Meyers and Meyers adopt the traditional 'access' interpretation, which I have rejected, but some of their comments also apply within the framework of interpretation which suggests a less immediate link with the heavenly council: 'if Joshua's increased responsibilities entail an absorption of certain functions previously performed by the king, then one would expect that Joshua would have the same relationship to prophetic pronouncements that the king previously had'. This might suggest a situation 'with prophets now addressing Joshua as they formerly spoke to kings and in that way constituting access to the Divine Council'.[119] Though this seems a more plausible interpretation, it is not completely without problems either: if the מהלכים were not heavenly beings but prophets, it is difficult to understand why they were not simply referred to as 'prophets (who go between these attendants)'.

### d. *Summary*

In the phrase וגם־אתה תדין את־ביתי וגם תשמר את־חצרי in Zech. 3.7 one can find an extension of the powers of the high priest,[120] though the precise nature of this extension is a matter of dispute. Depending on one's interpretation of the clauses וגם־אתה תדין את־ביתי וגם תשמר את־חצרי this extension would comprehend either jurisdiction over matters of temple and cult, or, more likely, government and administration of the temple.

---

119. Meyers and Meyers, *Haggai, Zechariah*, p. 197.

120. On the presence of at least a 'chief priest' in pre-exilic times, see the discussion in I.M. Duguid, *Ezekiel and the Leaders of Israel* (VTSup, 56; Leiden: E.J. Brill, 1994), pp. 59-63.

In the pre-exilic period these were prerogatives of the king: the chief priest was subject to the will of the king, even in matters of the temple and the worship of YHWH.[121] In whatever way one interprets the precise nature of the extension, it implies that the high priest is taking over prerogatives which once belonged to the king.[122] At the same time the limits of this extension to matters of temple and cult should be acknowledged.

In the final clause of v. 7, ונתתי לך מהלכים בין העמדים האלה, the word מהלכים should not be interpreted as a noun for 'access', for which interpretation there is no solid evidence whatsoever, but as a verb, a piel participle of הלך. 'Persons who go between these attendants' refers to intermediaries between heavenly council and the priest on earth. While the phrase is vague and not all details are completely clear, it seems best to interpret the function of these מהלכים as bearers of revelation, possibly prophets.

The relocation of prerogatives from the king to the priest raises the interesting question as to the reason for such a change. Was it because the king had failed to perform his duties, or was it because there was no provision for a king in the near future? Tollington affirms the latter position: an interpretation which finds here a transfer of former royal prerogatives to the senior priest, 'necessitates that no hopes were being fostered for a restored monarchy in the figure of Zerubbabel, and it would imply a significant rise in Joshua's status'.[123]

Such a conclusion is very tempting and particularly the comment on the absence of hopes for a restored monarchy would fit the overall thrust of the case I am arguing very well indeed, and yet I hesitate to adopt it. As Ezekiel 40–48 indicates, one can have a relocation of responsibilities between (still-) existing functions and offices.[124] So, as such one cannot conclude from the relocation of certain responsibilities

121. See, e.g., Duguid, *Ezekiel*, p. 63.

122. As observed by many scholars, e.g., Wellhausen, *Propheten*, p. 181; Marti, *Dodekapropheton*, p. 410; Driver, *Prophets*, p. 196; Nowack, *Propheten*, p. 340; Baldwin, *Haggai, Zechariah*, p. 115; Mason, *Haggai, Zechariah*, p. 51 (in contrast to Mason, I would not include 'the role of intermediary between God and the community' as a royal privilege; on this, see below); Rudolph, *Haggai, Sacharja*, p. 97; Jeremias, *Nachtgesichte*, p. 216; Schöttler, *Gottesvolk*, p. 335; VanderKam, 'Joshua', p. 559; Nelson, *Priest*, p. 121; Tollington, *Tradition*, p. 159; Rokay, 'Stadttor', p. 462.

123. Tollington, *Tradition*, p. 159.

124. See Duguid, *Ezekiel*.

from one institution to another that the institution which has responsibilities removed ceased to exist. In the absence of a reason stated in the oracle, any answer to the question of the reason for the transfer of prerogatives from the king to the priest must remain speculative.

## 5. *Conclusion*

In this chapter I have studied the setting of the צמח oracles in words addressed to members of the priesthood, and the presence of priests within the oracles themselves. Priests are the recipients of the צמח oracles because they have been given the position of men of portent (Zech. 3.8): the presence of the priesthood is a sign guaranteeing that YHWH will certainly fulfil his promise concerning the coming of Zemah. As the head of the college of priests, Joshua the high priest is singled out (6.11) to receive a crown on his head. The word used for 'crown' should be interpreted as singular, and the crown is indeed to be set on the head of Joshua. עטרה is a rather general word for 'crown', and not the one which is elsewhere found in contexts dealing with a coronation. Setting a crown on someone's head is in itself not an act of coronation, but may serve other purposes, in this particular case as a symbolic action which in a more dramatic way serves the same function found in 3.8: guaranteeing the coming about of the LORD's promise.

A priest is mentioned in the second צמח oracle (Zech. 6.14). His description is extremely vague and elusive, in contrast to a detailed description of the royal figure and his activities. The most that can be said about his role is that he functions as a counsellor to the king, and evidence for supremacy of the priest, or an equal status for ruler and priest, is absent.

In Zech. 3.7, Joshua, the high priest, is given certain prerogatives which formerly belonged to the king, but these are limited to the temple and its cult. No reasons are given for this transfer, and details are unclear. Evidence for increased civil power of the priest is absent,[125] and so is evidence for a form of government called 'diarchy'.

---

125. An in many ways similar conclusion (though details of interpretation differ) concerning the position of the high priest in the early postexilic period and concerning evidence to be found in Zechariah for the alleged acquiring of civil authority by the high priest has been reached by Rooke (*High Priesthood*, pp. 135-50).

## *Excursus 1: -ōt as a Feminine Singular Ending*

In this excursus I will discuss the evidence for the claim that the ending -ōt of the form עטרות in Zech. 6.11 can be explained as a feminine singular form. The same form עטרות with final -ōt has also been interpreted as a singular in Job 31.35-36:[126]

> Oh, that I had the indictment written by my adversary! / Surely I would carry it on my shoulder; I would bind it on me as a crown [אענדנו עטרות לי].

Some more traces of this singular feminine ending -ōt, possibly of Phoenician origin,[127] can be found in the Old Testament. I will start with the two cases which seem to be the clearest. Prov. 9.1 reads:

חכמות בנתה ביתה חצבה עמודיה שבעה

Wisdom has built her house, she has set up her seven pillars.

In this verse, the verbal forms in the singular (בנתה and חצבה) and particularly the singular suffixes (ביתה and עמודיה) indicate that חכמות is a singular form.[128] There is a similar appearance of חכמות followed by a combination of singular verbal forms[129] and suffixes in Prov. 1.20:

---

126. Lipiński, 'Zacharie', pp. 34-35; cf. Beuken, *Haggai–Sacharja 1–8*, p. 275 n. 1; Rudolph, *Haggai, Sacharja*, p. 128; A.R. Ceresko, *Job 29–31 in the Light of Northwest Semitic* (BibOr, 36; Rome: Biblical Institute Press, 1980), p. 184.

127. Rudolf Meyer, *Hebräische Grammatik* (4 vols.; Berlin: W. de Gruyter, 1966–72), II, p. 39 §41.5c; he reconstructs the origin of the form in the following way: *-ōt < *-at < *-atu (according to S. Segert, *A Grammar of Phoenician and Punic* [Munich: Beck, 1976], p. 74 §36, 46 [cf. p. 87 §43, 412, 1] the development was *at > *āt > ōt). See also Beuken, *Haggai–Sacharja 1–8*, p. 275 n. 1; Lipiński 'Zacharie', pp. 34-35; cf. Ceresko, *Job 29–31*, p. 184.

128. So Meyer, *Grammatik*, II, p. 39 §41.5c; his position is adopted in *HALAT* s.v. רנן, p. 1164.

129. The first verbal form, תָּרֹנָּה, also appears in 8.3, with the singular חכמה as its subject. תָּרֹנָּה is not simply a third person feminine singular, which would have been *תָּרֹן (cf. וְתָרֹן in Isa. 35.6). It is neither a simple third person feminine plural, which would have been something like תִּרְנֶינָה.* One way to interpret the form is to see it as an third person singular feminine imperfect, ending in -ā (cf. *HALAT* s.v. רנן). It would then be one of those few third person singular feminine forms with an afformative -ā; usually found in the cohortative (first person), like יְחִישָׁה in Isa. 5.19, and תָּעֻפָה in Job 11.17 (the noun which some propose to read here, תְּעֻפָה, is

חכמות בחוץ תרנה ברחבות תתן קולה

Wisdom cries aloud in the street; in the markets she raises her voice.

Another case is עגלות in Hos. 10.5, עגלות בית און 'the calf of Beth-Aven'. Rudolph suggests[130] that עגלות belongs to this category of singular endings in -*ōt* (the plural is always עֲגָלִים). That suggestion would remove the need for the emendation עֵגֶל.[131] Less clear is a case like the form עֵדֹתִי in Ps. 132.12, which RSV translates as 'my testimonies'. Kraus suggests the punctuation עֵדֹתַי,[132] apparently a plural of עֵדוּת.[133] Allen writes, '[t]he form of the suffix is unusual, עֵדוֹתַי being expected'.[134]

However, the problem is not solved by reading -*ay* instead of MT -*ī*. It is not just the suffix -*ī* which is unusual: for a plural of עֵדוּת one needs a waw as a *consonant*. The plural of עֵדוּת with suffix is not עֵדוֹתָיו ('*ēdōtāw*) as one finds in *HALAT*,[135] but עֵדְוֹתָיו '*ēdwōtāw* (note the *š°wā* with the ד).[136] The absence of the waw in MT עדתי makes a vocalization as a plural of עֵדוּת highly unlikely.

The alternative is to read the singular of עֵדוּת with suffix, that is, עֵדְתִי. That this would be the only occasion where עֵדוּת in the singular has a suffix is not an insuperable objection. More problematic is once again the absence of the waw. Because there is no עֵדוּת in the singular with a suffix attested one cannot speak with absolute certainty, but it is worthwhile mentioning the following. Nominal forms ending in -*ūt* can be written in defective spelling, for example מַלְכֻתוֹ, but nominal forms of the type Consonant-Vowel-Consonant *ūt* (like עֵדוּת) when with suffix are always written plene (even when the form without suffix may

not attested in the Old Testament); Imperfect וְתָבוֹאֶה in Isa. 5.19; Imperfect Consecutive וַתַּעְגְּבָה in Ezek. 23.20 (and 23.16 *Q*).

130. Rudolph, *Haggai, Sacharja*, p. 128; cf. *idem*, *Hosea* (KAT, 13.1; Gütersloh: Gerd Mohn, 1966), p. 195.

131. So *BHS* and *HALAT*.

132. Kraus, *Psalmen*, p. 1055.

133. This is also one of the suggestions in *HALAT* s.v. עֵדוּת.

134. L.C. Allen, *Psalms 101–150* (WBC, 21; Waco, TX: Word Books, 1990).

135. It comes as a surprise to see that *HALAT* refer to BL 605h [= p. 605 §76h] and M §56, where one finds the correct form עֵדְוֹתָיו.

136. See 1 Kgs 2.3; 2 Kgs 17.15; 23.3; Jer. 44.23; Ps. 119.14, 31, 36, 99, 111, 129, 144, 157; Neh. 9.34; 1 Chron. 29.19; 2 Chron. 34.31; for the form of the plural, see also Joüon and Muraoka, *Grammar*, §88Mj and 97Gb.

be written in defective spelling [as one finds with עֶדְרַת]),[137] that is, they are always written with the waw of the *šūreq* (וּ).[138] While there is nothing close to consistency in the choice of defective or plene spelling, in this case the regularity is noteworthy. If the absence of the waw is of any significance, then we might be forced to give up all attempts to derive עֵדֹתִי from עֵדוּת, and עֵדֹת as a feminine singular would become a possibility.[139]

## Excursus 2: The Crown in Ps. 21.4

Ps. 21.4 reads:

> For thou dost meet him with goodly blessings; thou dost set a crown of fine gold upon his head.

The precise nature of the setting of Psalm 21 is disputed. A number of scholars consider Psalm 21 as a song on the occasion of the coronation of a king,[140] or an anniversary of that coronation.[141] Others find the

137. גָּלוּת is sometimes written גָּלֻת, but before a suffix one always finds גָּלוּת.

138. It is interesting to notice that *HALAT* also give the form עֵדוּתִי.

139. So G.A. Rendsburg, 'Regional Dialects', in W.R. Bodine (ed.), *Linguistics and Biblical Hebrew* (Winona Lake, IN: Eisenbrauns, 1992), pp. 65-88; he interprets זוּ in עֵדֹתִי זוּ אֲלַמְּדֵם as a demonstrative pronoun ('Regional Dialects', p. 79; his earlier statement [G.A. Rendsburg, *Linguistic Evidence for the Northern Origin of Selected Psalms* (SBLMS, 43; Atlanta: Scholars Press, 1990), p. 89] was more cautious and left the possibility of זוּ being a relative pronoun open). I think it is more natural to take זוּ here as a relative pronoun. I admit that the vocalisation is unique: one usually finds זֶה or זוּ, e.g., Ps. 17.9 רְשָׁעִים זוּ שַׁדּוּנִי 'the wicked who despoil me'. However, I find it difficult to make sense of the phrase אֲלַמְּדֵם זוּ וְעֵדֹתִי on the assumption that זוּ is a demonstrative pronoun. Like אֲשֶׁר, זֶה or זוּ are used 'without distinction of gender or of number' (Joüon and Muraoka, *Grammar*, §36b and §145c). If this line of interpretation is to be preferred, then Rendsburg's second argument to support the interpretation of עֵדֹתִי as a singular feminine form, that is, 'the feminine singular demonstrative pronoun which follows', should be abandoned.

140. E.g. A. Weiser, *Die Psalmen: Übersetzt und erklärt* (ATD, 14; Göttingen: Vandenhoeck & Ruprecht, 1950), p. 143; ET *The Psalms: A Commentary* (OTL; London: SCM Press, 1962), p. 212.

141. E.g. P.C. Craigie, *Psalms 1–50* (WBC, 19; Waco, TX: Word Books, 1983), p. 190; H. Spieckermann, *Heilsgegenwart: Eine Theologie der Psalmen* (FRLANT, 148; Göttingen: Vandenhoeck & Ruprecht, 1989), p. 216; J. Day, *Psalms* (OTG; Sheffield: JSOT Press, 1990), p. 96; O. Loretz, *Die Königspsalmen. Die altorientalisch-kanaanäische Königstradition in jüdischer Sicht. I. Ps 20, 21, 72, 101 und*

setting in the role of the king in battle (either a prayer before battle,[142] or thanksgiving after victory in battle[143]).

A connection with a coronation or its anniversary would provide evidence for the use of עטרה in the context of a coronation, and would invalidate the statement I have made, namely that עטרה is not found in such contexts. I am aware that at a point like this it is very difficult to maintain one's integrity as an open-minded reader of the text. The issue becomes even more complex when one finds scholars stating that the language of the psalm is not specific enough to make a compelling case for either position.[144] The only unequivocal feature which warrants a link with a coronation (anniversary) setting is the clause 'thou dost set a crown of fine gold upon his head'. Yet I find that taking the mere mention of setting a crown on the king's head as proof for a coronation setting begs the question. If one allows for a distinction between a crowning and a coronation as I have argued above,[145] then the need to limit the interpretation of the Psalm as a whole to a coronation (anniversary) setting disappears, and the possibility of other interpretations can be evaluated.

There are two observations which in my view tip the balance in favour of an interpretation which finds the setting of the psalm in the role of the king as warrior. (a) Victory in battle is a major theme throughout the psalm (vv. 2, 6, 9-13; the battle theme is also present in the preceding Psalm 20, which a number of scholars connect with Psalm 21). (b) The parallel line 'thou dost meet him with goodly

---

144 (Mit einem Beitrag von I. Kottsieper zu Papyrus Amherst; Ugaritisch-Biblische Literatur, 6; Münster: Ugarit-Verlag, 1988), p. 92 (his Chapter 4 includes a survey of the history of the interpretation of the psalm).

142. S. Mowinckel, *Psalmenstudien. III. Kultprophetie und prophetische Psalmen* (Amsterdam: Schippers, 1966), p. 76.

143. M. Dahood, *Psalms. I. 1–50: Introduction, Translation, and Notes* (AB, 16; Garden City, NY: Doubleday, 1966), p. 131; L. Jacquet, *Les Psaumes et le coeur de l'homme: Etude textuelle, littéraire et doctrinale. Introduction et premier livre du Psautier. Psaumes 1 à 41* (Gembloux: Duculot, 1975), p. 503.

144. J.W. Rogerson and J.W. McKay, *Psalms 1–50* (CBC; Cambridge: Cambridge University Press, 1977), p. 93, 'the language is not sufficiently specific to limit the psalm to either setting'; cf. Kraus, *Psalmen*, p. 316, 'Eine genaue Situationserklärung wird kaum möglich sein'; he then lists several options for the setting of the psalm without committing himself to any one in particular.

145. In that discussion I pointed to Song 3.11, which shows that even a king can be 'crowned' at an occasion different from his coronation.

blessings' (v. 4) suggests that the crown is 'less a symbol of earthly authority here than a token of the rich blessings and prosperity…that God has in store for the king'.[146] The mentioning of the outstanding quality (פז, 'of fine gold') of the material of which the crown is made may be another element in support of this interpretation. If these observations are correct, then one can conclude that in Psalm 21 we do not have an example of עטרה in a passage referring to a coronation.

### Excursus 3: The Unusual Vocalisation of מַהְלְכִים

The usual form of the plural of the participle of the piel of הלך is מְהַלְּכִים. And that is the problem with taking the form in Zech. 3.7 as a piel participle: the Masoretes have vocalised the form as מַהְלְכִים. Kutscher explains[147] the unusual form in Zech. 3.7 (מַהְלְכִים) as a result of haplology (מַהְלְכִים > מְהַלְכִים > מְהַלְּכִים), a phonetic process on other occasions found—he claims—in the piel participle of First-Guttural verbs, for example מַחְלְמִים in Jer. 29.8, מַעְזְרִים in 2 Chron. 28.23, and the *qere* מחצרים forms in 1–2 Chronicles.[148] Kutscher also points to the similar form מַהְלְכִין in biblical Aramaic (Dan. 3.25; 4.34).

I believe that Kutscher is looking in the right direction, but his association of מַהְלְכִים with the forms מַחְלְמִים in Jer. 29.8 and מַעְזְרִים in 2 Chron. 28.23 is somewhat problematic: these verbs are attested in the qal only (חלם 27 times; עזר 75 times), but never in the piel (pual, or hitpael) stem. Kutscher's proposal would imply the postulation of a piel of these verbs not attested elsewhere in the Old Testament. If we don't count Jer. 29.8, there is one attestation for the hiphil of חלם, Isa. 38.16. חצר, Kutscher's third parallel, is attested in the piel once: the *kethib* לַמְחַצְּרִים in 2 Chron. 5.13 suggests a *qere* לַמְחַצְרִים.

---

146. Rogerson and McKay, *Psalms*, p. 94.

147. E.Y. Kutscher, 'מהלכים ואחיותיה', *Leš* 26 (1960–61), pp. 93-96 (93-95).

148. The *qere* is meant to correct different forms with different vocalizations: מחצרים *Q*—מַחְצְרִים *K* 1 Chron. 15.24; 2 Chron. 29.28; *K* מַחְצְרִים—*Q* מחצרים 2 Chron. 5.12; *K* מַחַצְּרִים—*Q* מחצרים 2 Chron. 7.6; 13.14; *Q*—לַמְחַצְּרִים *K* מַחַצְּרִים—*Q* מחצרים 2 Chron. 5.13.

Figure 10. חלם, עזר, *and* חצר *in Qal, Piel, and Hiphil Stem.*

| | qal | piel | hiphil |
|---|---|---|---|
| חלם | 27 × | – | Isa. 38.16 [Jer. 29.8?] |
| עזר | 75 × | – | 2 Sam. 18.3 [K לעזיר; Q לעזור] |
| חצר | - | 2 Chron. 5.13 [K לַמְחַצְצְרִים; Q לַמְחַצְּרִים] | 5 × |

The form מַהְלְכִין in Dan. 3.25 and 4.34 has commonly been interpreted as a participle of the piel of (Aramaic) הלך.[149] Eitan interprets the form in Dan. 3.25; 4.34 as a result of a phonetic process (as the examples discussed by Eitan indicate, apparently operating in both Hebrew and Aramaic) which he labels 'Vowel Receding'.[150] Eitan describes the process thus:

> whenever a *vocalized* half-consonant, א, ו, י, or also ה, though this more particularly in prefixes, immediately follows a vowelless consonant (in Heb. and Aram. any kind of šewa), there is a tendency for these letters to drop out in pronunciation, then further in writing, while thus yielding their vowel to the preceding consonant. In Hebrew and Aramaic this vowel, then, seems to recede in order to displace a šewa.

In formalized language this process could be described in the following way:

$$\partial \left\{ \begin{array}{c} {}^{,} \\ h \\ w \\ y \end{array} \right\} \rightarrow \emptyset \, / \, C{-}V$$

149. E.g. J. Goldingay, *Daniel* (WBC, 30; Dallas: Word Books, 1987), p. 66, on Dan. 3.25; BLA §76n p. 274 'für מַהְלְכִין...ist vielleicht Part. Pa. מְהַלְכִין zu lesen'. The form is interpreted as a hiphil participle in, e.g., *HALAT* p. 1698; Rosenthal, *Grammar*, §169.

150. I. Eitan, 'Some Philological Observations in Daniel', *HUCA* 14 (1939), pp. 13-22.

The change which results from this phonetic process is a conditioned sound change: the change is restricted to a particular environment. The single slash (/) introduces the environment. The line (— em-dash), indicates the location of the changing sound with respect to the conditioning environment: the half-consonant (|'|, |h|, |w|, or |y|) preceded by $š^ewâ$ ($ə$) which in the process disappears (→ ø), comes after a consonant (C), and before a vowel (V). The process as a whole could be called 'partial phonemic loss': the phoneme (the half-consonant) disappears, but only in a specific environment.[151] On the basis of this process of 'Vowel Receding' or 'partial phonemic loss' Eitan is able to explain forms like וַתַּזְרֵנִי in 2 Sam. 22.40 (= וַתְּאַזְּרֵנִי in Ps. 18.40), מַחְצְפָה in Dan. 3.22 (= מְהַחְצְפָה in Dan. 2.15).

The difference between these examples and the form מַהְלְכִין in Dan. 3.25 and 4.34 is that in מַהְלְכִין the consonant (in this case the ה) is still present in the orthography, but this is not completely unusual, as a form like יְראוּ (Josh. 24.14, 1 Sam. 12.24 and Ps. 34.10; < יִרְאוּ) shows. It seems that Eitan himself did not put Zech. 3.7 in this category. In a footnote he refers to a Hebrew commentary by one Lambert, about which he writes, 'where however מַהְלְכִים of Zech. 3, 7 is quite irrelevantly referred to'. Unfortunately he does not explain why this is irrelevant. In my view Eitan's analysis could also help explain Hebrew מַהְלְכִים in Zech. 3.7 just as it does מַהְלְכִין in Dan. 3.25 and 4.34.

The forms of the participle of the piel show a certain measure of irregularity: in many forms the doubling has disappeared (מְאַסְפָיו Isa. 62.9; מְבַקְשֵׁי Prov. 29.26; מְבַקְשֵׁי Ps. 105.3; Prov. 28.5; הַמְהַלְלִים 2 Chron. 23.12; הַמְמַלְאִים Job 3.15; מְשַׂנְאַי Ps. 81.16). Something along these lines may have happened in Zech. 3.7.

151. I have derived these writing conventions for formalised language and categories for different types of phonetic change from T. Crowley, *An Introduction to Historical Linguistics* (Oxford: Oxford University Press, 2nd edn, 1992), pp. 66-72.

Chapter 3

WHAT'S IN A NAME?—THE MEANING OF צמח

The main subject of this chapter is one Hebrew word, the noun צמח. The word occurs twice in the oracles of Zechariah; in both cases it is the name of the coming ruler (Zech. 3.8, 'my servant צמח'; Zech. 6.12, 'a man called צמח'). The justification for devoting one complete chapter to only one word is found in the presence of a considerable amount of confusion in the scholarly literature (and this includes the dictionaries) about the meaning of the word.

The chapter will be divided into two parts. In the first part I will determine the meaning of the word צמח. In the second part I will discuss the use of צמח in the Old Testament in contexts dealing with kingship.

1. *The Meaning of the Word* צמח.

a. *Survey*
The well-known English Bible translations (KJV, RSV, NJPS, NEB, NRSV) show a remarkable unanimity in the way they have rendered the word צמח in Zech. 3.8 and 6.12. In all these translations צמח is translated by the word 'branch'.[1] This is also the translation found in a great number of commentaries. I call this consensus remarkable because of a comment Driver made at the beginning of the twentieth century. In a note on the phrase 'my servant the Branch' (the translation of the phrase עבדי צמח in Zech. 3.8 as found in RV) he wrote:[2]

---

1. The translation of צמח with a word for 'branch' is only found in English language translations. Other modern language translations usually have an equivalent of 'sprout' (e.g. French: BJ and TOB translate 'Germe'; German: EÜ translates 'Sproß').
2. Driver, *Prophets*, pp. 197-98. An identical note is found in his commentary on Jer. 23.5 (S.R. Driver, *The Book of the Prophet Jeremiah* [London: Hodder & Stoughton, 1906], p. 364).

**the Shoot** (or rather, since there is no art., as a pr. name, Ẓemaḥ, 'Shoot'). The Heb. *ẓemaḥ* cannot mean 'branch': as its other occurrences show, it is a general term for what *sprouts* or *shoots* from the ground (see e.g. Gen. XIX. 25 'the growth of the ground', where 'branch' would obviously be unsuitable). In Is. IV. 2 the 'growth' or 'shooting' of Yahweh means generally the produce of the soil, quickened and blessed by Yahweh in the blissful future which the prophet is there looking forward to: in Jer. XXIII. 5...and in the parallel passage, XXXIII. 15...it is a fig. designation of Israel's future king, represented as a *sprout* or *shoot*; and here and in Zech. VI. 12, obviously on the basis of the two passages of Jeremiah, it is used actually as a title of the Messiah.

Dictionaries like BDB and *HALAT* are in line with Driver's choice of 'sprout'.[3] BDB gives the following translation equivalents:

> **sprout, growth**...**1.** coll. *sprouting, growth*... **2.** process of *growth*... **3.** future ruler, under fig. of *sprout* from Davidic tree...[4]

In *HALAT* one finds:

> 1. **das Spriessen**: ...das was sprosst, Gewächs: coll. ...—2. **der einzelne Spross** (als Nachkomme Davids u. König der Heilszeit)...

> 1. **sprouting**...what sprouts: collective... 2. a particular shoot, referring to an individual person, a descendant of David and of the king in the Messianic era of salvation...

Actually, the difference between the two translations 'branch' and 'sprout' is perhaps not that big: what is called a branch has started life as a (shoot or) sprout, as the following definitions of the words 'shoot' and 'sprout' suggest (the definitions can be found in the *Oxford English Dictionary*):

> [s.v. shoot] A young branch which shoots from the main stock of a tree, plant, etc.
> [s.v. sprout] A shoot from a branch, root, or stump of a tree, shrub or plant; a new growth developing from a bud into a branch, stalk, sucker, etc.

---

3.   LXX usually translates צמח (the noun) with forms of (the verb) ἀνατέλλω (LSJ gives the following translations: make to rise up; bring forth, give birth; rise, appear above the horizon; grow [of hair, or teeth]); ἀνατολή is found in Jer. 23.5 and Zech. 3.8 and 6.12 (LSJ 'rising above the horizon [heavenly body], east; growing [teeth, etc.]). In Vulgate צמח is usually translated *germen* 'sprout', but *oriens* 'east' in Zech. 3.8 and 6.12.

4.   For this meaning, BDB mentions passages like Jer. 23.5 and 33.15, which will be discussed later in this Chapter.

So, both 'sprout' and 'shoot' have to do with the initial stages of growth of new parts of a plant or tree. What the translations 'branch' and 'shoot/sprout' have in common is that they take צמח to refer to a part of the plant or tree, even though they disagree on the precise identification of which part. It is precisely this aspect of the usual interpretation of the meaning of the noun צמח—that is, that it is used for a part of a plant or tree—that was challenged by Rüthy in 1942 in his study of Hebrew words for plants and their constituent parts (*Die Pflanze und ihre Teile*). Rüthy concludes his discussion of the meaning of the noun צמח:[5] 'The meaning 'sprout' as a part of the plant cannot be substantiated anywhere in B[iblical] H[ebrew]'. According to Rüthy, צמח is used (1) 'as an infinitive, 'The [process of] sprouting'' (*das Sprießen*), (2) 'as a collective noun for everything that sprouts, vegetation' (*alles was spriesst, die Gewächse*).[6]

An extensive study of the root צמח has been made by Dambrine. She finds it used in three ways:[7] (a) the verb צמח describes the physiological life (of plants and of humans); (b) צמח expresses the growth of the plant; (c) צמח characterizes the life principle of the plant. Dambrine's extensive discussion would have been clearer and more useful if she had not dealt generally with 'the root צמח', but had made a proper distinction between the use of the verb צָמַח and the noun צֶמַח, and had given a description of the meaning of the verb and of the noun separately. Her discussion on pp. 4-7 makes clear that meanings (a) and (b) apply to the verb (at times she uses the verb 'to sprout' [*germer*] as a

---

5. 'Die Bedeutung «Spross» als Teil der Pfl. lässt sich demgemäss im B[ibel]h[ebräischen] nirgends nachweisen' (A.E. Rüthy, *Die Pflanze und ihre Teile im Biblisch-Hebräischen Sprachgebrauch* [Bern: Francke, 1942], pp. 48-49); the words quoted can be found on p. 49; cf. his remark on p. 48 that צמח 'im AT nirgends den einzelnen Spross bedeutet'. Löw's position (I. Löw, *Die Flora der Juden. Bd. IV. Zusammenfassung, Nachträge, Berichtigungen, Indizes, Abkürzungen* [Hildesheim: Georg Olms, 1967]) comes somewhere in the middle between the usual interpretation and that of Rüthy: he seems to make a distinction between the use of צמח in the Hebrew of the Old Testament and in later (mishnaic) Hebrew, 'b[ibel]h[ebräisch] Sproß...ist mišnisch Pflanze allgemein' (p. 42); and, 'Die Pflanze, ṣemaḥ, ist schon biblisch der Messias' (p. 351).

6. Compare H. Ringgren, 'צמח', *ThWAT*, VI, cols. 1068-72 (1071), 'Das Subst. ṣemaḥ bezeichnet das, was sproßt, d.h. "Gewächs o.ä".

7. L. Dambrine, 'L'Image de la croissance dans la foi d'Israël: Etude de la racine צמח et de ses dérivés' (Mémoire de l'Institut des Sciences bibliques de l'Université de Lausanne; 1971), pp. 4-7.

translation equivalent for these meanings). The only thing that Dambrine says about the meaning of the noun is (c), but this meaning only covers two of the occurrences of the noun (Ezek. 17.5-6; Hos. 8.7b), but does not fit in other contexts.

### b. *The Semantics of the Noun* צמח—*A Structural Approach*

The survey has made it clear that there is no agreement on the meaning of the noun צמח. There are basically two options.[8] (a) צמח is used for a part of the plant, and means either 'branch' or 'sprout' (usual translation). (b) צמח is used for the plant (or plants) as a whole, and means 'vegetation' (Rüthy). Either option would locate צמח in a different lexical field (see Fig. 11). The question can be put like this: where does צמח belong, with words for branch or shoot/sprout, or with more general words for vegetation, or perhaps somewhere else?

Figure 11. *Lexical Fields of 'Branch', 'Shoot/Sprout', and 'Plant(s)/Vegetation'*

| branch | shoot/sprout | plant(s)/ vegetation |
|---|---|---|
| בַּד | יֹנֶקֶת | דֶּשֶׁא |
| דָּלִית* | נֵצֶר | חָצִיר |
| חֹטֶר | [פֶּרַח] | עֵץ |
| עָנָף | | עֵשֶׂב |
| פֹּארָה | | שִׂיחַ |
| קָצִיר | | |
| שָׂרִיג | | |

The noun צמח occurs 12 times in the Old Testament. In four cases the noun is used in a figurative sense (Jer. 23.5; 33.5; Zech. 3.8; 6.12). Leaving these four passages out, the list comes down to eight occurrences.

1. ויהפך...צמח האדמה
   'and he overthrew...the X of the ground' (Gen. 19.25; cf. Exod. 10.15).
2. יהיה צמח יהוה לצבי ולכבוד
   'the X of the LORD shall be beautiful and glorious' (Isa. 4.2).
3. כארץ תוציא צמחה
   'as the earth brings forth its X' (Isa. 61.11).

8.  Since Dambrine does not adequately discuss the meaning of the noun, I leave her analysis out of the discussion here.

4.  רבבה כצמח השׂדה
    'grow up like the X of the field' (Ezek. 16.6-7).
5.  ויבשׁ כל־טרפי צמחה
    'all the leaves of its X will wither' (Ezek. 17.9).
6.  על־ערגת צמחה תיבשׁ
    'on the bed of its X it will wither' (Ezek. 17.10).
7.  קמה אין־לו צמח בלי יעשׂה־קמח
    'The standing grain has no X, it shall yield no meal' (Hos. 8.7).
8.  צמחה תברך
    'you bless its X'
    [that is, 'the X of the land', cf. ארץ in v. 10] (Ps. 65.9-10).

Figure 12. צמח *in Some English Translations.*

|            | KJV                      | RSV=NRSV          | JPS                    | REB                                          |
|------------|--------------------------|-------------------|-----------------------|----------------------------------------------|
| Gen. 19.25 | that which grew          | what grew         | vegetation            | everything growing                           |
| Isa. 4.2   | branch                   | branch            | radiance              | the plant that the LORD has grown            |
| Isa. 61.11 | bud                      | shoots            | growth                | blossom                                      |
| Ezek. 16.6-7 | bud                    | plant             | plants                | an evergreen plant growing in the field      |
| Ezek. 17.9 | the leaves of her spring | fresh sprouting   | its entire foliage    | freshly sprouted leaves                      |
| Ezek. 17.10 | where it grew           | where it grew     | where it is growing   | where it ought to sprout                     |
| Hos. 8.7   | bud                      | heads             | ears                  | heads                                        |
| Ps. 65.11  | springing                | growth            | growth                | growth                                       |

There is a rich diversity in the way the well-known translations translate the word צמח (see Fig. 12) in these passages. Is there a way to determine the meaning of the word with more precision than a label like 'possible translation' and come to a reasoned preference for one translation over another? I think there is, and the way forward is to adopt a structural approach. I will first try to establish with which words צמח is found in a relationship of combination (so-called syntagmatic relationships). In all but one (no. 7) of these cases, צמח is found in a construction of the type 'the צמח of Z' (or can be rewritten as such a construction). In five of these cases the reference of the Z is a word for field/earth/ground (nos. 1, 3-4, 8; in my view[9] no. 2 also belongs here), in the

9.  In the phrase צמח יהוה in Isa. 4.2, the 'Z' of the construction 'the צמח of Z'

remaining two the reference is a word for vine (nos. 5-6 [גֶפֶן Ezek.
17.6-8]). I will now look at both combinations.

*The צמח of the Earth/Ground/Field*. I will first discuss the phrase 'the
צמח of the earth/ground/field' (nos. 1-4, 8). In this phrase צמח stands in
a so-called syntagmatic relationship (a relationship of combination)
with words for 'earth/ground/field'. If צמח belongs with words for
'branch' or 'shoot/sprout' one would expect to find other words of the
same lexical field in the same slot as one finds צמח, that is one would
find phrases like 'branch(es) of the earth' or 'shoots/sprouts of the
earth'. On the other hand, if צמח belongs with words for 'plant(s)/vege-
tation' one would expect to find other words of the same lexical field in
the same slot as one finds צמח, that is one would find phrases like
'plant(s)/vegetation of the earth'.

Here we are looking for words which stand in a so-called paradigmatic relationship (a relationship of choice) with צמח, that is, words
that can occupy the same slot as צמח in a phrase like 'the צמח of the
earth/field/ground'. Interestingly, there are no cases[10] in the Hebrew
Bible of the type 'branch of the earth/field/ground', or 'sprout of the
earth/field/ground', neither does one find cases where the earth/field/
ground is said to produce branches or sprouts. A branch or a sprout is
always presented as a part or product of a plant, or a tree, not as the
(immediate) product of the earth.[11]

So there is an interesting difference in the use of Hebrew words for
'sprout' or 'branch' on the one hand, and the noun צמח on the other
hand. Sprout and branch are presented as part or product of plant or
tree, whereas צמח is presented as a product of the soil. This difference

does this time not refer to the place where צמח is present, but to the one who is its
ultimate cause (YHWH). The parallel line פְּרִי הָאָרֶץ identifies אֶרֶץ as the place of
צמח. See the discussion below.

10. The only word which one finds like צמח in a syntagmatic relationship with
words for 'earth/ground/field' is קְצִיר (e.g. Lev. 19.9; 23.22; Deut. 24.19; Joel
1.11), but in those cases we are dealing with a different root (קָצִיר[i] 'harvest', קָצִיר[ii]
'branch'; see BDB or *HALAT* s.v.).

11. As an example one could look at the words for 'sprout': יוֹנֶקֶת is presented
as a part or product of a cedar (Ezek. 17.22), of an unspecified plant or tree (Hos.
14.7; Job 8.16; 14.7; 15.30 [3 × singular]), or of a vine (Ps. 80.12). Similarly, נֵצֶר is
presented as a product coming from roots (Isa. 11.1; Dan. 11.7; in both cases the
roots of an unspecified plant or tree), or as something that has been planted (Isa.
60.21).

in options for syntagmatic relationships makes the idea that צמח belongs with words for 'sprout' or 'branch' difficult to maintain. What category, then, does צמח belong to? The way to provide an answer to this question is to observe which words from the world of flora are, just like צמח, used in syntagmatic relationship with words like earth/field/ground. Other words from the world of flora which are similarly presented as a product of the soil are דשא 'grass, vegetation', חציר 'grass', עץ 'tree', עשב 'plant, herb', שיח 'plant, bush'.

To conclude: the words which stand in a paradigmatic relationship with צמח, that is, the words which can stand in the same slot as צמח in phrases like 'צמח of the earth/ground/field' are all more general words for plant(s)/tree(s) or vegetation. In the five cases where צמח is used in this phrase the most natural meaning is 'vegetation'. Though one may want to have some reservations about his use of the words 'sprouts or shoots' (see his full definition and my discussion above), Driver was surely correct in identifying the origin of צמח as 'from the ground',[12] and so is Wanke (though I would substitute צמח for 'sprout' and 'growing' for 'coming forth'), 'The expression "sprout" means a plant breaking forth from the earth'.[13]

צמח *and a Vine.* I now turn to the discussion of two cases where the word צמח is used in connection with a vine (nos. 5-6, Ezek. 17.9, 10). These cases are less straightforward than the one discussed so far. In both cases the form is צִמְחָהּ, a form which from the point of view of

12. Driver, *Jeremiah*, p. 364.

13. 'Der Ausdruck «Sproß» meint eine aus der Erde hervorbrechende Pflanze' (G. Wanke, *Jeremia. I. Jeremia 1,1–25,14* [ZBAT, 20.1; Zürich: Theologische Verlag, 1995], p. 205). I have argued that the fact that צמח is presented as having its origin 'from the ground' speaks against 'shoot, sprout' as the meaning of the word. However, the first clauses of Isa. 53.2 read: 'For he grew up before him like a young plant [יונק], and like a root [שרש] out of dry ground [ארץ ציה]'.

Would clauses like these not suggest that it is not impossible for a shoot or sprout to grow up out of the ground? This would only be the case when the two clauses can only be understood as standing in synonymous parallelism, in such a way that the final words of the second clause do double duty, that is, the words מארץ ציה should be thought to also relate to the first clause, in which the word יונק is used. One can also read the two clauses as standing in synthetic parallelism, in which case the two clauses each in its own way evoke the idea of vulnerability. In that case there is no reason to connect the words מארץ ציה with יונק.

morphology could also be interpreted as an infinitive.[14] The two phrases are:

ויבש כל־טרפי צמחה 'all the leaves of its X will wither' (Ezek. 17.9).

and

על־ערגת צמחה תיבש 'on the bed of its X it will wither' (Ezek. 17.10).

Translations of the phrase טרפי צמחה in Ezek. 17.9 vary widely: 'the leaves of her spring' (KJV), 'fresh sprouting leaves' (RSV=NRSV), 'its entire foliage' (JPS), 'freshly sprouted leaves' (NEB). The withering of כל טרפי צמחה (of the vine) comes as a result of the pulling up of the roots and the cutting off of the fruits of the vine. If טרף means 'fresh',[15] something like 'all its fresh growth' fits more naturally with the comprehensiveness of the picture[16] than 'all its fresh sprouts', which would limit the withering to the initial stages of growth. Similarly, if טרף means 'leaf' (in my view the more attractive option), something like 'all the leaves it has grown' would fit the context better than 'all the leaves it has made sprout'.

In Ezek. 17.10 (ערגת) צמחה the translations have either 'where it grew' (KJV and RSV, compare NJPS 'where it is growing') or 'where it ought to sprout' (REB). Depending on whether one interprets שתל as either 'plant' or 'transplant',[18] the phrases ערגות מטעה (v. 7) and ערגת צמחה (v. 10) refer either to one and the same plot of ground or to two different plots. Some interpret v. 8 as referring to a new process of being planted, that is, the vine is being transplanted from one place to

---

14. *HALAT* mentions this as a possibility. With final ה verbs, the vowel of the infinitive construct with suffix is usually /o/, but a small number of cases with /i/ is attested (בְּטְחֵךְ, פְּתְחִי, פִּתְחוֹ [usually שַׁלְחִי], שֶׁלְחוֹ).

15. So *HALAT*; *ThWAT*, III, cols. 375-76; on the confusing statements surrounding the derivation of the word, see J. Kaltner, *The Use of Arabic in Biblical Hebrew Lexicography* (CBQMS, 28; Washington: Catholic Biblical Association, 1996), pp. 40-41.

16. Compare vv. 6, 8, and also indicated by the use of כל in v. 9.

17. So Rüthy, *Pflanze*, p. 63; M. Greenberg, *Ezekiel 1–20* (AB, 22; New York: Doubleday, 1983), p. 313. To assume a semantic development from 'fresh, freshly plucked' to 'leaf' (so *DCH*, III, p. 376 s.v. טֶרֶף) is in my view implausible, particularly when the leaf is presented as still being on the tree.

18. See the discussion in W.H. Brownlee, *Ezekiel 1–19* (WBC, 28; Waco, TX: Word Books, 1986), pp. 256, 267; Greenberg, *Ezekiel 1–20*, p. 312; L.C. Allen, *Ezekiel 20–48* (WBC, 29; Waco, TX: Word Books, 1990), p. 251, note on 8a; and compare K.-M. Beyse, 'שתל', *ThWAT*, VIII, cols. 535-37.

another (so RSV). Others (like NJPS) consider v. 8 as a description of the events mentioned already in vv. 5-6. In either case, evidence from the context that only the initial stages of growth are in view is lacking, and it is more natural to interpret the phrase ערגת צמחה in v. 10 as 'the bed where it grew'.[19]

צמח *and Standing Grain.* The final passage where one finds צמח is Hos. 8.7, 'The standing grain has no צמח, it shall yield no meal'. There is nothing in the context to indicate that an initial stage of growth is in view here. The perspectives of harvest and of yielding food actually makes the option of the concept of 'producing sprouts' less likely: in order to produce food for a meal, grain must not just produce sprouts but grow and mature. That is, the process of growth in its entirety is presupposed.

צמח in this verse is usually translated as 'heads', or 'ears' (that is, once again a part of a plant, but one different from 'sprout'). One can say that concepts like these provide the reference of צמח in this verse. However, rather than taking this particular translation equivalent as a meaning of the noun, it seems better not to introduce an unprecedented usage for this particular case but to translate the noun as 'growth': 'standing grain with no growth, it shall yield no meal'.

c. *The Verb* צמח
I will now take a brief look at the meaning of the verb צָמַח. The dictionaries provide two meanings:

> **Qal** ...*sprout, spring up...*
> **Pi.** *grow abundantly*, always of hair...
> **Hi.** ... **1.** *cause to grow...* **2.** of rain, *cause* the earth *to sprout...* (BDB).

> qal... 1. to **sprout...** 2. to **grow...**
> pi. to cause to produce
> outgrowth...**produce...**
> hif.... 1. to **make plants sprout...**
> 2. to **cause to sprout...**[20]

---

19. E.g. Allen, *Ezekiel 20–48*, p. 250, 'the bed where it is growing'.
20. **qal** ... 1. **sprossen...** 2. **wachsen...**
   **pi.** gesprosst machen..., **hervorbringen**
   **hi.** 1. **sprossen lassen...** 2. **zum Spriessen bringen...** (*HALAT*).

*'To Grow'*. The verb צמח occurs 33 times, 15 times in the qal, 4 times
in the piel, and 14 times in the hiphil. In most of these cases, the logical
subject of the verb, who or which does צמח or is made to צמח, is (a)
some agricultural or floral entity, (b) a human or divine quality or virtue, or (c) hair/beard (the piel is reserved for this third option). For the
non-metaphorical meaning we will have to look at those instances
where some agricultural or floral entity is the logical subject (11 times).

In most cases, to make the verb refer to an initial stage of growth
does not fit very well in the context (Gen. 2.5, 9; 3.18; 41.6, 23; Exod.
10.5; Isa. 44.4; 55.10; 61.11; Job 38.27; Ps. 104.14; 147.8; Eccl 2.6). In
a small number of cases the context does not immediately exclude one
or the other option. In Deut. 29.22 the clauses

לא תזרע ולא תצמח ולא־יעלה בה כל־עשב

do not necessarily present three stages in a sequence, but can be read as
two different processes arranged side by side. The change of subject
(ארץ in the first two clauses, כל־עשב in the last) marks the border
between the two processes: 'it is not sown, it does not cause growth, no
herb whatsoever grows up from it'.[21] In Ezek. 17.6 ויצמח ויהי לגפן
סרחת שפלת קומה can be translated, 'and it sprouted and became a low
spreading vine' (RSV) or, 'It grew and became a spreading vine of low
stature' (NJPS). In a case like this one can either posit a so-far-unat-
tested meaning ('sprout', referring to the initial stages of growth), or
read the usual meaning ('grow'). In the absence of compelling contex-
tual reasons for the first option the second seems far more preferable.

In those cases where a divine or human quality or virtue is the subject
of צמח, assuming the technical sense of 'to sprout' would be implausible. In a sentence like אמת מארץ תצמח וצדק משמים נשקף 'Faithfulness will spring up from the ground, and righteousness will look down
from the sky', an interpretation of צמח as referring to the initial stage of
growth would make little sense.

This brief survey shows that the meaning of the verb צמח is most
likely, 'to grow'.[22]

21. Compare J.H. Tigay, *The JPS Torah Commentary: Deuteronomy* דברים.
*The Traditional Hebrew Text with the New JPS Translation* (Philadelphia: Jewish
Publication Society of America, 1996), p. 279, who translates, 'all its soil devas-
tated by sulfur and salt, beyond sowing and producing, no grass growing in it'.
22. So also J.C. Greenfield, 'Lexicographical Notes ii. IX The Root שמח',
*HUCA* 30 (1959), pp. 141-51 (147, 149-50).

*No Meaning 'to Shine'*. Grossberg has argued recently[23] that צָמַח (the verb) can mean both 'sprout' and 'shine'. In spite of Grossberg's appeal to sound method when dealing with semantics, the article defies all principles of semantics (and of logic). I make three comments.

(a) Grossberg's statement, 'The Syriac cognate, however, denotes either "shine forth" or "spring"', is true, but irrelevant: whereas Hebrew has two roots, צמח and שׁמח, in Aramaic and Syriac שׁמח has disappeared, and Aramaic צמח has taken over the meaning of Hebrew שׁמח.[24] This is a not unusual phenomenon in languages, called homonymy.

(b) Grossberg claims as the source of his view that Hebrew צמח may mean 'shine' Jastrow's dictionary: 'Jastrow, too, identifies *ṣmḥ* in biblical Hebrew as "to break forth, shine, bloom, sprout, grow"'. This statement is inaccurate. As the title of Jastrow's dictionary indicates, this is *A Dictionary of the Targumim, the Talmud Babli and Yerushalmi, and the Midrashic literature*.[25] So, all passages cited by Jastrow under צָמַח are non-biblical, including the one on which Jastrow apparently has based his translation gloss 'shine', 'Cant. R. to III, 6 וְעמוּד...הִיה t אֵשׁ צוֹמֵחַ he pillar of cloud came down, and the pillar of fire grew brighter'.

(c) Grossberg's own attempt to show that צמח may also mean 'shine' is seriously flawed, largely because his approach suffers from what Barr has called an 'illegitimate totality transfer', the error of reading 'the "meaning" of a word (understood as the total series of relations in which it is used in the literature)...into a particular case as its sense and implication there'.[26] According to Grossberg, אוֹר means both 'light' and 'field'.[27] If אוֹר means both 'light' and 'field', one can translate Isa. 58.8

---

23. D. Grossberg, 'The Dual Glow/Grow Motif', *Bib* 67 (1986), pp. 547-54. His views have been adopted by J. Lust, 'Messianism and Greek Jeremiah', in C.E. Cox (ed.), *VII Congress of the International Organization for Septuagint and Cognate Studies Leuven 1989* (SBLSCS, 31; Atlanta: Scholars Press, 1991), pp. 87-122 (91), 'It should be noted that the root צָמַח appears to have assumed a second meaning: "to shine, to glow"', referring (p. 117 n. 9) to Grossberg.

24. See Greenfield, 'Notes', pp. 149-50.

25. (London: Luzac; New York: Putnam's Sons, 1903).

26. J. Barr, *The Semantics of Biblical Language* (Oxford: Oxford University Press, 1961), p. 218.

27. Grossberg, 'Glow/Grow', p. 547. This questionable statement is based on Dahood's discussion on the meaning of אוֹר (in *Psalms*, p. 223); for a critical

both, 'Then your light will break forth as the dawn/And your healing shine forth speedily' and, 'Then your field will break up as the dawn/And your healing will sprout quickly'. In this way, Grossberg finds dual meanings in all sorts of passages, including Jer. 23.5: 'We need but to recognize the dual meaning of *ṣmḥ*. The Lord is promising here, as in Jer. 33,15, both a "righteous [or 'rightful'] brilliance" and a "righteous [or 'rightful'] shoot" for the Davidic line'.

The same is true for Zech. 3.8 and 6.12: the traditional translations '"My servant, Branch" or "Shoot"' are correct, but 'the associative fields suggest also, "My servant, Brightness" and "a man whose name is 'Brightness' will shine."' Support for this interpretation is then found in the vision of the lampstand with the olive trees:

> Just as the word *ṣemaḥ* can be construed as illuminating and growing, so
> the menorah sheds light and recalls the branching olive tree. God's
> presence symbolized by the lampstand and God's annointed [*sic*] called
> *ṣemaḥ* share the identical light/growth ambivalence.[28]

A less sympathetic observer might call this a Humpty Dumpty approach. It certainly fails to make a convincing case for 'shine' as a meaning of Hebrew צמח.

### d. *Cognates of* צמח *in Other North-West Semitic Languages*

Does the use of cognates of צמח in other North-West Semitic languages either support or contradict my claim that the meaning of Hebrew צמח has usually been mistaken? I will first look at the meaning of *ṣmḥ* in Ugaritic, and then at the meaning of *ṣmḥ* in Phoenician (and Punic).[29]

*ṣmḥ in Ugaritic.* The evidence for *ṣmḥ* in Ugaritic is very meagre. *HALAT* (s.v. צמח) lists two passages, one in KTU 7.63, the other in KTU 1.19. For these two passages *HALAT* suggests the glosses 'Spross' and 'Sprösslinge' respectively. As the number 7 assigned to the text indicates, KTU 7.63 belongs to those texts which scholars have found difficult to classify.[30] The word *ṣmḥ* is found in line 9, the last line of

discussion of this proposal, see D.M. Howard, *The Structure of Psalms 93–100* (BJS, 5; Winona Lake, IN: Eisenbrauns, 1997), p. 73.

28. Grossberg, 'Glow/Grow', p. 550.

29. I have not been able to find any occurrences of צמח in Aramaic of the first millennium BCE.

30. According to some scholars, the text is a building inscription (e.g. E. Lipiń-ski, 'Recherches ugaritiques', *Syria* 50 [1973], pp. 35-51 [40]); others consider it a

the text. In *KTU/CAT*, the last two lines of the text read:

w/k . *lb* . *mlk*
[    ]ṣmḫ

The reading of the final word is somewhat problematic, because of the condition of the text. Olmo Lete adds asterisks to the three last letters of the last line;[31] Gray comments, 'The fragmentary nature of the text makes it impossible to tell whether ṣmḫ is to be read at all, though we consider this highly probable'.[32] The precise interpretation of the word is a matter of dispute. Gray reads ṣmḫ as a noun, which he interprets in the light of Jer. 23.5; 33.15; Zech. 3.8; 6.12; Isa. 11.1 as 'scion'. Olmo Lete reads the word as a verb by restoring a *y* before the remaining three letters. In his reconstruction the whole line reads: *[amd.y]ṣ\*m\*ḫ\**. He translates 'May he *flourish* [for ever (?)]! (emphasis original: '[¡Por siempre (?) *floreat!*'). The text is too fragmentary to make a conclusive choice about which proposal to adopt.

In the second passage, KTU 1.19 I 17, ṣmḫ is used by Dijkstra and De Moor to restore a lacuna in the Aqhat text.[33] The restored line reads: *wbmt[ḥ . t]ḥmṣ . ṣ[mḫ]t*, which they translate 'and because of his death the sprouts turn sour'. This emendation is based on the presence of the phrases *pr' qẓ*, 'the first of the summer fruit' and *šblt bġlph*, 'the ear in its sheath' in the next two lines. It seems that De Moor has now given up this emendation: in their recent edition of religious texts from Ugarit, De Moor and Spronk read,[34] *wbmt[ḥ.]ḥmṣ.ṣrr*, which De Moor translates,[35] 'And through [his] death the young ear of corn is parched'.

piece of an official letter (e.g. A. Caquot, 'La littérature ugaritique', *DBSup*, IX, cols. 1361-17 [1361]).

31. Olmo Lete, G. del, 'Los nombres "divinos" de los reyes de Ugarit', *AuOr* 5 (1987), pp. 39-69 (47); reprinted in *idem, La religión Cananea: Según la litúrgia de Ugarit. Estudio textual* (AuOrSup, 3; Barcelona: Editorial AUSA, 1992), pp. 116-26 (120-21).

32. J. Gray, *The Legacy of Canaan: The Ras Shamra Texts and their Relevance to the Old Testament* (VTSup, 5; Leiden: E.J. Brill, 2nd edn, 1969), p. 227.

33. M. Dijkstra and Johannes C. de Moor, 'Problematical Passages in the Legend of Aqhâtu', *UF* 7 (1975), pp. 171-215 (197, 199).

34. J.C. de Moor and K. Spronk, *A Cuneiform Anthology of Religious Texts from Ugarit: Autographed Texts and Glossaries* (SSS: NS 6; Leiden: E.J. Brill, 1987), p. 111.

35. J.C. de Moor, *An Anthology of Religious Texts from Ugarit* (Nisaba: Religious Texts Translation Series, 16; Leiden: E.J. Brill, 1987), p. 248.

This particular restoration is also found in *KTU/CAT*.[36]

Margalit in his edition of the Aqhat poem[37] agrees with reading an *ṙ* as the penultimate letter of the line, but he keeps the final *ḥ*, though put in brackets. He reads the whole line thus: *wbmt̊ ṣ*[h. y]*ḥmṣ*(.) *ṣṙ*[ḥ], 'And behind there loom[ed] a to[wer]'. **ṣrḥ* would then be a *hapax legomenon*, related to Arabic *ṣarḥ* and Hebrew צְרִיחַ. This is not the place to decide which of the proposals is the most plausible. One thing is clear: the proposal to read *ṣmḥ* in KTU 1.19 I 17 has been abandoned by several scholars, including by (at least) one of those who originally made the proposal.

In conclusion: of the two passages in Ugaritic which have been claimed to contain the noun *ṣmḥ*,[38] one is now no longer read as containing *ṣmḥ*, while the other is too fragmentary to allow any conclusive statement about the meaning of Ugaritic *ṣmḥ*.

*ṣmḥ in Phoenician and Punic*. I now turn to a discussion of the meaning of *ṣmḥ* in Phoenician and Punic. The noun *ṣmḥ* is relatively rare, and the contexts in which it occurs are in most cases not particularly clear. *DNWSI* lists one occurrence for Phoenician,[39] and three occurrences for

36. Compare K.T. Aitken, *The Aqhat Narrative: A Study in the Narrative Structure and Composition of an Ugaritic Tale* (JSSMS, 13; Manchester: University of Manchester Press, 1990), pp. 56-57: wbmt […]ḥmṣ ṣr[…] 'and through his death… turn sour'. *KTU*[1] read: w b*mt*(?)xḥ*mṣ ṣr*(?)x(?).

37. B. Margalit, *The Ugaritic Poem of AQHT: Text, Translation, Commentary* (BZAW, 182; Berlin: W. de Gruyter, 1989), pp. 131, 157, 219-20.

38. There is a third passage in the Ugaritic corpus where one finds the root *ṣmḥ*. KTU 4.12, a list of personal names, reads in line 4: *bn . yṣmḥ . bn ṯrn w nḥlh*. Such a personal name does not provide any independent information about the meaning of the root.

39. There may be a second occurrence of the noun *ṣmḥ*, in an inscription on a Cypro-Phoenician store jar from the fifth century, if the word is actually a noun. Opinions differ whether *ṣmḥ* in this inscription is a noun or a proper name. In a recent article (F.M. Cross, 'A Phoenician Inscription from Idalion: Some Old and New Texts Relating to Child Sacrifice', in M.D. Coogan, J.C. Exum and L.E. Stager (eds.), *Scripture and Other Artifacts: Essays on the Bible and Archaeology in Honor of Philip J. King* [Louisville, KY: Westminster/John Knox Press, 1994], pp. 93-107 [101]), Cross takes it as a noun and translates the inscription 'holocaust of a scion'. Others interpret the word as a proper name (so W. Spiegelberg, *Die demotischen Denkmaler 30601-31166. I. Die demotischen Inschriften* [Catalogue general des antiquites egyptiennes du Musee du Caire. Nos. 30601-31166; Leipzig, 1904], p. 89; M. Lidzbarski, *Ephemeris fur Semitische Epigraphik: Dritter Band*

Punic. The dictionary provides 'offspring, scion' as a gloss for the meaning of *ṣmḥ*.

The one Phoenician occurrence is found in the Lapethos ii inscription (KAI 43), dating from around 275 BCE.[40] The relevant lines are (in Gibson's edition):[41]

ושׁב----הח---יﬡ פּﬠלת קמת עם ומזבחת לאדן אשׁ לי למלקרת
על חיי ועל חי זרעי ים מד ים ולצמח צדק ולאשׁתו ולאדמי

... I made...and altars for the lord who is mine, Melcarth (to be serviced) on behalf of my life and on behalf of the life of my seed, day by day, and (altars) for the legitimate shoot and for his wife and for my folk (Lapethos ii, lines 10-11).

The person speaking in the inscription, Yatanbaal, has been identified by Gibson as a high official of Lapethos.[42] Usually, the phrase צמח צדק is interpreted as 'legitimate offspring' (see the discussion of the phrase below) and taken to refer to the royal heir in Cyprus, an interpretation which is often connected to the conventional interpretation of Hebrew צמח. If—as I have argued—'sprout' as a translation of Hebrew צמח is wrong, does this have any implications for the translation of Phoenician *ṣmḥ*? There are at least two possibilities. (a) Phoenician *ṣmḥ* has the same meaning as Hebrew צמח: 'vegetation, growth'. (b) Phoenician *ṣmḥ* has undergone a semantic development unparalleled in Hebrew (or Hebrew צמח a semantic development unparalleled in Phoenician), and one has to conclude that while Hebrew צמח is used for plants as a whole ('vegetation'), Phoenician *ṣmḥ* is used for a part of the plant: 'sprout'. Unfortunately, the Lapethos inscription is the only text where Phoenician *ṣmḥ* is found, and there is therefore no material to support or disprove either of the two possibilities.

*1909–1915* [Giessen: Alfred Töpelmann, 1915], p. 125). Z.S. Harris, *A Grammar of the Phoenician Language* (AOS, 8; New Haven, CT: American Oriental Society, 1936), p. 141, lists a noun as one option, for which he suggests the translation '"plant, garden"(?)', and a proper name as another option (which he translates '"Gardener"?'). The inscription is too short to allow any final conclusions on the nature of the form *ṣmḥ* (the complete inscription, or the Phoenician part of it, consists of one line of six characters, and reads '*lt ṣmḥ*).

40. For the dating of the inscription see, *KAI* II, p. 60; J.C.L. Gibson, *Textbook of Syrian Semitic Inscriptions*. III. *Phoenician Inscriptions Including Inscriptions in the Mixed Dialect of Arshlan Tash* (Oxford: Clarendon Press, 1982), p. 134.

41. Gibson, *Phoenician Inscriptions*, pp. 136-37.

42. *Phoenician Inscriptions*, p. 134.

Finally, let us consider the meaning of Punic ṣmḥ. On two of the
(Neo-) Punic cases (second half of the second century BCE) the editors
of *DNWSI* comment, 'uncert. interpr., obscure context', and on the
third, 'heavily dam. and diff. context'.[43] Usually Punic ṣmḥ is translated
'offspring, scion',[44] apparently on the basis of the usual interpretation
of Hebrew צמח as 'sprout'. The fragmentary nature of the evidence
makes it very difficult to establish the meaning of the word with certainty[45] or to use Punic ṣmḥ as an independent witness to the meaning
of North-West Semitic ṣmḥ.

To conclude: the low frequency of occurrences of cognates of צמח in
other North-West Semitic languages (Ugaritic [1] and Phoenician-Punic
[1+3]) and the problems surrounding the interpretation of these few
instances make it impossible to find in these languages an independent
witness to either support or contradict a particular interpretation of the
meaning of Hebrew צמח.

### e. *Conclusion*
A structural approach to the Hebrew noun צֶמַח and its use in the Old
Testament suggests the meaning of this word is neither 'branch' nor
'shoot/sprout', as is commonly thought, but (a) 'vegetation, greenery,
growth', and (b) 'growth' (as a process). Similarly, the verb צָמַח means
'to grow'. Evidence from cognate languages is too scarce to either
support or contradict this interpretation.

### 2. צמח *and Kingship in Other Parts of the Old Testament*

In the first part of this chapter I have discussed the meaning of the
Hebrew noun צמח where it is used in its literal sense. I left out the four
passages where it was used in a non-literal way: Jer. 23.5; 33.15; Zech.

---

43. The second century date of KAI 162-63 is given in *KAI* II, pp. 152-53. With
regard to the difficulties in the interpretation of these two texts, compare the
comment on p. 152, 'Die Schrift in der Kartusche ist klar zu lesen, doch bleiben
wegen der Vieldeutigkeit der Buchstaben viele Unsicherheiten'.

44. So *KAI* II, pp. 152-53; R.S. Tomback, *A Comparative Semitic Lexicon of the
Phoenician and Punic Languages* (SBLDS, 32; Missoula, MT: Scholars Press,
1974), p. 278; *DNWSI*; Cross, 'Phoenician Inscription', pp. 99, 101.

45. The discussion by Cross ('Phoenician Inscription', pp. 98-101) of the Punic
passages is marked by a tone of great confidence. Given the poor nature of the
material, this confidence does not rest on secure evidence.

3.8; 6.12. In the second part of this chapter I will now discuss those passages which have generally been seen to provide the background for the interpretation of Zech. 3.8 and 6.12: these passages are Isa. 11.1 and Jer. 23.5 (and 33.15). The next chapter will be devoted to the two passages in Zechariah.

### a. צמח *and Isa. 11.1*

Before I examine Isa. 11.1 and its role in the interpretation of the צמח oracles in Zechariah 3 and 6, I will make a brief comment on Isa. 4.2, a passage where the noun צמח occurs, and which has been interpreted as a messianic prophecy by some. The verse reads:

> In that day the branch of the LORD [צמח יהוה] shall be beautiful and glorious, and the fruit of the land [פרי הארץ] shall be the pride and glory of the survivors of Israel.

Here I take issue with the translation of RSV, which seems to be influenced by the translation 'branch' for צמח in the passages in Jeremiah and Zechariah. As the parallel 'fruit of the land [פרי הארץ]' indicates, the phrase צמח יהוה refers to the growth which YHWH will bring,[46] just as the phrase עצי יהוה (Ps. 104.16) refers to 'the cedars of the Lebanon, which YHWH himself has planted'.[47] This makes a messianic interpretation of the phrase צמח יהוה implausible.[48] I have similar problems with making צמח a messianic title already in the Old Testament: צמח דוד certainly is a messianic title in the Dead Sea Scrolls, but

46. So J. Skinner, *The Book of the Prophet Isaiah Chapters I–XXXIX* (CBC; Cambridge: Cambridge University Press, 1915), p. 32, who takes both expressions literally, and comments that '*afterwards* the Heb. word for "growth" (*ṣemaḥ*) came to be used as a title of the Messiah'. On the phrase, see also R. Clements, *Isaiah 1–39* (NCB; Grand Rapids: Eerdmans, 1980), p. 54, 'a reference to the wonderful growth which Yahweh will cause to spring up in the age of salvation'; Pomykala, *Davidic Dynasty Tradition*, p. 54, 'the growth the Lord will bring in the age of salvation'. H. Wildberger, *Jesaja 1–12* (BKAT, 10.1; Neukirchen–Vluyn: Neukirchener Verlag, 1972), pp. 154-55 'Da Jahwe die Fruchtbäume aus der Erde sprießen läßt (צמח hi. Gn 2 9), kann es nicht befremden, daß vom צמח יהוה gesprochen wird, auch wenn dieser Ausdruck im Alten Testament sonst nicht zu belegen ist'.

47. 'Die Zedern des Libanon, die Jhwh selbst gepflanzt hat' (Rüthy, *Pflanze*, p. 11).

48. Contra, e.g., Baldwin, '*Ṣemaḥ*', pp. 93-94; cf. K. Nielsen, *There is Hope for a Tree: The Tree as Metaphor in Isaiah* (JSOTSup, 65; Sheffield: JSOT Press, 1989), pp. 184-85.

the use of צמח in the Old Testament is too restricted to be called a title, even in Zechariah 1–6.[49]

I now move on to Isa. 11.1, which reads:

ויצא חטר מגזע ישי ונצר משרשיו יפרה

> There shall come forth a shoot from the stump of Jesse, and a branch shall grow out of his roots.

Here the prophet confronts a situation of decline of the Davidic dynasty. In that context he uses language of a shoot coming forth from the stump of Jesse, and of a branch growing out of Jesse's roots, 'to designate the future king not as a fortuitous member of the line of David but in fact as a new David', as Nielsen puts it.[50] Such imagery in which a part of a plant or a tree, like a root or a sprout, is used to refer to someone's offspring is not uncommon in ancient Near Eastern texts.[51]

A number of scholars interpret the צמח passages in Zechariah 3 and 6 in the light of or using language derived from this passage. For example Mowinckel, 'Zechariah announces that he [Zerubbabel] is *semah*, the Branch, the Rod, which has shot up again from the stump of David's fallen family tree'.[52] Such an interpretation fails to consider the difference in terminology.[53] The Hebrew words חטר and נצר in Isa. 11.1 are

49. Cf. Mowinckel, *He that Cometh*, pp. 19-20.

50. Nielsen, *Hope for a Tree*, p. 133. There is probably a connection between the tree imagery in Isa. 11.1 and the language of forest destruction in Isa. 10.33-34 (see, e.g., H. Barth, *Die Jesaja-Worte in der Josiazeit: Israel und Assur als Thema einer produktiven Neuinterpretation der Jesajaüberlieferung* [WMANT, 48; Neukirchen–Vluyn: Neukirchener Verlag, 1977], pp. 57-58).

51. See, e.g., Barth, *Jesaja-Worte*, p. 70; compare *CAD* s.v. *kisittu*, meaning 3, and *AHW* s.v. *kisittu*, meaning 4, and *per'u(m)*, *perhu*. Esarhaddon is called *pir'u Baltil šūquru...kisitti ṣâti* 'a precious branch of Baltil...an enduring shoot' (R. Borger, *Die Inschriften Asarhaddons Königs von Assyrien* [AfOB, 9; Graz: E. Weidner, 1956], p. 32 §20.17); compare *šrš 'dny* 'the scion of my lord' in the Azitiwada inscription (KAI 26 A i), l.10.

52. *He that Cometh*, p. 120; compare W. McKane, *Jeremiah 1–25* (ICC; Edinburgh: T. & T. Clark, 1986), p. 562; Roberts, 'Messianic Expectations', p. 46; Redditt, *Haggai, Zechariah*, p. 66. The influence of Isa. 11.1 on the interpretation of (Jer. 23.5 and 33.15 and) Zech. 3.8 and 6.12 may explain the almost universal choice of 'branch' as a translation equivalent of צמח in Jer. 23 and 33 and Zech. 3 and 6 (e.g. Thompson, *Jeremiah*, p. 489, who notices the difference in terminology but nevertheless merges the interpretation of the passages in Isaiah, Jeremiah and Zechariah).

53. Skinner, *Isaiah*, p. 32 (on צמח in Isa. 4.2), 'Observe that it is an entirely

indeed words used for 'branch' and 'sprout' in the Old Testament, but the word used in Zechariah 3 and 6 is a different word, צמח, with a different meaning. Unlike חטר and נצר, the noun צמח does not refer to a part of a plant, but, I have argued, is a noun used for 'vegetation' in a general sense. This difference should caution scholars against making their interpretation of Zech. 3.8 and 6.12 depend on Isa. 11.1.[54]

To conclude: it can be useful to relate one's interpretation of Zech. 3.8 and 6.12 to the interpretation of Isa. 11.1. In both passages kingship is an issue, and in both passages plant imagery can be found. There is, however, one important caveat. Every discussion which fails to take into account the difference in terminology and details of the imagery will hinder a correct interpretation of Zech. 3.8 and 6.12. What use one can make of Isa. 11.1 in the interpretation of Zech. 3.8 and 6.12 is a matter which I will discuss in the next section of this chapter.

### b. צמח *and Jer. 23.5*

The noun צמח is found twice in Jeremiah, once in Jer. 23.5, and once in Jer. 33.15.[55] In both cases we are dealing with a non-literal use. Since the second occurrence is found in an oracle in many ways similar to the first, I will concentrate my discussion on the first occurrence. Jer. 23.5 reads:

> Behold, the days are coming, says the Lord, when I will raise up for David a righteous Branch [והקמתי לדוד צמח צדיק], and he shall reign as king and deal wisely, and shall execute justice and righteousness in the

different word which is translated "Branch" in Is. xi, 1'; also W. Drake, 'Zechariah', in F.C. Cook (ed.), *The Holy Bible According to the Authorized Version (A.D. 1611), With an Explanatory and Critical Commentary and a Revision of the Translation, by Bishops and Other Clergy of the Anglican Church*. VI. *Ezekiel—Daniel—The Minor Prophets* (London: John Murray, 1876), p. 711. In the Dead Sea Scrolls the נצר/חטר of Isa. 11.1 is already identified with the צמח דוד; see 4Q161 (4QpIsaᵃ) 8-10 lines 11-17 and 4Q285 frg. 5 lines 3-4, and the discussion in J. VanderKam, 'Messianism in the Scrolls', in E. Ulrich and J. VanderKam (eds.), *The Community of the Renewed Covenant: The Notre Dame Symposium on the Dead Sea Scrolls* (CJAS, 10; Notre Dame: University of Notre Dame Press, 1994), pp. 211-34 (216-18).

54. Compare W. Rudolph (*Jeremia* [HAT, 12; Tübingen: J.C.B. Mohr (Paul Siebeck), 3rd edn, 1968], p. 147) and Petitjean (*Oracles*, p. 203), who sound a similar warning against interpreting Jer. 23.5 on the basis of Isa. 11.1.

55. On the relationship between the two passages, see, e.g., M. Fishbane, *Biblical Interpretation in Ancient Israel* (Oxford: Clarendon Press, 1985), pp. 471-74.

land. In his days Judah will be saved, and Israel will dwell securely. And
this is the name by which he will be called: 'The Lord is our righteousness'.

Unlike Isa. 11.1, in Jer. 23.5 exactly the same word צמח is found, once
again in a context dealing with kingship. The passage is part of quite a
long section containing a collection of oracles concerning kingship
which begins in ch. 21 and ends in 23.8. Several scholars identify one
or two of the following issues to be at stake in Jer. 23.5: (a) legitimacy;
(b) descent from David. Holladay is representative of this line of interpretation. He asserts that there must have been argument in Judah as to
which king was legitimate. 'Here is Zedekiah, whose name carries the
same nuance as the word "legitimate" here, but whose legitimacy is
dubious. By contrast Yahweh will in time raise up a legitimate descendant of David'.[56]

The issue of legitimacy is derived from the interpretation of צדיק in
the phrase צמח צדיק as 'legitimate'. The issue of descent from David is
connected with the presence of the words לדוד צמח. I will now discuss
the meaning of both phrases.

*Legitimacy—The Meaning of* צדיק. צמח in Jer. 23.5 (and 33.15) is
accompanied by the adjective צדיק. The usual meaning of צדיק is
'righteous',[57] but a great number of scholars interpret צדיק in this verse
as 'legitimate'. If this interpretation is correct, then this would be the
only occasion in the Old Testament where צדיק is considered to mean
'legitimate'. The evidence to support this interpretation came initially
from the Phoenician inscription from Kition (Lapethos ii), Cyprus,
which was mentioned earlier in this chapter, where a phrase similar to
צמח צדיק is found: ṣmḥ ṣdq.[58] In a later stage, Swetnam set out[59] 'to

---

56. Holladay, *Jeremiah*, p. 618; see also Dambrine, *Croissance*, pp. 41-44;
Thompson, *Jeremiah*, p. 489; McKane, *Jeremiah*, p. 561; Ringgren, 'צמח', col.
1071; Tollington, *Tradition*, p. 171.

57. E.g. BDB s.v., and *HALAT* s.v.

58. This is actually the only one occurrence of a phrase like ṣmḥ ṣdq in North-
West Semitic languages other than Hebrew. Remarks like '[t]he royal title *ṣemaḥ
ṣedeq* appears in North-west Semitic inscriptions' (Fishbane, *Biblical Interpretation*, p. 472 n. 36), or 'one must conclude that Jrm is here using a general North-
west-Semitic term for the legitimate king' (Holladay, *Jeremiah*, p. 618) suggest a
distribution of the phrase for which there is no evidence.

59. J. Swetnam, 'Some Observations on the Background of צדיק in Jeremias
23,5a', *Bib* 46 (1965), pp. 29-40 (29).

gather together the evidence for the interpretation of *ṣdq* in the sense of "legitimate"' and so made a collection of a total of ten passages in North-West Semitic texts (Ugaritic, Phoenician and Aramaic) which all supported the interpretation of *ṣdq* as 'legitimate'.

Elsewhere I have reviewed that evidence,[60] and I will briefly summarise the conclusions here. Of the nine passages which Swetnam has referred to there is only one (to be more precise: two sets of narrowly circumscribed sets of contexts) where the translation 'legitimate' is indisputedly correct (more on this below). One passage[61] is irrelevant for the discussion, and even Swetnam himself uses the translation equivalent 'righteousness' there. There are two passages[62] where Swetnam's interpretation is based on an incorrect translation of the relevant passage. There are four[63] where the context does not support the translation

60. W.H. Rose, 'The meaning of *ṣdq* in North-West Semitic', [forthcoming].

61. Nerab ii inscription (Aramaic): KAI 226, 1.2; J.C.L. Gibson, *Textbook of Syrian Semitic Inscriptions*. II. *Aramaic Inscriptions Including Inscriptions in the Dialect of Zenjirli* (Oxford: Clarendon Press, 1975), pp. 97-98 (no. 19); also in V. Hug, *Altaramäische Grammatik der Texte des 7. und 6. Jh.s v. Chr* (HSAO, 4; Heidelberg: Heidelberger Orientverlag, 1993), pp. 13-14.

62. (a) Krt epic (Ugaritic), KTU 1, 14 ll. 12-13: De Moor, *Religious Texts*, p. 192; the recent translation of the Krt epic by Dennis Pardee in W.W. Hallo and K.L. Younger (eds.), *The Context of Scripture: Canonical Compositions, Monumental Inscriptions, and Archival Documents from the Biblical World*. I. *Canonical Compositions from the Biblical World* (Leiden: E.J. Brill), p. 333, makes the same translation error as Swetnam. (b) Azatiwada inscription (Phoenician): KAI 26 A i, ll. 11-13; K.L. Younger, Jr, 'The Phoenician Inscription of Azatiwada: An Integrated Reading', *JSS* 43.1 (1998), pp. 11-47 (15).

63. (a) Yehimilk (Phoenician): KAI 4, ll. 6-7; Gibson, *Phoenician Inscriptions*, pp. 17-19 n. 6; on this passage, see S.E. Loewenstamm, *Comparative Studies in Biblical and Ancient Oriental Literatures* (AOAT, 204; Kevelaer: Verlag Butzon & Bercker; Neukirchen–Vluyn: Neukirchener Verlag, 1980), p. 212 n. 3. (b) Yehaumilk (Aramaic): KAI 10, ll. 9-11; Gibson, *Phoenician Inscriptions*, pp. 93-99 n. 25. (c) Barrakib i (Aramaic); KAI 215, ll. 4-7; Gibson, *Aramaic Inscriptions*, pp. 87-93, no 15; H.S. Sader, *Les états araméens de Syrie depuis leur fondation jusqu'à leur transformation en provinces assyriennes* (BTS, 36; Wiesbaden: Franz Steiner Verlag, 1987), pp. 156-72, esp. pp. 170-71; J. Tropper, *Die Inschriften von Zincirli* (ALASP, 6; Münster: Ugarit-Verlag, 1993), pp. 132-39, 163; the Barrakib i inscription should be read in conjunction with the Barrakib ii (KAI 216) inscription and the Panammu inscription (see below); for the historical background of these inscriptions, see J.D. Hawkins, 'The Neo-Hittite States in Syria and Anatolia', CAH, III/1², pp. 372-441 (408); and S.B. Parker, 'Appeals for Military Intervention: Stories from Zinjirli and the Bible', *BA* 59 (1996), pp. 213-24 (217). (d) Panammu

'legitimate' and the translation 'righteous' is more natural. There are two passages[64] where it is difficult to reach any firm conclusions on the meaning of *ṣdq*, because the interpretation is based partially on Jer. 23.5, and partially on the two sets of contexts where the meaning is undisputed.[65]

These sets of contexts, however, are quite far removed in time and language geography, which makes their position as a witness to the meaning of Hebrew צמח or Phoenician *ṣmḥ* somewhat controversial.

(Aramaic); KAI 215, ll. 11, 19; Gibson, *Aramaic Inscriptions*, pp. 76-86 n. 14; Sader, *États Araméens*, pp. 165-69; Tropper, *Inschriften*, pp. 98-131, 159-62.

64. (a) Bodaštart (Phoenician): KAI 15 (longer version); KAI 16 (shorter version); J. Élayi, *Sidon, cité autonome de l'empire perse* (Paris: Editions Idéaphane, 1989), pp. 41-45 (# VI-XVII for the longer version, # XVIII-XIX for the shorter version). (b) Lapethos ii (Phoenician): KAI 43, ll. 10-11; Gibson, *Phoenician Inscriptions*, pp. 134-41 n. 36.

65. In the first edition of the Lapethos ii inscription, Berger refers to the phrase *'ṣdq b'ṣdq* in the Nabataean tomb inscriptions from Mada'in Salih as the basis of his translation of Phoenician *ṣmḥ ṣdq* as 'for my legitimate offspring' (*pour ma progéniture légitime*; P. Berger, 'Mémoire sur une inscription phénicienne de Narnaka dans l'île de Chypre', *RA* 3 [1895], pp. 69-88 [83]). In 1940, Honeyman translated 'and to the rightful scion', referring to 'close parallels in Phoenician and Biblical Hebrew' (A.M. Honeyman, 'Observations on a Phoenician Inscription of Ptolemaic Date', *JEA* 26 [1940], pp. 57-67 [63 and nn. 8, 9]; the Phoenician parallels are the Yehaumilk inscription and the Bodaštart inscription; the biblical Hebrew parallels are Jer. 23.5; 33.15). In the first edition of the Bodaštart inscription, Berger provides no comments on philological details and makes no reference to the Lapethos inscription (P. Berger, '[Communication in] "Livres Offerts"', in *idem, Comptes rendus des séances de l'Académie des inscriptions et belleslettres* [1904], pp. 721-22). The translation 'legitimate son' was called into question by Torrey in the same year as being 'highly improbable', mainly because of the absence of parallels apart from the Lapethos ii inscription (C.C. Torrey, 'Two Letters from Professor Porter in Regard to the Bod'aštart Stones in Beirut', *JAOS* 25 [1904], pp. 324-31 [328-29]). One year later, Clermont-Ganneau discussed the inscription and made the link with *ṣmḥ ṣdq* in the Lapethos ii inscription (C. Clermont-Ganneau, 'La nouvelle inscription phénicienne du Temple d'Echmoun à Sidon', *RAO* 6 [1905], pp. 162-67 [164]), while Lidzbarski in 1908 based his interpretation 'und der Erbprinz Jathonmilk' on Nabataean *'ṣdq* (M. Lidzbarski, *Ephemeris fur Semitische Epigraphik: Zweiter Band 1903–1907* [Giessen: Alfred Töpelmann, 1908], p. 155). Donner and Röllig in *KAI* translated 'Legitimer Sohn, Erbsohn'. They commented that this expression is so far (1968; they do not mention Swetnam's article from 1965) without parallels, but that it can be considered certain on the basis of *ṣmḥ ṣdq* in the Lapethos ii inscription in connection with Jer. 23.5; 33.15.

The texts in which the word is found are dated to the first century CE or later, and all belong to a fairly restricted set of contexts: most of them belong to (a) tomb inscriptions from one location, Mada'in Salih, ancient Hegra,[66] and two occurrences are found in (b) private legal documents from Naḥal Ḥever.[67] The word is written with an 'aleph at the beginning: *'ṣdq*, and on its own is taken to mean 'legitimate heir, legal heir, person with legitimate claims', or 'true relative, legal kinsman'.[68] In most cases,[69] however, the word is found in the phrase *'ṣdq b'ṣdq*, 'by legal inheritance', or 'by hereditary title'.[70] As was mentioned, the language is Nabataean, but the word *'ṣdq* is considered to be an Arabic/Lihyanite loan,[71] which suggests that there was no word readily available in the Nabataean language which could express what Arabic/Lihyanite *'ṣdq* expressed.

It is difficult to maintain that on the basis of this evidence צדיק in Jer. 23.5 'must' mean 'legitimate'. It is fair to say, as some scholars have

66. A recent edition is provided by J.F. Healey, *The Nabataean Tomb Inscriptions of Mada'in Salih* (edited with introduction, translation and commentary; JSSSup, 1; Oxford: Oxford University Press, 1993).

67. See K. Beyer, *Die aramäischen Texte vom Toten Meer samt den Inschriften aus Palästina, dem Testament Levis aus der Kairoer Genisa, der Fastenrolle und den alten talmudischen Zitaten: Ergänzungsband* (Göttingen: Vandenhoeck & Ruprecht, 1994), pp. 168-72, 186-87, and p. 402 s.v. *'ṣdq*.

68. Healey, *Nabataean Tomb Inscriptions*, p. 91.

69. M. O'Connor, 'The Arabic Loanwords in Nabatean Aramaic', *JNES* 45 (1986), pp. 213-29 (219), states that *'ṣdq* occurs once on its own, and ten times in the phrase *'ṣdq b'ṣdq*; see also *DNWSI* s.v.

70. Healey, *Nabataean Tomb Inscriptions*, p. 91. A similar analysis of the meaning of *'ṣdq* can be found with other scholars, e.g. J. Cantineau, *Le Nabatéen. II. Choix de textes Lexique* (Paris: Librairie Ernest Leroux, 1932), p. 139; N.I. Khairy, 'An Analytical Study of the Nabataean Monumental Inscriptions at Medā'in Ṣāleḥ', *ZDPV* 96 (1980), pp. 163-68 (167); O'Connor, 'Arabic Loanwords', p. 219; *DNWSI* p. 98 s.v. *ṣdq*.

71. Healey, *Nabataean Tomb Inscriptions*, pp. 59, 60-61 n. 66 and p. 91; J.F. Healey, 'Lexical Loans in Early Syriac: A Comparison with Nabataean Aramaic', *SEL* 12 (1995), pp. 75-84 (78-79); *DNWSI* p. 98 s.v. O'Connor investigated Cantineau's list of 29 Arabic loans which made it into the Nabataean language and reduced it to 15, in which list *'ṣdq* is still included (see Cantineau, *Le Nabatéen*, II, pp. 171-72). On *'ṣdq* see also J. Cantineau, *Le Nabatéen. I. Notions générales: Ecriture Grammaire* (Paris: Librairie Ernest Leroux, 1930), p. 88; O'Connor, 'Arabic Loanwords', pp. 216-17, 219.

remarked, that Swetnam generalizes too much.[72] So there are serious problems with the evidence for 'legitimate' as a meaning of North-West Semitic *ṣdq*.[73] On the other hand, the context of Jer. 23.5 contains elements which allow a satisfactory interpretation of צדיק in its usual sense 'righteous'. The use of צדיק may be explained partly from the context (Jer. 22-23), where 'justice and righteousness' was the critical issue in the evaluation of the kings (22.3, 13, 15), and partly as a play on the name of King Zedekiah, during whose reign these words were probably spoken.[74] Against that background, the most natural interpretation of the adjective in the phrase צמח צדיק is to relate it to the continuation of the verse,[75] which provides a description of the nature of the rule of צמח צדיק and states that he will 'reign as king and deal wisely, and shall execute justice and righteousness [משפט וצדקה] in the land'.[76]

*Descent from David—The Meaning of* צמח לדוד. This bring us to the second issue: descent from David, an issue linked with the presence of the words צמח לדוד. As we have seen, the phrase is usually taken to

72. H.H. Schmid, *Gerechtigkeit als Weltordnung: Hintergrund und Geschichte des alttestamentlichen Gerechtigkeitsbegriffes* (BHT, 40; Tübingen: J.C.B. Mohr, 1968), p. 88, on Swetnam, 'der allerdings zu viele Stellen undifferenziert über einen Leisten schlägt'. The same criticism is raised by J. Krašovec, *La justice (ṣdq) de Dieu dans la Bible Hébraïque et l'interprétation juive et chrétienne* (OBO, 76; Freiburg: Universitätsverlag; Göttingen: Vandenhoeck & Ruprecht, 1988), p. 46, who states that Swetnam tends towards generalisation in his treatment of North-West Semitic epigraphic material, and that there appears to be no justification for the meaning 'legitimate'.

73. Some scholars see the need for greater caution regarding the interpretation of צדיק as 'legitimate' in Jer. 23.5. E.g. D.F. Jones, *Jeremiah: Based on the Revised Standard Version* (NCB; London: Marshall Pickering; Grand Rapids: Eerdmans, 1992), p. 299. Tollington (*Tradition*, p. 170 n. 3) dismisses the evidence of Phoenician *ṣmḥ ṣdq* as irrelevant, because of the late date.

74. For this historical setting, see Rudolph, *Jeremia*, pp. 134-35, and the discussion in McKane, *Jeremiah*, pp. 560-65.

75. So, e.g., Rudolph, *Jeremia*, pp. 145-46; A. Weiser, *Das Buch Jeremia* (ATD; 20/21; Göttingen: Vandenhoeck & Ruprecht, 1981), pp. 198-99; Jones, *Jeremiah*, p. 299; P.C. Craigie, P.H. Kelley and J.F. Drinkard, Jr, *Jeremiah 1-25* (WBC, 26; Waco, TX: Word Books, 1991), p. 330.

76. Notice the contrast with the qualification of former kings: בלא־צדק...בלא משפט (Jer. 22.13). For the composition of the phrase compare אילי הצדק 'oaks of righteousness', in Isa. 61.3.

refer to something like '(a legitimate) descendant of David'. There are in my view two problems with this descent view.

The first problem concerns the use of the word צמח. In the first part of this chapter I have argued that Hebrew צמח refers to plant(s) as a whole, not to parts of a plant. Now, the words which are used in Hebrew (and also in other North-West Semitic languages) as metaphors for offspring are all words for different parts of the plant, like a root, or a shoot or sprout, or a branch (see above). There is therefore a need to ask whether there is any significance in the fact that the prophet Jeremiah chose not the usual imagery of a part of a plant, but a word for plants as a whole or, collectively, as a group. I want to argue that this choice is deliberate.

The key to the understanding of the צמח oracle in Jer. 23.5 is again found in the wider context of the passage. In the preceding oracles the prophet has announced the rejection from the office of kingship of both Coniah, the present king (22.24-29), and of his offspring (22.30). The oracle concerning the offspring of the king says about Coniah:

> Write this man down as childless, a man who shall not succeed in his days; for none of his offspring shall succeed in sitting on the throne [כי לא יצלח מזרעו איש ישב על־כסא] of David, and ruling again in Judah (Jer. 22.30).

The unequivocal rejection of the offspring (זרע) of Coniah for future kingship raises the question of the future of the Davidic dynasty as such.[77] This is the issue addressed in the first part of ch. 23. After a prophecy of judgment on the wicked shepherds and a promise that God will provide good shepherds (vv. 1-4), the prophet proclaims God's promise to raise צמח צדיק for David.

The choice of the word צמח is meant to create a contrast with the word זרע in the earlier oracle concerning the rejection of Coniah's offspring, as a small number of scholars have pointed out, though they usually develop the contrast in ways with which I would disagree. Amsler construes a contrast between simple (*einfachem*) זרע 'seed, offspring' on the one hand, which signifies the uninterrupted line of

77. Cf. H.G.M. Williamson, 'Messianic Texts in Isaiah 1–39', in J. Day (ed.), *King and Messiah in Israel and the Ancient Near East: Proceedings of the Oxford Old Testament Seminar* (JSOTSup, 270; Sheffield: Sheffield Academic Press, 1998), pp. 238-70 (270), who finds an 'openness to the possibility of the end of the dynasty' in Jer. 22.24, 30.

descendants of a dynasty (2 Sam. 7.12), and צמח צדיק on the other, a phrase which the prophet uses to proclaim a legitimate heir through whom the threatened and imperilled would be completely renewed and restored to its privileged position.[78] Wanke comments that for human offspring one normally finds זרע, and so the use of צמח here might in this context point to something extraordinary, but he then develops it along the lines of Isa. 11.1.[79]

This interpretation of the צמח imagery is an example of one of the uses of plant imagery in the Old Testament. That is, to portray a dramatic reversal of events, dramatic because there was no reason to expect this to happen. That this reversal is a result of a direct intervention of God, in which the usual historical causation is bypassed, seems to be the underlying thought, and is sometimes expressed explicitly.[80] Exam-

---

78. S. Amsler, 'צמח', *THAT*, II, cols. 563-66 (565).

79. Wanke, *Jeremia*, p. 205, 'Da jedoch für die Bezeichnung der menschlichen Nachkommen–schaft gewöhnlich der Ausdruck "Same" gebraucht wird, dürfte die Verwendung von "Sproß" hier etwas in diesem Rahmen Außergewöhnliches andeuten'. Cf. H. Gressmann, *Der Messias* (Göttingen: Vandenhoeck & Ruprecht, 1929), pp. 253-54, 'Das Wort צמח ist auch keineswegs sonst für "Nachkommen–schaft" gebräuchlich; ja, man darf bezweifeln, daß es diese Bedeutung je gehabt hat... So denkt auch Jeremia nicht an einen leiblichen Nachfahren Davids, sondern an einen fremden, aber von Gott legitimierten Nachfolger, der auf dem Throne Davids sitzen wird'; W.H. Schmidt, 'Der Ohnmacht des Messias: Zur Überlieferungsgeschichte der messianischen Weissagungen im Alten Testament', in Struppe (ed.), *Messiasbild*, pp. 67-88, who also sees a contrast between Jeremiah 23 and 22.30, 'So richtet sich auch diese messianische Weissagung...gegen die Wirklichkeit'.

80. Cf. E. Jacob, *Esaïe 1–12* (CAT, 8a; Geneva: Labor et Fides, 1987), p. 73, comments on the use of צמח in Isa. 4.2 that whatever will sprout and is destined to become a wonderful burgeoning, is all created by God: every sprout is a renewal, whether in creation, history, the life of the people, or the Davidic dynasty. Cf. also Amsler on the use of the root צמח (verb and noun) in Deutero-Isaiah ('צמח', col. 564-66), 'Der Israelit staunt über dieses Wachsen, das umso wunderbarer erscheint, als im palästinischen Klima der Vegetationsrhytmus beschleunigt ist (Jes 35,1f.; 40,6f.)'. He finds a comparison between the certainty of the growth of plants as a result of rainfall and the certainty of the salvation of the people as a result of the personal intervention of YHWH, and observes that the vocabulary of plant life is here transferred to the order of history, where it serves to express 'nicht eine kontinuierliche Entwicklung, sondern vielmehr das Wunderbare, die Harmonie und die Gewißheit des Heilshandelns Jahwes'. F. Lundgreen, *Die Benützung der Pflanzenwelt in der alttestamentlichen Religion* (Giessen: Alfred Töpelmann, 1908), p. 153,

ples of this use of plant imagery may be found in Isa. 4.2; 11.1; 42.9 (cf. the description of God as creator in v. 5); 43.19; 61.11.

Without making an explicit connection with the choice of the word צמח, McKane makes a more or less similar point, based on the content of the oracle as a whole: the oracle of Jer. 23.5 'does not introduce a prediction which will be effected by replacing one Judaean king with another within the framework of a continuing historical institution of monarchy'. What is announced is not a matter of simple historical progression, 'the future hope which is here proclaimed accepts as inevitable the downfall of the historical institution of Davidic monarchy and does not foresee or indicate any connection in terms of historical probabilities between the present circumstances and the future hope'.[81]

The issue in Jer. 23.5 is the discontinuity with respect to historical probabilities. There is, therefore, a difference between Jer. 23.5 and Isa. 11.1. The difference in terminology reflects a difference in the historical and political background, and is used to convey a different message. In Isaiah 11, in a situation of decline of the monarchy, the words חטר and נצר, 'shoot' and 'branch', are used to express the idea that there is still hope for the restoration of the monarchy (see my discussion of the verse above) and for an active role for the Davidic dynasty in that restoration. On this verse, Wildberger comments, 'daß ein Baumstrunk noch einmal Schoße treibt, bezeugt auch so jenes Handeln Jahwes, das Jesaja als "wunderbar" bezeichnet (28 29 29 14), ohne daß es darum dem gewöhnlichen Ablauf der Vorgänge in Natur und Geschichte widersprechen muß'.[82]

The final words of this comment ('dem gewöhnlichen Ablauf der Vorgänge in Natur und Geschichte') express the difference between the thrust of Isa. 11.1 and that of Jer. 23.5, the latter passage being marked by an absence of 'any connection in terms of historical probabilities' (McKane). This absence must be understood against the background of a development from decline of the monarchy (Isaiah's time)[83] to its near

comments on Ps. 104, 'Das besingen der Flora, als eines wunderbaren Werken Jahwes, stand in der Poesie der Hebräer obenan'.

81. *Jeremiah*, pp. 560, 561.

82. *Jesaja*, p. 447; ET *Isaiah 1–12*, p. 470, 'the very fact that the stump of a tree is able to produce shoots once again testifies to the direct action of Yahweh, which Isaiah terms "wonderful" (28.29; 29.14), without thereby contradicting the general flow of events which take place in nature and history'.

83. The authenticity of this prophecy is debated. For a defence of a setting in the

collapse (Jeremiah's time). The clause והקמתי לדוד צמח is used to express the idea that no simple historical development, but only an intervention by God can provide a future for the monarchy.

There is another detail in the wording of the oracle which supports this interpretation. At the same time, this detail creates a second problem for the descent view. The detail I have in mind is the prepositional phrase לדוד. The first thing that is somewhat unusual about this phrase is its position in the syntax of the clause:

והקמתי לדוד צמח צדיק

The word order [Verb]–[Prepositional Phrase]–[Object] makes one wonder whether the position of the prepositional phrase before the object of the verb is deliberate. Is it possible to discover something special about the phrase לדוד which the prophet tries to highlight by giving the prepositional phrase the potentially prominent position immediately after the verb and before the object? In my view there is indeed something special about the phrase, and that is the use of the preposition ל, rather than מן 'from'. Compare the phrase in Jer. 23.5 with 2 Sam. 7.12:

> When your days are fulfilled and you lie down with your fathers, I will raise up your offspring after you, who shall come forth from your body [והקמתי את־זרעך אחריך אשר יצא ממעיך], and I will establish his kingdom.

The last three words of the clause which I have set in Hebrew characters echo an identical phrase in Gen. 15.4 (אשר יצא ממעיך), and similar phrases are found elsewhere.[84] The preposition מן is also found in Isa. 11.1 (ויצא חטר מגזע ישי ונצר משרשיו יפרה), and in Jer. 22.30, though in this verse the construction is somewhat different (לא יצלח מזרעו איש ישב על־כסא דוד ומשל עוד ביהודה).

What the dynastic oracles in 2 Sam. 7.12 and Jer. 23.5 have in common is the verb 'I will raise up' (והקימתי). They differ, however, in the choice of the preposition: מן versus ל. The use of the preposition ל rather than מן has usually gone unnoticed (as the frequent appearance of a translation like 'from David' in discussions of Jer. 23.5 indicates), but the position of the prepositional phrase could well have been chosen to point the attention to the presence of precisely this preposition. The

---

life of Isaiah see Barth, *Jesaja-Worte*, pp. 62-63, 73; Wildberger, *Jesaja*, pp. 442-46; ET *Isaiah 1–12*, pp. 465-67.

84. 2 Sam. 16.11, of Absalom; 2 Chron. 6.9, of Solomon; 2 Chron. 32.21, of unnamed descendants of the Assyrian king Sennacherib.

difference in the choice of the preposition makes good sense when it is connected with the צמח–זרע opposition. In Jer. 23.5, 'David' is not the origin or source of a new sprout or the like, as in Isa. 11.1, but only the recipient of the צמח.

The input of 'David' is reduced. In the dynastic oracle in 2 Samuel 7 the question of who will act to guarantee that there will be a future for the Davidic dynasty was left open. There was room for the input of David and his house, and for the involvement of God: '*I will raise up your offspring after you, who shall come forth from your body*'. In the course of the history of the monarchy, a history marked by a great deal of unfaithfulness on the side of the Davidic dynasty, the picture changes: the role of the house of David with respect to the future of the monarchy is more and more reduced and the dynasty comes increasingly to depend on God alone.

A reflection of this process of change is found in Isa. 11.1: only a stump is left of the house of David, which is no more named after David, but after his father Jesse. But that is at least something which leaves open the possibility of some input from the house of David. Jeremiah 22–23 offers yet another perspective:[85] one of the last kings belonging to the house of David is told that none of his offspring will sit on the throne and rule, and only a divine intervention (the exact nature of which is left in the dark) will guarantee the future of the Davidic dynasty. This is what is expressed in the clause והקמתי לדוד צמח צדיק. The righteous growth will be raised up by YHWH for David. David will be at the receiving end. Once the nuances of the phrase לדוד צמח have been taken into account, it becomes extremely difficult to interpret the oracle along the lines of *descent from* David.

In sum, then, this would be the translation which I propose for Jer. 23.5:

> Behold, the days are coming, says the Lord, when I will raise up for David righteous growth, and a king shall reign and deal wisely, and shall execute justice and righteousness in the land.

That the change of the picture which I have outlined does not fit a chronological framework of a gradual reduction of the input in the

---

85. B.S. Childs, *Old Testament Theology in a Canonical Context* (London: SCM Press, 1985), p. 242 writes, 'The description of the coming ruler varies greatly from prophet to prophet, and is consistently joined to contingent historical events in the life of Israel'.

continuing existence of the house of David can be seen in a passage like
Ezek. 17.22-24: there a future ruler in the line of David is presented as a
sprig which will be taken by YHWH 'from the lofty top of the cedar
[מצמרת הארז]' to plant it 'on the mountain height of Israel'. In this
picture (most likely later than Jeremiah 22–23) the plant imagery is
more similar to that in Isaiah 11.

### 3. *Conclusion*

In this chapter I have studied the meaning of the word צמח which is
used as the personal name of the coming ruler in Zech. 3.8 and 6.12. I
have argued that the traditional understanding of צמח as meaning either
'sprout/shoot' or 'branch' (that is, a part of a plant) is flawed. Instead,
an investigation of the syntagmatic and paradigmatic relationships in
which צמח can be found suggests that the meaning of the word is
'vegetation, greenery, growth' (that is, plants as a whole, possibly in a
collective sense).

This interpretation of the meaning of צמח has implications for the
relationship of the צמח oracles to the passages which have often been
considered to provide the key to the understanding of them: Isa. 11.1
and Jer. 23.5. The difference in terminology between Isa. 11.1 and the
צמח oracles (those in Jeremiah and in Zechariah) implies that the overall thrust of these passages is substantially different. The imagery in Isa.
11.1 of 'a shoot from the stump of Jesse' and 'a branch...out of his
roots' leaves room for the Davidic dynasty to make a contribution to its
own future. The צמח imagery in Jer. 23.5 suggests that only a divine
intervention can safeguard the future of the Davidic dynasty. The relationship between Isa. 11.1 and the צמח oracles in Zechariah is indirect,
and probably of a contrastive nature. The message of Jer. 23.5 and the
צמח oracles in Zechariah seems more analogous. I will discuss the
nature of that relationship in more detail in the next chapter.

## Chapter 4

## A CASE OF MISTAKEN IDENTITY—WHO IS ZEMAH?

In the previous chapter I have discussed the precise meaning of the word צמח, the word used as the name of the royal figure in Zechariah 3 and 6. All this was done with a view to preparing the stage for the discussion of the content of the צמח oracles, which I will deal with in this chapter.

The two portraits of צמח in Zechariah 3 and 6 are complementary. In the first section of this chapter I will look at the portrait in Zechariah 3. In the second section I will discuss the portrait in Zechariah 6. In the final section I will consider the question of the identification of צמח.

### 1. Zemah in Zechariah 3

The portrait of צמח in Zechariah 3 takes up one verse only: that is, verse 8.[1] The acts in the next verse, the engraving of the inscription on the stone with seven eyes and the removal of the guilt of the land, are both ascribed to YHWH ('I will...'), not to צמח. It is therefore unclear why some scholars[2] credit צמח with these actions.

The portrait of צמח in 3.8 is therefore brief, and as a result not much more than a silhouette. In this stage of the vision reports, the figure of צמח in a sense dawns at the horizon of the visions. A number of the questions (but perhaps not all) which this sketchy portrait raises are dealt with in the more extensive portrait in 6.12-13. I will first discuss those features which are found only in 3.8, and next those that are found in both 3.8 and 6.12-13.

---

1. Compare Reventlow, *Haggai, Sacharja*, p. 55.
2. E.g. T. Chary, *Agée, Zacharie*, pp. 82-83, 'purification...attachée à la personne du messie'; Baldwin, *Haggai, Zechariah*, p. 118, 'The Branch, like Moses and Joshua, will act in a representative capacity, remove the guilt of the land...'

### a. *Unique Features*

*YHWH Will Bring him.* Most of the features in the portrait of צמח in Zechariah 3 appear again in Zechariah 6. There are two exceptions. The first exception concerns the person who is said to be the agent of his coming. In Zech. 3.8 it is YHWH who says, 'Behold, I will bring my servant צמח'. On this point there is a similarity with the צמח oracles in Jer. 23.5 (and 33.15), where it is also YHWH who says, 'I will raise up for David righteous growth'.

*The Designation of צמח as עברי 'My Servant'.* The second unique feature is the epithet which צמח receives in Zech. 3.8, where he is called עברי 'my servant'. I will discuss the use and the meaning of the phrase 'my servant' more extensively in chapter 7. There I will conclude that it cannot be said to be a typical royal title. There are in fact only two kings with this title: one finds the title with David 40 times ('my/your/ his servant' [the personal pronoun refers to YHWH]), including four cases where עברי דוד refers to a future ruler, and once with Hezekiah ('his servant').

It is fair to say that as such the title 'my servant' does not specify what kind of function or office the person bearing the title has, but it clearly suggests a special status and a special relationship with God. Most of the other examples of the phrase 'my servant PN'[3] refer to persons from the past or the present, but at least one more refers to a person of the future: the servant in Isaiah 40–55. Whether Zech. 3.8 also belongs to the first category (past or present), or to the second (future), depends on the identification of the person to whom the name צמח refers. I will deal with this later in the chapter.

### b. *Shared Features*

*The Link with the Priesthood.* I now turn to the discussion of the features which the portraits of צמח in Zechariah 3 and 6 have in common. The first common feature is the fact that both oracles have the same addressee: (members of) the priesthood. In 3.8-10 the oracle is addressed to 'Joshua the high priest, you and your friends who sit before you', who are said to be 'men of good omen'. In 6.9-15 the promise of the coming of צמח is part of the message embedded in a symbolic action in which Joshua, the present high priest, is involved and spoken

3.    The cases (20 in total; the reversed order [PN–*'abdī*] is found 26 times) are listed by Lemaire, 'Zorobabel', p. 51.

to. I have discussed the significance of this embedding of the צמח oracles in words addressed to members of the priesthood in chapter 2.

*The Future Reference of the Coming of* צמח. The second feature shared
by both portraits is that the time reference of the promise of the coming
of צמח is consistently future. In 3.8, where the bringing of צמח is presented as the result of an act of God, the construction is הנה + participle. In 6.12-13 one finds a sequence of an Imperfect form followed
by Perfect Consecutive forms. Both constructions indicate future reference.[4]

*The Name* צמח. The third shared feature is the name of the royal figure.
The name צמח is not attested as a personal name in the Old Testament.
As far as I know there is only one example of this personal name in
extra-biblical Hebrew: there is a '[so]n of צמח' mentioned in a list of
offerings on a bowl from Arad, dated to the second half of the eighth
century BCE.[5]

While in Hebrew צמח is apparently acceptable as a proper name, it
may not always work in the same way in other languages, and conse-
quently it may be difficult to retain a close link between noun and
proper name as found in Hebrew. So, in the English language, the

4. On the future reference of the participle, see the comments in Joüon and
Muraoka, *Grammar* §121e, on the 'use of the participle to express the near future
and the future in general'; and Waltke and O'Connor, *Syntax* §37.6-7: the participle
denotes 'certainty, often with immanency [*sic*]...הנה often occurs with all these
constructions because that particle calls to a situation either for vividness...or for its
logical connection with some other event...' While in a number of cases הנה +
participle is used to indicate imminent future, this is not always so, as examples like
1 Kgs 21.21; 2 Kgs 21.12; 22.16 show.

5. Y. Aharoni, *Arad Inscriptions* (Judean Desert Series; Jerusalem: The Bialik
Institute and The Israel Exploration Society, 1975), pp. 82-86 [Hebrew]; ET *Arad
Inscriptions* (Jerusalem: The Israel Exploration Society, 1981), pp. 80-84; also
noted by A. Lemaire, 'L'Epigraphie paléo-hébraïque et la Bible', in J.A. Emerton,
(ed.), *Congress Volume Göttingen 1977* (VTSup, 29; Leiden: E.J. Brill, 1978),
p. 171. In Ugaritic *yṣmḥ*, a form of the verb *ṣmḥ*, appears once as a personal name,
also in the 'son of X' construction (*bn yṣmḥ*). The text (KTU 4, 12 l. 4) can be
found in C.H. Gordon, *Ugaritic Manual. Newly Revised Grammar. Texts in Transliteration. Cuneiform Selections. Paradigms–Glossary–Indices* (AnOr, 35; Rome:
Pontificio Istituto Biblico, 1955), p. 132 Text 10; and p. 316 #1633. Dambrine,
*Croissance*, p. 11, interprets *bn yṣmḥ* as a shortened form of *bn yṣmḥ dgn* (with the
theophoric element left out) 'the son of Dagan-will-make-grow'.

equivalents of צמח, 'Vegetation', 'Greenery', or 'Growth', would sound somewhat odd as proper names. In some other European languages, however, one finds proper names closely related to the noun *flora* (the equivalent of English *flora*, vegetation, originally a loan from Latin), a word in the same lexical field as Hebrew צמח, names like *Flo(o)r*, *Floris* in Dutch and *Florian* in German.

In languages where it is difficult to find a proper name which is clearly and closely related to a noun meaning 'vegetation, greenery, growth', one could choose to use a transliteration in the body of the text, and add a footnote explaining that the Hebrew word can be used both as a noun meaning 'vegetation' and as a proper name.[6] In this book I have adopted a similar practice by using (the [simple] transliteration) 'Zemah' as the equivalent of Hebrew צמח in Zech. 3.8 and 6.12.

## 2. Zemah in Zechariah 6

### a. Matters of Syntax
Before I consider the content of the צמח oracle in Zechariah 6, I will look at the syntax of Zech. 6.12-13. The reason for this is the presence of a few special syntactic features. The first special feature is the waw before the clause starting with מתחתיו. The waw is best interpreted as marking the first clause as a casus pendens construction:[7] without this waw one would have had a normal and correctly formed sentence:

---

6. Another option would be to have both the transliteration of the proper name and the translation of the noun in the body of the text, as is done in UB, which translates Zech. 3.8, 'Oui, me voici, je fais venir mon serviteur, Ṣèmaḫ, Germe' (UB, V, p. 127; similarly, Zech. 6.12, on p. 131); cf. Lemaire ('Zorobabel', p. 50), who translates the beginning of Zech. 6.12, 'Voici un homme, dont le nom est Ṣemaḥ/Germe...'

7. On this use of the waw see: GKB §143d; W. Groß, *Die Pendens-Konstruktion im Biblischen Hebräisch* (Studien zum althebräischen Satz, 1; ATSAT, 27; Erzabtei St. Ottilien: EOS Verlag, 1987), pp. 188-89; Joüon and Muraoka, *Grammar* §156l; cf. Van der Woude, *Zacharia*, p. 116. See also G. Khan, *Studies in Semitic Syntax* (LOS, 38; Oxford: Oxford University Press, 1988), p. 69, section 3.2 'An extraposed item may be connected to the rest of the clause by conversive *wāw*'. It is not clear why Khan would want to limit this usage to 'conversive *wāw*': there are also examples of a waw followed not by a perfect consecutive or imperfective consecutive (Khan's terminology) but by other constructions (see Groß, *Pendenskonstruktion*, pp. 106-107).

*הנה־איש צמח שמו מתחתיו יצמח ובנה את־היכל יהוה

The usual function of a casus pendens construction is 'to highlight or focus one element of the main clause'.[8] On a casus pendens construction with waw (apodosis), GKB comments (§143d), 'The isolation and prominence of the principle subject is in this case still more marked than in the instances treated above' ('instances treated above' refers to casus pendens constructions without waw). The specific purpose of focusing on one constituent of the clause may also serve to mark contrast.

The second special syntactic feature is the position of the prepositional phrase מתחתיו before the verbal form יצמח. Such a prepositional phrase in initial position usually has a similar function of emphasis or contrast.[9] There is a third marker of emphasis in this short passage: the independent personal pronoun is used two times[10] in v. 13 as a separate subject indicator. Though there is reason to be cautious with the use of emphasis as a grammatical category,[11] the accumulation of emphasis markers in such a brief passage is remarkable and cannot be ignored.

b. *More Features*
After this grammatical note, I now continue the descriptions of the other features in the portrait of Zemah.

*Third Party.* The absence of the article before איש suggests that the person spoken about should not be identified with the person spoken to, Joshua (or Zerubbabel according to those who change the name in v. 11). That this would create a problem is apparently felt by those who

8. Waltke and O'Connor, *Syntax*, §4, 8. The waw is a waw apodosis in the casus pendens construction, see GKB §143d, 'Die Isolierung und Hervorhebung des Hauptsubjekts ist dann eine noch stärkere, als in den oben behandelten Fällen'; Joüon and Muraoka, *Grammar* §156l.

9. T. Muraoka, *Emphatic Words and Structures in Biblical Hebrew* (Jerusalem: Magnes Press; Leiden: E.J. Brill, 1985), pp. 41-43.

10. On the suggestion that the two 'and he [והוא]' in v. 13 refer to two different persons, see Chapter 5 (section 5.3.a 'Literary Layers in 6.9-15').

11. Cf. B.L. Bandstra, 'Word Order and Emphasis in Biblical Hebrew Narrative: Syntactic Observations on Genesis 22 from a Discourse Perspective', in Bodine, (ed.), *Linguistics*, p. 112, 'Emphasis has tended to become "the great explanation" of syntactic irregularities... If some particle, word, or construction is difficult to explain, the notion of emphasis is invoked and the problem is considered solved'.

alter the text by adding the article (הנה האיש).[12] That alteration on its
own would not have been enough: if the one spoken to was the same as
the one whom the prophet is speaking about, one would have expected
(as one finds it in, e.g., Hag. 2.23) a second person, that is, something
like,[13] 'You are the man...'

Only an interpretation which takes הנה איש as referring to a third
party is able to make sense of the construction איש + PN + שמו, which
is used in narrative to introduce a person.[14] The fact that only one name
is mentioned would make it difficult to interpret this situation like those
which involve a change of name or the giving of a new name. In such a
situation usually both the old name and the new name are mentioned
(e.g. Gen. 17.5, 15; 32.29; Dan. 1.7).The figure who appeared at the
horizon in Zech. 3.8 has now come in closer vision, and is further introduced by the prophet.

When the word for the name is a noun or adjective, or is not a real
personal name, the function of PN + שמו can be to focus the attention
on a particular characteristic of the person which finds expression in the
name.[15] In prophetic speech a construction including the same constituents ('Behold' + [noun for male figure, 'man' or 'son'] + [remark on his
origin][16] + 'X his name' + [description of an action he will do]; the
order of the constituents varies), is used twice to refer to a future figure
(once near, once distant future):

הנה־בן נולד לך הוא יהיה איש מנוחה

והנחותי לו מכל־אויביו מסביב

כי שלמה יהיה שמו

ושלום ושקט אתן על־ישראל בימיו

הוא־יבנה בית לשמי

---

12. See the section 'A Crown on the Head of Zerubbabel' in Chapter 5.

13. Cf. Hanhart, *Sacharja 1–8*, p. 409; Laato, *Josiah*, p. 247.

14. 1 Sam 17.4, 23; Job 1.1; 2 Chron. 28.9 (without איש). Cf. the use of the
Aramaic phrase PN + שמה to refer to an unfamiliar figure (Ezra 5.14; see Japhet,
'Zerubbabel', p. 93; E.Y. Kutscher, *Hebrew and Aramaic Studies* (Jerusalem:
Magnes Press, 1977), p. 71; H.G.M. Williamson, 'Ezra and Nehemiah in the Light
of the Texts from Persepolis', *BBR* 1 (1991), pp. 41-61 (46).

15. Of human beings: 1 Sam. 25.25 (Nabal, 'fool'). Of God: Exod. 34.14 (worship no other god 'for the Lord, whose name is Jealous, is a jealous God [כי יהוה
קנא שמו אל קנא הוא]'); Isa. 54.5 (יהוה); Isa. 57.15 (קדוש); Jer. 33.2; Amos 4.13;
5.8, 27; 9.6.

16. I take ומתחתיו יצמח in Zech. 6.12 as referring to the origin of צמח; see
below.

והוא יהיה־לי לבן ואני לו לאב
והכינותי כסא מלכותו על־ישראל עד־עולם (1 Chron. 22.9-10)

and

הנה־בן נולד לבית־דוד יאשיהו שמו וזבח עליך (1 Kgs 13.2)

All these features together make it clear that the prophet is talking about a third party, not about the one to whom he is speaking.

*Where צמח Is from.* The use of the name צמח is now explained by the following words: ומתחתיו יצמח. מתחתיו literally means 'under him', or 'from under him'. In Exod. 10.23 ולא־קמו איש מתחתיו is translated 'nor did any rise from his place', or 'no one could get up from where he was' (NJPS). It is suggested by several scholars that the enigmatic phrase ומתחתיו יצמח expresses the result of the presence or action of צמח: the blessing of which צמח will be the cause, for example, '[w]here he is there is flourishing'.[17] I doubt whether this can be expressed in Hebrew in this way:[18] when the verb is used to express a general state of affairs there is always a subject stated (in literal use, e.g. Gen. 2.5, 'no herb of the field had yet sprung up'; in metaphorical use, e.g. Isa. 58.8, 'your healing shall spring up speedily'). The closest parallel to the suggested impersonal use in Zech. 6.12 seems to be Isa. 55.10, but there the verbal form is הצמיח (צמח hi.), 'as the rain and the snow come down from heaven, and return not thither but water the earth, making it bring forth and sprout [והולידה והצמיחה]...'[19] Another problem is that in 6.12 for the next verbal form (ובנה) one needs איש צמח שמו as subject, which makes a construction in which something else (and what it is, is not mentioned!) is the subject of יצמח awkward.

It seems better to relate ומתחתיו יצמח to the origin or the nature of the growth of צמח.[20] It may be that the cryptic nature of the phrase is

17. J. Touzard, 'L'âme juive au temps de Perses', *RB* 35 (1926), p. 201 (a messianic dynasty); Ackroyd, *Exile*, p. 194; also in Nowack, *Propheten*, p. 353; Elliger, *Propheten*, pp. 129-30; K.-M. Beyse, *Serubbabel*, p. 81; Amsler, *Aggée; Zacharie 1–8*, p. 109; Hanhart, *Sacharja 1–8*, p. 224.

18. For similar objections of a syntactical nature, see Hanhart, *Sacharja 1–8*, pp. 409-10.

19. As I made clear in the previous Chapter, I would prefer 'bring forth and grow' for RSV's 'bring forth and sprout'.

20. With Köhler, *Sacharja*, p. 206; Mitchell, *Haggai and Zechariah*, p. 187; Ridderbos, *Profeten*, p. 103; Baldwin, *Haggai*, p. 135; Van der Woude, *Zacharia*, p. 116; Hanhart, *Sacharja 1–8*, pp. 409-10 (but I disagree with Hanhart when he

deliberate, and that its primary function is negative: to say what the origin of צמח is not, without specifying positively what it is. צמח is presented here not as growing from something which is already present, a trunk, or a stump (as a sprout or a branch do [e.g. Isa. 11.1]); with צמח things will be different, 'he will grow from his (own) place', or[21] 'he shall grow up in his place'. There is something mysterious about the origins of Zemah, in a way similar to Mic. 5.1-3, where the words, 'whose origin is from of old, from ancient days' suggest 'that the future king would come into existence in a wonderful way'.[22]

Perhaps the prepositional phrase מתחתיו has a parallel[23] in the למטה in 2 Kgs 19.30 (= Isa. 37.31), 'the surviving remnant of the house of Judah shall again take root downward [שרש...למטה...ויספה], and bear fruit upward' (an event ascribed to God's intervention: קנאת יהוה תעשה־זאת [2 Kgs 19.31 = Isa. 37.32]). The combination of צמח verb and noun is also found in Jer. 33.15, where the hiphil stem of the verb (אצמיח לדוד צמח) is used to state that YHWH is the one responsible for the growing of the צמח צדקה.

I have already pointed to a striking difference between Zech. 3.8 and 6.12-13: YHWH as the agent who will make צמח come is an element present in (Jeremiah 23 and 33 and) Zech. 3.8, but not in 6.12-13.[24] There is a possibility that the mysterious quality of the phrase מתחתיו may be related to this.

gives the nature of the growth of צמח this specific content: 'der Ausdruck יצמח מתחתיו zeigt nicht anderes als die nicht abreißende Folge der davidischen Dynastie'; for 'reign in his stead' וימלך תחתיו is used, never וימלך מתחתיו). For other suggestions, see Marti, *Dodekapropheton*, p. 420 ('neue Phase der davidischen Dynastie'); Petitjean, *Oracles*, p. 286 (appearance on political scene); Rudolph, *Haggai, Sacharja*, pp. 127-28, 130 ('aus seinem eigenen Boden', 'im Heiligen Lande selbst'); Meyers and Meyers, *Haggai, Zechariah*, p. 355 ('from his loins ("under him") or "after him", later on, another Davidide will arise or "shoot up" '); Tollington, *Tradition*, p. 172, 'dynastic succession'.

21. So R.P. Gordon, 'Nahum–Malachi', in *The Targum of the Minor Prophets* (translated, with a critical introduction, apparatus, and notes by Kevin J. Cathcart and Robert P. Gordon; Edinburgh: T. & T. Clark, 1989), p. 198.

22. Mowinckel, *He that Cometh*, p. 184.

23. Another possible parallel of the phrase מתחתיו may be found in Job 8.18 (about a plant to be 'destroyed from his place [ממקומו]').

24. Cf. Petersen, *Haggai and Zechariah*, p. 276, 'we should expect Yahweh to be the source of the luxuriant growth of the branch as that is described, albeit enigmatically, in 6.12'.

## c. *Zemah and the Temple*

Prominent in the description of the royal figure in 6.12-13 is that צמח will build the temple of YHWH. This is the first action in the description, even preceding the mentioning of the rule of צמח, and it is the only action the description of which is repeated.[25] The question whether the priority in description of the action of building the temple over the action of ruling corresponds to a priority in chronology, is difficult to answer with any certainty.

Rebuilding a temple is usually a task for a king,[26] but it is difficult to claim that it is exclusively the king's prerogative. In an earlier passage in the vision cycle one finds Zerubbabel already involved in the rebuilding of the temple (4.8-10). There is no evidence that at that particular moment in the process of the reconstruction of the temple Zerubbabel was rebuilding the temple in the capacity of a king. In a sense it can be said that the temple was built by a king, but Zerubbabel was not that king, but only his agent: in 2 Chronicles and Ezra the Persian kings are presented as the temple builders; for example, 'Cyrus the king of Persia' (Ezra 4.3), and 'Cyrus and Darius and Artaxerxes king of Persia' (Ezra 6.14). In spite of its prominence in other sources dealing with this period,[27] one does not find this thought in Zechariah.

## d. *The Rule of* צמח

In the further description of the royal figure words are used which express the prerogatives and privileges associated with a king. First we read about the status of צמח, 'he shall bear royal honour'. הוד is often (though not exclusively)[28] used for the majesty of a king; for example, 1 Chron. 29.25; Ps. 45.4; Jer. 22.18. Next we read about his authority:

25. See the discussion of the repetition in Chapter 5, where I conclude that it functions to express emphasis (and possibly also to mark the transition from words addressed to Joshua to words addressed to the prophet).

26. Petersen, *Haggai and Zechariah*, p. 240; and see D.R. Runnals, 'The King as Temple Builder', in E. Furcha (ed.), *Spirit within Structure* (Festschrift George Johnston; Pittsburgh: Pickwick Press, 1983), pp. 18-22, for the ancient Near Eastern setting of this notion.

27. 2 Chron. 36.23 = Ezra 1.2; Ezra 4.3; 5.13, 17; 6.3, 12; cf. Isa. 44.28.

28. See, e.g., Schöttler, *Gottesvolk*, p. 396 n. 360. Rignell's attempt to play down the royal connotation of הוד in Zech. 6.12 (Rignell, *Nachtgesichte*, pp. 231-32; he takes it as referring to the 'glorious office' of the priest [cf. my remarks in Chapter 5 on his interpretation of the double והוא]) is rightly criticised by Petitjean, *Oracles*, pp. 294-96.

he will 'sit and rule on his throne'. While 'sit on the throne' is the usual description of a king in office (e.g. 1 Kgs 1.46; 16.11),[29] the word used for 'to rule', משל, is somewhat unusual:[30] usually מלך is used for the rule of a king (e.g. 1 Kgs 1.17; 16.11). But other passages can be found which deal with kingship without using a form of the root מלך, for example Ps. 110, where the only persons for whom מלך is used are the rivals of the royal figure. In the context of Zech. 6.9-15, features like the crown and the sitting on the throne, make it abundantly clear that צמח is indeed a royal figure. What is perhaps somewhat striking is the absence of anything that in one way or another may be associated with David or his house (for example why not 'the throne *of David*'?).

### e. *A Priest by his Throne*
The description of צמח ends with the mentioning of a priest at his throne. I have discussed the interpretation of this part of the description in Chapter 2 (section entitled 'The Lack of Specificity in the Description of the Priest').

### 3. *The Identity of Zemah*

In the introductory Chapter of this book I have listed the different views concerning the identity of the 'man called Zemah'. The views can be grouped in two categories: a great number of scholars conclude that the figure called Zemah is no one else than Zerubbabel, the governor (in the rest of this Chapter I will call this the ZZ view), while a minority of scholars opt for an unspecified and unknown future figure as the person to whom צמח refers (the FF view).

Having looked into the portraits of Zemah in some detail in the two preceding sections of this Chapter, I now move on to see whether the details of the portrait may enable us to come to a plausible solution of the problem of the identification of Zemah. It must be admitted that the FF view provides in a sense unfair competition: since it introduces an

---

29.  See the discussion in Chapter 2, and Jan P. Lettinga, 'Het "gezeten-zijn" van koning en rechter', *De Reformatie* 32 (1956–57), p. 360.

30.  There is a possibility that משל echoes Mic. 5.1 ממך לי יצא להיות מושל בישראל ומוצאתיו מקדם מימי עולם, where the same verb is used in a passage that could be interpreted as messianic (cf. Williamson, *1 and 2 Chronicles*, p. 226 on a possible echo of Mic. 5.1 in מושל בישראל in 2 Chron. 7.18). But the absence of בישראל in Zech. 6.13 makes the link tenuous.

unspecified future figure, it is not too difficult to make all the details of the portrait fit. As I will show, there remain things for discussion also for the FF view.

a. *The View that Zemah and Zerubbabel Are One and the Same Person*
I will begin with the view that Zemah and Zerubbabel are one and the same person. There are certainly things which can be said in favour of this identification, in particular the temple building by צמח and his association with the priest. Such elements naturally direct our thoughts to Zerubbabel and Joshua, as we know them from the book of Ezra (chs. 3–5), where they are presented as leaders of the community in Jerusalem and as organising the rebuilding of the temple. However, a closer look at the details of the oracle uncovers some major problems for the ZZ identification.

*A Crown on the Head of Joshua.* If Zerubbabel was the one with whom Zemah should be identified, it is not clear why the crown was not set upon his head, in stead of on the head of Joshua.

*Future Reference.* Identifying Zerubbabel as the person to which צמח refers does not explain the consistent future reference[31] concerning his coming and his bearing honour and sitting and ruling on his throne.[32] This is the place where the importance of the issue of the dating of the oracle becomes clear (more on this in chapter 5). The date in 1.7 suggests that the visions were seen in the time when the rebuilding of the temple was in progress (Zech. 4.9-10). For the ZZ view to be possible, a date before the beginning of the rebuilding of the temple has to be postulated. So scholars have argued for a setting of 6.9-15 before the visions,[33] either when Zerubbabel was already in Jerusalem, or when he

31. So also Lagrange, 'Prophéties', pp. 71-72; cf. A.H. Edelkoort, *De profeet Zacharia: Een uitlegkundige studie* (Baarn: Bosch & Keuning, 1945), p. 74.

32. If the verb בנה is taken in the sense of 'finish building' or the like (see the discussion of the meaning of the verb below), then the action described in the phrase ובנה את־היכל יהוה would be one feature fitting within an interpretation which identifies Zemah and Zerubbabel.

33. Horst, *Propheten*, pp. 210-11, 222, 226, 232, 239; Rignell, *Nachtgesichte*, pp. 228, 240-41; Ackroyd, *Exile*, p. 197; Petitjean, *Oracles*, pp. 269, 286; Mason, *Haggai, Zechariah*, p. 62; Smith, *Parties*, p. 189 n. 50; S. Amsler, 'Des visions de Zacharie à l'apocalypse d'Esaïe 24–27', in J. Vermeylen (ed.), *The Book of Isaiah— Le livre d'Isaïe. Les oracles et leurs relectures: Unité et complexité de l'ouvrage*

was still in Babylon. The latter view can only be held if the end of 6.10 ('who have arrived from Babylon') is seen as secondary.[34]

There is only one reason for such dating proposals: the identification of Zemah with Zerubbabel. Only if there are other arguments which make a compelling case for the ZZ identification, are there good reasons to conclude that it is necessary to date this oracle before the visions and accept the implications of such a dating. So I continue the assessment of the case for the ZZ view.

*The Use of the Name Zemah.* The next problem is the use of the name Zemah. If Zerubbabel was the one referred to as צמח, why did the prophet not use his name in Zechariah 3 and 6, as he did in Zechariah 4 (vv. 6-10)?[35] Those who argue for the ZZ identification sometimes explain the absence of Zerubbabel's name in 6.12 by pointing to the potentially explosive content of the oracle which might have threatened Zerubbabel's position as governor under the authority of the Persians.

While one can understand this as a possible explanation of the use of צמח instead of Zerubbabel in 6.12, this hypothesis does not explain the use of צמח in 3.8: there nothing was said of צמח which could possibly have compromised Zerubbabel's position before the Persians, if he was the one referred to by צמח. In 3.8 the angel of YHWH announces only that YHWH will bring his 'servant צמח' (compare זרבבל בן־שאלתיאל עבדי in Hag. 2.23), while nothing is said about his status or authority. If Zerubbabel was the one referred to by צמח, why was his name not mentioned in this 'politically safe' context, as there was apparently no problem in mentioning his name in 4.6-10?[36]

Scholars have pointed to the pun which the choice of the word צמח creates with the name Zerubbabel (usually interpreted as Akkadian *zēr*

(BETL, 81; Leuven: University Press and Uitgeverij Peeters, 1989), pp. 263-73 (265-66); Redditt, 'Night Visions', p. 255; Redditt, *Haggai, Zechariah*, p. 42.

34. And this is exactly what Ackroyd proposes (*Exile*, pp. 197-98): we must assume 'that the last words of 6, 10 "who came from Babylon" is a latter addition made in the light of the events, at a time when the words were being grouped together or re-expounded by the prophet himself'. Unfortunately, Ackroyd does not specify which the events were, in the light of which it is not an unreasonable assumption that these specific words 'who came from Babylon' were added.

35. Cf. Schöttler, *Gottesvolk*, p. 158: צמח cannot be identified with Zerubbabel, 'sonst müßte es הנה־האיש heißen und das Fehlen der namentlichen Nennung wäre unerklärlich'.

36. Cf. Eichrodt, 'Symbol', p. 513; Redditt, 'Night Visions', p. 257.

*Bābili*, 'seed of Babylon').[37] Perhaps this suggestion should be reconsidered somewhat if צמח does not mean sprout, and should not be interpreted as a metaphor for offspring. In any case, the possibility of a pun here does not help us to settle the issue of the identification in one direction or another.[38] On the one hand one could argue that this points to the identification of the two, but on the other hand one could argue that the pun is meant to contrast the two (that is, צמח, not Zerubbabel).

*A Double Name? (Lemaire)* Recently, Lemaire has added a new feature to the ZZ view.[39] He argues that Zerubbabel had a double name, one Hebrew and one Babylonian, and that Zemah is not a symbolic, but a real name, the Hebrew name of Zerubbabel. He mentions other examples, in the Old Testament, like Daniel and his friends, and the Akkadian name *Nabū-šēzibanni* for the later Egyptian pharaoh Psammetichus I. He points to the semantic correspondence between these two names, *ṣemaḥ* meaning 'germe, pousse, rejeton' ('sprout, shoot, offshoot'), and *zēr(u)* meaning 'graine, semence, descendance' ('seed, semen, offspring').

Lemaire is correct in pointing to the fact that צמח is attested as a proper name (see the discussion in the first section of this Chapter), but I am not convinced by his case that it is used, in Zech. 3.8 and 6.12 as a name referring to a contemporary of the prophet, namely Zerubbabel. The other example from the Old Testament to which Lemaire refers, the old and new names of Daniel and his friends, has one feature which in the case of Zerubbabel–Zemah is absent: the explicit equation of the names with one and the same person:

> And the chief of the eunuchs gave them names: Daniel he called Belteshazzar, Hananiah he called Shadrach, Mishael he called Meshach, and Azariah he called Abednego (Dan 1.7).

37. E.g. Rignell, *Nachtgesichte*, pp. 225, 226; Bauer, *Zeit*, p. 146; Lemaire, 'Zorobabel', pp. 49, 50. Bauer's suggestion to take 'Zerubbabel' not as the name of an individual, but as a code (*Chiffre*) for a group (corporate personality) is unconvincing. The idea that there is a pun here is rejected by Tollington (*Tradition*, p. 169), because Zechariah's audience would have missed such a pun, 'since the name Zerubbabel is Babylonian and derived form a Semitic word *zeru*, rather than a Hebrew word'. But I guess Zechariah's audience would have known the word זרע.

38. So, rightly, K. Koch, *Die Profeten*. II. *Babylonisch-persische Zeit* (UT, 281; Stuttgart: W. Kohlhammer, 1980), p. 168; ET *The Prophets*. II. *The Babylonian and Persian Periods* (London: SCM Press, 1983), p. 164.

39. Lemaire, 'Zorobabel', pp. 50-52.

One could add other examples of persons who are given a new name and where the identification is made explicitly, like, for example, Joseph/Zaphenath-paneah (Gen. 41.45), Eliakim/Jehoiakim (2 Kgs 23.34; 2 Chron. 36.4), and Hadassah/Esther (Est. 2.7). The situation is different, however, in Zechariah 1–6. There we would have two names for one and the same person used in different sections (Zemah in 3.8, Zerubbabel in 4.6, 9, and once again Zemah in 6.12), but nowhere does one find an explicit remark which connects the two names to one and the same person. Lemaire does not explain for what reason Zechariah would have failed to make the connection explicit, and why he would have alternated between the two names throughout the sections of chs. 1–6.

In the other text to which Lemaire refers, a section in one of the cylinder texts of Assurbanipal (*ARAB*, II, 774), one does not find the two names, but only one of the two, *Nabū-šēzibanni*, whereas the name Psammetichus is not mentioned. Again, it is not unusual that someone is given a different name, the moment he is installed in a ruler position. What is unusual is a situation where in one document one finds the two different names used alternatingly, without an explicit connection between the two being made in any possible way. That is what Lemaire claims for Zechariah 1–6, and he would have made his case stronger if he had provided parallels for that. Now his proposal is only an educated guess.

*The Meaning of the Name Zemah.* The ZZ identification holds that the use of צמח as the name of the future ruler evokes the idea of descent from David and points to the restoration of the monarchy. The choice of the name Zemah with its reminiscences of Jer. 23.5 is problematic for this view. If Zechariah wanted to bring up the notion of descent from David, then one must conclude that it is highly peculiar that he did not choose imagery that unambiguously expressed that idea, like the shoot/branch imagery from Isa. 11.1. I have argued in Chapter 3 that this imagery in Isa. 11.1 communicates a message which is different from the message conveyed by the vegetation imagery from Jer. 23.5, which indicates discontinuity with respect to historical developments and the need for an intervention by YHWH.

By making צמח a symbolic name, Zechariah unmistakably identifies the צמח which God announced to raise up (Jer. 23.5), as a person. The choice of this particular name suggests that, after a period of several decades (a period which included exile into Babylon), the situation and prospects with regard to the Davidic dynasty in the time of the prophet Zechariah is not much different from that in the time of the prophet Jeremiah. What Jeremiah's oracle conveyed is still true in this new situation: historical developments as such will not bring in a new monarchy. A personal intervention by God is still called for.

In a sense, what we have here is a second stage in which the fulfilment of the צמח oracle of Jer. 23.5 is pushed even further into the future. The first stage is Jer. 33.14-16, where the original oracle was taken up in a situation where it had not yet been fulfilled.[40] The use of the צמח imagery in Zechariah 3 and 6 together with the future orientation of the oracle once again locates the fulfilment in the future. 'The promise first given to preexilic prophets is repeated'.[41] As such, the repetition conveys a message: we are *not yet* there. In a sense, it is also another call, be it an implicit one, to pay attention to the message of the prophets (cf. Zech. 1.4-6).

Perhaps one should add that the repetition of the promise does not exclude further development: there is an interesting difference between Jer. 23.5 and 33.14-16 on the one hand and Zech. 3.6 and 6.12 on the other hand. Whereas the Jeremiah passages use the word מלך (both verb and noun) and mention the name David, in the Zechariach oracles one finds the related משל, but the name David is absent. This absence fits in with the reticence concerning the explicit mentioning of the house of David in the oracles of both Haggai and Zechariah dating to this particular period.

*The Emphasis Markers.* The ZZ identification does not really explain the abundance of markers of emphasis or contrast present in vv. 12-13. These emphasis markers highlight the person of Zemah (the casus pendens construction, and the repetition of the personal pronoun הוא), and the origin and nature of his growth (ומתחתיו יצמח). If Zerubbabel was the person referred to, with whom is he contrasted? One could think of the high priest Joshua, perhaps, but there seems little evidence

---

40. See Fishbane, *Biblical Interpretation*, pp. 472-73.

41. W.S. LaSor, D.A. Hubbard and F.W. Bush, *Old Testament Survey: The Message, Form, and Background of the Old Testament* (Grand Rapids: Eerdmans, 1982), p. 497; compare Cook's comment on 3.8 (*Prophecy*, p. 136), 'The divine promise is a simple messianic reminder'.

to support the idea that there was something like a conflict between
Zerubbabel and Joshua.[42]

*'Zerubbabel' Replaced by 'Joshua'.* Redditt has recently argued that
though originally צמח may have been used for Zerubbabel, the text has
been modified to make צמח 'refer to Joshua in light of the rising influence of the high priesthood'. Redditt does not want to exclude the possibility, which he considers less likely, 'that the reference is to some
future, unspecified person'.[43] So, the person with whom צמח should be
identified is most probably the high priest Joshua.

Redditt's proposal is based on an implausible reconstruction of the
redaction of the צמח oracles which makes vv. 11b-13 a secondary addition. In the next Chapter I will give a more extensive discussion of
Redditt's proposal, and show to what problems it leads. Apart from
that, there are several details in vv. 11b-13 which do not fit Joshua as
the one whom the words are referring to, like the use of the third person, the future reference, the presence of two persons in v. 13, and so
on.[44]

b. *Zemah a Future Figure*
As I said above, it is much easier to accommodate the details of the
portrait of צמח with a future figure whom we know very little about.
So, those elements which create a problem for the ZZ view fit nicely in
the FF view: the future reference, the use of the name צמח and its
meaning.

*Which Temple?* There is one feature that requires discussion, and that is
that Zemah will build the temple. How does that fit, when in an earlier
vision it is proclaimed that Zerubbabel who has started the rebuilding of

42. Barker, 'Two figures', p. 43, also sees צמח contrasted here with Zerubbabel,
but she identifies צמח with Joshua, a view which is untenable (see my discussion
below).
43. Redditt, *Haggai, Zechariah*, p. 66; compare Redditt, 'Night Visions', pp.
258-59; Barker, 'Two Figures', pp. 41-43; and G.W. Ahlström, *The History of
Ancient Palestine from the Palaeolithic Period to Alexander's Conquest* (JSOTSup,
146; Sheffield: JSOT Press, 1993), p. 820, 'The term "branch", which is a royal
epithet, is here used for the high priest Joshua. The crown must have been made for
Zerubbabel, but because he was no longer in command the high priest came to fill
his place'.
44. Cf. Tollington, *Tradition*, p. 172.

the temple will also be the one to finish it? The passage from the earlier vision reads:

> The hands of Zerubbabel have laid the foundation of this house; his hands shall also complete it. Then you will know that the LORD of hosts has sent me to you. For whoever has despised the day of small things shall rejoice, and shall see the plummet in the hand of Zerubbabel (Zech. 4.9-10).

What temple is there to build, if Zerubbabel is going to finish the temple which is at that moment under construction, and if—as I am arguing—Zemah is not the same person as Zerubbabel? Adherents of the ZZ identification usually identify the temple in 6.12-13 with what we now call the Second Temple, which at the time of the prophetic ministry of Zechariah was in the process of being rebuilt under the direction of Zerubbabel (cf. 4.9-10).

Others have interpreted the phrase, 'he shall build the temple of YHWH' in 6.12-13 as a reference to the building of a future temple:[45] the modest appearance of the present temple (Hag. 2.3, 9; Zech. 4.10)[46] would leave open the possibility for a future more glorious temple (cf. Ezek. 37.26; 40–48; Hag. 2.7-9). Among them is Lagrange, who states that it would have been difficult for Zechariah to be persuaded that the messianic age had already begun and in particular that the Messiah was already present, and that it is enough to assume that the present temple building project did not meet his expectations, so that from then on he lists the construction of the true temple among the attributes of צמח.[47]

---

45. Rudolph, *Haggai*, p. 131, 'die Ankundiging, daß der neue "Sproß" den Tempel weiterbauen werde'; Smith, *Micah–Malachi*, p. 219; Meyers and Meyers, *Haggai, Zechariah*, pp. 203, 356-57; Murmela, *Prophets*, p. 65.

46. Cf. W. Dommershausen, 'Der "Spross" als Messias-Vorstellung bei Jeremia und Sacharja', *TQ* 148 (1968), pp. 321-41 (331), who comments on the temple dedicated in 515 BCE, 'In den damaligen ärmlichen Verhältnissen blieb er an Pracht und Ausstattung hinter dem alten Tempel weit zurück, so daß unser Text mit der Hoffnung auf einen prachtvollen Tempel auch über das Jahr 515 hinaus Geltung behielte'.

47. Lagrange, 'Prophéties', p. 72; cf. Ridderbos, *Profeten*, p. 102; Meyers and Meyers, *Haggai, Zechariah*, pp. 356-57; Van der Woude, *Zacharia*, p. 116; Van der Woude, 'Serubbabel', pp. 151-53. Cf. the theme of the provisionality of the Second Temple in 1–2 Chronicles (see R. Mosis, *Untersuchungen zur Theologie des chronistischen Geschichtswerkes* [FTS, 92; Freiburg: Herder, 1973], pp. 226-27, 233-34).

The use of Hebrew בנה covers a range of nuances, including 'rebuild', 'continue building', 'finish building' or 'add to a present construction'.[48] On this interpretation בנה can be interpreted as 'rebuild' (*wiederbauen*) or 'add to a present construction' (*ausbauen, weiterbauen*). So it would not necessarily contradict the reference to Zerubbabel finishing the building of the temple in Zech. 4.9.[49] This prospect of a future more glorious temple may explain the presence of the phrase היכל יהוה[50] in these verses, rather than the usual ביתי (1.16; 3.7; 4.9).[51] Some scholars point to the presence in Jewish apocalyptic literature of traditions of a new eschatological temple to be rebuilt in the place of Zerubbabel's Temple.[52] Such traditions could then be interpreted as a

48. S. Wagner, 'בנה', *ThWAT*, I, cols. 689-706 (691), lists the following words as being within the horizon of the core meaning of בנה: '"aufbauen", "wiederaufbauen", "ausbauen", "anbauen", "abbauen", "gründen", "errichten", "hochziehen", "(be-) festigen", "restaurieren", "verfertigen", "(Wall) aufwerfen"'. Cf. Rudolph, *Haggai*, p. 80 (on 1.16; 'fertigbauen', 'weiterbauen'); p. 131 ('weiterbauen'); Elliger, *Propheten*, p. 117 n. 1 (on 1.16; 'wiederbauen', 'neubauen', 'fertigbauen'); Meyers and Meyers, *Haggai, Zechariah*, p. 357; Van der Woude, 'Serubbabel', p. 151.

49. Van der Woude, 'Serubbabel', p. 151. Meyers and Meyers, *Haggai, Zechariah*, p. 357, note that while 'it may seem odd to the modern reader to find a prophecy that Yahweh's temple will be built by a Davidide when such an edifice is about to be completed, the biblical mentality did not preclude the erection of a new structure in addition to the existence of an actual temple in the restoration community'. The extent of the work, either creating a new structure or refurbishing an old one, 'would be far less relevant than the fact that actual work would take place'.

50. In general, היכל is used for the central sanctuary (twice for the sanctuary in Silo [1 Sam 1.9 and 3.3]; frequently for the temple in Jerusalem [e.g. 2 Kgs 18.16; 23.4; Isa. 44.28; Jer. 7.4; Ezek. 8.16]); it is used for the Second Temple in Hag. 2.18 and Ezra 3.10.

51. Van der Woude, 'Serubbabel', p. 151; Cook, *Prophecy*, p. 136 n. 48. The difference in terminology is also noted by Marinkovic, 'Zechariah 1–8', p. 101, but he does not interpret it as referring to a future temple.

52. See R.G. Hamerton-Kelly, 'The Temple and the Origins of Jewish Apocalyptic', *VT* 20 (1970), pp. 1-15 (1-4). Compare R.E. Clements, *God and Temple* (Oxford: Basil Blackwell, 1965), p. 133, 'the post-exilic Jewish community did have a real experience of the divine presence, usually interpreted in terms of the spirit, even though they held to the promise that they would experience the full and complete enjoyment of it in the future'. See also the discussion of the notion in Jewish literature of the Second Temple period that the exile was not yet over by M.A. Knibb ('The Exile in the Literature of the Intertestamental Period', *HeyJ* 17 [1976], pp. 253-72 [271-72]) and N.T. Wright (*Christian Origins and the Question*

development from elements present in Zech. 6.12-13.

At the end of the oracle, the angel says that 'those who are far off shall come and help to build the temple of the LORD'. This has been taken as another element that may support a future temple interpretation.[53] This may be right, but it is difficult to be absolutely certain. The case would be much stronger if one could be sure that 'those who are far off' include Gentiles. Unfortunately, as Meyers and Meyers write,[54] 'it is nearly impossible to determine with certainty whether the statement here pertains to the exiled Judeans and/or to other non-Yahwist groups'. An exclusive interpretation (exiled Judeans only)[55] could be supported from passages like Zech. 2.11 (cf. Isa. 57.19; 60.4, 9). An inclusive interpretation (exiled Judeans and also Gentiles)[56] could be supported from passages like Zech. 8.22-23 (cf. Hag. 2.7-9; Isa. 49.1).

*The Emphasis Markers.* If Zemah is a future figure, and if the emphasis markers (in particular the casus pendens construction, and also the repeated personal pronoun) are there to indicate contrast, who then is the figure with whom Zemah is contrasted? The most obvious answer is Zerubbabel, to whom at least part of the elements of the prophecy (like the building of the temple) could be applied. That is, the building of the היכל יהוה and the ruling on the throne—these are things which Zemah will do, and in these he is distinguished from Zerubbabel, who built the בית יהוה and who was a governor under Persian authority.

It is tempting to extrapolate from this contrast to a particular reason for stating this contrast, for example that the prophet is combating strong messianic aspirations either on the side of Zerubbabel or on the side of other people. This is possible, and one could imagine a situation in which this happened. It is not impossible that a segment of the

*of God*. I. *The New Testament and the People of God* [London: SPCK; Minneapolis: Fortress Press, 1992], pp. 268-70, 299-301; *Christian Origins and the Question of God*. II. *Jesus and the Victory of God* [London: SPCK, 1996], pp. xvii-xviii, 126-27).

53. Lagrange, 'Prophéties', p. 72.

54. Meyers and Meyers, *Haggai, Zechariah*, p. 364.

55. So Rignell, *Nachtgesichte*, p. 238; Wallis, 'Erwägungen', p. 235; P.R. Ackroyd, *Studies in The Religious Tradition of the Old Testament* (London: SCM Press, 1987), p. 160; Meyers and Meyers, *Haggai, Zechariah*, pp. 364-65.

56. So Marti, *Dodekapropheton*, p. 421; Mitchell, *Haggai and Zechariah*, p. 193; Petitjean, *Oracles*, p. 300; Van der Woude, *Zacharia*, pp. 111, 118; Hanhart, *Sacharja 1–8*, pp. 440, 443.

society of Yehud directed their expectations of the restoration of the monarchy towards the figure of Zerubbabel. This has actually been argued by a number of scholars.

There is, however, no direct evidence in the visions to support this speculation. Attempts to find evidence for such royal aspirations in the prophecies of Zechariah's contemporary Haggai are misguided, as I will argue in Chapter 7. What Zechariah does is to repeat (in his own words and with a particular emphasis) the old promise of a future ruler, and to give the high priest a crown as a sign that this promise will one day be fulfilled. If my interpretation of the identity of Zemah is correct, then it cannot be maintained that Zechariah was one of the propagandists of giving Zerubbabel a role in the restoration of the monarchy.

## 4. *Conclusion*

In this Chapter I have studied the double presentation of Zemah in the silhouette in Zechariah 3 and the more detailed portrait in Zechariah 6. I have reviewed the diverse features of the two portraits, and then tested proposals for the identification of Zemah against these features. I have argued that the view which identifies Zemah with Zerubbabel faces a number of problems. These include (a) the crowning of Joshua rather than Zerubbabel, (b) the use of the name Zemah rather than Zerubbabel, (c) the discontinuity conveyed by the name Zemah when properly understood, and (d) the future reference of most of the elements in the description of Zemah. The way these problems are addressed within the framework of an interpretation which identifies Zemah with Zerubbabel fail to satisfy.

The view which considers Zemah to refer to an unidentified future figure can deal with the details of the portrait of Zemah in a much more satisfactory way. If Zemah is indeed a future figure, who will build the temple, and who will rule, then this oracle can be said to be messianic in the sense described in Chapter 1. It would imply that around the year 520, at the time the temple was rebuilt, and yet in 'a day of small things',[57] the prophet Zechariah pointed the people of Jerusalem to look

---

57. Scholars have rightly raised the question whether Zechariah would view his own time, which he described as 'a day of small things' (Zech. 4.10), as a messianic age; as Siebeneck writes, the miserable conditions of Jerusalem make 'it unbelievable that Ag and Za proclaim Zorobabel as the Messias and ascribe to him future

to the future, when better things would come, including a ruler who would truly build the temple. The choice of the name Zemah implied that Zerubbabel was not that ruler.

Perhaps I can clarify my argument if I use the adjective *royal* for 'pertaining to a king, his dignity or office' and use the adjective *royalist* for 'supporting a king or a king's rights'.[58] When the words are taken in this way, I can present my position like this. The צמח oracles in Zechariah 3 and 6 are royal, that is they deal with a figure who is a king, hence my phrase 'royal figure'; however, the צמח oracles are not royalist, that is, they do not announce, encourage or instigate a restoration of the monarchy in the person of Zerubbabel, the presumed referent of the royal figure called צמח. The discontinuity evoked by the use of the name צמח (with its background in Jeremiah 22–23) and the fact that YHWH will bring him are features which suggest that this is a messianic, rather than a royalist, oracle.

This may be a correct interpretation of the text as we have it now, but what if the present text is actually a combination of separate oracles, or a rewritten version of an original oracle? Would that not show that the ZZ identification is true after all? I will deal with that question in the next chapter.

universal domination' ('Messianism', p. 327 [abbreviations original]; cf. Lagrange, 'Prophéties', p. 72).

58. These definitions correspond to the ones found in *OED* s.v. royal: '2. Of rank, etc. Of or pertaining to a sovereign, or the dignity or office of a sovereign'; and s.v. royalist: '1. A supporter or adherent of the sovereign or the sovereign's rights, esp. in times of civil war, rebellion, or seccession' (the dictionary notes that the word can also be used as an adjective, but does not provide a definition of the meaning of the word in this use).

Chapter 5

VISIONS AND ORACLES—ON THE ORIGIN AND COMPOSITION OF
ZECHARIAH 3.8-10 AND 6.9-15

In the first Chapter of this book (section entitled 'Visions and Oracles')
I mentioned the issue of the relationship between the oracles and the
visions in Zechariah 1–6. A great majority of scholars hold to the view
that part of the oracular material in Zechariah 1–6 (usually 1.16-17;
2.10-17; 3.8-10; 4.6b-10a; 6.9-15; see Fig. 6 in Chapter 1) should be
considered as oracles which have been added to the vision reports. Over
the last 15 years or so, a small number of scholars has abandoned this
view and they interpret these portions as integral parts of the vision
reports.

Both מצא oracles which I have studies in the previous Chapters
belong to the disputed material. In the first Chapter I adopted the
strategy to explain the text as we have it now, and then in a later
Chapter to come back to the whole issue. This is what I propose to do in
this Chapter. In the first part I will discuss the criteria used for establishing the origin of Zech. 3.8-10 and 6.9-15. In the second part I will
discuss how these criteria are applied with respect to the composition of
Zech. 3.8-10. In the third part I will do the same with respect to the
composition of Zech. 6.9-15.

## 1. Criteria for Establishing the Origin of the Oracles in Zechariah 3 and 6

Redditt has recently complained that there is often not much method in
deciding that part of the oracles are secondary:[1] scholars 'routinely
eliminate the oracles and exhortations as additions'. A discussion of the
grounds on which such decisions rest is often lacking. This is unsatisfactory.

1.  Redditt, *Haggai, Zechariah*, p. 39.

a. *The Quest for Grounds*

In itself the possibility that oracle material ends up in a context where it does not belong originally is one that cannot be dismissed from the outset. There is enough evidence from prophetic books that this was one of the techniques used in the composition of prophetic literature. The prophetic books do not provide a chronological record of the prophet's utterances. Concerns other than chronology may have operated in the arranging of material. The issue is not whether material from a different context was added, but what criteria and arguments are used to decide that it happened in a particular case.

*What Makes the Case of Zechariah 1–6 Special.* The quest for arguments becomes even more imperative when one looks at the situation in Zechariah 1–6. When one looks at the dates given to the material which is considered to be secondary one finds that scholars date some of the material later than the vision cycle, and some earlier. The earlier material is dated to a time before the arrival of Zerubbabel in Judah–Jerusalem, and therefore before the visions,[2] and even before what as far as the evidence goes seems to be the start of Zechariah's prophetic ministry, which Zech. 1.1 dates in October or November 520.

So then, the first special assumption these scholars have to make is this: Zechariah had a prophetic ministry before the one recorded in Zech. 1.1. There is no independent evidence available to support such a claim of a prophetic ministry of Zechariah before the date given in 1.1.[3] As such this observation does not prove that there was no such ministry, but it raises the issue of the reason for assuming such an earlier ministry. What is it that makes it necessary to assume a prophetic ministry of Zechariah dating to a period before the ministry mentioned in Zech. 1.1?

The second special assumption concerns the nature of the process of composition of the book one then has to reconstruct in order to accom-

2.    Horst, *Propheten*, pp. 210-11, 222, 226, 232, 239; Petitjean, *Oracles*, pp. 269, 286; Amsler, 'Visions', pp. 265-66; Redditt, 'Night Visions', p. 255; Redditt, *Haggai, Zechariah*, p. 42. A small number of scholars date not only oracles, but also complete visions to a setting in Babylon before 520. E.g. Galling, *Studien*, pp. 109-26 (on 1.16-17; 2.10-16; 6.9-15) and pp. 127-48 (on 3.8-10 and 4.6-10); Sinclair, 'Redaction', pp. 38-39. For a discussion of Galling's proposals, see Seybold, *Bilder*, pp. 17-18.

3.    Eichrodt, 'Typos', p. 511.

modate the theory in this particular case. If part of the oracles date from a time before the visions, a reconstruction of the redaction of the book should be made which contains at least this element, that the prophet or the redactor had the vision cycle before him and decided to add some earlier material at different places throughout the visions block. While such a procedure cannot be said to be impossible, it is a highly unusual one. In other cases scholars usually reconstruct a redaction process which goes just the other way around: material of a later date is added to an existing body of earlier material. So, again, this raises the issue of the reasons scholars give for the assumption of this unusual procedure.

What, then, are the reasons for assuming a prophetic ministry of Zechariah before the date in Zech. 1.1, and for assuming that material from before the visions was inserted into the collection of vision reports, with its unusual implications for the nature of the composition of the book? The reason is not difficult to find: it is to safeguard a particular interpretation of certain parts of the oracles. To be more precise: it is to safeguard the identification of the royal figure called Zemah with Zerubbabel.

In the צמח oracles, Zemah is a future figure, as most scholars agree. Now, Zerubbabel was already present in Jerusalem at the time of the date of the visions given in Zech. 1.1 (15 February 519).[4] So, in order to maintain the ZZ identification, one is forced to date the oracles to an earlier period, before Zerubbabel's arrival in Jerusalem, and therefore before the visions. This implies that the accuracy of the ZZ identification determines whether it is really necessary to adopt these assumptions concerning the oracles being earlier than the visions. If the ZZ identification is correct, then there is a problem which can be solved by dating the oracles to a time before the visions, with all its implications. If the identification is incorrect, then there would be no need to date the צמח oracles to a time before the visions.

I elaborate these points because the implications of the ZZ identification for the nature of the composition of the book are in most cases not realized. Those who at the start of their investigation of the צמח oracles commit themselves to these assumptions of an earlier date of the צמח oracles expose themselves to the charge of begging the question: the assumptions only become necessary once a particular interpretation is accepted. But one should not make that result of the investigation the

---

4.   See Chapter 1 (section entitled 'Whatever Happened to Zerubbabel?').

point of departure. The position to start from is to investigate whether it is possible to make sense of these oracles without adopting the popular but unusual assumptions concerning an earlier date of the material. That is what I have tried to do in the preceding Chapters.

In the discussion of the question of the secondary origin of part of the oracular material in Zechariah 1–6 one needs to distinguish two issues: (a) the composition technique used in prophetic books of combining material from different contexts and backgrounds, and (b) the application of that in this particular case, with its unusual implications for the composition of this part of the book, that is, that in an existing unified core of material oracles are inserted which predate that core.

### b. *The One-Point Principle*

Those scholars who do present arguments for their position usually mention one or two specific reasons, which I will call the One-Point Principle and the Coherence Principle. In this and the next section I will discuss these two principles.

Rothstein, who was the first to make a case for separating within the oracles between original and secondary material, argued[5] that each vision intends to convey only one main point (*nur einen Hauptgedanken ausspricht und aussprechen soll*). Everything that is not related to the one point falls outside the framework of the original vision report and is considered secondary. Rothstein applies this to the first vision report and concludes that 1.16-17 is secondary. These verses contain statements of Zechariah, but are not original in the vision report. The same is true for 2.10-17, 3.8-10, 4.6b-10a and 6.9-15.

This principle assumes a very specific relationship between visions and oracles. The vision sets the agenda for the oracles. Rothstein does not give reasons why he believes that this One-Point Principle is operating in the visions in Zechariah 1–6. He simply states it, without providing a justification. Another problem with principles like the One-Point Principle is that they are difficult to prove or disprove. The absence of oracular material that goes beyond the presumed one point proves the principle, but if on the other hand there is material in an oracle that goes beyond the one point it can be labelled as secondary, and once again the principle is established.

Other scholars have claimed that with respect to the dynamics of vision and oracle more or less the opposite of what Rothstein suggests

5. Rothstein, *Nachtgesichte*, pp. 55, 70-71, 87-88.

is true. The agenda is not so much set by the vision: the oracles may explain elements of the vision, but at times they may go beyond such an explanation. Tigchelaar comments that the oracles came to Zechariah by mediation of the angel, and that the angel not only gave a decipherment of the obscure visions, but sometimes added divine oracles which went beyond a simple explanation of the symbols.[6]

After a study of the first vision report in Zechariah 1, Hanhart reaches a similar conclusion, indicating the implications for the other vision reports in Zechariah 1–6: vision and explanation are organised in such a way that the more important role is given to an explanation and proclamation, the specific contents of which go far beyond what could be interpreted as explanation of elements of the vision.[7]

Rudolph, who endorses Rothstein's One-Point Principle when he discusses 3.7-10 (and concludes to the secondary nature of these verses),[8] apparently has a problem with applying the principle to the situation in Zechariah 1. The oracles in the first vision report in that chapter are found in vv. 14-17:

> So the angel who talked with me said to me, 'Cry out, Thus says the LORD of hosts: I am exceedingly jealous for Jerusalem and for Zion.

6.    Tigchelaar, 'Ange', pp. 353-54, 'les oracles arrivent à Zacharie par l'intermédiaire de l'ange. L'ange qui parlait à Zacharie ne donne pas seulement des déchiffrements des visions obscures, il y ajoute aussi quelquefois des oracles divins qui dépassent une simple explication des symboles'. Cf. Long's discussion ('Reports of Visions', pp. 357-63), in which he shows that the connection between divine proclamation and vision in vision reports is not necessarily as static as an approach like that of Rothstein would suggest. For a brief survey of different proposals for the classification of vision reports, see S. Amsler, 'La parole visionnaire des prophètes', *VT* 31 (1981), pp. 359-63 (363 n. 8); Niditch, *Symbolic Vision*, pp. 2-7. Niditch (pp. 5-7) criticizes Long's classification of visions for lacking sufficient precision, and offers a diachronic approach instead of the usual synchronic approaches.

7.    Hanhart, *Sacharja*, p. 77, 'Als besonders ausgeprägtes Formelement, in dessen Licht die analogen Elemente der folgenden Gesichte erst deutlich erkennbar sind, muß in ersten Gesicht eine Zuordnung von Bildhälfte und Sachhälfte, Gleichnis und Deutung von der Art gesehen werden, daß das Gewicht der Aussage auf einer Deutung bzw. Verkündigung liegt, deren Einzelaussagen weit über das hinausgehen, was sich als Deutung der Bildelemente erklären läßt...' Cf. Seybold, *Bilder*, p. 108, 'Der Textfolge Bild und Bilddeutung über den Sprecher-Boten und Interpreten Jahwes korrespondiert die gegenläufige Sinnfolge Jahwewort und dramatisierte Bildidee, wodurch die scheinbare Balance aufgehoben ist und das Deutewort mit dem Endgewicht versehen wird...'

8.    See his discussion of 3.8-10 (Rudolph, *Haggai, Sacharja*, p. 94).

And I am very angry with the nations that are at ease; for while I was angry but a little they furthered the disaster. *Therefore, thus says the LORD, I have returned to Jerusalem with compassion; my house shall be built in it, says the LORD of hosts, and the measuring line shall be stretched out over Jerusalem. Cry again, Thus says the LORD of hosts: My cities shall again overflow with prosperity, and the LORD will again comfort Zion and again choose Jerusalem'.*

The first two verses of this passage are generally held to be original, the last two (in italics) are considered to be secondary. Rudolph argues[9] that there is such a clear connection between vv. 16-17 and vv. 12-15 that there are no grounds to eliminate vv. 16-17. He then makes the observation that the words עוד קרא לאמר at the beginning of v. 17 (resuming קרא לאמר of v. 14) indicate that the Interpreting Angel is still speaking.[10] One can add to this[11] that not only do vv. 16-17 connect well with what precedes, the vision report would have a somewhat strange ending with the reference to YHWH's anger towards the nations in v. 15. Only vv. 16-17 give a satisfying answer to the complaint of the community expressed by the angel of YHWH in v. 12 (compare עד־מתי אתה לא־תרחם in v. 12 with שבתי לירושלם ברחמים in v. 16).

In my view, these are good reasons for considering vv. 16-17 as an original part of the vision report. The next thing to look at is what this tells us about the relationship between the vision (vv. 8-13) and the oracles (vv. 14-17). There is actually very little explanation in the oracles: various elements of the vision, such as the 'the myrtle trees in the glen', the colours of the horses, and also the observation, 'all the earth remains at rest', are left unexplained. The oracles take up only one element, the complaint of the angel in 1.12, and develop that particular element.

In a sense one could still call this a One-Point approach, but this is apparently not what Rothstein had in view. In the first vision report it is only one point from the vision that is picked up and developed in the oracles, while other elements (like the observation, 'all the earth remains at rest', not a minor point in a time when memories of usurpation and power struggles in the Persian empire are still fresh) are left to speak

9. Rudolph, *Haggai, Sacharja*, pp. 79-80.
10. The only alternative is to see the phrase עוד קרא לאמר as a deliberate attempt to imitate the style of the Interpreting Angel who spoke קרא לאמר of v. 14, which I find unsatisfactory.
11. With Van der Woude, 'Serubbabel', pp. 141-42.

for themselves. This is different from Rothstein's claim that the visions actually have only one main point. His approach is unduly restrictive and makes the relationship between vision and oracles too static.

The absence of a justification for the One-Point Principle and its failure to deal satisfactorily with the situation in the first vision report are weaknesses which impair the usefulness of this principle. The situation appears to be somewhat more complex than the One-Point Principle suggests. The vision can make more than one point, out of which the oracular material may take up just one, which it then develops, even in a way that goes beyond an explanation of elements in the vision. If this is true in the first vision report, there is no reason to exclude that the same situation occurs in the other vision reports.

Rothstein constructs too static a relationship between visions and oracles, and makes the visions too prominent, undervaluing the oracles. The first vision report in Zechariah 1 suggests that it is better to see the relationship between visions and oracles as more dynamic.

c. *The Coherence Principle*
A second reason for distinguishing within the oracles between original and secondary material is the presence of tensions or contradictions within the oracles themselves (this is what I call the Coherence Principle). Most recently, Redditt states this principle in the following words: 'visions frequently include oracles...and later apocalyptic literature characteristically combined visions with exhortations. The real issue is whether all the material in the second section is self-consistent'.[12]

So, when one talks about coherence here it is not coherence between visions and oracles, but coherence within the oracular material itself. In general, scholars recognize a continuity between oracles and the preceding visions,[13] even those scholars who assign a secondary origin to the oracles.[14] As such, it is an interesting thing to observe that those who

12. Redditt, *Haggai, Zechariah*, p. 39.
13. E.g. Amsler, 'Parole Visionnaire', p. 361.
14. E.g. Rothstein, *Nachtgesichte*, p. 88 on Zech. 3.8-10, 'Der Inhalt von v. 8-10 knüpft zwar an das vorausgehende Gesicht an...' Cf. Baldwin, *Haggai, Zechariah*, p. 93; Horst, *Propheten*, pp. 210-11; Seybold, *Bilder*, pp. 16-17, 19; Petersen, *Haggai and Zechariah*, pp. 120-22. With respect to the connection between 6.9-15 and what precedes, scholars (including those who assume a different origin for vv. 9-15, e.g. Ackroyd, *Exile*, pp. 182-83; Rignell, *Nachtgesichte*, p. 241; Beuken, *Haggai–Sacharja 1–8*, p. 317; Rudolph, *Haggai, Sacharja*, pp. 126, 128) point to the arrival

find secondary material in the oracles also find this continuity. At the same time it makes it difficult to argue convincingly against the notion of secondary material: apparently unity of theme is not enough to secure unity of origin.

But with the Coherence Principle one at least has a specific criterion, and so in the next two parts of the Chapter I will discuss the application of the Coherence Principle to the צמח oracles. Two things will become clear: (a) criteria for the evaluation of the presence or absence of coherence appear to be quite subjective and may vary from one scholar to another. And (b) it is at times difficult to avoid the impression of a certain amount of circular reasoning, and I realize that my discussion below is open to that charge as well.

### d. *Conclusion*

Scholars employ two criteria for establishing the secondary origin of parts of the oracles in the vision reports in Zechariah 1–6: the One-Point Principle and the Coherence Principle. I have tried to show that the One-Point Principle is an unduly restrictive principle, and that the situation in the first vision report (in Zechariah 1) shows that the relationship between vision and oracles is more dynamic. I will leave an evaluation of the Coherence Principle until after we have seen it at work in the discussion concerning the origin of Zech. 3.8-10 and 6.9-15. I have also indicated that the view that dates the צמח oracles to a time before the visions has some unusual complications for the composition of Zechariah 1–6.

### 2. *The* צמח *Oracle in Zech. 3.8-10*

The elements in Zech. 3.8-10 which have raised the suspicion of indicating the secondary nature of the passage or some of its parts are mainly of a formal nature. They include (a) the appeal to 'listen' in v. 8 (which is thought to be out of place in the middle of a passage), (b) the introduction of Joshua's associates, which had not been mentioned before, and (c) the reference in the third person to Joshua in v. 9, while in v. 8 he was addressed in the second person.

---

of exiles from Babylon as a first instalment of the fulfilment of the promise in the preceding vision that God has set his Spirit at rest in the north country (6.8).

Petersen, for example, writes about the 'call to attention' שִׁמְעוּ־נָא in v. 8:[15] 'The presence of this formula suggests strongly that v. 8 begins a new unit rather than continues an earlier speech'. I agree that v. 8 'begins a new unit', but seeing this as excluding the possibility that v. 8 'continues an earlier speech' is in my view an argument based on a false dilemma. Verse 8 both 'begins a new unit' and 'continues an earlier speech'. The presence of שִׁמְעוּ־נָא in the course of speech is not a problem for coherence: it can be paralleled from examples elsewhere.[16] In Zech. 3.8 the appeal to listen may also serve as a marker of the transition of speech addressed to Joshua only to speech addressed to Joshua and his colleagues.

The extension of the addressees to include Joshua's colleagues without them being mentioned before is, for Redditt,[17] an indication of the secondary nature of v. 8 (and v. 10; v. 9 is original in his view). I find it hard to see why this extension would be so significant as to point to secondary origin, given the fact that the high priest operates within a body, which makes an inclusion of the other members of the body quite a natural development.

I now come to the third supposed indication of the secondary nature of 3.8-10: the reference in the third person to Joshua in v. 9. It may be noted that the shift from second to third person already occurs in v. 8 and is linked to the change in perceived audience, Joshua on his own in v. 7, Joshua and his colleagues in vv. 8-10. There is no need to consider the shift in number in v. 8 as evidence of secondary status:[18] in Hebrew it is not unusual for a vocative to be followed by a statement about the people just addressed, but now in the third person. Waltke and O'Connor write in their study of Hebrew syntax, 'After a vocative, a modifying phrase or clause regularly uses the third-person pronoun (as also in Classical Arabic) and not the second-person pronoun as in English and other languages'.[19] As an example, they mention Mic. 1.1

---

15. Petersen, *Haggai and Zechariah*, p. 208; cf. Reventlow, *Haggai, Sacharja*, p. 55.

16. Van der Woude, *Zacharia*, p. 71, mentions Gen. 27.43; Exod. 18.19; Deut. 6.3; Jer. 34.4.

17. 'Night Visions', p. 254.

18. Contra Galling, *Studien*, p. 146 n. 3.

19. See Waltke and O'Connor, *Syntax* §4.7d, and GKB §144p; cf. Keil, *Propheten*, p. 558; Mitchell, *Haggai and Zechariah*, p. 160; Rudolph, *Haggai, Sacharja*,

שמעו עמים כלם, where the suffix attached to כל is a third person suffix. Once this shift of audience has been made in v. 8, the continuation by referring to Joshua in the third person in v. 9 is not a problem.

In conclusion, two of the three elements that have been taken to indicate the secondary nature of Zech. 3.8-10 can be relatively easily interpreted in a way in which they are not so disjunctive as to indicate that these verses have been added. The third can be explained as a grammatical peculiarity of the Hebrew language. From the perspective of coherence, therefore, there are no strong reasons to consider vv. 8-10 as secondary.

### 3. *The Composition of Zech. 6.9-15*

I now turn to the discussion of 6.9-15. Matters are far more complicated here. The literary integrity of Zech. 6.9-15 has been questioned from different perspectives. The views on the composition of 6.9-15 can be grouped into three categories. (a) MT is a combination of two (or more) oracles of separate origin. (b) MT is a reworking by a redactor of an original text which is not impossible to reconstruct; in the original text either (i) there was no command to set a crown on the head of someone, or (ii) there was a command to set a crown on the head of Zerubbabel, or (iii) there was a command to set a crown on the head of Joshua and one on the head of Zerubbabel.[20] (c) MT is not without difficulties, but it is preferable to stick to the text as we have it in MT.

This is an issue of considerable complexity, among other things because the reasons for suspicion about MT being a reworking partly arose from a particular interpretation of certain elements of the passages. Having discussed the interpretation of the צמח oracles in the preceding Chapters I now proceed to an evaluation of these proposals.

#### a. *Literary Layers in 6.9-15*
Different proposals have been made by those who find literary layers in Zech. 6.11-15. I will discuss the four as set out in Figure 13:

p. 98; Amsler, *Aggée; Zacharie 1–8*, p. 82 n. 1; Van der Woude, p. 72; Laato, *Josiah*, pp. 240-41.

20. With some scholars, one finds a combination of (a) and (b).

Figure 13. *Original and Secondary in the Oracles in Zech. 6.11-15*

| original | secondary |
|----------|-----------|
| 11, 14-15 | *12-13* |
| 11a, 14-15 | *11b-13* |
| 11-12 | *13-15* |
| 11-13 | *14-15* |

*The Secondary Origin of vv. 12-13.* The first proposal is to find the secondary material in vv. 12-13.[21] In that case the first layer would have run like this:

ויהי דבר־יהוה אלי לאמר
לקוח מאת הגולה מחלדי ומאת טוביה ומאת ידעיה
ובאת אתה ביום ההוא ובאת בית יאשיה בן־צפניה אשר־באו מבבל
ולקחת כסף־וזהב ועשית עטרות
ושמת בראש יהושע בן־יהוצדק הכהן הגדול
והעטרת תהיה לחלם ולטוביה ולידעיה ולחן בן־צפניה לזכרון בהיכל יהוה
ורחוקים יבאו ובנו בהיכל יהוה
וידעתם כי־יהוה צבאות שלחני אליכם
והיה אם־שמוע תשמעון בקול יהוה אלהיכם

And the second layer would be:

ואמרת אליו לאמר כה אמר יהוה צבאות לאמר
הנה־איש צמח שמו ומתחתיו יצמח
ובנה את־היכל יהוה
והוא יבנה את־היכל יהוה
והוא־ישא הוד וישב ומשל על־כסאו
והיה כהן על־כסאו
ועצת שלום תהיה בין שניהם

The problem with this proposal is that it reconstructs a first layer which includes the command to set a crown on the head of Joshua, but does not contain an explanation of the meaning of that symbolic action. Such a text would have been impossible to understand for its first audience, which makes this a highly unlikely proposal.[22] We would have a symbolic action without a prophetic message.

---

21. Wallis considers vv. 9-10abα, 11, 14 as original, and vv. 10bβ, 12-13, 15 a later addition (Wallis, 'Erwägungen', pp. 234-35); Petersen finds the following layers: vv. 10-11, 14 + vv. 12-13 (*Haggai and Zechariah*, pp. 121, 173). Schöttler considers vv. 12, 13b-14 as secondary (*Gottesvolk*, pp. 380-81).

22. Amsler, *Aggée; Zacharie 1–8*, p. 106; Van der Woude, 'Serubbabel', p. 149. It would be saying too much that there are no symbolic actions without an expla-

*The Secondary Origin of vv. 11b-13.* Redditt has tried to solve this problem by proposing to consider v. 11b as part of the secondary material.[23] In that case there is no command to set the crown on the head of someone in the original text, and thus no symbolic action which invites an explanation. The original edition was directed to exiles who were still in Babylon and speaks only of the crown (not necessarily a royal crown) to be made and to be deposited in the temple, and invites people far off to come and help to build the temple:

ויהי דבר־יהוה אלי לאמר
לקוח מאת הגולה מחלדי ומאת טוביה ומאת ידעיה
ובאת אתה ביום ההוא ובאת בית יאשיה בן־צפניה אשר־באו מבבל
ולקחת כסף־וזהב ועשית עטרות
והעטרת תהיה לחלם ולטוביה ולידעיה ולחן בן־צפניה לזכרון בהיכל יהוה
ורחוקים יבאו ובנו בהיכל יהוה
וידעתם כי־יהוה צבאות שלחני אליכם
והיה אם־שמוע תשמעון בקול יהוה אלהיכם

Redditt reconstructs two layers of redaction of the original edition. In the first redaction vv. 11b-13 were added, at that stage v. 11b read ושמת בראש זרבבל:

ושמת בראש זרבבל
ואמרת אליו לאמר כה אמר יהוה צבאות לאמר
הנה־איש צמח שמו ומתחתיו יצמח
ובנה את־היכל יהוה
והוא יבנה את־היכל יהוה
והוא־ישא הוד וישב ומשל על־כסאו
והיה כהן על־כסאו
ועצת שלום תהיה בין שניהם

In a later redaction, the name of Zerubbabel was replaced by that of Joshua:

nation, but it is unusual; compare G. Fohrer, *Die symbolische Handlungen der Propheten* (ATANT, 54; Zürich: Zwingli-Verlag, 1968), p. 18, pp. 70-71 (on Zech. 6.9-15), and pp. 96-97, 'Die meisten Berichte haben ein Wort bei sich, das die symbolische Handlung deuten soll'. This is what in his view distinguishes prophetic actions from magic practices, which have power in themselves, but lack an explanation. But occasionally one does not find an explanation, so that one can conclude that the explanation 'ist also weder regelmässig vorhanden noch unbedingt erforderlich'.

23. Redditt, 'Night Visions', p. 253; also Redditt, *Haggai, Zechariah*, p. 40.

וְשַׂמְתָּ בָרֹאשׁ יְהוֹשֻׁעַ בֶּן־יְהוֹצָדָק הַכֹּהֵן הַגָּדוֹל
וְאָמַרְתָּ אֵלָיו לֵאמֹר כֹּה אָמַר יְהוָה צְבָאוֹת לֵאמֹר
הִנֵּה־אִישׁ צֶמַח שְׁמוֹ וּמִתַּחְתָּיו יִצְמָח
וּבָנָה אֶת־הֵיכַל יְהוָה
וְהוּא יִבְנֶה אֶת־הֵיכַל יְהוָה
וְהוּא־יִשָּׂא הוֹד וְיָשַׁב וּמָשַׁל עַל־כִּסְאוֹ
וְהָיָה כֹהֵן עַל־כִּסְאוֹ
וַעֲצַת שָׁלוֹם תִּהְיֶה בֵּין שְׁנֵיהֶם

One of the problems with Redditt's proposal is that it does not explain the future reference of the coming of Zemah (both in 3.8 and 6.12), whom Redditt identifies with Zerubbabel (in the first redaction; the second redaction was meant to provide for the identification with Joshua), who was already in Jerusalem at the time the first redaction occurred.[24] Apart from that, it suffers some major weaknesses, which it shares with all proposals which assume a rewriting of the text in which a clause about setting the crown on the head of Joshua is either added or replaces a similar clause which mentions Zerubbabel. I will give a more extensive discussion of these problems in the next section ('Zech. 6.9-15 as a Rewritten Oracle'), and will only briefly mention five problems here.

If my interpretation of the meaning and the function of the name צמח is correct, (a) a simple identification of Zemah with Zerubbabel (first redaction) will not do. If Zerubbabel (or, in the later redaction: Joshua) were the one to whom 'a man called Zemah' refers, (b) why is the oracle set in the third person, not in the second, and (c) why is it 'a man called Zemah', and not a phrase with the article, 'the man called Zemah'? (d) If Joshua in the second redaction ends up as the one Zemah refers to, who is the other person in the form שניהם? The motive of the redactors which Redditt reconstructs for the second edition in which Joshua takes the place of Zerubbabel, that is, the elevation of the priesthood,[25] can only be held on the basis of (e) a reconstruction of the his-

---

24. 'Night Visions', p. 256. In his commentary on 3.8 he states (*Haggai, Zechariah*, p. 66; cf. 'Night Visions', p. 258) that the present text should be interpreted as indicating Joshua as the one about whom the צמח passages are speaking, though originally 3.8 and 6.12 'designated Zerubbabel as the Branch'; he then adds, 'It is possible, though on the whole it seems less likely, that the reference is to some future, unspecified person'. On the clause וּמִתַּחְתָּיו יִצְמָח, the only comment is, 'the prophet employed a word play based on the root *ṣmḥ*: "Branch... will branch out", nothing is said about the future reference.

25. 'Night Visions', p. 257.

tory of this part of the Persian period and the position of the priesthood in that period which has become more and more implausible.

*The Secondary Origin of vv. 13-15.* Others think that originally the passage included v. 12, and the secondary material starts in v. 13.[26] The original oracle finished at v. 12:

ויהי דבר־יהוה אלי לאמר

לקוח מאת הגולה מחלדי ומאת טוביה ומאת ידעיה

ובאת אתה ביום ההוא ובאת בית יאשיה בן־צפניה אשר־באו מבבל

ולקחת כסף־וזהב ועשית עטרות

ושמת בראש יהושע בן־יהוצדק הכהן הגדול

ואמרת אליו לאמר כה אמר יהוה צבאות לאמר

הנה־איש צמח שמו ומתחתיו יצמח

ובנה את־היכל יהוה

The rest is secondary:

והוא יבנה את־היכל יהוה

והוא־ישא הוד וישב ומשל על־כסאו

והיה כהן על־כסאו

ועצת שלום תהיה בין שניהם

והעטרת תהיה לחלם ולטוביה ולידעיה ולחן בן־צפניה לזכרון בהיכל יהוה

ורחוקים יבאו ובנו בהיכל יהוה

וידעתם כי־יהוה צבאות שלחני אליכם

והיה אם־שמוע תשמעון בקול יהוה אלהיכם

The reasons for this way of dividing the passage are various, as the following discussion will show.

*Rignell.* Rignell claims[27] that in vv. 13-15 we have a later commentary of Zechariah himself, in which the prophet looks back and presents what is now a reality: things have happened as he predicted, Zerubbabel builds the temple, and Joshua enjoys high priestly honour, so that the new age has already started.

There are several problems with this view. (a) Rignell claims that the two 'and he [והוא]' in v. 13 refer to two different persons, the first one to Zerubbabel and the second one to Joshua.[28] This suggestion must be

---

26. Rignell, *Nachtgesichte*, pp. 230, 241; Petitjean, *Oracles*, pp. 289, 299-303; Amsler, *Aggée; Zacharie 1–8*, pp. 106-107.

27. Rignell, *Nachtgesichte*, pp. 230, 233, 241-42.

28. Rignell, *Nachtgesichte*, p. 231-33; a similar view in Ackroyd, *Exile*, p. 198. Redditt ('Night Visions', p. 252) attributes this view to Beuken, but that appears to

rejected[29] for reasons of Hebrew syntax. While הוא may be used as a demonstrative (or 'quasi-demonstrative', as it is called in recent studies of the syntax of biblical Hebrew),[30] it is never used to express the opposition 'this one...that one', a function of the 'true demonstrative' זה.[31]

(b) Rignell clearly struggles with the different verbal forms used in vv. 13-15 and fails to provide an adequate explanation of them. The Imperfect forms in v. 13 are interpreted as 'he is about to build' (*er ist im Begriff zu bauen*), that is, they present a process which at that moment is still going on. This is a possible use of an Imperfect form.[32] The problems start with the two Perfect forms in the second half of the verse. Rignell explains, 'The Perf[ect] is used, because Yahweh has destined him to rule as king. The second clause is in analogy with the first formed with the same "tense" of factuality: "He is a priest on his throne."'[33]

This is not a satisfying explanation of the change of verbal forms from Imperfect to Perfect forms. With verbs of action, events or actions which are simultaneous with the moment of speaking are expressed with Imperfect forms, not with Perfect forms.[34] Whether the action is commissioned by YHWH or not does not change this matter of syntax. The only way to make sense of the different verbal forms in vv. 13-15 is to take them as pointing to events in the future. This explains the

---

be a mistake: in Beuken's interpretation, the priest is subject only in the clause והיה כהן על־כסאו, not before (*Haggai–Sacharja 1–8*, p. 277), 'Vom Priester wird nur eines gesagt: והיה כהן על־כסאו'.

29. Amsler, *Aggée; Zacharie 1–8*, p. 109.

30. Waltke and O'Connor, *Syntax*, §17.3; Joüon and Muraoka, *Grammar*, §143j.

31. E.g. Job 1.16; see Waltke and O'Connor, *Syntax*, §17.3c; cf. Joüon and Muraoka, *Grammar*, §143c; Chary, *Aggée, Zacharie*, p. 112.

32. Joüon and Muraoka, *Grammar*, §113d.

33. 'Es wird Perf. gebraucht, denn es ist von Jahve über ihn bestimmt, dass er als König regieren soll. Der zweite Satz ist in Analogie zu dem ersten mit dem gleichen »Tempus« der Faktizität gebildet: »Er ist ein Priester auf seinem Thron.«' (*Nachtgeschichte*, p. 232); cf. p. 228 on the significance of the change in verbal forms.

34. See Joüon and Muraoka, *Grammar*, §112. The only exceptions are so-called performative utterances (not *Grammar*'s terminology, there it is 'an instantaneous action which, being performed at the very moment of the utterance, is assumed to belong to the past'), which are first person forms (Joüon and Muraoka, *Grammar*, §112f).

Imperfect forms,[35] and also the Perfect Consecutive forms in the verb-initial clauses.[36]

To sum up: the reasons which led Rignell to distinguish an original oracle and a later commentary by the prophet himself are defective, because they interpret the text in a way which goes against some basic rules of Hebrew grammar.

*Petitjean.* Petitjean finds three differences which point to the different origins of vv. 10-12 and 13-14: the difference in the name of one of the returned exiles (Heldai in v. 10 and Helem in v. 14), the difference in the destination of the crown (for Joshua in v. 11, to be deposited in the temple in v. 14), a difference in the role and the position of the high priest and the Davidide.

Petitjean's first point is the change from Heldai to Helem.[37] Some of

---

35. Joüon and Muraoka, *Grammar*, §113.

36. Joüon and Muraoka, *Grammar*, §119c.

37. For the interpretation of the phrase לחן בן־צפניה in v. 14, in which is a difference with יאשיהן בן־צפניה in v. 10, see A. Demsky, 'The Temple Steward Josiah ben Zephaniah', *IEJ* 31 (1981), pp. 100-102 (adopted by Petersen, *Haggai and Zechariah*, p. 278), who suggests that לחן is a noun, a title to refer to an official in charge of cultic apparel in the temple, a 'temple steward'. He compares the word to the Neo-Assyrian *laḫḫinnu* and the Aramaic לחן (e.g. Ananiah son of Azariah 'לחן of YHW the God in Elephantine the fortress' in some of the Elephantine Papyri). The masculine word is not found in the Old Testament, but the feminine לחנה is, so Demsky argues, present in the Aramaic of Dan. 5.2, 3, 23, where he proposes to translate 'a female administrator of the royal household', instead of the usual 'concubine, courtesan'. Zech. 6.14 would then be a case (and the only one) where the word is used in Hebrew. The preposition ל, which would be expected before it, was possibly lost by haplography or because of an inconsistency in the use of a series of prepositions (as in v. 10). Demsky considers it possible that the family name was associated with the office (as was the practice in the Second Temple period), which would explain the use of the patronymic only.

The weakest part of Demsky's case is the appeal to the use of לחנה in Dan. 5 (Schöttler, *Gottesvolk*, p. 160 n. 464). Demsky's translation ('a female administrator of the royal household') is not very probable because לחנה is used in parallel with שגלה: the phrase שגלתה ולחנתה seems to refer to two classes of women of the palace and harem (cf. the discussion in Goldingay, *Daniel*, pp. 100-101). But even though we have to reject this problematic interpretation by Demsky, this does not really affect his case concerning לחן in Zech. 6.14: the Aramaic word is found in some of the Elephantine Papyri and לחן in our verse may be the equivalent Hebrew word (perhaps the presence of the feminine לחנה with a different meaning in Dan. 5 should be explained as a case of homonymy).

the early versions[38] harmonize the readings, in two different directions: Peshitta reads Heldai on both occasions, Vulgate and Targum read Helem. This is an indication of the high antiquity of the two different readings of the name. The best way to explain the two forms seems to be that they are variants of the same name,[39] but the measure of the difference and the presence of the variants in one and the same passage make this a unique case. This solution is to be preferred above the suggestion that one of the two forms[40] was a nickname, because it is not clear why a nickname should have been used on either occasion.[41] Even if the two names are explained as variants of one name, this case of the two different names remains perplexing. The proper weight of this problem can only be assessed once the other differences have been reviewed.

Petitjean's second point concerns the destination of the crown. To find a difficulty with the crown being put on the head of Joshua the high priest first and then being deposited in the temple, is a judgment which

---

Another problem is that 'the son of Zephaniah' is referred to only by his patronymic. This is not uncommon in narrative (see Clines, 'X, X ben Y, ben Y: Personal names in Hebrew Narrative Style', *VT* 22 [1972], pp. 266-87 [282-87]), but it is more difficult to find a parallel to the use of the patronymic only in a list of names such as we have here. A list of offerings on a bowl from Arad, dated to the second half of the eighth century BCE (Aharoni, *Arad Inscriptions*, pp. 82-86, inscription 49 [ET *Arad Inscriptions*, pp. 80-84, inscription 49), seems to provide the closest parallel, but here either בן is plural (e.g. [on the base] 'the sons of בצל / the sons of קרח'), or the proper name is most likely a geographical name ([on the base] בנ.גלגל 'the son of Gilgal'); in the only line were בן seems to be used in the singular the text is defective ([row 4] צמה.נ... '[So]n of צמה'). Though not completely without problems, Demsky's proposal provides perhaps the least unattractive solution of the problem of the difference between לחן בן־צפניה in v. 14 and יאשיהן בן־צפניה (Demsky's proposal is adopted by, e.g., Petersen, *Haggai and Zechariah*, p. 278, but rejected by, e.g., Schöttler, *Gottesvolk*, p. 160 n. 464).

38. The LXX has translated the three names of the exiles as nouns, with different nouns for the first name (see the discussion in Petitjean, *Oracles*, pp. 274-76).

39. So Wellhausen, *Propheten*, p. 185; Meyers and Meyers, *Haggai, Zechariah*, p. 340; cf. Baldwin, *Haggai, Zechariah*, p. 137. Meyers and Meyers and Baldwin refer to the name חלב in 2 Sam. 23.29, which is written חלד in 1 Chron. 11.30, and חלדי in 1 Chron. 27.15. Rudolph (*Haggai, Sacharja*, p. 127), Van der Woude (*Zacharia*, p. 113), Schöttler (*Gottesvolk*, p. 160 n. 464), and Hanhart (*Sacharja*, p. 410) assume a scribal error in v. 14.

40. Either חלדי (Rignell, *Nachtgesichte*, p. 235), or חלם (Petersen, *Haggai and Zechariah*, p. 278).

41. Cf. Mason, *Preaching*, p. 211, who calls this suggestion a 'desperate shift'.

in my view creates disjunctions that are not necessary. It is not altogether impossible to imagine a situation in which the crown is first set on the head of the high priest and later finds its final destination in the temple, which is the high priest's sphere of operation, the more so if one is not dealing with a coronation, but with a crowning which has a different purpose: a sign to guarantee the fulfilment of a promise given by God.

Petitjean's final point has to do with the difference in the role and the position of the high priest and the Davidide.[42] In (3.8-10 and) 6.12 the only role of the high priest is to announce the arrival of (so Petitjean) the Davidic prince, but in v. 13 one finds the high priest at the same height as the royal heir: both are presented as being seated in majesty. Here, the problems are created by exegetical choices which Petitjean makes, but which in my view are flawed. Things are very different (and far less problematical) once one realises (a) that Joshua the high priest in v. 11 and the priest in v. 13 are not one and the same person (see Chapter 2, section entitled 'The Lack of Specificity in the Description of the Priest'), and (b) that it is incorrect to interpret the situation in v. 13 as indicating an equal position for royal figure and priest (see Chapter 2, 'Equal Status, Supremacy or Submission?').

To sum up: of the three differences between Zech. 6.12-13 and 14-15 which Petitjean points out as a reason for the suggestion that vv. 14-15 are secondary, there are two which disappear once some implausible elements in Petitjean's interpretation of the passage are abandoned. The one difference which is left, the change of the name of Heldai into Helem, remains a puzzling case, but when the other alleged differences do not carry conviction it would mean overrating its significance to make this difference the only reason for considering vv. 14-15 secondary.

*Amsler*. Amsler[43] finds evidence for a break between v. 12 and v. 13 in the abandonment of the use of the first person for God ('V. 13 abandons the divine *I* style and does no more belong to the oracle proper; it is a development added by the prophet to make the point of the oracle explicit'). However, the abandonment of the 'divine I' style is a feature

---

42. Petitjean, *Oracles*, pp. 293-94.

43. 'Le v. 13 quitte le style du *je* divin et ne fait plus partie de l'oracle proprement dit; c'est un développement ajouté par le prophète pour expliciter la porté de l'oracle' (Amsler, *Aggée; Zacharie 1–8*, p. 106).

that marks the whole of 6.9-15 (contrast the first person reference 'my Spirit' in 6.8), and it cannot be used as a criterion to distinguish between original and secondary within 6.9-15. Amsler suggests[44] that v. 12b may also be secondary, because of the use of the third person in that verse (הֵיכַל יְהוָה rather than בֵּיתִי), but even when one grants that, there is still no first person used of God to be found anywhere in 6.9-15. Meyers and Meyers point[45] to the 'set phrase' character of הֵיכַל יְהוָה, and indeed one will never find a first person suffix (referring to YHWH) with הֵיכַל. This would further weaken Amsler's argument.

*On the Repetition in v. 13.* I have examined the different arguments which have been advanced in support of the claim that Zech. 6.13-15 is secondary. The arguments presented by Rignell and Amsler suffered from several weaknesses, which deprived them of their power of conviction. Of Petitjean's case, only one of the three points remains, but the change of the name Heldai (v. 10) into Helem (v. 14) is on its own not a strong enough reason to adopt a division of vv. 9-15 in original and secondary material.

When I reject the proposal to find secondary material from v. 13 onwards, I do not want to deny that the beginning of v. 13 with its repetition of what was said at the end of v. 12 requires discussion.[46] Different proposals for dealing with this repetition have been presented. (a) Wallis interprets the first part of v. 13 as a conditional clause:[47] 'And if he is the one who will build the temple of Yahweh, then he will assume majesty and sit and rule on the throne'. I doubt whether Hebrew syntax allows for this interpretation: while it is never formulated as a rule, a conditional clause with waw at the beginning of the protasis and of the apodosis usually has waw + Perfect in the protasis, even when something separates the Perfect from the waw.[48] This could of course be the

44. *Aggée; Zacharie 1–8*, p. 109.
45. Meyers and Meyers, *Haggai, Zechariah*, p. 356.
46. Some commentators propose to delete one of the two phrases that צֶמַח will build the temple of the Lord (Wellhausen, *Propheten*, p. 185; Rothstein, *Nacht-gesichte*, p. 203; Chary, *Aggée, Zacharie*, p. 112). The LXX seems to delete the beginning of v. 13, the Peshitta deletes the end of v. 12. This is taken as an indication that their Vorlage read as MT by Rignell, *Nachtgesichte*, p. 229; Petitjean, *Oracles*, p. 289; Baldwin, *Haggai, Zechariah*, p. 134.
47. 'Und ist er es, der den Tempel Jahwes bauen wird, so soll er Hoheit annehmen und sitzen und herrschen auf dem Throne' ('Erwägungen', p. 235).
48. For examples see Joüon and Muraoka, *Grammar*, §167.

exception which confirms the rule, but before I draw that conclusion I will look for alternative suggestions for resolving the issue.

(b) According to Beuken,[49] והוא at the beginning of v. 13 indicates the beginning of a citation from 2 Sam. 7.13 (הוא יבנה־בית לשׁמי). While I agree that there are allusions to the dynastic oracle in this passage (the reference to building the temple, the sitting on the throne) am not convinced that there is a kind of formal citation here: the differences in terminology would speak against that (בית versus היכל, כסא ממלכתו versus וישׁב ומשׁל על־כסאו).

(c) The repetition of 'he will build...' is often interpreted as expressing emphasis.[50] The waw before הוא can be interpreted as an emphatic waw ('yea'):[51] 'Yea, he shall build...', or '*He* shall build...' This seems a satisfying explanation to me, the more so when there are more emphasis markers in this passage, as I have discussed in Chapter 4. There I suggested that the emphasis markers may have served to draw a contrast between Zerubbabel and his temple building project and Zemah and his temple building project. It is perhaps possible to take this explanation together with the next one.

(d) In his most recent study of the passage, Van der Woude offers a new suggestion for the interpretation of v. 12-15: he argues that the easiest way to explain the first words of v. 13 is to assume that the words to Joshua accompanying the symbolic action finish at the end of v. 12, and that in vv. 13-15 the Interpreting Angel explains the saying in v. 12 to the prophet.[52] In general it seems to be assumed that the words to Joshua finish at the end of v. 13,[53] but formally there is nothing in the

---

49. Beuken, *Haggai–Sacharja 1–8*, pp. 277-78.

50. Dommershausen, 'Spross', p. 330; Rudolph, *Haggai, Sacharja*, p. 129; Petersen, *Haggai and Zechariah*, pp. 276-77; Meyers and Meyers, *Haggai, Zechariah*, p. 358.

51. See Waltke and O'Connor, *Syntax*, §39.2, 4, and Joüon and Muraoka, *Grammar*, §177n.

52. 'Serubbabel', p. 145; the same division is suggested by B. Duhm, 'Anmerkungen zu den Zwölf Propheten. VII. Buch Sacharja I. (Kapitel 1–8)', *ZAW* 31 (1911), pp. 161-75 (172): vv. 13-15 do not belong to (what in his view are) the words to Zerubbabel, but continue the statements of the Angel to Zechariah. Similarly, according to Hanhart, *Sacharja*, p. 410, the repetition either marks the boundary between the words addressed to צמח, or emphasize what is the essence of his presence.

53. See the inverted commas in the commentaries (e.g. Petersen, *Haggai and Zechariah*, pp. 272-73; Meyers and Meyers, *Haggai, Zechariah*, p. 336), mono-

Hebrew to indicate the end of the words to Joshua at any place in particular. So, from a formal perspective, Van der Woude's proposal is as
good as any proposal concerning the end of the words to Joshua.

The only, perhaps minor, problem I have with this proposal is that it
leaves the message the prophet is told to deliver to Joshua quite short,
and extremely enigmatic: the prophet is to crown Joshua the high priest
and to say to him, 'Behold, a man called 'Growth'—from his place he
will grow and he will build the temple.' Only on the assumption that
Zechariah also told the rest of the words of the Interpreting Angel to
Joshua (perhaps not an unreasonable assumption) can one expect that
this symbolic action was meaningful and understandable for Joshua.

*The Secondary Origin of vv. 14-15.* Finally, there are those who find
secondary material in vv. 14-15.[54] The material was added to alter the
overall thrust of the oracle after Zerubbabel had failed to meet the
expectations raised in vv. 12-13, by giving the crown a new destination.
As I have argued above with reference to Petitjean, the depositing of
the crown in the temple does not necessarily exclude that it first served
in a symbolic action. This proposal is further based on the identification
of Zemah with Zerubbabel, an identification which on the basis of
vv. 12-13 alone (which this view considers original) is untenable, as I
have tried to show in Chapter 4.

*Conclusion.* Different proposals have been made to find two literary
layers in Zech. 6.9-15. I have reviewed those proposals and pointed out
their weaknesses, some minor, some major. Finding secondary material
in vv. 12-13 would leave us with a symbolic action without an explanation. Redditt's proposal to locate the secondary material in vv. 11b-13
solves the problem of the proposal just mentioned, but leaves a number
of issues unaccounted for, including the future reference, and is based
on a debatable reconstruction of the priesthood and its role in the early
Persian period. Most of the reasons given for taking vv. 13-15 as secondary are flawed, or are based on an interpretation of details in vv. 12-
15 which I have argued to be unsatisfactory (the same is true for the
view which takes vv. 14-15 as secondary). There is only one problem

graphs (Beyse, *Serubbabel*, p. 77), and in Bible translations (e.g. RSV, NJPS).
    54.  Horst, *Propheten*, p. 238: compare Fohrer, *Symbolische Handlungen*, p. 70
n. 164; Elliger, *Propheten*, p. 130.

which one of the advocates of this proposal points out that is really difficult to resolve, the change of name between v. 11 and v. 14.

### b. *Zechariah 6.9-15 as a Rewritten Oracle*

Having discussed the views which hold that Zech. 6.12-15 is a combination of two (or more) oracles of separate origin, I now turn to an examination of the view that what we have in MT is the result of a reworking by a redactor of an original text which is not impossible to reconstruct. Several suggestions for altering the text have been made. The alterations concern seven points: (a) the precise form of the word עטרות in v. 11; (b) the act of crowning, and whose head is to be crowned; (c) the identity of the one(s) to whom the words in vv. 12-13/12-15 were spoken, and therefore the suffix attached to אל at the end of v. 11 (singular or plural); (d) איש without or with an article; (e) the description of the activities of צמח; (f) the absence or presence of the name Joshua in the line concerning the priest; and (g) the phrase על-כסאו.

Not all of the seven elements in these reconstructions are of equal significance. The one concerning (b) the destination of the crown seems to be the most crucial. Some of the other elements are in comparison less significant, for example (e) the precise details of the description of the activities of צמח, or (g) the phrase על-כסאו. Other changes are only there because they are an implication of the change of destination of עטרות, for example (c) the alteration of אליו to אליהם.

The proposals can be grouped in three categories:[55] no command to set a crown on the head of someone; a command to set a crown on the head of Zerubbabel; a command to set a crown on the head of Joshua and one on the head of Zerubbabel

*A Crown but No Head.* The first proposal suggests that the original text would have read something like the left hand column in the following figure. The left hand column presents the text as scholars claim it was originally, before the intervention of the redactor. The right hand column presents the text as we have it now: <u>words underlined</u> indicate

---

55. The categories are based upon looking at the significant alterations of the text. I leave out small details which do not make a difference, like על ימינו instead of the usual alteration מימינו for על-כסאו in v. 13 (Mitchell, *Haggai and Zechariah*; Gressmann's על-מימינו (*Messias*, p. 257) is apparently a mistake: it is not attested in the Hebrew of the Old Testament).

what the redactor has altered, <words between sharp brackets> indicate what the redactor has added, ~~words in strikethrough~~ indicate what the redactor has removed.

| | |
|---|---|
| ולקחת כסף־וזהב ועשית עטרת | ולקחת כסף־וזהב ועשית <u>עטרות</u> |
| | <ושמת בראש יהושע בן־יהוצדק הכהן הגדול> |
| ואמרת אליהם לאמר | ואמרת <u>אליו</u> לאמר |
| כה אמר יהוה צבאות לאמר | כה אמר יהוה צבאות לאמר |
| הנה־איש צמח שמו ומתחתיו יצמח | הנה־איש צמח שמו ומתחתיו יצמח |
| | <ובנה את־היכל יהוה> |
| והוא יבנה את־היכל יהוה | והוא יבנה את־היכל יהוה |
| והוא־ישא הוד וישב ומשל על־כסאו | והוא־ישא הוד וישב ומשל על־כסאו |
| והיה יהושע כהן מימינו | והיה ~~יהושע~~ כהן <u>על־כסאו</u> |
| ועצת שלום תהיה בין שניהם | ועצת שלום תהיה בין שניהם |

That is, (a) the word for 'crown' should be read עֲטֶרֶת; (b) originally there was only a command to make a crown, and the whole phrase about setting the crown on the head of someone (v. 11b) is a later addition; (c) in v. 12 the prophet is addressing the four men of v. 10, therefore the original text read אליהם instead of אליו; (e) one of the two lines on 'he will build the temple of the LORD' is secondary and should be omitted, preferably the first one (the end of v. 12); (f) the name of Joshua was originally part of the text, but has been omitted from v. 13 by the redactor; and (g) the phrase על־כסאו is a replacement for an original מימינו. This is the view of Wellhausen (some later commentators attribute the next reconstruction [a crown on the head of Zerubbabel] to Wellhausen, but that is a mistake), and of a few other commentators around the beginning of the twentieth century.[56]

56. Wellhausen, *Propheten*, pp. 43, 185; Marti, *Dodekapropheton*, p. 420; Mitchell, *Haggai and Zechariah*, pp. 185-86, 188-89. Wellhausen writes on v. 11 (p. 185), 'Der Satz nach dem Atnach ist zu streichen; das Diadem ist von Zechariah für Zerubbabel als künftigen König bestimmt, erst von einem späteren Diaskeuasten für den Hohenpriester Josua'. This suggests not a replacement of MT בן־יהוצדק זרבבל בן־שאלתיאל by הכהן הגדול יהושע, but a complete deletion of the second half of v. 11, ושמת בראש יהושע בן־יהוצדק הכהן הגדול (MT has an *atnāḥ* with עטרות), as also the translation on p. 45 indicates: 'mach eine Krone, und sag zu ihnen'. This is how Wellhausen has been interpreted by Mitchell (pp. 185-86): 'If, therefore, a name was mentioned here, it must have been that of Zerubbabel. Perhaps, as Wellhausen maintains, the latter half of the verse entire is an addition; which means that the prophet left it to his readers to supply the name of Zerubbabel'. Mitchell also mentions the option of replacing the name of Joshua by that of Zerubbabel, but in the end prefers omitting the whole of v. 11b (pp. 188, 189): in

*A Crown on the Head of Zerubbabel*. According to the second proposal, the original text would have been:

ולקחת כסף־וזהב ועשית <u>עטרות</u>

ושמת בראש <u>יהושע בן־יהוצדק הכהן הגדול</u>

ואמרת אליו לאמר

כה אמר יהוה צבאות לאמר

הנה־<u>ה</u>איש צמח שמו ומתחתיו יצמח

‹ובנה את־היכל יהוה›

והוא יבנה את־היכל יהוה

והוא־ישא הוד וישב ומשל על־כסאו

והיה <u>יהושע</u> כהן <u>על־כסאו</u>

ועצת שלום תהיה בין שניהם

ולקחת כסף־וזהב ועשית עטרת

ושמת בראש זרבבל בן־שאלתיאל

ואמרת אליו לאמר

כה אמר יהוה צבאות לאמר

הנה־האיש צמח שמו ומתחתיו יצמח

והוא יבנה את־היכל יהוה

והוא־ישא הוד וישב ומשל על־כסאו

והיה יהושע כהן מימינו

ועצת שלום תהיה בין שניהם

The crucial element in this reconstruction is found in the second point: (b) there was indeed a command to set the crown on someone's head, but the person to be crowned was Zerubbabel, not Joshua. Zerubbabel was also (c) the one addressed by the prophet, and therefore אליו can be retained. Originally there was (d) an article before איש, which has been omitted later. Scholars taking this line would agree with points (a), (e), (f) and (g) of the first view. This reconstruction is found in a number of commentaries,[57] monographs[58] and articles.[59]

v. 12 only the words הנה־איש צמח שמו are original, the rest (ומתחתיו את־היכל יהוה יצמח ובנה) is 'of secondary origin'. In the last line of v. 13 he does not read the name 'Joshua', but והיה כהן על ימינו.

57. E.g. Nowack, *Propheten*, p. 353 (but: אליהם [referring to the four men]); Edelkoort, *Zacharia*, p. 81; Horst, *Propheten*, pp. 236-38; Chary, *Aggée, Zacharie*, pp. 110-15 (he adds the title of Zerubbabel in the second line [ושמת בראש זרבבל בן־שאלתיאל פחת יהודה], does not reconstruct an article before איש, and does not have the name Joshua in the line concerning the priest [והיה כהן מימינו]); Elliger, *Propheten*, pp. 128-29; Amsler, *Aggée; Zacharie 1–8*, p. 105 (apart from reading עטרת instead of עטרות, Amsler has exactly the same reconstruction as Chary); Redditt, *Haggai, Zechariah*, p. 79 (he finds it 'difficult to avoid the conclusion argued by many scholars that the name Zerubbabel originally stood in the text, either alongside Joshua or [more likely] alone').

58. E.g. Galling, *Studien*, p. 147; E. Hammershaimb, *Some Aspects of Old Testament Prophecy from Isaiah to Malachi* (Teologiske Skrifter, 4; Copenhagen: Rosenkilde of Bagger, 1966), p. 106 (who states that this reconstruction is '[o]n exegetical grounds...as certain as anything'); Fohrer, *Symbolische Handlungen*, pp. 70-71 (in Fohrer's reconstruction the clause הנה־האיש צמח שמו ומתחתיו יצמח is also secondary); Becker, *Messiaserwartung*, p. 60 [ET *Expectation*, p. 65]. Gressmann has something more or less along the same lines (*Messias*, pp. 257-58). He also suggests that originally a phrase like 'Siehe, ich kröne dich hiermit zum König'

*Crowns on the Heads of both Zerubbabel and Joshua.* The third proposal is to read:

| | |
|---|---|
| ולקחת כסף־וזהב ועשית עטרות | ולקחת כסף־וזהב ועשית עטרות |
| ושמת בראש זרבבל פחת יהודה | ושמת בראש זרבבל פ̶ח̶ת̶ ̶י̶ה̶ו̶ד̶ה̶ |
| וראש יהושע בן־יהוצדק הכהן הגדול | ו̶ר̶א̶ש̶ יהושע בן־יהוצדק הכהן הגדול |
| ואמרת אליהם לאמר | ואמרת <u>אליו</u> לאמר |
| כה אמר יהוה צבאות לאמר | כה אמר יהוה צבאות לאמר |
| הנה־איש צמח שמו ומתחתיו יצמח | הנה־איש צמח שמו ומתחתיו יצמח |
| ובנה את־היכל יהוה | ובנה את־היכל יהוה |
| | ⟨והוא יבנה את־היכל יהוה |
| | והוא־ישא הוד וישב ומשל על־כסאו⟩ |
| והיה כהן מימינו | והיה כהן <u>על־כסאו</u> |
| ועצת שלום תהיה בין שניהם | ועצת שלום תהיה בין שניהם |

In this reconstruction (a) עֲטָרוֹת is a plural; (b) two persons are crowned, both Zerubbabel and Joshua; (c) the prophet addresses the four men of v. 10 (אליהם). In (e) the description of the activities of צמח, the first reference to the building of the temple of YHWH is original, but the second is secondary (והוא יבנה את־היכל יהוה), as are the words concerning the bearing of honour, the sitting and the ruling (והוא־ישא הוד וישב ומשל על־כסאו). (g) מימינו was the original reading, later replaced by על־כסאו. A relatively small number of scholars adopt this reconstruction.[60]

---

preceded הנה־איש צמח שמו, and that מתחתיו יצמח is a meaningless addition to explain צמח שמו. Beuken, *Haggai–Sacharja 1–8*) seems a bit reluctant on pp. 275-76, but on p. 310 he writes, 'Es ist gut möglich, daß sie [die Überlieferung] den Namen Serubbabel durch den Josuas ersetzte'. Carroll seems to favour this view (*Prophecy*, p. 166), 'verse 11 could have originally had Zerubbabel as the recipient of the crowns', but when he goes on it becomes unclear whether Carroll holds that Joshua was originally also to be crowned: 'The plural crowns may have been intended for king and priest and the subsequent failure of Zerubbabel to become king necessitated the removal of his name at this point...[H]e was removed from the coronation reference'.

59. E.g. Dommershausen, 'Spross', pp. 332-33; Sinclair, 'Redaction', pp. 40-42, 46-47; Lescow, 'Sacharja 1–8', p. 85 n. 20; Marinkovic, 'Zechariah 1–8', p. 101; Bianchi, 'Zorobabel', pp. 160-61; Lemaire, 'Zorobabel', p. 55.

60. In the last century a similar view was proposed by H. Ewald, *Die jüngsten Propheten des alten Bundes mit den Büchern Barukh und Daniel* (Göttingen: Vandenhoeck & Ruprecht, 2nd edn, 1868), pp. 206-207 and Hitzig, *Propheten*, p. 357. For this century, see Beyse, *Serubbabel*, pp. 77-78; Carroll, *Prophecy*, p. 167; Hanson, *People Called*, p. 265; J.A. Soggin, *Introduction to the Old Testament. From its Origins to the Closing of the Alexandrian Canon* (London: SCM Press, 3rd edn,

*Scholars' Reasons and the Redactor's Motives.* For a better understanding and evaluation of the view that MT is a reworking it is important to know for what reasons suspicions against MT have arisen. The misgivings were based on one or more of the following observations. The first observation is that the nature of the headdress does not fit with the person on whose head the crown is to be set. According to Amsler,[61] for example, the crown is an insignia of a king: a priest has a turban, but never (*jamais*) a crown. The second observation is that there is a discrepancy between the recipient of the crown (Joshua, the priest) and the contents of the oracle (the oracle is not about Joshua but about someone else [שמו צמח איש]), and it deals with royal functions, including building the temple).[62] Redditt has a number of objections taken from the immediate context against the conclusion that Joshua is the recipient of the crowns: 'Verse 12 specifically calls the recipient the Branch, which is a messianic title... the verse specifically said that the Branch would build the Temple, a task reserved exclusively for Zerubbabel in 4.6b-10a'. He therefore finds it 'difficult to avoid the conclusion argued by many scholars that the name Zerubbabel originally stood in the text, either alongside Joshua or (more likely) alone'.[63]

1989), pp. 389-90. In an earlier study, P.R. Ackroyd ('Zechariah', in Matthew Black and H.H. Rowley [eds.], *Peake's Commentary on the Bible* [London: Nelson, 1962], pp. 646-55 [649]; cf. Ackroyd, *Exile*, p. 196-97) mentions this reconstruction as an 'attractive' alternative but seems somewhat reluctant to adopt it. But in recent discussion he seems to be more willing to take this line, as can be seen from a comment in an article from 1984 ('Historical Problems of the Early Achaemenian Period', *Orient* 20 [1984], pp. 1-15 [reprinted in Ackroyd, *Chronicler*, pp. 141-55 (153)]), 'Neither in ch. 3 nor in ch. 6 is Zerubbabel mentioned by name, and it may be right to suppose that his name has been eliminated in a process of reinterpretation pointing to a later understanding of the nature of the temple with stress on the priesthood rather than on any royal figure'. Cf. Ackroyd, *Chronicler*, pp. 86-111 (107), on the probability of the removal of the name Zerubbabel from the text of Zech. 3 and 6 ('It has often seemed most probable...'). On the basis of his use of words like 'eliminated' and 'removed', I take it to mean that in Ackroyd's view originally both the names of Joshua and Zerubbabel were there (cf. Ackroyd, *Exile*, pp. 196-97), rather than that there was an original reference to Zerubbabel only, later to be replaced by reference to Joshua. That is the reason why I group Ackroyd with Beyse.

61. Amsler, *Aggée; Zacharie 1–8*, p. 107; cf. Dommershausen, 'Spross', p. 332.

62. Nowack, *Propheten*, p. 353; Dommershausen, 'Spross', p. 332; Chary, *Aggée, Zacharie*, pp. 110-13; Amsler, *Aggée; Zacharie 1–8*, pp. 107-108.

63. Redditt, *Haggai, Zechariah*, p. 78.

Scholars who take this view have also made an attempt to uncover the motives of the redactor to alter the text. Usually two motives have been detected. Some scholars say the alteration of the text was for historical reasons: the text was corrected to accommodate the facts of historical reality.[64] In the end not a king, but the high priest became the ruler of the Jewish community.[65] Others say the text was altered for ideological reasons. The text fell in the hands of the priests, who were not willing to accept Zerubbabel's position of priority over Joshua.[66] An example of this approach is Hanson. In his book *The Dawn of Apocalyptic*, in a discussion of the Zadokite revision of the Ezekielian program of restoration (which he dates to the decades following the rebuilding of the temple), Hanson writes about Zech. 6.9-15, 'This Zadokite attempt to degrade the role of the *nāsî'* in favor of the Zadokite priesthood may underlie the textual disruption in Zech. 6.9-14, where the crowning of Zerubbabel seems to have been deleted from the account'.[67]

*Reasons and Motives.* How credible are these reasons for suspicions against MT? Concerning the first observation: a royal crown on the head of a priest is only a problem if the action implies a coronation. That we are dealing here with a coronation is usually assumed by scholars, but in my view this assumption needs to be challenged. In Chapter 2 I have set out the case for the view that the act of setting a crown on the head of someone does not necessarily imply a coronation, a thesis for which support from elsewhere in the Old Testament can be adduced.

The second observation (the oracle is not about Joshua) is in my view

---

64. E.g. Beyse, *Serubbabel*, pp. 38-39: a later redactor wanted 'die Aussagen des Propheten Sacharja den Verhältnissen seiner Gegenwart anpassen'.

65. Wellhausen, *Propheten*, p. 185; Marti, *Dodekapropheton*, p. 420; Mitchell, *Haggai and Zechariah*, p. 186; Nowack, *Propheten*, p. 353; Mason, *Haggai, Zechariah*, p. 63. Compare the views of Chary and Amsler who consider the alteration as being made after the disappearance of Zerubbabel, either by the prophet himself (Chary, *Aggée, Zacharie*, p. 115), or by a later redactor (Amsler, *Aggée; Zacharie 1–8*, p. 108).

66. Gressmann, *Messias*, p. 258; Mason, *Haggai, Zechariah*, p. 28. R.J. Coggins, *Haggai, Zechariah, Malachi* (OTG; Sheffield: JSOT Press, 1987), p. 47, describes this view thus: 'because of an increasing belief among the Jewish community that the priestly office was the all-important one'.

67. Paul D. Hanson, *The Dawn of Apocalyptic: The Historical and Sociological Roots of Jewish Apocalyptic Eschatology* (Philadelphia: Fortress Press, 1975), pp. 263-64.

not a problem at all. I find it difficult to see what the problem is when a prophet talks to A about B, or even announces to A the coming of B. Such a situation makes sense in general, I would say, and in this particular case the more so when A had already been told about the arrival of B, in an oracle where A was addressed as one of the 'men of good omen' (3.8).

I now turn to a discussion for the motives attributed to the redactor for altering the text: the position of the high priest in history or ideology. There are two factors that need to be discussed here: the historical issue of the emergence of the high priesthood as an institution of civil power, and the position of the priest in Zech. 6.9-15.

(a) To begin with the historical issue: the hypothesis is based on a particular reconstruction of the history of the early Persian period which has fallen into disfavour. In Chapter 1 I have set out how recent scholarship suggests that the emergence of a high-priestly theocracy occurred much later than is assumed in this theory.

The impression which one gets from books in the Old Testament related to the Persian period agree with this historical reconstruction. In the prophetic books relating to the period we find the high priest only mentioned in connection with matters related to temple and priesthood. In the book of Haggai Joshua is mentioned five times,[68] of which four are in the narrative framework. In none of these cases is he mentioned on his own: he is always accompanied by Zerubbabel and mentioned after him.[69] In the book of Zechariah Joshua is mentioned 5 times (on his own) in ch. 3, and once in 6.12. In both chapters the context is the temple and its rebuilding. As I have argued in Chapter 2, the evidence for a position of authority in civil matters, which some have found in these chapters (particularly in 3.7 and 6.13) is weak.

In the historical books of Ezra and Nehemiah, again the high priest is mentioned only in the context of matters dealing with temple and priesthood. A striking example of this is that the rebuilding of the destroyed walls of Jerusalem is initiated not by the high priest but by an official of the Persian court of Jewish origin, Nehemiah, who leaves his job to go to Jerusalem. Interestingly, the high priest is not mentioned in the account of the covenant renewal in Nehemiah 10. All these data are difficult to match with the idea of the emergence of the priesthood as a

68. Hag. 1.1, 12, 14; 2.2, 4.
69. Besides these five occurrences together with Joshua, Zerubbabel is mentioned twice on his own: 2.21, 23.

political authority already in this part of the Persian period.

(As an aside, there are similar problems of a historical nature with Rudolph's view[70] that the reference to Zemah is a later correction by the prophet himself. The expectations which Zechariah had focused originally on Zerubbabel did not materialize, so Rudolph argues, which forced the prophet to change his mind and set his hopes on a future figure which he gave the name Zemah. The issue in which Zerubbabel failed to meet Zechariah's expectations concerns the finishing of the temple building project: according to Rudolph it is certain that Zerubbabel was not present at the dedication of the temple, despite Zechariah's promise that he would finish the temple.

Rudolph's case is based on the assumption that the absence of Zerubbabel in the record of the temple dedication in Ezra 6 is evidence that he was not present at the occasion. In Chapter 1 I have pointed to the difficulties with this conclusion. As Japhet points out, it is not only Zerubbabel who is not mentioned in Ezra 6, but one does not hear about Joshua either. There may have been other reasons for the absence of these two leaders in the narrative about the temple dedication. Japhet attributes the failure to mention Zerubbabel and Joshua at the temple dedication to a tendency of the author of Ezra which she describes as[71] 'highlighting and centering of the public's role in the events, and the resultant dimming of the figures and roles of the leaders'. So, it is dubious to base a case concerning the failure of Zerubbabel to finish the temple building on his absence in Ezra 6.[72] In fact, some scholars think that he was still around at that time,[73] and present at the occasion.[74])

(b) Concerning the second issue, the position of the priest in Zech. 6.9-15: scholars claim that the present text in Zech. 6.9-15 elevates the position of the high priest at the expense of that of the royal figure. As I have argued in Chapter 2 ('The Relationship between Royal Figure and Priest in Zech. 6.13'), there is no evidence to support such a reading. When one compares what the oracle (in its present form) tells us about the royal figure, Zemah, with what it tells us about the priest, one has to conclude that the priest is a shadowy figure at best. Evidence for an equal position of royal figure and priest is difficult to find, let alone

70. Rudolph, *Haggai, Sacharja*, pp. 55, 130.
71. Japhet, 'Zerubbabel', p. 86.
72. Beyse, *Serubbabel*, p. 48; Van der Woude, 'Serubbabel', p. 140.
73. Reventlow, *Haggai, Sacharja*, p. 55.
74. Galling, *Studien*, p. 148; Beyse, *Serubbabel*, pp. 48-49.

evidence for a supremacy of the priest. My interpretation of Zech. 6.9-15, which I have developed in this book, confirms the conclusion which Cook has recently arrived at. He considers Wellhausen's assumption of a downfall of the Davidides resulting in a stagnant priestly hegemony over restoration polity to be no longer tenable, '[i]t has been a misreading to see either a reflection of increasing priestly power, or tendentious pro-priestly editing in this pericope. Far from arguing for acceptance of any hierocratic status quo, the text points forward to a coming messianic reign.'[75]

*Consistency.* To sum up the argument so far: the features which have raised suspicions against MT—a royal crown on the head of the high priest, and the fact that Joshua is the addressee of an oracle which deals with a third party—can both be explained in a satisfactory way without assuming that the text is rewritten. The motives which scholars attribute to the redactor to explain why he altered the text—a priestly hierocracy as a fact of history or a piece of ideology—are difficult to maintain for historical reasons, and because there is no prominent role for the (high) priest in MT.

But these are not the only problems. Another factor is the matter of consistency. Some of the scholars who find evidence for a reworking of the text judge that the redactor has done a poor job. Mitchell is particularly scathing in his assessment of the work of the redactor who was responsible for altering the text to what it is now: he calls it 'a clumsy attempt, by an anxious scribe, to bring the prophet into harmony with history'.[76] Amsler remarks that a redactor altered the text in spite of the difficulties of ascribing to a priest titles and functions which are typically royal.[77] In the opinion of Beyse, such a lack of sophistication is more or less typical, 'As often happens with interventions of this nature, in this case also it has not been applied with all thoroughness; the editors were satisfied when the name "Zerubbabel" had been deleted'.[78]

For other scholars the fact that one must assume such a lack of sophistication on the part of the redactor is a reason to express strong

---

75. Cook, *Prophecy and Apocalypticism*, pp. 135-36.
76. Mitchell, *Haggai and Zechariah*, p. 186.
77. Amsler, *Aggée; Zacharie 1–8*, p. 108.
78. 'Wie es aber oft mit Eingriffen solcher Art zu gehen pflegt, so ist auch hier nicht mit aller Gründlichkeit zu Werke gegangen worden; man war zufrieden, als der Name "Serubbabel" getilgt worden war' (Beyse, *Serubbabel*, p. 91).

reservations against or even completely to reject the idea of an original text referring to Zerubbabel being reworked in order to adapt to new historical circumstances. In response to Mitchell's phrase 'a clumsy attempt', Rignell remarks[79] that the attempt must be considered too clumsy to be true: if it was the objective of the redactor to remove anything which might recall Zerubbabel he should have done something about v. 12 as well. In an earlier study of the passage Ackroyd wondered,

> why if editing were carried out to avoid any reference to Zerubbabel this was not done sufficiently consistently to remove his name from 4, 6b-10a and also from the book of Haggai where equally plain claims are made on his behalf.[80]

One also has to assume that the clumsiness and inconsistency were limited to the macro level (like the points mentioned by Amsler and Ackroyd), because at the levels of small details the redactor is given credit for really minor alterations, like writing אליו for original אליהם (Mitchell; Beyse), איש for האיש (Amsler), and על־כסאו for מימינו (Mitchell [על ימינו]; Beyse; Amsler). There is even more inconsistency (or is it consistency?) here than scholars have assumed.

I conclude that once one takes a closer look at the hypothesis of a rewritten text and thinks through its implications, it loses any attractiveness which it might have had at first sight.

*The Early Versions.* When one studies the early versions one finds that while for some elements of the reconstructions mentioned above it is possible to appeal to the early versions for support, this is the case only for the less significant elements, not for the most crucial element, the (change of) destination of the עטרות.[81]

---

79. Rignell, *Nachtgesichte*, p. 224, 'Dagegen lässt sich einwenden, daß der Versuch allzu plump sein würde, um wirklich zu sein'.

80. Ackroyd, *Exile*, p. 196; he then continues, 'If the Persian secret service were thought to be likely to investigate Jewish nationalistic aspirations by reading their prophetic books—a supposition which does not appear so very probable—then we must suppose that the editing would have been consistent'. Cf. D. Buzy, 'Les symboles de Zacharie', *RB* 15 (1918), pp. 136-91 (186); Rignell, *Nachtgesichte*, p. 12; Petitjean, *Oracles*, p. 285; Carroll, *Prophecy*, p. 167; and Van der Woude, 'Serubbabel', p. 148. As I have mentioned above, later statements of his opinion indicate that Ackroyd now seems to be more open to the idea of a reworking of the text ('Early Achaemenian Period', p. 153; 'Persian Period', p. 107).

81. Cf. Schöttler, *Gottesvolk*, p. 155.

So one finds in LXX a plural στεφάνους in v. 11 (but note the singular στέφανος in v. 14), which presupposes an interpretation of עטרות as a plural, which also seems to be the interpretation underlying כליל רב 'a large crown' of Targum.[82] Furthermore, LXX does not provide a translation for והוא יבנה את־היכל יהוה in v. 13a (but Targum has a reference to building the temple both at the end of v. 12 and at the beginning of v. 13). Finally, LXX reads ἐκ δεξιῶν αὐτοῦ for MT על־כסאו in v. 13 (in Targum both occurrences of על־כסאו in v. 13 are translated על כורסותי 'upon his throne'). But on the issue of the destination of עטרות, both LXX (καὶ ἐπιθήσεις ἐπὶ τὴν κεφαλὴν Ἰησοῦ τοῦ Ιωσεδεκ τοῦ ἱερέως τοῦ μεγάλου) and Targum unequivocally support MT ושׂמת בראשׁ יהושׁע בן־יהוצדק הכהן הגדול .

Once again, a statement by Cook sums up my findings in this Chapter well: 'no textual support exists for the suggestion, often adopted since Wellhausen, that the crowning was originally of Zerubbabel but was changed to Joshua'.[83]

## 4. *Conclusion*

### a. *Summary*

At the beginning of this Chapter I wrote that in prophetic books the possibility exists that in a given case oracles end up in a context where they did not originally belong. I noted that when one applies this general statement to the oracles in the vision reports in Zechariah 1–6 (where scholars distinguish between original and secondary), one is confronted with an unusual feature: the date which scholars often assign to (part of) the secondary material is a date *before* the core of material they were inserted in. This would imply a prophetic ministry of Zechariah before the date given in Zech. 1.1 (possible, but without evidence[84]) and a quite unusual process of composition of Zechariah 1–6.

The attribution of the label 'secondary addition' in general, and in

82. Gordon ('Targum Nahum–Malachi', p. 198 n. 9) takes MT עטרות as a plural, and interprets the addition in Targum of רב as indicating that Targum takes the plural as a *pluralis excellentiae*, so that the singular in Targum should 'not be taken to support the reading "crown" (sing.), though its evidence is commonly misinterpreted in this way'.

83. Cook, *Prophecy and Apocalypticism*, p. 134.

84. Cf. Reventlow, *Haggai, Sacharja*, p. 55, on the dating of the צמח passages, 'Für eine Datierung vor dem Auftreten Serubbabels oder nach seinem Abgang… gibt es keinen Hinweis, ebensowenig für nachträgliche Einfügung des Wortes'.

this case with its unusual implications for the composition of Zechariah 1–6 in particular, raises the question as to the grounds on which this enterprise is based. I discussed the principles which scholars employ to decide what part of the oracles is original to the vision reports, and what should be considered a secondary addition. I examined the One-Point Principle (everything in the oracles that goes beyond the one point the vision intends to convey is secondary) and concluded that its view of the relationship between visions and oracles was too static. I then introduced the Coherence Principle (lack of consistency within the oracles points to secondary additions), and reviewed how this principle was applied to the oracles which are the subject of this book, Zech. 3.8 and 6.9-15.

The three features in Zech. 3.8-10 which have been pointed to as indicating the secondary status of these oracles were reviewed. With respect to two of these features the tension they were thought to create was only apparent, and the third involved a peculiar feature of Hebrew grammar.

The views on the composition of Zech. 6.9-15 were far more complex. I first reviewed the proposals to find two literary layers in this passage, and argued that on closer inspection the grounds for these proposals in most cases failed to carry conviction. It is not possible to solve all the problems (particularly with respect to the difference in the names in v. 11 and v. 14), but the problems that remain are overrated if they are taken as indicating the secondary origin of part of the oracles.

I then discussed the different proposals for reconstructing an original text in Zech. 6.9-15 which was later rewritten into what we have now in MT. What set scholars on the track of reconstructing an original text, was the inappropriateness of a royal crown on the head of a high priest, the discrepancy between the recipient of the crown (Joshua, the priest) and the contents of the oracle (a royal figure). Referring to my interpretation of these features in this book I argued that there is a satisfactory explanation of these features. The motive which—so the scholars claim—guided the redactor in his alteration of the passage was the elevation of the high priest, either as a matter of historical fact, or as a piece of propaganda. I argued that the historical situation in the Persian period makes the presence of such a motive difficult to locate in that period, and that the present text—which is said to be a result of an alteration guided by that motive—gives no support for this reconstruction of the motive of the redactor.

The alteration hypothesis leads to the assumption of a considerable amount of incompetence on the part of the redactor, because he failed to carry out all alterations which one would expect to have happened on this scenario, and at the same time one is confronted with conflicting evidence consisting in changes of minor details which suggest that the redactor must have done his job with substantial sophistication. Finally I discussed the possible evidence of the early versions for the alteration hypothesis, and concluded that there is little.

If the quality of arguments determines the plausibilty of a specific proposal to label certain oracles as secondary, then in this case there is good reason to abandon the proposal because the grounds are dubious at best. There would be even less justification for the additional hypothesis to assign an early date to the alleged secondary material: only the determination to identify Zemah with Zerubbabel leads to this unusual hypothesis.

### b. *Struggling with MT*

Some years ago, Koch commented that the more he had been engaged in the interpretation of prophetic books of the Old Testament, the more sceptical he had become about current literary criticism, 'which with an easy hand selects a lot of unauthentic material, once stylistic doublets or so-called factual contradictions have been found'.[85]

After the long discussion in this Chapter one can sympathize with such a comment. When there are such serious problems with proposals to distinguish different layers or to reconstruct an original text underneath the present one, one can understand that a number of scholars[86] prefer to accept the integrity of the text of MT. This is not to deny that there are a number of difficulties in the text. But it has become clear that attempts to reconstruct an original do not improve things. So,

---

85. 'Die mit leichter Hand eine Fülle von unechtem Gut aus diesen Schriften aussortiert, weil stilistische Doppelungen oder sog. sachliche Widersprüche beobachtet werden' (Koch, *Profeten*, II, p. 192) (ET *Prophets*, II, p. 189, 'With insouciant confidence, it sifts out a profusion of non-genuine material from these writings, on the grounds of stylistic 'doublets', or what it takes to be factual contradictions').

86. Buzy, 'Symboles', p. 186; H. Junker, *Die zwölf kleinen Propheten*, II (HSAT, 8; Bonn: Peter Hanstein Verlagsbuchhandlung, 1938), p. 148; Rignell, *Nachtgesichte*, p. 224; Eichrodt, 'Symbol', p. 513; Baldwin, *Haggai, Zechariah*, p. 134; Meyers and Meyers, *Haggai, Zechariah*, pp. 350-53; Hanhart, *Sacharja*, pp. 409, 426-27; Reventlow, *Haggai, Sacharja*, p. 71; Tollington, *Tradition*, p. 166.

several scholars have noticed a recent tendency to move away from such attempts and to face the text with all its difficulties.

One example is Stacey: after a discussion of different proposals to reconstruct an original text he comments,

> These solutions are all imaginative and they all depend on reading details into the text rather than out of it. Recent commentators have been more inclined to wrestle with the text as it is and to solve problems of meaning without depending on a hypothetical literary history.[87]

Similarly, Reventlow writes, 'In recent studies, scholars attempt more and more to cope with the text as it has been transmitted, and to overcome what is offensive by an understanding of the content'.[88] It seems therefore best to conclude—with a growing number of scholars[89]—that the oracles are most likely to be seen as being part of the vision, and that the attempt to distinguish within the oracles between original and secondary material should be abandoned.

---

87. Stacey, *Prophetic Drama*, p. 211.

88. 'Neuerdings sucht man aber immer häufiger mit dem überlieferten Text auszukommen und seine Anstöße durch inhaltliches Verständnis zu überwinden' (Reventlow, *Haggai, Sacharja*, p. 71). Already in 1974, Seybold, 'Königserwartung', p. 76, wrote, 'Neuere Auslegungen sind gegenüber solchen literarkritischen Operationen zurückhaltender'.

89. E.g. Harrelson, 'Trial', p. 119*; Van der Woude, *Zacharia*, p. 30; Meyers and Meyers, *Haggai, Zechariah*, p. 132; Tigchelaar, 'Ange', p. 352 and n. 13; Van der Woude, 'Serubbabel', pp. 141-46; Hanhart, *Sacharja*, p. 46. Rooke (*High Priesthood*, pp. 138-39) considers the cleansing episode (Zechariah 3) and the crowning episode (6.9-15) as integral to the visions.

Chapter 6

## THE TWO SONS OF OIL WHO STAND BY
## THE LORD OF THE WHOLE EARTH

In the preceding Chapters there has been reason a number of times to mention Zech. 4.14. In RSV the passage in which this verse is found reads:

> Then I said to him, 'What are these two olive trees on the right and the left of the lampstand?' And a second time I said to him, 'What are these two branches of the olive trees, which are beside the two golden pipes from which the oil is poured out?' He said to me, 'Do you not know what these are?' I said, 'No, my lord.' Then he said, 'These are the two anointed who stand by the Lord of the whole earth' (Zech. 4.11-14).

The phrase translated, 'the two anointed who stand by the Lord of the whole earth' was referred to in the discussion of the nature of the relationship between royal figure and priest at his throne as found in Zech. 6.13 (3.3), and in the discussion of the issue of access to the heavenly council in Zech. 3.7 (3.4). Scholars often make a direct connection between Zech. 4.14 and either of the two passages, for example Petersen on Zech. 4.14 and 6.9-15, 'Commentators uniformly view these anointed figures as signifying the diarchic polity recoverable in the oracular material, e.g. Zech. 6.9-15'.[1]

The link between the passages is found in the idea of access for the high priest to the divine council, found in Zech. 3.7, and the idea of a diarchy of Zemah and the priest, found in Zech. 6.13. I have argued in Chapter 2 that the interpretation of these passages which leads to finding the ideas of access to the divine council and diarchy is flawed. If these features are not to be found in these two passages, what is the situation in 4.14, with which they are so often connected? That is the question I want to answer in this Chapter by investigating the identi-

---

1. Petersen, *Haggai and Zechariah*, p. 118; cf. Tollington, *Tradition*, pp. 175-76.

fication of the בני היצהר העמדים על־אדון כל־הארץ, usually translated 'the anointed ones who stand by the LORD of the whole earth'. For the understanding of this clause, the interpretation of two phrases are of particular importance: the one translated 'the two anointed' and the one translated 'who stand by', and so the following discussion will find its focus in an investigation of the meaning of these two phrases.

## 1. *Preliminary Remarks*

Before I proceed to the interpretation of v. 14 I need to make two remarks of a more general nature, which are in some way related to each other. The two remarks concern the identification of the lampstand in the vision of Zechariah 4, and the authenticity of Zech. 4.12.

### a. *On the Identification of the Lampstand*
The central element in the vision in Zechariah 4 is a golden lampstand. In spite of its prominent place in the picture, the precise identification of the lampstand is highly problematic, and that for a very simple reason: while the vision report provides an identification of several elements of the lampstand, it does not explain what the lampstand itself is a symbol for.[2]

Given the absence of the explanation of what the lampstand refers to, it comes as no surprise that scholars have not reached a consensus on its identification. The two most favourite options are (a) the lamp stand as a symbol representing the community of the people of God[3] (or—more specifically—the Jewish community[4]); and (b) the lampstand as a sym-

---

2. In the same way, the tabernacle lamp stand in Exodus does not receive an identification (as pointed out by Smith, *Micah–Malachi*, p. 205).

3. Keil, *Propheten*, pp. 564, 566, 571; T. Laetsch, *The Minor Prophets* (Concordia Classic Commentary Series; St Louis: Concordia Publishing House, 1956), p. 428 ('church, God's people'); R.E. Clements, *God and Temple*, p. 133, 'The whole vision of Zech. iv. with its seven-branched lamp stand fed by the oil of two olive trees, is interpreted as the spirit of God flowing to the community through the two anointed ones; i.e. Zerubbabel and Joshua'.

4. Köhler, *Sacharja*, p. 146; J. Boehmer, 'Was bedeutet der goldene Leuchter Sach. 4, 2?', *BZ* 24 (1938–39), pp. 360-64 (364); Bič, *Sacharja*, pp. 57, 59 ('die *eine* Gemeinde, d.h. Jerusalem'); Baldwin, *Haggai, Zechariah*, p. 124; E. Achtemeier, *Nahum–Malachi* (Interpretation; Atlanta: John Knox Press, 1986), p. 124 ('the lights [NB!] of the lampstand represent Israel, the covenant people of God, who are to shine forth in the world').

bol representing YHWH[5] (or one of his attributes, like his presence,[6] or his omniscience and/or providence[7]). A small number of scholars reject these two options and interpret the vision lampstand as either a symbol for the temple,[8] or as a symbol for Zerubbabel.[9]

5.    K. Möhlenbrink, 'Der Leuchter im fünften Nachtgesicht des Propheten Sacharja', *ZDPV* 52 (1929), pp. 267-86 (257-58; already at that time he wrote that there is now a consensus on the symbolic meaning of the lamp stand, 'daß er letztlich Jahwe selber darstelle'); Chary, *Aggée, Zacharie*, p. 85 ('le chandelier de Zacharie un symbole de la personne de Yahwé lui-même'); Jeremias, *Nachtgesichte*, pp. 180-82 ('dem Bild eines Leuchters, der für Jahwe steht'); Rudolph, *Haggai, Sacharja*, p. 107 ('der Leuchter...das Symbol für Jahwe selbst'); Petersen, *Haggai and Zechariah*, p. 227 ('the lampstand itself symbolizes the deity'). In spite of their major disagreements, Keel and Weippert agree at least on the identification of the lampstand as a symbol of the deity (O. Keel, *Jahwe-Visionen und Siegelkunst* [SBS; 84-85; Stuttgart: Verlag Katholisches Bibelwerk, 1977], p. 315; H. Weippert, 'Siegel mit Mondsichelstandarten aus Palästina', *BN* 5 [1978], pp. 43-58 [45-46]). Few scholars have been convinced that the picture in the lampstand vision would have been derived from the lunar cult or astral cult (for a critical discussion of the Keel–Weippert exchange, see Amsler, *Aggée; Zacharie 1–8*, p. 89 n. 3 and n. 5; Schöttler, *Gottesvolk*, pp. 239-42; Hanhart, *Sacharja*, pp. 256-57; Reventlow, *Haggai, Sacharja*, p. 58; E.J.C. Tigchelaar, *Prophets of Old and the Day of the End: Zechariah, the Book of Watchers and Apocalyptic* (OTS, 35; Leiden: E.J. Brill, 1996), pp. 27-29).

6.    Rothstein, *Nachtgesichte*, pp. 127-28 ('der Leuchter mit den sieben Lampen...ist ein Abbild des in seiner Gemeinde gegenwärtigen und über seiner Gemeinde waltenden Gottes'); Rignell, *Nachtgesichte*, p. 175 ('der Leuchter...ein Symbol der Gegenwart Jahves'); Ackroyd, *Exile*, pp. 192-93 ('the lampstand as the symbol of the divine presence'); Seybold, 'Königserwartung', p. 74 ('der Leuchter repräsentiert...Jahwes Gegenwart'); Mason, *Haggai, Zechariah*, p. 47 (the lamp stand 'represented the presence of God in the midst of his temple'); Meyers and Meyers, *Haggai, Zechariah*, p. 262 (the lampstand 'represents the presence of Yahweh himself'); Schöttler, *Gottesvolk*, p. 235 (the lampstand 'symbolisiert die Gegenwart Jahwes').

7.    Marti, *Dodekapropheton*, p. 414; Chary, *Aggée, Zacharie*, p. 85-86; Galling, *Studien*, p. 117: the lampstand is a 'Symbol der Weltherrschaft des einen und höchsten Gottes (4,10b)'; Amsler, *Aggée; Zacharie 1–8*, p. 89.

8.    Buzy, 'Symboles', p. 169 (the lampstand is the temple under construction and the completion stone in particular, the lamps (eyes) symbolize the care of the divine providence concentrated on the building under construction to watch over its quick completion); Ridderbos, *Profeten*, pp. 79-80; Niditch, *Symbolic Vision*, p. 106; Van der Woude, 'Zion as Primeval Stone in Zechariah 3 and 4', W. Claassen (ed.), *Text and Context: Old Testament and Semitic Studies for F.C. Fensham* (JSOTSup, 48; Sheffield: JSOT Press, 1988), pp. 237-48 (239; 'the lamp-stand is

This is not the place to resolve the dispute over the identification of the lampstand, if I were able to do so. Within the context of this chapter, however, there is one aspect of the discussion that needs our attention, and that is the argument behind the identification of the lampstand as representing YHWH. From the way this identification is presented, it seems that for its proponents this is the most logical and straightforward option. It is necessary to question this.

The identification is based on the following argument, recently presented by Petersen in these words:

> The lights of the lamp symbolize the deity's eyes, and by inference the lampstand itself symbolizes the deity. This is, of course, not stated explicitly. Israel's aniconic tradition was and remained strong. And yet this implication of the lampstand's function in the vision is difficult to gainsay.[10]

A similar kind of reasoning is adopted with regard to the sons of oil in v. 14: since they 'stand by the Lord of the whole earth', and the olive trees of which they are the identification are located on either side of the lampstand, therefore the lampstand should be identified as representing YHWH. The key to the identification is found in a simple substitution, which can be presented in a figure (see Figure 14).

---

explained as the temple mountain [v. 7], then the "bowl" on top of it as the temple building [vv. 8-9], then the lamps as the eyes of the Lord [v. 10], and finally the olives as the two "sons of the fresh oil" [v. 14]'). According to L. Rost, 'Bemerkungen zu Sacharja 4', *ZAW* 63 (1951), pp. 216-21 (220; reprinted in Leonhard Rost, *Das Kleine Credo und andere Studien zum Alten Testament* [Heidelberg: Quelle & Meyer, 1965]), in the original explanation the lampstand stood for the temple and the oil for the cult in the temple (this view is adopted by U. Kellermann, *Messias und Gesetz: Grundlinien einer alttestamentlichen Heilserwartung. Eine traditionsgeschichtliche Einführung* [Neukirchen–Vluyn: Neukirchener Verlag, 1971], p. 59).

9. K.A. Strand, 'The Two Olive Trees of Zechariah 4 and Revelation 11', *AUSS* 20.3 (1982), pp. 257-61 (258-59).

10. Petersen, *Haggai and Zechariah*, pp. 227-28 (note the words 'by inference'). One finds exactly the same argument in Elliger, *Propheten*, p. 110, 'Die sieben Augen sind...die Augen Gottes (10b). Der Leuchter ist also Gott selbst, wie auch aus V. 14 hervorgeht. Ausdrücklich gesagt wird es nicht... Wahrscheinlich ist ganz mit Absicht von einer Darstellung Gottes nicht die Rede. Symbolisiert wird nur seine Allwissenheit'. See also, Seybold, 'Königserwartung', p. 74; Rudolph, *Haggai, Sacharja*, p. 107, 'da die Leuchtstellen Symbole für die Augen sind, kann der Leuchter, der diese Fülle trägt, nur das Symbol für Jahwe selbst sein...'; and Smith, *Micah–Malachi*, p. 205.

Figure 14. *The Identification of the Lamp Stand and Some of its Details*

**identification**

| **provided** | suggested |
| **in the passage** | by commentator |

| **lights** | (on) the lampstand |
| = | = |
| **eyes** | (of) YHWH |

| **two olive trees** | (by) the lampstand |
| = | = |
| **two sons of oil** | (by) the Lord |
| | (of the whole earth) |

It is precisely this type of argument that requires discussion. At first sight it may seem very logical and straightforward, but closer inspection will show that the whole argument is flawed from the perspective of methodology. In my view what happens is a confusion of different genres. Those who use arguments such as these assume an immediate correspondence between the world generated in the picture of the vision (I will call this 'world-P') and the 'real' world ('world-R') where one finds the objects or persons which the details of the picture are symbols of. The relationship between realities in world-R is considered to be exactly identical to the relationship between corresponding objects in world-P, in something like a one-to-one correspondence.

It goes like this: the lights belong to the lampstand (world-P), and the eyes belong to YHWH (world-R). The lights on the lampstand equal the eyes of YHWH, therefore the lampstand equals YHWH. The olive trees are on either side of the lampstand (world-P), and the sons of oil stand by YHWH (world-R). The olive trees by the lampstand equal the sons of oil who stand by the Lord of the whole earth, therefore the lampstand equals YHWH .

Finding such a one-to-one correspondence assumes that one should interpret the vision as if it were an allegory.[11] Unfortunately, scholars

11. In an article about the identification of the lampstand, Boehmer quotes a maxim from the interpretation of parables, which is indeed an appropriate comment also in this context of the interpretation of Zechariah 4 (quoted from I.K. Madsen, 'Zur Erklärung der evangelischen Parabeln', *TSK* 104 [1932], pp. 311-36 [317]; the

do not indicate the grounds on the basis of which they allow themselves to apply rules from the interpretation of one literary genre, allegory, to the interpretation of another, visions, and it is not clear whether there are any. Particularly in cases where the passage itself refrains from providing identifications for all of the details, one should be very cautious in reading visionary material like an allegory.

In sharp contrast to this approach is the following statement by Tigchelaar, a statement which in my view is much sounder from the perspective of methodology: 'The fact that the olive trees are standing beside the menorah, and that the "sons of oil" stand beside the Lord of the entire earth, does not mean that the menorah is a symbol of Yahweh himself'.[12] I conclude that the argument used to support the identification of the lampstand as representing YHWH, which boils down to a simple substitution of objects in world-P with realities in world-R, is flawed because it confuses two different genres, vision and allegory.

As stated earlier, the passage itself does not provide an identification. All I have tried to do so far is to show that the case for the identification of the lampstand as a symbol for (the presence of) YHWH is far from compelling. Once its weakness is exposed it looses the force with which it is usually presented. This opens the possibility for considering an association of the lampstand with the temple or the community worshipping at the temple, which seems the most plausible option to me.[13] This identification fits best in the context of the chapter as a whole (see below).

### b. *On the Authenticity of Verse 12*
*A Difficult Verse.* In the opinion of a great number of scholars, Zech. 4.12 is something of a black sheep. The verse adds a second question while only one question is eventually answered in v. 14. The difficulties

original article was not available to me), 'Bildliche Züge, die der gewöhnlichen Erfahrung entsprechen und sich in ein Ganzes zusammenschließen, fordern nicht Zug für Zug, sondern nur als Totalität etwas Ähnliches in der Sachhälfte der Parabel...'

12. Tigchelaar, *Prophets*, p. 40.

13. This view comes close to the views of Baldwin and Niditch. Baldwin writes (*Haggai, Zechariah*, p. 124), 'The lampstand represents not the Lord but the witness of the Temple and the Jewish community to Him... Zechariah's lamp stood for the worshipping community of the post-exilic period'. According to Niditch the lampstand is 'an evoker of temple—more precisely tabernacle—and cult' (Niditch, *Symbolic Vision*, p. 106).

of the interpretation of the verse are immense. It goes beyond the scope of this investigation to provide an extensive discussion, let alone a reso-lution of the problems. Beginning with the less problematic: the word צנתרות is probably related to the cognate צנור ('shaft', 'cataract') in 2 Sam. 5.8 (a feature of the Jebusite water system of Jerusalem)[14] and in all likelihood means 'pipes' or 'tubes'. The fact that these 'pipes' are made of gold indicates that they belong to the lampstand,[15] not the trees. ביד means 'through'[16] (never 'beside' [RSV]).[17] צהב at the end of the question is either a poetical equivalent of,[18] or a transcriptional error for[19] יצהר. The phrase, 'which empty the gold [oil] from them' should be connected with the masculine (as indicated by the form of the nu-meral שני) צנתרות (ם)זיתים is also masculine but the presence of אשר ex-cludes זיתים from being the subject of מריקים). If one takes the olive trees (the word is found in the phrase שבלי הזיתים) as the antecedent

14. In spite of alternative proposals, this is still the most plausible interpretation of צנור; see the recent survey and discussion in T. Kleven, 'The Use of ṣnr in Ugaritic and 2 Samuel V 8: Hebrew Usage and Comparative Philology', *VT* 44 (1994), pp. 195-204 (195-202).

15. Van der Woude, *Zacharia*, p. 94; Van der Woude has now (n. 117 on p. 280) abandoned his earlier view ('Die beiden Söhne des Öls (Sach 4:14): Messianische Gestalten?', in M.S.H.G. Heerma van Vos, P.H.J. Houwink ten Cate and N.A. van Uchelen, *Travels in the World of the Old Testament: Studies Presented to Prof. M.A. Beek* [Assen: Van Gorcum, 1974], pp. 262-68 [267]) that the צנתרות are mountains.

16. E.g. Petersen, *Haggai and Zechariah*, p. 215; NJPS.

17. Contra BDB (p. 391); Hanhart, *Sacharja*, p. 242. See Schöttler, *Gottesvolk*, p. 107 n. 282.

18. E.g. Nowack, *Propheten*, p. 346; A. Brenner, *Colour Terms in the Old Testament* (JSOTSup, 21; Sheffield: JSOT Press, 1982), p. 168; Schöttler, *Gottes-volk*, p. 118. Cf. a translation like 'golden oil' in Chary, *Aggée, Zacharie and Mason, Haggai, Zechariah*. According to Meyers and Meyers, *Haggai, Zechariah*, p. 257, זהב 'refers to the color and not the substance of that which is being transferred from trees to lampstand'.

19. So, e.g., Rothstein, *Nachtgesichte*, p. 124 n. 1 (Rothstein argues that in the Old Hebrew Script there would have been a high degree of similarity of the letters of היצהר and הזהב, which could have resulted in confusion); Duhm, 'Anmer-kungen', p. 169. I prefer this reconstruction of a simple error to the more complex ones mentioned by Elliger in the apparatus in *BHS*, in which not only היצהר is added but also a word to express that into which the oil is poured out ('*the oil into the* golden *lamps*' (Elliger); '*the oil into the* golden *conduits*' (Nowack, *Propheten*, p. 346); the Hebrew text for these proposals can be found in the apparatus of *BHS*.

of the suffix הם- in מעליהם, then there is no need to alter the text by removing the first מ of מעליהם.

This leaves us with the phrase שבלי הזיתים. One interpretation of שבלי gives the meaning 'branches'.[20] The root from which this meaning is derived, שבלת[i] (plural שבלים), is used for ears (that is, the fruit, not the branches) of grain (not olive trees) as they grow or are harvested (e.g. Gen. 41.5; Ruth 2.2; Job 24.24; Isa. 17.5). So the presence of the word in the context of a description of olive trees is unusual, but may be based on analogy.[21] The word then would refer to the 'fruit-laden ends of olive branches',[22] or the 'tops of the olive trees' (NJPS).

There is also another root שבלת. שבלת[ii] is used for a 'flowing stream'. The word is only attested in the singular, and always in connection with water, but this may be a coincidence connected to the low frequency of the use of the word (only three times).[23] The problem with deriving the meaning from this root is that it is difficult to imagine the nature of the syntactical relationship between the שבלים and the זיתים. Petersen[24] translates the complete phrase as 'two streams of olive oil', but admits that one would expect שבלי זית (he compares it with the phrase שמן זית 'olive's oil' in Exod. 27.20; 30.24; Lev. 24.2) rather than שבלי הזיתים.

This difficulty and the fact that elsewhere the word only occurs in the singular is the reason why I prefer the interpretation of the word on the basis of the root שבלת[i] as ears or tops. The verse as a whole could then be translated: 'What are the two tops of the olive trees which [are] through the golden pipes which empty the gold from them'. In spite of

20. So RSV, and, e.g., Chary, *Aggée, Zacharie*, p. 88; Baldwin, *Haggai, Zechariah*, p. 123; Rudolph, *Haggai, Sacharja*, pp. 103, 109; Amsler, *Aggée; Zacharie 1–8*, pp. 87, 89; Meyers and Meyers, *Haggai, Zechariah*, pp. 228, 255; Schöttler, *Gottesvolk*, p. 107 ('fruchtbehangenen Zweigen'); Hanhart, *Sacharja*, pp. 242, 288; Reventlow, *Haggai, Sacharja*, pp. 57, 60.

21. Köhler, *Sacharja*, p. 143.

22. Smith, *Micah–Malachi*, p. 205.

23. In Ps. 69.3, 16 שבלת is used of a 'flood' sweeping over someone; in Isa. 27.12 it is used in the phrase 'from the river Euphrates [משבלת הנהר] to the Brook of Egypt'. I leave Judg. 12.6 out of this discussion, because it is not clear whether the word in this verse is שבלת[i] or שבלת[ii] (it does not make a difference for my present discussion anyway, since it does not address the issue of—if שבלת[ii]—what it is a stream of).

24. *Haggai and Zechariah*, pp. 215, 235.

the lack of clarity of many of the details, the overall picture seems to be reasonable clear: the olive trees supply the lamp stand with oil.[25]

*Original or Secondary.* The verse is usually considered a later addition and, as a result, deleted.[26] Without v. 12, the passage would read:

> Then I said to him, 'What are these two olive trees on the right and the left of the lampstand?' He said to me, 'Do you not know what these are?' I said, 'No, my lord.' Then he said, 'These are the two anointed who stand by the Lord of the whole earth' (Zech. 4.11-14).

Reading the passage without v. 12 provides a picture that is substantially different from the picture when v. 12 is included: there is no (physical) connection between the lampstand and the olive trees. As Driver puts it:[27] 'if v. 12 be omitted, the olive trees of v. 3 merely *stand beside* the candlestick; they are otherwise unconnected, and do not supply the lamps with oil'. I offer the following brief remarks on the authenticity of v. 12, which will make clear why I consider the verse as original.

(a) Verse 12 adds a second question, and this would certainly be a unique formal feature in the vision reports of Zechariah 1–6. However, ch. 4 introduces other formal features not found in the earlier vision reports. In the first verse we are told that the angel returns and awakens

25. E.g. Rost, 'Sacharja 4', p. 219; Beuken, *Haggai–Sacharja 1–8*, p. 259; Ackroyd, *Exile*, pp. 193-94; Petersen, *Haggai and Zechariah*, p. 234; Hanhart, *Sacharja*, p. 288.

26. Marti, *Dodekapropheton*, p. 414; Van Hoonacker, *Prophètes*, p. 619; Duhm, 'Anmerkungen', p. 169; Mitchell, *Haggai and Zechariah*, p. 164-65; A.C. Welch, 'Zechariah's Vision of the Lampstand', *ExpTim* 29 (1917–18), pp. 239-40 (240); Buzy, 'Symboles', p. 165; Nowack, *Propheten*, p. 346; Möhlenbrink, 'Leuchter', p. 262; Galling, *Studien*, pp. 117, 137; Beuken, *Haggai–Sacharja 1–8*, p. 26; Elliger, *Propheten*, p. 110-11; Ackroyd, *Exile*, p. 192-93; Chary, *Aggée, Zacharie*, pp. 88-89; Beyse, *Serubbabel*, p. 71; Seybold, *Bilder*, pp. 41, 43, 45, 55; Rudolph, *Haggai, Sacharja*, p. 109; Mason, *Haggai, Zechariah*, pp. 47-48; Amsler, *Aggée; Zacharie 1–8*, pp. 89-90; Petersen, *Haggai and Zechariah*, pp. 234-35; Tollington, *Tradition*, p. 37. Wellhausen, *Propheten*, p. 182, calls v. 12 '[e]ine sehr verdächtige Wiederholung', and considers it impossible that זיתים (v. 11) and שׁבלי הזיתים (v. 12) come from the same author, but he does not say explicitly that v. 12 is a secondary addition. Some others are similarly not completely clear about how they themselves consider v. 12, e.g. Driver, *Prophets*, p. 204; Reventlow, *Haggai, Sacharja*, p. 60. Schöttler considers only v. 12abα as an additional gloss to vv. 11, 12bβ, 13, which are already not original (*Gottesvolk*, pp. 118-19).

27. Driver, *Prophets*, p. 204. Compare Mitchell, *Haggai and Zechariah*, p. 168.

the prophet. Second, the angel asks the prophet, 'What do you see?'
(v. 2, then also in 5.2). Third, he asks the prophet, 'Do you not know
what they are?' (first in v. 5 and then once again in v. 13). A final new
feature is the resumption of speech, first in v. 4 (ואען ואמר), where it
has a clear purpose, to mark the change from description of the vision
to asking about its meaning, and then once again here in v. 12, where its
function cannot be so easily defined (in this respect the situation in
v. 12 is similar to that in 5.6, where one finds ויאמר twice). Therefore,
to find unique formal features is not so unusual in this chapter.[28] The
two features which make 4.12 unique is the second question and the
explicit indication that this is the second time of asking, (ואען שנית
(ואמר), but once one has got this far into the chapter it seems an exag-
geration to make much of this.

(b) Another element which has raised the suspicion that v. 12 is
secondary is the introduction in this verse of details of the vision not
mentioned before, like the olive 'ears'/'tops' and the golden conduits.
This argument seems to be based on an unwritten rule that the first
description of what is seen in a prophetic vision is the only place where
details of the vision can be reported, so that there is no place for details
not already mentioned in the part of the vision report which deals with
the explanation.

One may doubt whether such a rule ever existed. Admittedly, the
introduction of new elements in this stage in the vision report is unique
in the sequence of visions in Zechariah 1–6, but it is not unparalleled in
vision reports elsewhere in the Old Testament. In Daniel 7 Daniel first
describes (vv. 1-14) what he saw in the vision, and then (vv. 15-28) he
asks for and receives the explanation. In his question to the interpreter,
Daniel introduces two aspects of the vision which he had not mentioned
before (the claws of bronze, and the war between the beast and the
saints).

(c) It is often stated that v. 12 introduces a theological difficulty.
According to Rudolph, v. 12 would introduce a 'warped, indeed...blas-
phemous thought' (*schiefe ja...blasphemische Gedanke*): the two human
beings would provide food for and give strength to the lampstand, that
is, to YHWH. For this reason one then has to ascribe to the interpolator a
different explanation of the lampstand, for example as referring to the
Jewish community, which then would imply a striking contradiction

28. Compare the discussion of the unique formal features in Zechariah 3, in
Chapter 1 (section entitled 'The Origin of Zechariah 3').

with v. 14b.[29] As Rudolph's remark concerning 'a striking contradiction to v. 14b' (*ein krasser Widerspruch zu V. 14b*) indicates, this problem is created by a particular identification of the lampstand, namely as a symbol representing YHWH. This identification loses its compelling force once its faulty logic has been exposed (see my discussion above), and as a result the theological difficulty disappears.

(d) Petersen argues that the degree of difficulty of (the in his view secondary) v. 12 was deliberate and served the purpose of confusing the picture. He feels 'forced to suggest that v. 12 is difficult to translate because it was intended to be unclear. Some pious commentator took offense at the rather clear motif of divine–human interdependence and obfuscated that picture by the introduction of puzzling detail and cryptic syntax'.[30] Petersen's approach is problematic for several reasons. Petersen's comment, 'Some pious commentator took offense at the rather clear motif of divine-human interdependence' assumes (i) the identification of the lamp stand with YHWH, and (ii) the presence of a notion of 'divine–human interdependence'. I have argued above that such an identification of the lampstand is questionable. One wonders where Petersen finds a notion of 'divine–human interdependence', if not in v. 12, which he considers secondary (in Petersen's interpretation v. 14 does not say anything about the relationship between lampstand and trees; it only identifies the trees). If there were such a notion, it is introduced by v. 12, but in Petersen's position one cannot state that it is already there and that the addition of v. 12 then attempts to 'obfuscate the quite clear and potentially "blasphemous" picture created by the interpreted vision'.

The idea of a deliberate attempt to confuse the picture in general

---

29. Rudolph, *Haggai, Sacharja*, p. 109. The difficulty is noticed by many scholars, e.g. Van Hoonacker, *Prophètes*, p. 619; Buzy, 'Symboles', p. 171; Beuken, *Haggai–Sacharja 1–8*, p. 259; Ackroyd, *Exile*, pp. 193-94; Baldwin, *Haggai, Zechariah*, p. 123; Van der Woude, *Zacharia*, p. 94. Keel, *Visionen*, p. 310 n. 109, is less sympathetic to those who would attribute the alleged *theologischen Unsinn* of v. 12 (which he does not find there because he interprets בְּיַד as 'under the authority of' [on which see Schöttler, *Gottesvolk*, p. 107 n. 282]) to a glossator, 'Glossatoren mutet man jeden Unsinn zu. Warum nicht! Sie waren schließlich unsere Vorläufer'. Petersen, *Haggai and Zechariah*, p. 234, is able to give a positive evaluation of what others find a theological anomaly; he finds in the secondary v. 12 a development in theological thinking. In his view there is a notion of consubstantiality in the picture, 'A human-divine political symbiosis is constitutive for the postexilic community'.

30. Petersen, *Haggai and Zechariah*, p. 237.

seems an unsatisfactory approach. An approach like Van der Woude's seems more plausible: 'an interpolator does obviously not intend to cloud the sense of a text, but rather to make it more clear'.[31]

To sum up: Zech. 4.12 is an extremely difficult verse. However, the reasons for considering the verse secondary are far from compelling. The unusual formal features found in 4.12 match with other unprecedented formal features in the rest of the chapter. The introduction of details not mentioned before can be paralleled from Daniel 7. The theological difficulty found in the verse is only there for those who identify the lampstand with YHWH. Abandoning the identification of the lampstand with YHWH results in the disappearance of the alleged theological difficulty of YHWH being dependent on human beings. It is difficult to comprehend for what reason a redactor would have added such a difficult verse.

On the basis of these remarks, I take Zech. 4.12 as a verse that is original to the vision report,[32] and not a secondary addition. The function of the verse was most likely to make the question in v. 11 more specific.[33]

## 2. The Meaning of the Phrase 'The Two Sons of Oil'

After these two preliminary remarks I now turn to the main subject of this chapter, the interpretation of the clause, 'These are the two anointed who stand by the Lord of the whole earth'. The phrase which RSV translates 'the two anointed' is in Hebrew שְׁנֵי בְנֵי־הַיִּצְהָר. There are in Hebrew two words for oil: יִצְהָר is one of them, the other is שֶׁמֶן. יִצְהָר is used 15 times, but (with Zech. 4.14—the verse under discussion—as the only exception) only in set word-pairs or triplets, while שֶׁמֶן is used

---

31. 'Ein Interpolator hat ja nicht die Absicht den Sinn eines Textes zu verschleiern, sondern vielmehr ihn zu verdeutlichen' (Van der Woude, 'Söhne', p. 266); and similarly Rignell, *Nachtgesichte*, p. 168, 'Ein Interpolator dürfte sich übrigens einer durchsichtigeren Terminologie bedient haben, als sie der Text aufweist'.

32. With Köhler, *Sacharja*, p. 157; Keil, *Propheten*, p. 571; Koch, *Profeten*, II, p. 172 (ET *Prophets*, II, pp. 168-69); Van der Woude, pp. 93-95; Bauer, *Zeit*, p. 266; Hanhart, *Sacharja*, p. 253.

33. So Keil, *Propheten*, p. 571; Bauer, *Zeit*, p. 266; K.M. Craig, Jr, 'Interrogatives in Haggai–Zechariah: A Literary Thread?', in J.W. Watts and P.R. House (eds.), *Forming Prophetic Literature: Essays on Isaiah and the Twelve in Honor of John D.W. Watts* (JSOTSup, 235; Sheffield: JSOT Press, 1996), pp. 236-38 (238).

195 times, and in a great variety of contexts. Translations like that of
the RSV[34] are based on two convictions: (a) יצהר and שמן are synonymous; and (b) the phrase בני־היצהר (= בני־השמן) means 'anointed
ones'.

### a. *The Case for the Synonymy of* יצהר *and* שמן
The view that יצהר and שמן are synonymous goes back to a brief article
written by Köhler in 1928 on the phrase דגן (ו)(תירוש (ו)יצהר.[35] The
article has been very influential,[36] though more recently an increasing
number of scholars has challenged Köhler's conclusions. Köhler provided an analysis of the use of these three words in the phrase דגן
(ו)תירוש (ו)יצהר and its variants, and the use of the words on their own.
He argued that the three words דגן, יצהר and תירוש are archaisms, and
synonymous with לחם, שמן and יין respectively. The archaic words are
preserved in phrases, but used on their own only occasionally.

With respect to the use of יצהר on its own, that is, outside the phrase
דגן (ו)תירוש (ו)יצהר, Köhler states that since the phrase זֵית יִצְהָר in
2 Kgs 18.32 and זֵית שֶׁמֶן in Deut. 8.8 are interchangeable (*steht in
Wechsel mit*) and mean the same thing, the reference to Joshua and
Zerubbabel in Zech. 4.14 as בְּנֵי־הַיִּצְהָר is just a solemn way of saying
בְּנֵי־הַשֶּׁמֶן. On the basis of the same factual identity of שֶׁמֶן in Deut. 8.8
and יִצְהָר in 2 Kgs 18.32 he rejects the attempts of lexicographers to
find a distinction between יִצְהָר 'fresh oil' and שֶׁמֶן 'oil'. He then compares the phrase דָּגָן וְתִירוֹשׁ וְיִצְהָר with set phrases in German which
have retained archaic words no longer used on their own, that is outside
the set phrase.

*Confusion of Meaning and Reference.* Köhler's argument for establishing the synonymy of the שמן/יצהר pair is seriously flawed.[37] The main

34. Compare 'the two anointed ones' in NRSV, and 'the two anointed dignitaries' in NJPS.
35. L. Köhler, 'Eine archaistische Wortgruppe', *ZAW* 46 (1928), pp. 218-20
(219-20).
36. Those who adopt Köhler's thesis, include Rudolph, *Haggai, Sacharja*,
p. 108 n. 13; *HALAT*, p. 408 s.v. יצהר. H. Ringgren, 'יצהר', *ThWAT*, III, cols. 825-
26 (825), echoes Köhler: '*jishār* scheint mit *šaemoen* "Öl" gleichbedeutend zu sein.
*zêt šaemoen* Deut. 8, 8 und *zêt jishār* bezeichnen beide die Ölbäume'; see also
Ringgren, 'שמן', *ThWAT*, VIII, cols. 251-55 (252), 'Öl, das im AT entweder *šaemœn*
oder → יצהר *jishār* heißt...'
37. For similar criticism, see Schöttler, *Gottesvolk*, pp. 245-54.

problem is that he confuses meaning and reference. The proof for his case of synonymy is that '[t]he expression in 2 Kgs. 18.32 can simply be exchanged with Deut. 8.8; both expressions have the same meaning'.[38] The two passages read in the RSV:

> ...a good land, a land of brooks of water, of fountains and springs, flowing forth in valleys and hills, a land of wheat and barley, of vines and fig trees and pomegranates, a land of olive trees and honey, a land in which you will eat bread without scarcity, in which you will lack nothing, a land whose stones are iron, and out of whose hills you can dig copper (Deut. 8.7-9).

> ...a land like your own land, a land of grain and wine, a land of bread and vineyards, a land of olive trees and honey, that you may live, and not die (2 Kgs 18.32).

The passages make clear that both composite phrases זית יצהר and זית שמן may have the same reference, that is, an olive tree. But as such that does not make the two phrases synonymous. As Lyons writes, 'Expressions may differ in sense, but have the same reference; and "synonymous" means "having the same sense", not "having the same reference"'.[39]

Just quoting two contexts where the two phrases have the same reference is not sufficient to establish whether the two phrases have the same meaning. One has to look at other contexts were the phrases are used. In this particular case there are no such other contexts. Fortunately, it does not really matter for the issue under discussion here: the exact nature of the semantic relationships in the יצהר/שמן pair. Even if one concludes that the two compound phrases זית יצהר and זית שמן are synonymous, the only thing one has done is to make a statement about the sense relationship between these two composite phrases.

*Confusion of Phrases and Constituents.* And that is the second problem with Köhler's case: he fails to distinguish between a case for the synonymy of the composite phrases זית יצהר and זית שמן, and a case for the synonymy of יצהר and שמן. It is one thing to claim that the composite phrases זית יצהר and זית שמן are synonymous, it is another thing

---

38. '[D]er Ausdruck זֵית יִצְהָר II Reg 18 32 steht in Wechsel mit זֵית שֶׁמֶן Dtn 8 8 und bedeutet dasselbe'(Köhler, 'Eine archaistische Wortgruppe').

39. J. Lyons, *Semantics* (Cambridge: Cambridge University Press, 1977), p. 199.

to establish the nature of the sense relationship between the individual constituents out of which the phrases are built, including those components which appear in the same paradigmatic slot, in this case יצהר and שמן.

*Lack of Interchangeability.* One of the things to look at, when one wants to find out whether words are synonymous, is interchangeability: if two lexical items are synonymous then either of them can be found in contexts where the other is found. And here one finds a major problem with Köhler's thesis. The two words are not equally distributed over different contexts. Even though both יצהר and שמן are found to refer to the produce of the land, yet in contexts dealing with oil for anointing and (apart from Zech. 4.14) also in contexts dealing with oil for burning lamps, the word for oil is always שמן, *never* יצהר[40] (see Fig. 15).

Figure 15. *The Distribution of Words for 'Oil'*

| oil as produce of the land | oil for lighting a lamp | oil for anointing |
|---|---|---|
| יצהר or שמן | שמן | שמן |

This state of affairs, particularly the restriction of the use of יצהר to contexts dealing with the produce of the land, strongly suggests that the two words, though clearly related in meaning, are not synonymous. It provides strong evidence in support of the decision to make a distinction between the meaning of יצהר and the meaning of שמן. The latter is the more general word for oil, including oil as a final product, prepared for use in lighting or anointing. The precise nuance of יצהר is perhaps difficult to capture. Scholars usually interpret it as 'fresh oil', the raw material, freshly squeezed, before it is prepared,[41] though evidence is

40. Several scholars rightly point this out, e.g. Petersen, *Haggai and Zechariah*, p. 231. Cf. V. Maag, *Text, Wortschatz und Begriffswelt des Buches Amos* (Leiden: E.J. Brill, 1951), p. 192, 'Es ist sogar zu vermuten, dass die Salbung nur mit dem lauter gewordenen שמן, nicht aber mit יצהר ausgeführt werden durfte'.

41. So, e.g., Driver, *Prophets*, p. 202: יצהר 'denotes the freshly expressed juice of the olive; and is not the word (*shémen*) which denotes the oil as prepared for use, and ready, for example, to be employed for a lamp...or in anointing...'; G. Dalman, *Arbeit und Sitte in Palästina. IV. Brot, Öl und Wein* (Gütersloh: C. Bertelsmann, 1935), p. 255, 'Dem biblischen Hebräisch ist eigen, daß das dem Traubenmost parallele flüssige Produkt der Olive als *jishār* von *šémen*, dem fertigen Öl, unter-

lacking to be absolutely certain about this nuance. I conclude that the semantic relationship between the two words in the שׁמן/יצהר pair is most likely not one of synonymy.

*Zech. 4.14 an 'Isolated' Occurrence.* I now want to consider one possible objection to the semantic analysis I have proposed. It may be asked whether I have given due consideration to the fact that the use of the word יצהר is almost completely restricted to set phrases like דגן (ו)תירושׁ (ו)יצהר. Does this not make the semantics of the יצהר/שׁמן pair somewhat more complicated than my analysis suggests? Should one not reckon with the possibility that if the word יצהר were found more often outside the context of formulaic phrases, then it would become clear that יצהר and שׁמן are actually synonymous?

I would agree that this is a possibility but that the nature of the situation makes it impossible to go further than calling it a possibility: the reason we have a problem is precisely because we do not have much evidence. So a scarcity of evidence makes it extremely difficult to resolve the issue. But if the restricted occurrence of the word יצהר possibly distorts the semantic picture, then it also points to the uniqueness of the choice of precisely this word in Zech. 4.14.

The presence of this word in this context provides us with at least some evidence. Here one finds the word outside its usual context of a formulaic phrase, in a relatively late text within the corpus of the Hebrew Old Testament. If, as Köhler argues, the words יצהר and שׁמן are synonymous, one has to consider this question: for what reason would Zechariah choose to use here a word that elsewhere is found only as part of a composite phrase, and is—in Köhler's view—supposed to be archaic? Calling בני־היצהר a 'solemn expression' fails by far to do justice to the peculiarity of the choice of the word יצהר, rather than the more usual שׁמן.

This late occurrence of an 'isolated' יצהר would not call into question

schieden wird'; Maag, *Amos*, p. 192; Van der Woude, 'Söhne', pp. 264-65; Petersen, *Haggai and Zechariah*, p. 231; Meyers and Meyers, *Haggai, Zechariah*, p. 258; Schöttler, *Gottesvolk*, p. 247; *HAH* s.v. יצהר gives 'frisches Öl (versch. v. → שׁמן)'; Tollington, *Tradition*, p. 177, 'the freshly harvested oil from olives'. A different suggestion is made by O. Borowski, *Agriculture in Iron Age Israel* (Winona Lake, IN: Eisenbrauns, 1987), p. 126, 'Besides being used for lighting... oil had a prominent place in cultic life as an offering. In this context a different word is used, i.e., *yiṣhār*'.

Köhler's statement concerning the archaic nature of the words יצהר, דגן and תירוש, and the occasional nature of their appearance (*dann auch isoliert noch gelegentlich gebraucht*), if it were the only late case of one of the three elements of the phrase occurring as an 'isolated' word. But the case does not stand on its own. When one studies the use of the word דגן, another element in the set phrase, one discovers that דגן as part of the composite phrase (or one of its variants) occurs 30 times, and isolated דגן 10 times, with no less than five cases in relatively late texts (sixth century BCE and later).[42] The use of labels like 'archaic' and 'occurring only occasionally' fails to do justice to these data.

*Conclusion*. To sum up: Köhler's case for the synonymy of שמן/יצהר cannot be maintained because it is built on a confusion first of (a) meaning and reference, and next of (b) composite phrases and their constituents. The two words appear not to be interchangeable: while in some contexts either יצהר or שמן may be found, in other contexts, that is, those dealing with oil for anointing and also contexts dealing with oil for burning lamps, one finds always שמן, and never יצהר. So, the word used for oil in Zech. 4.14, יצהר, is most likely not synonymous with שמן.

Zechariah 4.14 is unique in that it is the only case where the noun יצהר is found on its own, that is, not as part of a formulaic phrase. This in itself makes the presence of the noun יצהר highly significant, and Köhler's explanation of the phrase בני־היצהר as a solemn expression for בני־השמן fails to do justice to the peculiarity of the choice of precisely this word.

### b. *No Evidence for the Interpretation 'Anointed Ones'*
While Köhler stated that בני־היצהר is a solemn expression for בני־השמן, he did not provide any further discussion of what either phrase actually meant. Up until recently, most scholars would interpret the phrase בני־היצהר as 'anointed ones'.[43] This raises another problem. Those who

---

42. The phrase דגן (ו)תירוש (ו)יצהר is not found in Ezekiel, isolated דגן occurs once (Ezek. 36.29), either of the other two constituents never. Isolated דגן occurs three times in Nehemiah (5.2, 3, 10), the phrase (complete or incomplete) five times (Neh. 5.11; 10.38, 40; 13.5, 12). Isolated דגן occurs once in Joel (1.17), the phrase (complete or incomplete) three times (Joel 1.10; 2.19, 24).

43. E.g. Mitchell, *Haggai and Zechariah*, p. 165; Niditch, *Symbolic Vision*, pp. 90, 109-10.

interpret the phrase as 'anointed ones' are unable to produce any evidence that the phrase as a whole, בְּנֵי־הַיִּצְהָר, or its alleged counterpart, בְּנֵי הַשֶּׁמֶן, could be used for 'anointed ones'. To be precise, there are no other passages where either expression in precisely this form is found, but a similar phrase without the article is found once, in Isa. 5.1, this time in the singular: כֶּרֶם...בְּקֶרֶן בֶּן־שָׁמֶן, translated in RSV as 'a vineyard on a very fertile hill'. Here the phrase בֶּן־שָׁמֶן is used as a substitute for an adjective. The meaning of this phrase is rather different from the idea of an anointed leader figure, which a number of scholars want to find in Zech. 4.14 (a phrase like מָשִׁיחַ נָגִיד [see Dan. 9.25] would qualify much better for expressing that idea).

As such, the absence of evidence for the interpretation 'anointed ones' is not conclusive proof that this is a wrong interpretation. But when one takes this problem of the absence of evidence together with the problems in the case for the synonymy of the שֶׁמֶן/יִצְהָר pair, then the case for 'anointed ones' breaks down. With Petersen, one has to conclude that 'there is little warrant for understanding the phrase "sons of oil" to designate them as anointed'.[44]

### c. *The Meaning of the Phrase* בְּנֵי־הַיִּצְהָר

So, what does the phrase בְּנֵי־הַיִּצְהָר mean? The phrase [בֵּן + Noun] belongs to a group of phrases which also include [אִישׁ + Noun] and [בַּעַל + Noun]. Phrases like these are used in two ways: (a) 'to represent the nature, quality, character, or condition of (a) person(s)', and (b) to 'indicate the relationship of an individual to a class of beings'.[45] The word יִצְהָר falls outside the category of words which one finds in usage (b). So we are left with (a) nature, quality, character, or condition. As Schöttler has argued, when [בֵּן + Noun] is used in this way, it is either in an active or in a passive sense. If passive, 'anointed' would be a possibility, but we have seen that this is problematic because of the use of יִצְהָר.

Those scholars who reject the interpretation 'anointed ones' usually take the phrase in an active sense and interpret it as expressing something like 'full of oil'.[46] It is tempting to call them 'oilmen', but that

44. Petersen, *Haggai and Zechariah*, p. 231.
45. See Schöttler, *Gottesvolk*, p. 244; Waltke and O'Connor, *Syntax*, §9, 5, 3b; cf. Joüon and Muraoka, *Grammar*, §129j; H. Haag, 'בֵּן', *ThWAT*, I, pp. 670-82 (674-75).
46. Driver, *Prophets*, p. 203 ('rather the idea of *full of oil*,—as indeed an olive

would suggest that they are human beings, which would prejudge the identification of the two sons of oil. The choice of the word יצהר, rather than שמן, can then be explained as highlighting one of the major differences between the lampstand in the vision and other lampstands, including the one in the temple. Every lamp stand needs human hands to tend it. For example:

> And you shall command the people of Israel that they bring to you pure beaten olive oil for the light, that a lamp may be set up to burn continually. In the tent of meeting, outside the veil which is before the testimony, Aaron and his sons shall tend it from evening to morning before the LORD (Exod. 27.20-21; cf. Lev. 24.2-4).

The lampstand in the vision is different (assuming that v. 12 is original):[47] it has a direct supply of oil, and there is no need for what Wolff in another context has called 'the processing hand of a human being' (*die verarbeitende Menschenhand*).[48]

### d. *Conclusion*

The usual interpretation of the Hebrew phrase בני היצהר as 'anointed ones' is flawed. יצהר is not synonymous with שמן, the usual word for oil, and the word used for anointing oil and oil used to burn a lamp. The phrase בני היצהר should be understood as referring to those who provide oil, that is, they are the oil suppliers. The oil for the lampstand is not the usual oil, prepared by human hands (for which normally שמן is used), but oil coming directly from the trees on either side of the lampstand.[49]

tree might be metaphorically said to be,—than anointed with oil'); F. Haeussermann, *Wortempfang und Symbol in der alttestamentlichen Prophetie* (BZAW, 58; Giessen: Alfred Töpelmann, 1932), p. 99 ('daß die Ölbäume nicht "Gesalbte", mit Öl Ausgestattete, sind, sondern Ölspender'); Rignell, *Nachtgesichte*, p. 171 ('die welche Öl haben'); Baldwin, *Haggai, Zechariah*, p. 124 ('full of oil'); Strand, 'Olive Trees', p. 258 ('"sons of oil" because they *furnish* oil'). Cf. already LXX: οἱ δύο υἱοὶ τῆς πιότητος 'the two sons of fattiness, prosperity'.

47. S.R. Driver, *The Book of Exodus* (CBSC; Cambridge: Cambridge University Press, 1911), p. 261, 'the lamps are differently supplied with oil'.

48. H.W. Wolff, *Hosea* (BKAT, 14.1; Neukirchen–Vluyn: Neukirchener Verlag, 2nd edn, 1965), p. 44.

49. Someone could argue that because יצהר is never used elsewhere for either anointing oil or fuel for a lamp, any identification of the referent of יצהר in Zech. 4.14 is ambiguous. However, there are two reasons why interpreting it as fuel is more attractive. (a) It fits more naturally in the context, where a lampstand and its

## 3. *The Meaning of the Phrase 'Who Stand by'*

The two sons of oil are said to 'stand by the Lord of the whole earth'. It is now time to discuss the meaning of the phrase עמד על.

### a. עמד *Followed by the Preposition* על

עמד is a common Hebrew word for 'to stand'. With a preposition it can have a purely local meaning (עמד על 'to stand on, by';[50] עמד לפני 'to stand before'[51]), but sometimes the meaning is slightly more specific (עמד על 'to stand by [someone who is sitting]' [sometimes with מעל or ממעל],[52] 'to stand [as head] over',[53] 'to stand [to protect]',[54] and 'to stand against [= oppose]';[55] עמד לפני 'to stand before = to serve').[56] Occasionally, the verb without the preposition may have a more technical meaning, for example, 'to stand' = 'to be in attendance' (an example of this usage is Zech. 3.7: העמדים האלה,[57] which NJPS translates correctly as 'these attendants').

A number of scholars interpret the phrase עמד על in Zech. 4.14 as referring to being in the service of YHWH, for example Rudolph:[58] 'The two men symbolised by the olive trees, are in the service of Yahweh...' The survey of the use of עמד with and without certain prepositions

---

lamps figures prominently; (b) there is no evidence that the phrase בני היצהר can be used for 'anointed ones'.

50. E.g. Gen. 18.8; 24.30; 41.17; Josh. 11.13; 1 Kgs 13.1; 2 Kgs 9.17.

51. E.g. Deut. 4.10; 1 Kgs 1.28; 19.11.

52. E.g. Exod. 18.13, 'Moses sat to judge the people, and the people stood about [עמד...על] Moses'; see also Isa. 6.2 (v. 1, 'I saw the Lord sitting upon a throne...'), 'Above [or: by] him stood [עמדים ממעל] the seraphim'; Jer. 36.21, 'all the princes who stood beside [העמדים מעל] the king'.

53. E.g. Num. 7.2; 1 Sam. 19.20.

54. E.g. Est 8.11.

55. Ezra 10.15 (on the interpretation of עמד על as 'to oppose', see Williamson, *Ezra, Nehemiah*, p. 156); Dan. 8.25.

56. Gen. 41.46; Deut. 1.38; 10.8 (// שרת); Judg. 20.28; 1 Sam. 16.21; 1 Kgs 1.2; 10.8; 17.1; 18.15; 2 Kgs 3.14; 5.16; Jer. 15.19; 35.19; Ezek. 44.15 (// שרת).

57. See also 1 Chron. 6.18.

58. 'Die beide Männer, die durch die Ölbäume symbolisiert werden, stehen also in Dienst Jahwes...' (Rudolph, *Haggai, Sacharja*, p. 107); see also Köhler, *Sacharja*, p. 159; Driver, *Prophets*, p. 203; Rignell, *Nachtgesichte*, p. 172; Laetsch, *Minor Prophets*, p. 430; Chary, *Aggée, Zacharie*, p. 88; Amsler, *Aggée; Zacharie 1–8*, p. 90; Reventlow, *Haggai, Sacharja*, p. 60.

above has indicated that either עמד (without preposition) or עמד לפני is used for 'to serve', but not עמד על.[59] If one wants to do justice to the presence of the preposition על,[60] one cannot maintain[61] an interpretation along the lines of 'to serve'.[62]

59. I was not able to find a single case where עמד על is used for 'to serve'. Similarly, in all the examples which Ringgren gives for 'vor jem. stehen' in the sense of 'ihm dienen', 'in seinem Dienst stehen', one finds עמד לפני, not עמד על (Ringgren, 'עמד', *ThWAT*, VI, cols. 194-204 [198-99]). Someone might want to suggest the meaning 'to serve' for עמד על in Gen. 18.8, where Abraham has a meal prepared for the three men who were visiting him, and he 'set it before them; and he stood by [והוא־עמד עליהם] them under the tree while they ate'. The passage certainly shows an attitude of servanthood in Abraham, but עמד על probably does not so much express that idea but rather the local 'to stand by (someone who is sitting)', as also the phrase 'under the tree' suggests.

60. The preposition על in the phrase עמד על in Zech. 4.14 is the same as the one used in vv. 3, 11: 'And there are two olive trees by it, one on the right of the bowl and the other on its left [ושנים זיתים עליה אחד מימין הגלה ואחד על־שמאלה];'. 'these two olive trees on the right and the left of the lampstand [הזיתים האלה על־ימין המנורה ועל־שמאולה]'. In my view this is purely coincidental, given the fact that על is a very common preposition. It would be reading too much into this to interpret the presence of the preposition על in vv. 3, 11 as an anticipation of the phrase עמד על in v. 14 (contra Rudolph, *Haggai, Sacharja*, p. 107).

61. Rost is right in pointing to the distinction between עמד לפני and עמד על ('Sacharja 4', pp. 218-20), but his further discussion is somewhat confused. He makes a move from 'to stand by someone [who is sitting]' via 'to be a servant' ('Diener des Herrn der ganzen Erde') to 'to serve in the cult'. Those who 'stand by' a king of course are those who serve him, but that is not the nuance which is expressed in the phrase עמד על. Of all the servants of a ruler it could be said in principle that they 'stand before', that is 'serve', him (עמד לפני), but only a specific group out of those who can be said to 'stand before' the king have the privilege to 'stand by' him (עמד על), that is to be the king's 'court officials'.

62. Cf. Nelson, *Priest*, p. 123, 'These two do not simply stand *before* Yahweh in order to serve him, but as prominent dignitaries their position is *beside* Yahweh (note the Hebrew preposition and compare 1 Kings 22.19)'. Others have suggested that the idea of divine protection is expressed in the use of the phrase עמד על here (Wellhausen, *Propheten*, p. 183; Marti, *Dodekapropheton*, p. 414; Nowack, *Propheten*, p. 345; cf. Rudolph, *Haggai, Sacharja*, p. 107, 'in Jahwes Dienst und damit zugleich—das liegt im Wesen des Dienstverhältnisses—unter seinem Schütz'), but I do not think that is possible. The one who is the subject of the phrase עמד על is the one who protects (Est 8.11 עמד על נפשׁו, 'to defend one's life'; cf. possibly Dan. 12.1), not the other way around.

b. *Royal Courts and the Heavenly Court*

Several scholars have pointed to the use of verbs for to 'to stand' (עמד,
and also נצב [niphal and hithpael]) in contexts of royal or heavenly
courts. Malamat writes concerning the Hebrew עמד and its Akkadian
counterpart *i/uzuzzum*, 'This verb serves in various contexts in both
Akkadian and Hebrew, also to indicate service before a high authority
and participation in an assembly in general'.[63] Various scholars have
pointed to the significance of the preposition על in such contexts.

Cross speaks of an idiomatic use of על with עמד or a related verb,
'applying to the courtiers (heavenly or earthly) standing by a seated
monarch or judge (divine or human)'.[64] Mullen makes a similar observation, 'The various scenes of the council in Hebrew literature frequently depict the position of the other gods of the assembly by the
idiomatic usage of *'l* with a verb of standing'.[65] Van der Woude concludes, 'The expression of Zech. 4.14 does not simply mean "to serve",
but relates to being in the *presence* of Yahweh.'[66]

The picture of the heavenly court corresponds to the picture of a
royal court on earth.[67] One would therefore expect to find similar
phraseology used in descriptions of the royal court. An example of the

63. A. Malamat, 'The Secret Council and Prophetic Involvement in Mari and
Israel', in R. Liwak and S. Wagner (eds.), *Prophetie und geschichtliche Wirklichkeit im alten Israel: Festschrift für Siegfried Herrmann zum 65. Geburtstag* (Stuttgart: W. Kohlhammer, 1991), pp. 231-36 (233); cf. G. Cooke, 'The Sons of (the)
God(s)', *ZAW* 76 (1964), pp. 22-47 (40).

64. F.M. Cross, 'The Council of Yahweh in Second Isaiah', *JNES* 12 (1953),
pp. 274-77 (274-75 n. 3). He refers to '1 Kings 22:19; Zech. 4:14 (both of council
of Yahweh; cf. Isa. 6:2), and Exod. 18:13, 14 (Moses sitting in judgement)'.

65. 'Die Wendung meint in Sach 4,14 also nicht bloß ›dienen‹, sondern bezieht
sich auf die *Anwesentheit* bei Jahwe' (Mullen, *Divine Council*, p. 256). For
Mullen's 'other gods of the assembly' I would suggest reading 'other participants in
the assembly'. As will become clear below, participation in the heavenly court is
not restricted to heavenly beings.

66. 'Die Wendung meint in Sach 4,14 also nicht bloß >dienen<, sondern bezieht
sich auf die *Anwesentheit* bei Jahwe' (Van der Woude, 'Serubbabel', p. 155 n. 58
[italics original]). So one has to disagree with Driver who states about 'stand by'
(עמד על), 'The expression hardly differs from "stand *before*", iii, 4' (Driver, *Prophets*, p. 203).

67. Compare Goldingay's remark about the various designations of heavenly
beings who participate in the Council of YHWH as found in the book of Daniel
(*Daniel*, p. 88), 'These terms utilize the arrangements of a human court to picture
God's management of the affairs of heaven and earth'.

use of על עמד in a description of a royal court can be found in Judg. 3.19, a scene in the royal court of Eglon the king of Moab. Ehud has just paid tribute to the king and then returned to announce that he has a secret for the king. At that moment, the king 'commanded, "Silence." And all his attendants [העמדים עליו] went out from his presence'.[68]

So the wording of v. 14, 'who stand by the Lord of the whole earth', indicates that the scene of the vision is the heavenly court and presents God in his role as the sovereign ruler of the whole earth. Of course, this is not an unfamiliar theme in the visions of Zechariah 1–6, and it appeared already earlier in this chapter in the phrase 'the eyes of the LORD, which range through the whole earth' (v. 10), which can be interpreted as referring to attendants of the heavenly court.[69] Some of the more recent studies have adopted this interpretation of the setting of v. 14, for example Van der Woude, 'It is stated next that the two figures "stand by the Lord of the whole earth"; the most appealing explanation of this further detail is that they have access to the heavenly court [...]'.[70]

However, in my view these scholars seem to have failed to see the full implications for the identification of 'the sons of oil who stand by the Lord of the whole earth'. I will discuss that identification in the next section.

---

68. Another case where על עמד is used to refer to members of the royal court is Jer. 36.21 (in this verse the preposition is מעל).

69. Koch also makes the connection with the eyes in v. 10, but he develops the idea in a way different from mine (Koch, *Profeten*, II, p. 172): 'Wie immer zu erklären, die beiden Öhlsöhne sind in jedem Fall den Augen Jahwäs zugeordnet, erfüllen also wie diese eine globale Funktion, und dies vom Tempel in Jerusalem aus, der Mitte der Welt'. (ET *Prophets*, II, p. 169, 'However they are explained, the two 'sons of oil' certainly have to do with the eyes of Yahweh, which means that, like the eyes, they exercise a global function, and do so from the temple in Jerusalem, the centre of the world'.) Niditch, *Symbolic Vision*, p. 112, and Tigchelaar, *Prophets of Old*, p. 31, identify the eyes as members of the heavenly court. On the interpretation of the phrase 'the eyes of the LORD' see also Petersen, *Haggai and Zechariah*, pp. 225-27.

70. 'Wenn es nun weiter heißt, daß diese zwei Gestalten ›bei dem Herrn der ganzen Erde stehen‹, ist die ansprechendste Erklärung dieser Näherbestimmung die, daß sie Zutritt zur himmlischen Ratsversammlung haben' (Van der Woude, 'Serubbabel', pp. 154-55); cf. Koch, *Profeten*, II, p. 172 [ET *Prophets*, II, pp. 168-69]; Petersen, *Haggai and Zechariah*, p. 232; Meyers and Meyers, *Haggai, Zechariah*, pp. 259, 275-76; Reventlow, *Haggai, Sacharja*, pp. 54, 60; Floyd, 'Cosmos', p. 134.

## 4. *The Identification of the Two Sons of Oil who Stand by the Lord of the Whole Earth*

So far I have argued that the phrase 'the two sons of oil' should most likely not be interpreted as anointed ones, and that the phrase 'stand by the Lord of the whole earth' locates the two sons of oil in the heavenly court. Now I will discuss what this implies for the identification of the two sons of oil. The most crucial element in this phase of the discussion is the heavenly court setting: abandoning the 'anointed ones' interpretation appears not to change scholars' identification of the two sons of oil.[71]

### a. *The Traditional Identification: Zerubbabel and Joshua*
Irrespective of the interpretation they give for the phrase 'the two sons of oil' scholars almost universally identify the two sons of oil as Zerubbabel and Joshua.[72] Those scholars who adopt the heavenly court setting, usually maintain the traditional identification of the sons of oil with Joshua and Zerubbabel (or a priestly leader and a political leader).[73] I now want to discuss the question whether it is really possible to

71. E.g. Niditch, *Symbolic Vision*, p. 114.

72. Interpretations identifying the two sons of oil as Joshua and Zerubbabel, or a future priest and prince, go back to the rabbinic period; some rabbinic sources give other human leader figures, like Moses and Aaron, or Aaron and David, as an identification (see H.L. Strack and P. Billerbeck, *Kommentar zum Neuen Testament aus Talmud und Midrasch*. III. *Die Briefe des Neuen Testaments und die Offenbarung Johannis* [Munich: Beck, 1926], pp. 811-12). It would not be difficult to compose a long list of modern scholars, but I will quote only Petersen, who writes (*Haggai and Zechariah*, pp. 118, 231, 233), 'Commentators uniformly view these anointed figures as signifying the diarchic polity recoverable in the oracular material, e.g. Zech. 6.9-15… [I]t would appear to be the case that Joshua and Zerubbabel are symbolized in this vision and its interpretation…if, as many have suggested, Joshua and Zerubbabel are the "sons of oil", then this vision appears to emphasize the diarchic character of the postexilic polity'. The view that the two sons of oil should be identified not with Zerubbabel and Joshua, but with the future messianic prince and priest, as in Zech. 6.13 (Van der Woude, 'Serubbabel', p. 155; cf. Cook, *Prophecy and Apocalypticism*, pp. 132, 143), or with a not further specified priestly leader and political administrator (Meyers and Meyers, *Haggai, Zechariah*, pp. 259, 275-76), is in my opinion just a slight variant on this consensus.

73. E.g. Petersen, *Haggai and Zechariah*, pp. 118, 231, 233; Meyers and Meyers, *Haggai, Zechariah*, pp. 259, 275-76; Nelson, *Priest*, p. 124. Compare also

adopt the heavenly court setting and yet maintain the traditional identification.

*Prophets as Innovators.* In Chapter 2 (section entitled 'Joshua and the Council of YHWH in Zech. 3.7') I have discussed the question concerning which human beings are said to have access to heavenly council, and concluded that only prophets fall into this category. It would obviously be wrong to say that a prophet like Zechariah just repeats things and ideas from the past: a prophet can also be an innovator. So one cannot exclude the possibility that there is something completely new in this oracle. Whereas in the past only prophets enjoyed the privilege of participation in the heavenly court, the possibility cannot be dismissed that what one witnesses in this passage is an inauguration of a new era, in which not just prophets, but also other human beings, in this case a prince and a priest, share this privilege. It would explain the amazement one finds expressed in the comments of some scholars, for example Petersen, 'we now hear of two persons who apparently have access to the divine council'.[74]

On the other hand, one could argue that the element of innovation would be less substantial if participation in the heavenly court were what was granted to Joshua the high priest in the preceding chapter (Zech. 3.7), as many scholars have argued. There are two problems with this view. In the first place, as I have argued in Chapter 2, this is not a satisfying interpretation of that passage: what is promised to the high priest in Zech. 3.7 is not direct access to the heavenly court, or participation in it, but something less immediate, namely the provision of intermediaries between heavenly council and high priest. In the second place, even if for the sake of the argument one accepts the idea that Joshua has already been granted access to the heavenly court, there is another difference between Zech. 3.7 and 4.14: in 3.7 the promise is given to one person, the high priest only; in 4.14 not just a priest, but also a prince—so the argument goes—is given this privilege.

To be clear, I am not arguing that there may not be something very innovative in 4.14, but there needs to be evidence available to support

Floyd, 'Cosmos', p. 134, 'the temple's co-regents occupy a human position that corresponds to the role of the angelic attendants closest to Yahweh's heavenly throne (cf. 6.5). It is in this sense that Joshua, the high priest, and Zerubbabel, the governor both stand beside the heavenly king'.

74. Petersen, *Haggai and Zechariah*, pp. 232-33.

such an interpretation. My problem with the Zerubbabel and Joshua identification is that I cannot escape the impression that far more is read into the passage than one can really find in it. Let us consider what scholars are really saying when they make this identification. If the two sons of oil are to be identified as Joshua and Zerubbabel, it would mean that the phrase אלה בני־היצהר העמדים על־אדון כל־הארץ indicates (a) human beings, who are (b) leaders of the community, holding (c) a different office each. Furthermore, while the same thing (or—in my view—something related but of a more indirect nature) was promised to Joshua the high priest only in 3.7, it is presented here as given to both Joshua and (d) Zerubbabel. Finally, another element is often found in the phrase, (e) the idea that king and priest are now of equal standing.

The real problems start with the third element (two different offices), for which I find no evidence. The next elements in particular (access to the divine court as the privilege of both priest and prince, and equal standing of prince and priest) are innovative. It seems unlikely that such innovative ideas would be expressed in so condensed a manner. If such reservations are correct, then one has to consider two options. The first one is to assume that the prophet was extremely obscure, so that indeed 'we are faced with a lack of identification that is puzzling', as Ackroyd[75] puts it. The alternative is to consider the possibility that the prophet meant something altogether different.

### b. *An Alternative Suggestion: Heavenly Beings*
I want to suggest that the best way forward is to consider once more the heavenly court setting of the passage. If it is right, on the basis of the phrase העמדים על אדון כל־הארץ, to identify the setting as that of a heavenly court, then one should consider the possibility of an identification which in a sense is more traditional, or less innovative. If in the rest of the Old Testament only heavenly beings and prophets are portrayed as participants in the heavenly court, then it would be worth considering whether members of either of these two categories qualify for being the persons referred to as 'the two sons of oil who stand by the LORD of the whole earth'. If so, then the two sons of oil could be either prophets or heavenly beings.

If the sons of oil are prophets, then one immediately thinks of Haggai

---

75. Ackroyd, 'Persian Period', in *Chronicler*, p. 108.

and Zechariah. The two prophets are mentioned together in Ezra 5.1 and 6.14.[76] If this is the correct identification, then the picture is something like the following. Just as the two olive trees provide oil for the lampstand to burn, so the two prophets, presumably by speaking the word of YHWH, provide the means of sustenance for the people of God.

The possibility that the sons of oil are prophets cannot be excluded, and it is particularly appealing in that it goes perfectly well with the number two in the phrase 'the two sons of oil' (see the discussion below). Yet I find the complete lack of explicit identification of the two sons of oil as prophets somewhat puzzling. The question to ask is this: for what class of persons would a phrase like 'who stand by the Lord of the whole earth' be sufficient?

The only category for which such a phrase, without the need of any further qualification, would be sufficient, seems to be heavenly beings who are attendants in the heavenly court (compare another concise phrase referring to members of the heavenly court, העמדים האלה 'these attendants', in 3.7). Another reference to heavenly beings as members of the heavenly court in the same chapter, Zechariah 4, may be found in the phrase 'the eyes of the Lord which range over the whole earth' in v. 10b. Is it perhaps possible that the two sons of oil also are heavenly beings?

When one looks back into the history of the interpretation of Zech. 4.14 one finds that an identification of the two sons of oil as heavenly beings is precisely what a small minority of scholars have argued for, though it seems that they have gone almost completely unnoticed. At the end of the last century Perowne questioned the traditional identification with Zerubbabel and Joshua, as representing the kingly and priestly offices, and wondered 'whether the angel does not purposely avoid giving a definite, and especially a *human* meaning to these symbols'. Given the tenor of the vision as a whole, which he finds summarized in the phrase 'by my Spirit, says the Lord of hosts', he then concludes, 'These

---

76. Another reference to the prophets Haggai and Zechariah may be found in Zech. 8.9, though in that verse neither their number nor their identity is given: 'Thus says the LORD of hosts: "Let your hands be strong, you who in these days have been hearing these words from the mouth of the prophets, since the day that the foundation of the house of the LORD of hosts was laid, that the temple might be built'.

"sons of oil," then, are agents or agencies, near to God and beyond our ken, "that stand by the Lord of the whole earth." '[77]

Back in 1932 Haeussermann came to a similar conclusion: the traditional identification is flawed because 'the olive trees [are] not "anointed ones", those who have been equipped with oil...but oil suppliers'. He chooses to interpret the sons of oil as angels of the council of YHWH who provide blessing and prosperity in the community.[78] Welch also seems to think of the sons of oil as agents of the council of YHWH, '[the] eyes of Yahweh, these ministers of His will, are directed and supplied, kept vigilant by the two who (v. 14) stand beside the Lord of the whole earth'.[79] For Junker, the phrase עמד על provides the key to the identification: it is used of heavenly spirits, who stand around the throne of God. Since in the vision the seven lamps already are used as symbols for angels, 'the interpretation of the olive trees given by Welch as referring to angels belongs within the frame of representation of the vision, and at the same time fits in the overall interpretation (symbolic presentation of the divine provision)'.[80]

77.  T.T. Perowne, *Haggai and Zechariah* (CBSC; Cambridge: Cambridge University Press, 1888), p. 88.

78.  'Die Ölbäume [sind] nicht "Gesalbte", mit Öl Ausgestattete...sondern Ölspender' (Haeussermann, *Wortempfang*, p. 99); '[D]ienende Engel im Hofstaat Jahwes, die Glück und Segen spenden sollen' (Haeussermann, *Wortempfang*, p. 99). Haeussermann argues his case for the identification of the sons of oil as heavenly beings on the basis of the interpretation of בני־היצהר as oil suppliers (rather than anointed ones). But the reason why the (apparently only) alternative to the Joshua and Zerubbabel identification is the heavenly beings identification which he suggests, is not clear. It may be based on the phrase העמדים על־אדון כל־הארץ, but he does not discuss the phrase as such.

79.  Welch, 'Lampstand', p. 240.

80.  'Liegt Welchs Deutung der beiden Ölbäume auf Engel in der einheitlichen Vorstellungslinie der Vision, und sie fügt sich zugleich in die Einheit der Gesamtdeutung (symbolische Darstellung der göttlichen Vorsehen) ein' (Junker, *Propheten*, p. 141). The interpretation given by Koch (*Profeten*, II, p. 172 [ET *Prophets*, II, pp. 168-69]) seems somewhat ambiguous: on the one hand he takes the standing by the Lord of the whole earth as presupposing that they are in heaven. On the other hand he speaks about the two sons of oil as exercising a global function which they do from the temple in Jerusalem, the centre of the world. In a recent article, R.P. Carroll, 'So What Do we Know about the Temple? The Temple in the Prophets', in Eskenazi and Richards (eds.), *Second Temple*, pp. 34-51 (42), draws a parallel with the vision in Isa. 6: 'A golden *menôrâ* flanked by two olive trees—cf. Isaiah 6's

There may even be a trace of an identification along these lines in one of the early Jewish interpretations: *Targum Jonathan* to the Prophets translates Zech. 4.14 thus:

ואמר אלין תרין בני רברביא דקימין קדם רבון כל ארעא

And he said: 'These are the two sons of the great ones, who stand before the lord of all the earth'.

If 'the two sons of the great ones' points to heavenly beings, then this interpretation would clearly have been a minority opinion in the early Jewish tradition.[81] It is not clear, however, whether one can be completely sure that בני רברביא refers to heavenly beings, since Aramaic רב(רבא)[82] is also commonly used for 'great man' or 'chief'. However, one could support an interpretation of בני רברביא as referring to heavenly beings with the observation that precisely the same phrase בני רברביא is used by *Targum Onqelos* and *Targum Pseudo-Jonathan* to translate MT בני אלהים 'sons of God' in Gen. 6.2.[83]

If we find in the phrase 'the two sons of oil' another reference to members of the heavenly court, then in this case they are not involved in world political affairs (so in several places in the visions, including 4.10b), but their commission lies in sustaining and supporting the community of the people of God which worships at the temple in Jerusalem. The picture would in some sense correspond to the promise of divine assistance in the oracle in 4.6: 'Not by might, nor by power, but by my Spirit, says the LORD of hosts'.

*An Unresolved Problem.* There remains one issue which is hard to explain within the framework of the proposal to identify the two sons of oil as heavenly beings: it does not provide a satisfying explanation for the fact that there are precisely 'two' sons of oil (this in contrast with

notion on YHWH superintended by $\check{s}^e r\bar{a}p\hat{i}m$—represents the all-seeing power of YHWH's (divine) council'.

81. As we have seen above, in early Jewish interpretations, the two sons of oil are usually identified as human leader figures (see Strack and Billerbeck, *Kommentar*, III, pp. 811-12).

82. Jastrow, *Dictionary*, lists רברביא as a plural of רברבא, 'great; great man; prince, officer'. M. Sokoloff, *A Dictionary of Jewish Palestinian Aramaic of the Byzantine Period* (Dictionaries of Talmud, Midrash and Targum, 2; Ramat Gan: Bar Ilan University Press, 1990), lists רברבין as a plural of רב, 'great, large, important, older, master, teacher, chief'.

83. Gordon, 'Targum Nahum–Malachi', p. 195 and n. 24.

the two prophets identification, discussed above). The number 'two' figures rather prominently in vv. 11-14. It is used first in the question in vv. 11-12 ('these two olive trees', and 'these two branches of the olive trees'). The number 'two' is also used before the phrase which describes how they are to be identified. The phrase is not something like, 'these two are the sons of oil who...' (cf. 'these seven are the eyes of the Lord...' in v. 10b), but 'these are the two sons of oil who...' As Petersen puts it,[84] 'the number two is more important in the interpretation than is the number seven in the interpretation of the eyes'.

Why are there precisely two agents of the heavenly court mentioned here? At this stage I am not able to give a satisfying explanation of this element of the text. It is possible to mention some other passages where we find the same number two used of unidentified heavenly beings. Two cherubim cover the lid of the ark in tabernacle and temple (Exod. 25.18; 1 Kgs 6.23; 2 Chron. 3.10). Daniel tells in one of his vision reports, 'Then I heard a holy one speaking; and another holy one said to the one that spoke, "For how long..."' (Dan. 8.13-14), and in another vision report: 'behold, two others stood, one on this bank of the stream and one on that bank of the stream' (Dan. 12.5). It is not clear in what way (if any) this supports my case.

Admittedly, the failure to provide a satisfactory explanation of this important detail that there are specifically *two* sons of oil remains a problem in the interpretation I have proposed. Nevertheless, I would suggest that on balance this interpretation is more attractive because it does not need a number of quite specific presuppositions for which evidence is lacking, and it also faces less difficulties than the Zerubbabel–Joshua identification.

## 5. *Conclusions and Implications*

The discussion in this Chapter can be summed up thus: the traditional identification of the two sons of oil in Zech. 4.14 as representing the anointed leaders of the community in Yehud/Jerusalem faces serious difficulties: in the first place it gives an unlikely meaning to the Hebrew phrase בני היצהר, which most probably does not mean 'anointed ones', but describes the two as the persons supplying oil for the lampstand which is at the centre of the vision. In the second place, the traditional interpretation fails to do justice to the heavenly court setting of the

---

84. Petersen, *Haggai and Zechariah*, p. 229.

verse (the significance of the fact that the phrase עָמַד עַל 'stand by', with its special nuance of 'being an attendant or court official', can be used in such contexts is generally overlooked). The two sons of oil are most likely not human leader figures, but heavenly beings, attendants of the heavenly court.

With such an interpretation of v. 14, it is possible to provide an overall interpretation of the vision of the lampstand in Zechariah 4 which integrates the message of both the vision and the oracular material in vv. 6-10 into a consistent whole. Perowne puts it like this:

> [the vision] is intended to encourage Zerubbabel in the work of re-building the Temple, by impressing upon him the truth, that as that candlestick gave forth its light, in silent, ceaseless splendour, unfed and untended by human agencies, so the work in which he was engaged, of restoring the material Temple and setting the golden candlestick in its place again, and so preparing the way, first for the Jewish Church, and then for the Christian Church, which that candlestick symbolised (Rev. i. 20), to shine in the world, should be accomplished, not by human resources, but by the Spirit of God, ver. 6.[85]

If the sons of oil are heavenly beings and not human leaders of earth, then it is no longer possible to refer to this verse as providing evidence that Zechariah envisaged a political organization called 'diarchy', in which two leaders, a prince and a priest, stand at the head of the Jewish community. This is then the second passage (compare my discussion of Zech. 6.13 in Chapter 2) on which the idea of diarchy was based, a passage which on closer inspection does not support such an interpretation. The conclusions of my interpretation of the passages in which scholars have found evidence for the idea of diarchy come close to that of Berquist:[86]

> Many scholars have envisioned a dyarchy that collapses into a rule by the high priest after the removal of Zerubbabel, but there is insufficient evidence for such a view. Instead, these two figures each play major roles within Yehudite society, and the general submission to the leadership of each is vital for Yehud, but in different ways. Zechariah does not equate the two or even present them in the same passage.

---

85. Perowne, *Haggai and Zechariah*, p. 84.
86. Berquist, *Judaism*, p. 72.

## Chapter 7

ZERUBABBEL LIKE A SEAL (HAGGAI 2.20-23)

In the book thus far I have studied the nature of the expectations in the צמח oracles and the identity of the royal figure called Zemah. I have argued that Zemah should not be identified with Zerubbabel, but he is a future royal figure. This interpretation implies that Zechariah's prophecies concerning Zemah can be called 'messianic' (see my definition of this term in Chapter 1).

In this final Chapter I will confront the results of my study of Zemah in Zechariah 1–6 with an examination of the final oracle in Haggai 2 (vv. 20-23), a passage which has been interpreted by many as pointing to the restoration of the monarchy or the inauguration of the messianic age. After a brief introduction of the book of Haggai, I will discuss first the vocabulary of the promise to Zerubbabel in v. 23, and then provide an interpretation of it within the context of vv. 20-23.

## 1. *Introduction*

The main theme in the prophecies of Haggai is the rebuilding of the temple in Jerusalem. The prophet urges the people to get their priorities sorted out and to redirect their building activities from their own homes to the temple. He confronts them with the situation of economic hardship in which they find themselves at present, which he links directly with the neglect of concern for the rebuilding of the temple, and holds before them a promise of reversal into a situation in which God will bless the produce of the land (1.1-11). Under the leadership of Zerubbabel the son of Shealtiel, the governor, and Joshua the son of Jehozadak, the high priest, the people accept the challenge and start the project of rebuilding the temple (1.12-15).

Two oracles introduced by the language of theophany follow (2.1-9, 20-23), with another promise of the blessing of God for a better economy sandwiched in between them (2.10-19). The first oracle concerns the future glory of the temple which will be greater than the glory of the former temple, and to which the treasures of the nations will contribute. The second and final oracle announces a dramatic change of the political and military landscape, engineered by YHWH, and finishes with a special promise for Zerubbabel the governor of the province Yehud. The oracle reads in RSV:[1]

> The word of the LORD came a second time to Haggai on the twenty-fourth day of the month, 'Speak to Zerubbabel, governor of Judah, saying, I am about to shake the heavens and the earth, and to overthrow the throne of kingdoms; I am about to destroy the strength of the kingdoms of the nations, and overthrow the chariots and their riders; and the horses and their riders shall go down, every one by the sword of his fellow. On that day, says the LORD of hosts, I will take you, O Zerubbabel my servant, the son of Shealtiel, says the LORD, and make you like a signet ring; for I have chosen you, says the LORD of hosts' (Hag. 2.20-23).

## 2. What Zerubbabel Already Is

The promise in Hag. 2.23 tells us two things about Zerubbabel. In the first place, it states what Zerubbabel already is in the eyes of YHWH at the moment he is spoken to by God through the prophet Haggai. YHWH addresses him as:

> my servant I have chosen you.

In the second place, it states what God will do with him:

> I will take you and make you like a חותם.[2]

In this section I will discuss the vocabulary used to describe Zerubbabel's position as it is at the moment he is addressed by the prophet. In the two following sections I will discuss the terminology used to describe what God will do to him: 'I will take you', and 'make you like a חותם'.

### a. Zerubbabel God's Servant (עבד)
In the Old Testament one finds a diverse number of individuals being referred to as עבד, 'my servant' (my = of God), or 'servant of YHWH'. The table in Figure 16 lists cases where an individual is referred to as

---

1. On the dates in Haggai (and Zechariah) see Chapter 1 (section entitled 'The Dates in Haggai and Zechariah').
2. The reason why I leave חותם untranslated will become clear soon.

'my/your/his servant' (with the pronoun referring to God), or 'servant of YHWH'.[3]

Figure 16. *'My/Your/His Servant' (Individuals)*

| | my servant | your[4] servant | his servant (or: of YHWH) |
|---|---|---|---|
| Abraham | Gen. 26.24 | | Ps. 105.6, 42; 1 Chron. 16.13 |
| Isaac | | Gen. 24.24 | |
| Jacob | Ezek. 28.25; 37.25 | | |
| Moses | Num. 12.7, 8; Josh. 1.2, 7; 2 Kgs 21.8; Mal. 4.4 | 1 Kgs 8.53 | Exod. 14.31; Josh. 1.1; 9.24; 11.15; 1 Kgs 8.56; Ps. 105.26; |
| Joshua | | | Josh. 24.29; Judg. 2.8 |
| Caleb | Num. 14.24 | | |
| Ahijah (prophet) | | | 1 Kgs 14.18; 15.29 |
| David (king) | 2 Sam. 3.18; 7.5, 8; 1 Kgs 11.13, 32, 34, 36, 38; 14.8; 19.34; 20.6; Isa. 37.35; Jer. 33.21, 22. 26; Ezek. 34.23, 24; 37.24, 25; Ps. 89.4, 21; 1 Chron. 17.4, 7 | 1 Kgs 3.6; 8.24, 25, 26; Ps. 132.10; 2 Chron. 6.15, 16, 17, 42 | 1 Kgs 8.66; 2 Kgs 8.19; Ps. 18.1; 36.1; 78.70; 144.10 |
| Elijah (prophet) | | 1 Kgs 18.36 | 2 Kgs 9.36; 10.10 |
| Jonah (prophet) | | | 2 Kgs 14.25 |
| Hezekiah (king) | | | 2 Chron. 32.16 |
| Isaiah (prophet) | Isa. 20.3 | | |
| Eliakim (steward) | Isa. 22.20 | | |

3. See, for a similar list, Touzard, 'L'âme juive', p. 181.

4. I list here only those cases where someone refers to a third person as 'your servant' (your = of God), not where someone uses 'your servant' for self-reference (including cases like 'thy servant David' in 2 Sam. 7.26 [= 1 Chron. 17.24]).

Figure 16. *(Continued)*

|  | my servant | your servant | his servant (or: of YHWH) |
|---|---|---|---|
| Nebuchadrezzar | Jer. 25.9; 27.6; 43.10 | | |
| Zerubbabel | Hag. 2.23 | | |
| Zemah | Zech. 3.8 | | |
| Job | Job 1.8; 2.3; 42.7, 8 | | |

It is not just individuals who are referred to as servants of God. The phrase is also used for groups (Fig. 17).

Figure 17. *'My/Your/His Servant' (Groups)*

|  | my servant(s) | your servant(s) | his servant(s) |
|---|---|---|---|
| Abraham, Isaac and Israel/Jacob | | Exod. 32.13; Deut. 9.27 | |
| Israel/Jacob (nation) | Isa. 41.8; 44.1, 2, 21; 45.4; Jer. 30.10; 46.27, 28; Ezek. 28.25; 37.25 | | Isa. 48.20; Ps. 136.22 |
| 'the prophets' | 2 Kgs 9.7; 17.13; Jer. 7.25; 26.5; 29.19; 35.15; 44.4; Ezek. 38.17; Zech. 1.6 | Dan. 9.6; Ezra 9.11 | 2 Kgs 17.23; 21.10; 24.2; Jer. 25.4; Amos 3.7; Dan. 9.10 |

Both tables show the rich diversity in the use of 'servant' for an individual's or a group's relationship with God. It is clear that a phrase with עבד 'servant' is most often used for David (some 40 times). Special mention should be made of four cases in Ezekiel 34 and 37 where an unspecified future ruler is called 'David my servant'. For example:

> And I, the LORD, will be their God, and my servant David shall be prince among them (Ezek. 34.24; cf. 34.23 and 37.24, 25).

On the other hand, the use of עבד in connection with individual members of the Davidic line is extremely rare. One could argue that the fact that the epithet 'servant' is hardly ever used for kings after David may be related to the fact that most of them were disappointing in their performance as kings appointed by YHWH. However, that still does not explain why even 'good' kings (like Josiah) hardly ever receive this accolade. There is in fact only one such case: in 2 Chron. 32.16, a text later than Haggai, Hezekiah is called 'his [= God's] servant':

> And his servants said still more against the Lord GOD and against his servant Hezekiah (2 Chron. 32.16).

b. *Chosen by God (בחר)*

בחר is used for the choice by God of a wide selection of persons and places (Fig.18).[5]

Figure 18. *'Chosen' by God*

|  | בחר **verb** | בחיר **noun** |
|---|---|---|
| **INDIVIDUALS** | | |
| Abraham | Neh. 9.7 | |
| Moses | | Ps. 106.23 |
| Aaron | 1 Sam. 2.28; Ps. 105.26 | |
| Saul | 1 Sam. 10.24; 2 Sam. 21.6 MT | |
| David | 2 Sam. 6.21; 1 Kgs 8.44; 11.34; Ps. 78.70; 1 Chron. 28.4; 2 Chron. 6.6 | Ps. 89.4 |
| Solomon | 1 Chron. 28.5, 6, 10; 29.1 | |
| the Servant | Isa. 41.9; 42.1; 43.10; 49.7 | |
| unnamed ruler | Jer. 49.19; 50.44 | |
| **COLLECTIVES** | | |
| God's people | Deut. 7.6, 7; 14.2 | |
| Jacob/Israel (nation) | Ps. 135.4; Isa. 41.8; 44.2; Ezek. 20.5 | Isa. 45.4 |
| Judah (tribe) | Ps. 78.68 | |
| the priests and/or Levites | Deut. 18.5; 21.5; 1 Chron. 15.2; 2 Chron. 29.10, 11 | |

---

5.   Again, compare Touzard, 'L'âme juive', p. 181.

Figure 18. *(Continued)*

| | בחר verb | בחיר noun |
|---|---|---|
| **PLACES** | | |
| the place for YHWH's name | Deut. 12.5, 11, 14, 18, 21, 26; 14.24, 25; 15.20; 16.2, 6, 7, 11, 15; 17.8, 18; 18.6; 26.2 | |
| Jerusalem | 1 Kgs 11.13, 32, 36; 14.21; 2 Kgs 21.7; 23.27; 2 Chron. 6.6; 12.13; 33.7; Neh. 1.9; Zech. 1.17; 2.12; 3.2 | |
| Zion | Ps. 132.13 | |
| temple | 2 Chron. 7.16 | |

As the figure shows, the use of בחר with a king as the object of the choice is not very common at all. It is used of Saul, and of David, but then there is only one king after David who is said to have been 'chosen' by YHWH, and this is again in a text later than Haggai: according to 1 Chron. 28.6, 10, Solomon was chosen by YHWH (for purposes of dynastic rule and temple building). YHWH's faithfulness to the Davidic dynasty did not depend on the choice of the current ruler, it was 'for the sake of David' (e.g. 1 Kgs 11).[6]

---

6. So Pomykala, *Dynasty Tradition*, p. 48, who takes the argument somewhat further, perhaps too far, in my opinion: 'The continuation of the Davidic line was secure, because God chose David, not because he chose the reigning Davidic monarch...if Haggai were invoking the Davidic dynasty promise, we would expect to find Zerubbabel's status as a Davidic king based on God's having chosen David, not on his having chosen Zerubbabel'. Adopting a suggestion of Meyers and Meyers (*Haggai, Zechariah*, p. 70), Pomykala then proceeds to state that the choice of Zerubbabel 'is more suggestive of a new era in the rulership of Judah', because the use of בחר seems to imply 'new beginnings of a sort' in the other occurrences (persons and places). Such an observation is based on the assumption that the choice of Zerubbabel was for the purpose of commission. This assumption may be true, and it seems plausible to associate the choice with the fact that Zerubbabel was governor (referred to in v. 21). But it is difficult to confirm the assumption, for two reasons. (a) The choice is an event in the past: it precedes the action of making like a seal. The choice and the (future) action of making like a seal can therefore not be identified: in fact, the choice is given as the *reason* for the future action. (b) The purpose

If one looks more specifically for the combination '(my) servant' and 'whom I have chosen', one can find at least five passages where the two phrases have (or may have) the same reference. There are four passages in 1 Kings 11 (the chapter which deals with the division of the united kingdom in two kingdoms) in which one finds both the noun עבד referring to David, and also the phrase אשר בחר. In one of out these four it is immediately clear that 'David my servant' is the chosen one:

> Nevertheless I will not take the whole kingdom out of his hand; but I will make him ruler all the days of his life, for the sake of David my servant whom I chose, who kept my commandments and my statutes (1 Kgs 11.34).

In two cases (1 Kgs 11.32, 36) it is clear that Jerusalem is the chosen one, because העיר precedes אשר בחרתי, for example:

> he shall have one tribe, for the sake of my servant David and for the sake of Jerusalem, the city which I have chosen out of all the tribes of Israel... (1 Kgs 11.34).

This leaves us with one case, where there is some ambiguity concerning the object of choice (1 Kgs 11.13): 'for the sake of David my servant and for the sake of Jerusalem which I have chosen'. If a decision can be made on whether in this verse David or Jerusalem is the chosen one, then the verse as a whole would suggest Jerusalem, because the focus in this verse is on the one tribe which will be given to the future king, which is also the focus in the two verses in which there is no doubt that Jerusalem is the chosen one (the focus of the verse in which David is clearly the chosen one is the person who will be the future ruler—see v. 34, above).

The combination of the two phrases '(my) servant' and 'whom I have chosen', is found in one passage of the people of God as a collective:

> 'You are my witnesses', says the LORD, 'and my servant whom I have chosen, that you may know and believe me and understand that I am He. Before me no god was formed, nor shall there be any after me' (Isa. 43.10).

for the choice itself is left unspecified by the prophet. It could also be related to his role as governor, or to his role in rebuilding the temple (Köhler, *Sacharja*, p. 114; T. André, *Le prophète Aggée: Introduction critique et commentaire* [Paris: Fischbacher, 1895], p. 352; Wolff, *Haggai*, p. 83.

One could mention here also Isa. 41.8, in which the two phrases '(my) servant' and 'whom I have chosen' are found in parallel clauses referring to God's people—but now under different names—once again: 'But you, Israel, my servant, Jacob, whom I have chosen, the offspring of Abraham, my friend'.

This survey shows that in the Hebrew of the Old Testament the combination of the two phrases '(my) servant' and 'whom I have chosen', in which both phrases have the same referent, is not a very frequent one. Out of these, there is only one where it is absolutely clear that David is the referent of the two phrases, then there is one more (found in the same chapter), in which David is called 'my servant' and where he could be the referent of the phrase 'whom I have chosen', though in its context it is more likely that Jerusalem is the chosen one. The combination '(my) servant' and 'whom I have chosen' is used in Isaiah 40–55 at least once to refer to Israel as a people.

### c. *Conclusion*

I conclude that when scholars immediately associate the presence of the words עבד and בחר with the notion of kingship[7] they overstate the case. Both words are used to relate to kings, but they are found also in a variety of contexts referring to a variety of persons. A survey of this range of contexts shows that the association with the notion of kingship is far less prominent[8] than scholars have thought.[9]

---

7.    E.g. Runnals, 'Temple Builder', p. 23.

8.    Compare Beyse's remark on the use of עבד (*Serubbabel*, p. 58), 'das Wort *'äbäd* [besitzt] eine so große Bedeutungsbreite, daß man es nicht spezifische Bezeichnung für einen König ansehen kann'. Similarly, Meyers and Meyers, *Haggai, Zechariah*, p. 68, 'Clearly 'servant' was not a normal designation for an incumbent king of Israel or Judah'; and Sérandour, 'Construction', p. 17, 'le titre de "serviteur"…n'a rien de spécifiquement royal…'

9.    The only other short passage apart from Hag. 2.23 where the three words together figure and refer to one person is Ps. 78.70-71: 'He chose David his servant, and took him from the sheepfolds; from tending the ewes that had young he brought him to be the shepherd of Jacob his people, of Israel his inheritance'. Here the one person is David, but this is in my view does not determine the meaning of the three words found in Hag. 2.23. Compare Wolff, *Haggai*, p. 85, 'Vielleicht is es bezeichnend, daß Ps 78,70 alle Stichworte unseres Haggai-Spruchs enthält…nur das Bild vom Siegel und damit das eigentliche Neue felht im Psalmwort; in Ps 78,70 steht jedoch der Name David, der wiederum bei Haggai fehlt'.

## 3. *'I Will Take you' (לקח)*

### a. לקח *for Service/Mission*

Several scholars interpret the use of the verb לקח in v. 23 as indicating selection for a special mission. According to Mitchell, the phrase 'I will take you' in v. 23 'implies selection for an important service or mission'. Along the same lines, Wolff argues that in similar passages לקח is used for interventions which entail a change of location, vocation, or function.[10]

There is no doubt that לקח with God as subject can function in this way (selection for service/mission), as examples like the ones mentioned by Mitchell[11] indicate. For example:

> I took you from the pasture, from following the sheep, that you should be prince over my people Israel (2 Sam. 7.8).

> [A]nd the LORD took me from following the flock, and the LORD said to me, 'Go, prophesy to my people Israel' (Amos 7.15).

> He chose David his servant, and took him from the sheepfolds; from tending the ewes that had young he brought him to be the shepherd of Jacob his people, of Israel his inheritance (Ps. 78.70).

However, these and the other passages mentioned by Mitchell all refer to the past: 'I have taken'. 1 Kgs 11.37 would be a perfect example of Mitchell's point (though Mitchell does not mention the verse), because this is one of the few occasions where—as in Hag. 2.23—the verb לקח (with God as subject) is used to announce something which is going to happen in the future,[12] but the important difference is the presence in

10. Mitchell, *Haggai and Zechariah*, p. 78, and Wolff, *Haggai*, p. 83, 'Eingriffe zum Ortswechsel, Berufs- und Funktionswechsel'; cf. Perowne, *Haggai and Zechariah*, p. 46; Amsler, *Aggée; Zacharie 1–8*, pp. 39-40; Van der Woude, *Haggai–Maleachi*, pp. 73-74.

11. Not all examples collected by Mitchell are convincing. See my discussion of Exod. 6.7 below.

12. An interesting passage in this part of the discussion is 1 Sam. 8.11, 13, 16 (here לקח is not used of God, but of the king): 'He said, "These will be the ways of the king who will reign over you: he will take [ולקח] your sons and appoint them to his chariots and to be his horsemen [ושם לו במרכבתו ובפרשיו], and to run before his chariots..." ' This is a clear example of 'taking' for service/mission, and the verb used immediately after לקח is the same as in Hag. 2.23: שׂים. As I will discuss below, the presence of the preposition כ in Hag. 2.23 is a problem for interpreting

1 Kgs 11.37 of words to describe what the mission entails:

> And I will take you, and you shall reign over all that your soul desires,
> and you shall be king over Israel (1 Kgs 11.37).

Such an explicit description of the mission is absent in Hag. 2.23.

### b. לקח *for Relationship*

Two somewhat similar passages in Numbers make clear that לקח may
express selection for mission, but not necessarily:

> Behold, I have taken the Levites from among the people of Israel instead
> of every first-born that opens the womb among the people of Israel. The
> Levites shall be mine (Num. 3.12).

> And behold, I have taken your brethren the Levites from among the
> people of Israel; they are a gift to you, given to the LORD, to do the
> service of the tent of meeting (Num. 18.6).

In Num. 18.6 the idea of service/mission is clearly present, but in Num.
3.12 the focus is on the special relationship between God and the Lev-
ites. There are many examples where the verb לקח does not express
selection for mission, but rather relationship, or protection. For example:

> [A]nd I will take you for my people, and I will be your God (Exod. 6.7).

> But the LORD has taken you, and brought you forth out of the iron
> furnace, out of Egypt, to be a people of his own possession, as at this day
> (Deut. 4.20).

> He reached from on high, he took me, he drew me out of many waters (2
> Sam. 22.17 = Ps. 18.16).

> Yet it was I who taught Ephraim to walk, I took them up in my arms; but
> they did not know that I healed them (Hos. 11.3).

In these examples the issue of mission is not prominent, but as the
context indicates it is the idea of relationship or protection which is
expressed by the verb לקח.

### c. *Conclusion*

In conclusion: the verb לקח with God as subject can indicate different
things, depending on the context in which the verb occurs. To restrict *a
priori* the use of לקח to just one notion, that is, the idea of taking for

the verb שׂים in that verse along the lines of 'appoint'.

service or mission, to the exclusion of the notion of taking for relation-ship or protection, fails to do justice to the range of contexts where לקח is found. In the end it is each individual context which decides what the verb conveys in a particular case.

### 4. *'I Will Make you Like a* חותם*'*

I will now look at the word translated 'signet ring' in RSV and which I have left untranslated so far. The Hebrew noun חותם shares a lexical field of Hebrew nouns for 'seal, signet' with טבעת. I will start by mak-ing some brief remarks on the use of טבעת, in order to find out how each of the two words function in the lexical field they share.[13]

### a. *The Meaning of* טבעת
The noun טבעת (used 50 times) is a word for different types of rings, for example, rings used for holding together objects or for transporting them,[14] rings as part of the priestly garments,[15] and rings worn on the body, either as ornament,[16] or—most relevant for the present discus-sion—with a seal set in them which could be used for purposes of authentication, that is, signet rings.[17] This last meaning, 'signet ring', is found in six cases, which all involve a ruler giving his signet ring to someone as a symbol of the delegation of authority to that person. A well-known example of this practice is found in the Joseph story in

---

13. Besides the dictionaries, for the semantics of חותם and טבעת see S. Moscati, 'I sigilli nell'Antico Testamento studio esegetico-filologico', *Bib* 30 (1949), pp. 314-38 (316); O. Keel, *Deine Blicke sind tauben: Zur Metaphorik des Hohen Liedes* (SBS, 114-15; Stuttgart: Verlag Katholisches Bibelwerk, 1984), p. 115 n. 426; S. Schroer, *In Israel gab es Bilder: Nachrichten von darstellender Kunst im Alten Testament* (OBO, 74; Freiburg: Universitätsverlag; Göttingen: Vandenhoeck & Ruprecht, 1987), p. 404.

14. Exod. 25.12, 14-15, 26-27; 26.24, 29; 27.4, 7; 30.4; 36.29, 34; 37.3, 5, 13-14, 27; 38.5, 7.

15. Exod. 28.23-24, 26, 28; 39.16-17, 19, 21.

16. Exod. 35.22; Num. 31.50; Isa. 3.21.

17. Gen. 41.42; Est. 3.10, 12; 8.2, 8, 10. Not being a native speaker of English myself I had to look up in a dictionary what exactly a 'signet' is: in the English language 'signet' is a hyponym of 'seal': 'seal' is the general word, and 'signet' is the more specific term, used for a 'small seal, usually one fixed in a finger-ring' (*OED*). So the words 'seal' and 'signet' are strictly speaking not synonyms: while every signet is a seal, not every seal is a signet.

Genesis, when Pharaoh gives authority over Egypt into the hands of Joseph:

> Pharaoh said to Joseph, 'Behold, I have set you over all the land of Egypt'. Then Pharaoh took his signet ring from his hand and put it on Joseph's hand, and arrayed him in garments of fine linen, and put a gold chain about his neck; and he made him to ride in his second chariot; and they cried before him, 'Bow the knee!' Thus he set him over all the land of Egypt (Gen. 41.40-42).

A similar transaction is recorded twice in the book of Esther:

> So the king took his signet ring from his hand and gave it to Haman the Agagite, the son of Hammedatha, the enemy of the Jews. And the king said to Haman, 'The money is given to you, the people also, to do with them as it seems good to you' (Est. 3.10-11).

> ...and the king took off his signet ring, which he had taken from Haman, and gave it to Mordecai (Est. 8.2).

The continuation of the story indicates the new authority which the person to whom the signet-ring is given now enjoys. The edict which was written on the command of Haman is 'written in the name of King Ahasuerus and sealed with the king's ring [ונחתם בטבעת המלך]' (Est. 3.12). Mordechai is told (Est. 8.8): 'you may write as you please with regard to the Jews, in the name of the king, and seal it with the king's ring [וחתמו בטבעת המלך]; for an edict written in the name of the king and sealed with the king's ring cannot be revoked'. And so it is said about the edict which was written on the command of Mordechai (Est. 8.8): 'The writing was in the name of King Ahasuerus and sealed with the king's ring [ויחתם בטבעת המלך]'.

In all these three cases the terminology used to describe the giving of the ring to a trusted subject is almost identical:

| | | | |
|---|---|---|---|
| ויתן אתה על־יד | מעל ידו | ויסר פרעה את־טבעתו | Gen. 41.42 |
| ויתנה ל | מעל ידו | ויסר המלך את־טבעתו | Est. 3.10 |
| ויתנה ל | אשר העביר מהמן | ויסר המלך את־טבעתו | Est. 8.2 |

### b. *The Meaning of* חותם

The noun חותם is attested 15 times in the Old Testament.[18] In Figure 19 I give a survey of how the word is translated in KJV, RSV and NJPS.

---

18. I include חותמת, which occurs once, with these 15.

Figure 19. חותם *in Some Translations*

| חותם | KJV | RSV | NJPS |
|---|---|---|---|
| 'seal' | 5 | 5 | 13 |
| 'signet' | 10 | 8 | 2 |
| 'signet ring' | – | 2 | – |

In some cases the use of the word has to do with the physical qualities of a seal or of the impression made with it (Job 38.14; 41.7[15]). The phrase חתם בחותם refers to the same action as the phrase חתם בטבעת, which was discussed above:

> So she wrote letters in Ahab's name and sealed them with his seal [ותחתם בחתמו ], and she sent the letters… (1 Kgs 21.8).

In one case חותם is used to evoke the connotation of intimacy and close relationship:

> Set me as a seal [שימני כחותם] upon your heart, as a seal [כחותם] upon your arm; for love is strong as death, jealousy is cruel as the grave. Its flashes are flashes of fire, a most vehement flame (Song 8.6).

In all these five cases the translations give 'seal'. Then there are eight cases where RSV (with KJV) translates 'signet', whereas a translation like NJPS has 'seal'. I want to argue that in each of these eight cases 'seal' is a more adequate translation than 'signet'. The eight cases are found in Genesis 38 (2 times) and in Exodus 28 and 39 (3 times in each).

In Genesis 38 there is nothing in the context to support the identification of the seal as a signet mounted in a ring, while the mentioning of the cord (v. 25 'the חותם and the cord and the staff', cf. v. 18) may provide a clue for an identification of the חותם here as a seal worn on a cord around the neck, as some commentators have suggested.[19]

---

19. '[T]he inclusion of the cord is further proof that no signet ring was involved', E.A. Speiser, *Genesis* (AB; Garden City, NY: Doubleday, 1964), p. 298; cf. G. Wenham, *Genesis 16–50* (WBC, 2; Dallas: Word Books, 1994), p. 368. The word which von Rad uses, 'Siegel' (G. von Rad, *Das Erste Buch Mose* [ATD, 2.4; Göttingen: Vandenhoeck & Ruprecht, 5th edn, 1958], p. 311), becomes 'signet ring' in the ET (*Genesis: A Commentary* [OTL; London: SCM Press, 1972], p. 356). He comments (p. 315 [ET p. 360]), 'Bei dem Siegel handelte es sich um ein sog. Rollsiegel, wie es bei Ausgrabungen gefunden wurde, einen kleinen Zylinder, den man zum siegeln über den weuchen Tonurkunden abrollte und an einer Schnur um den Hals bei sich trug'. Westermann comments (C. Westermann, *Genesis*. III. *Teilband*

Whether one agrees with this interpretation of the cord or not, it is clear that only the translation 'seal' does not prejudge the identification of the seal. In his commentary on Genesis, Sarna describes the function of the impression of the seal 'as a means of identifying personal possessions and of sealing and legitimating clay documents. It was a highly personal object that performed the function of the signature in modern society, a kind of extension of the personality'.[20]

In the six occurrences in Exodus 28 and 39, חותם appears in the phrase פתוחי חותם, 'the engravings of a חותם'. The stones to be attached to the garments of the high priest are to be engraved with the names of the sons of Israel. The gold plate on his turban is to be engraved with the words 'Holy to the LORD'. In both cases the process of engraving is compared to the engraving of a חותם, that is, any seal, not just a signet.

In conclusion, given the lack of any indication that the חותם mentioned in Genesis 38 and in Exodus 28 and 39 was a seal set in a ring (that is, a signet) it seems better to use the translation equivalent 'seal' in each of these eight cases, as does NJPS, rather than 'signet', with its association with a ring on the finger which is absent in the Hebrew. That would imply that in at least 13 out of 15 cases where חותם is used the English word 'seal' is the best translation equivalent (as in NJPS).

### c. *The Meaning of* חותם *in Jer. 22.24: 'Seal' or 'Signet-Ring'?*

This leaves us with two cases where both RSV and NJPS choose a word which they have not used before to translate חותם, namely 'signet ring' in RSV, 'signet' in NJPS. The two passages are Jer. 22.24 and Hag. 2.23. Are these two passages in some way special cases, which justify a departure from the usual translation 'seal', or is 'seal' also in these two cases the best translation equivalent? The verse in Jeremiah is generally seen as in some way providing the background to the verse in Haggai, and I think this observation is valid.

---

*Genesis 37–50* [BKAT, 1.3; Neukirchen–Vluyn: Neukirchener Verlag, 1982], p. 48), 'Der Siegelring oder das Rollsiegel (Zylinder-S.) diente dazu, Verträge zu signieren... Das Siegel wurde an der Schnur um den Hals getragen'. (ET *Genesis 37–50: A Commentary* [Minneapolis: Augsburg, 1986], p. 53). The presence of the cord does not necessarily identify the seal as a cylinder seal: stamp seals were most probably also worn on a cord around the neck (see Keel, *Blicke*, p. 114 n. 426).

20. N.M. Sarna, *The JPS Torah Commentary: Genesis. The Traditional Hebrew Text with the New JPS Translation* (Philadelphia: Jewish Publication Society of America, 1989), p. 268.

This justifies a more detailed discussion of the use of חותם in Jer. 22.24. The verse in its context reads:

> As I live, says the LORD, though Coniah the son of Jehoiakim, king of Judah, were the signet ring on my right hand, yet I would tear you off and give you into the hand of those who seek your life, into the hand of those of whom you are afraid, even into the hand of Nebuchadrezzar king of Babylon and into the hand of the Chaldeans. I will hurl you and the mother who bore you into another country, where you were not born, and there you shall die. But to the land to which they will long to return, there they shall not return (Jer. 22.24-27).

In this passage, the presence of the prepositional phrase 'on my right hand' identifies the position of the חותם as being on the hand of its owner. It is clear that here the referent of the word חותם is most likely a signet ring. Is it right, then, to conclude that at least in this case חותם means 'signet ring'?

Here it is useful to recall the distinction between reference and meaning. Barr describes reference as 'that to which a word refers, the actual or thought entity which is its referent,' and 'meaning' (which he calls 'information') as 'the difference which is conveyed, within a known and recognized sign system (a language like Hebrew or Arabic), by the fact that it is *this* sign and not another that is used'. He points out that '[m]any arguments in which biblical scholars adduce linguistic evidence appear to me, however, to involve some confusion between the former and the latter'.[21]

In this case, the reference of חותם is a signet ring, but the question to be asked is what information, if any, is conveyed by the choice of the more general word for 'seal', חותם, rather than טבעת, the word used specifically for 'signet ring'? The answer to that question is to a large extent related to the interpretation of the precise nature of the imagery conveyed by the use of חותם. Scholarly opinion is divided on this issue.

*Delegated Authority.* Some interpret the use of חותם imagery in Jer. 22.24 as signifying royal authority.[22] Clements states, 'No doubt kings

---

21. J. Barr, *Comparative Philology and the Text of the Old Testament* (Oxford: Clarendon Press, 1968), pp. 291-92.

22. In some cases it is not clear whether a scholar adopts one line of interpretation or the other; some seem to follow both. An example of this is McKane, *Jeremiah*, p. 541, who comments both that '[t]he signet-ring embodies power of the highest kind' and that the ring 'is made to symbolize the peculiar closeness of the

wore such rings as the mark of their divinely given office [...] the signet-ring was a badge of the kingly office'.[23] The problem with this interpretation is that the details of the picture simply do not fit. We have seen in the discussion of passages in Genesis 41 and Esther 3 and 8 that the ring is originally on the hand of the king and is then given to one of his subjects to symbolize the delegation of authority.

To reverse such an action, the ring would be taken from the hand of the king's subject and be put on the hand of the king again. Something like this happened in the case of Haman and Mordecai: 'the king took off his signet ring, which he had taken from Haman [אשר העביר מהמן], and gave it to Mordecai' (Est. 8.2). In the picture in Jeremiah 22 YHWH takes the role of the king, and his subject is Coniah. So, if this were a picture where the transfer of authority was reversed, then the ring would be found first on the hand of Coniah, to be taken from his hand, and to be put on the hand of YHWH. But as we find it here, it is not Coniah who wears the ring; the position of the ring is on the hand of YHWH. Also, the ring will not in some way be returned to the hand of its first owner, but thrown away and left to the enemy.

Clements admits that there is a problem, but he does so only in passing: 'The full implication of the imagery is not clear'.[24] McKane

relation between Yahweh and his anointed king'. Another example is Craigie, Kelley and Drinkard, *Jeremiah*, p. 319: they first state that 'the signet ring implies authority vested by Yahweh (Hag. 2.23). Since Jehoiachin was king, though only for a short time, he was in the very position of authority the signet ring implies'. They then continue, 'he was the signet, but... Yahweh tore him away (that suggests tearing away something very precious to Yahweh)'.

23. Clements, *Jeremiah*, p. 136. Clements does not produce evidence to support either statement. Weiser, *Jeremia*, p. 194, tries to find the origin in the enthronement ritual (the imagery 'scheint...aus dem mit der Thronbesteigung des Königs verbundenen religiösen Ideenkreis erwachsen zu sein').

24. R.E. Clements, *Jeremiah* (Interpretation; Atlanta: John Knox Press 1988), p. 136. The use of the word 'presumably' is perhaps an indication that Clines also has felt the problematic nature of the picture ('Haggai's Temple, Constructed, Deconstructed and Reconstructed', in Eskenazi and Richards (eds.), *Second Temple*, pp. 60-87 [78]), 'Zerubbabel is termed 'my servant' (עבדי), whom Yhwh will 'set as a signet ring' (חותם), presumably upon his own finger as a symbol of Zerubbabel's appointment as ruler'. There has been no evidence produced to support the idea that someone would set a signet ring upon his *own* finger as a symbol of the appointment of *someone else* as his representative. Compare the subtle shift in the following sentences in Wolff's discussion of the חותם imagery in Hag. 2.23 (Wolff, *Haggai*, p. 84): 'Wer jemandem sein Siegel schenkt, er verleiht ihm rechtskräftige

seems to be more aware of the seriousness of the problem:[25]

> The use of the signet ring in Jer. 22, 24 as a literary image involves quite an elaborate process of transference: it is not the ring on the vizier's finger conferring a delegated royal authority; it is the ring on the finger of Yahweh's right hand which symbolizes the Davidic king... The application of the image of the signet ring to Jehoiachin in Jer. 22, 24 may be an original literary departure—the creation of a new piece of imagery—...

Before one concludes that the literary image is the result of an 'elaborate process of transference', one should perhaps first ask whether one has understood the picture correctly.

*Preciousness—Intimate Relationship.* Other scholars interpret the חותם imagery as an indication of preciousness or personal value.[26] Rudolph

Vollmacht und gänzliches Vertrauen. Daß Jahwe Serubbabel einem Siegel gleichsetzen will, ist die eigentliche Aussage der Verheißung'.

25. McKane, *Jeremiah*, p. 541.

26. So already Kimchi (as quoted in McKane, *Jeremiah*, p. 541), 'Even if Coniah is like a signet ring on the right hand, which is never removed from it, I shall remove you from there and pull you off'. See also, e.g., André, *Aggée*, p. 357, 'quand bien même tu me serais aussi précieux qu'un cachet, dont on ne se sépare jamais, malgré cela je te repousserais loin de moi!'; B. Duhm, *Das Buch Jeremia* (KHAT, 11; Tübingen: J.C.B. Mohr, 1901), p. 179, 'Der Siegelring, den man nach dieser Stelle an der Hand, sonst auch wohl auf der Brust trug (Cnt 8 6), ist als Instrument zur Beglaubigung von Dokumenten so wichtig, wie bei uns die eigenhändige Handschrift, und wird daher sorgsam behütet'; P. Welten, 'Siegel und Stempel', *BRL²*, pp. 299-307 (299), 'S[iegel] stellen daneben Schmuckstücke und Wertgegenstände dar (Hag. 2 23)'; W.W. Hallo, '"As the Seal upon thine Arm": Glyptic Metaphors in the Biblical World', in L. Gorelick and E. Williams-Forte (eds.), *Ancient Seals and the Bible* (OPNE, 2.1; Malibu, CA: Undena, 1983), pp. 7-17 (9), where he describes the seal as a 'symbol of personal reliance on and affection for the recipient', and p. 10 on Jer. 22.24 and Hag. 2.23, 'Both prophets imply the intimacy of the signet-ring with its finger and both presumably have in mind a stamp-seal set in such a ring'; Holladay, *Jeremiah*, pp. 605-606, first describes the general use and value of a seal, 'The seal was one's signature and therefore represented one's identity; Cant 8.6 suggests the emotional identification with one's seal', and then contrasts Jehoiachin's fate with that of Zerubbabel, 'Hag. 2.23 suggests how great were the hopes invested in Zerubbabel when it is said that Yahweh will make him like a signet ring... The king, Jehoiachin, who should be like Yahweh's signet ring, will not be so treated by Yahweh'; P.J. King, *Jeremiah: An Archaeological Companion* (Louisville, KY: Westminster/John Knox Press,

constructs the seal imagery thus 'as valuable as the ring, which the important person always carries on his body, because his seal serves for his authentication'.[27] Jones points to the function of the seal, 'used for letters and official documents, a personal and valuable possession bearing the owner's characteristic mark', and then gives this analysis of the imagery: 'the image of the signet ring...stands for the indissoluble relationship between the LORD and his anointed king, a relationship which nevertheless the LORD will dissolve'.[28]

Some remarks on the use and distribution of seals in Israelite society may shed some light on the understanding of this kind of imagery. In ancient times a seal was used to produce a seal impression (in a small lump of [soft] clay, called a 'bulla'). A seal impression was used to certify personal possession of objects, and to authenticate documents.[29] A seal was seen as an object with high personal value. The stone of which the seal was made could be of precious material, which would add to its value. For both reasons, the seal was carefully guarded against loss,[30] and it was carried on the body.

It seems misguided to restrict the group of users of seals to kings, officials and civil servants, as is sometimes done.[31] Such a restriction can be explained from the fact that much study of seals has been done

1993), p. 92, 'Jeremiah used "signet ring" (*hotam*) metaphorically to describe something precious'.

27. 'So wertvoll wie der Ring, den der Vornehme immer bei sich trägt, weil sein Siegel ihm zur Beglaubigung dient' (Rudolph, *Jeremia*, p. 143).

28. Jones, *Jeremiah*, pp. 294-95.

29. See, e.g., King, *Jeremiah*, p. 93.

30. In a related culture, that of Mesopotamia, the loss of a seal could have serious legal consequences; one could issue a special statement with the precise date of the loss, to make documents sealed after that date invalid. The loss of a seal was also seen as a bad omen. See W.W. Hallo, 'Seals Lost and Found', in M. Gibson and R.D. Biggs (eds.), *Seals and Sealing in the Ancient Near East* (Bibliotheca Mesopotamica, 6; Malibu, CA: Undena, 1977), pp. 55-60 (56, 58).

31. E.g. 'Das Siegel scheint gleichsam Symbol der Königs- und Beamtenwürde zu sein' (B. Otzen, 'חתם', *ThWAT*, III, cols. 282-88 [284, 288]); 'the signet-ring was a badge of the kingly office', Clements, *Jeremiah*, p. 136; 'The ring which is inseparable from the person of the statesman...', McKane, *Jeremiah*, p. 541; Meyers and Meyers, *Haggai, Zechariah*, p. 69. The same idea is found in Y. Shiloh and D. Tarler, 'Bullae from the City of David: A Hoard of Seal Impressions from the Israelite Period', *BA* 49 (1986), pp. 197-209 (201), apparently a result of reading mediaeval practices into the Israelite society of the first millennium BCE.

from a literary or epigraphic perspective.[32] Many seals with an inscription may have belonged to those categories from the upper classes (but not necessarily all: there is no compelling reason, for example, to ascribe *all* seals carrying a name but not an indication of office to upper class circles).

However, it is only some ten per cent of the seals discovered which carry an inscription. And many of these seals with an inscription were inscribed not in a negative sense, resulting in a positive, readable image in the lump of clay, but 'in the positive sense...clearly not intended for impressing in clay'.[33] These two phenomena should make one aware of the fact that seals were not only worn for functional reasons, but also as ornamentation. It also should make one cautious about restricting the possession of seals to the upper class in society.[34]

32. As pointed out by Keel (*Visionen*, p. 93 n. 160; and 'Bildträger aus Palästina/Israel und die besondere Bedeutung der Miniaturkunst', in O. Keel and S. Schroer, *Studien zu den Stempelsiegeln aus Palästina/Israel*, I [OBO, 67; Freiburg: Universitätsverlag; Göttingen: Vandenhoeck & Ruprecht, 1985], pp. 7-45 [23]). For more recent developments in the research on seals, see Gorelick and Williams-Forte, *Ancient Seals*, and the review by O. Keel, review of *Ancient Seals*, pp. 307-11; Schroer, *Bilder*; Keel, 'Siegel und Siegeln in der Bibel', in O. Keel and C. Uehlinger (eds.), *Altorientalische Miniaturkunst: Die ältesten visuellen Massenkommunikationsmittel. Ein Blick in die Sammlungen des Biblischen Instituts der Universität Freiburg Schweiz* (Mainz: Philipp von Zabern, 1990), pp. 87-92; and Avigad, *Corpus*, pp. 21-46, an adaptation of earlier articles, including 'The Contribution of Hebrew Seals to an Understanding of Israelite Religion and Society', in P.D. Miller, P.D. Hanson and S.D. McBride (eds.), *Ancient Israelite Religion* (Philadelphia: Fortress Press, 1987), pp. 195-208, and 'Hebrew Seals and Sealings and their Significance for Biblical Research', in J.A. Emerton (ed.), *Congress Volume Jerusalem 1986* (VTSup, 40; Leiden: E.J. Brill, 1988), pp. 7-16. Note also the extensive bibliography in P. Bordreuil, 'Sceaux inscrits des pays du Levant', *DBSup*, LXVI, cols. 86-212.

33. Hallo, 'Glyptic Metaphors', p. 9; see also Keel, review of Gorelick and Williams-Forte, *Ancients Seals*, p. 311; Schroer, *Bilder*, p. 407 n. 274.

34. It seems difficult to improve on the way Koole has put it (*Haggai* [COT; Kampen: Kok, 1967], p. 101), 'Uit literaire en archaeologische gegevens blijkt dat koningen ervan gebruik maakten, maar verder ieder die zich een status wilde veroorloven'. ('From literary and archaeological sources it appears that kings used [seals], but also anyone who wanted to grant himself some status'.) See also Avigad, *Corpus*, p. 22; and Schroer, *Bilder*, pp. 405-406 (the unusual spelling is original), 'Selbst wenn nicht jedermann und jede Frau glücklicheR BesitzerIn eines persönlichen Exemplars gewesen sein sollte—obwohl anzunehmen ist, dass die meisten Leute ein Stück aus billigem Material wohl erschwingen oder auch selbst herstellen

The high personal value attached to a seal explains why it was used as a picture for the preciousness of one person in the estimation of another, as in the passage from Song 8.6, quoted above. Fox, in his commentary on Song of Songs from the perspective of ancient Egyptian love songs, points out different ways in which a seal could be kept, 'worn on a cord around the neck so that it rested on the chest (Gen. 38:18, 25) or kept on one's hand as a ring (Jer. 22:24; Sir. 49:11)'. On the seal imagery in Song 8.6 he comments, 'To be as a seal on the heart and the arm implies belonging and special intimacy; see Jer. 22:24; Hag. 2:23… The seal was like a signature and as such would be kept on one's person continuously'.[35]

Imagery similar to that in Song 8.6 is found in a passage from Egyptian love poetry which uses a root similar to חותם; here the man says about the woman:

konnten—ist sicher, dass JedeR IsraelitIn Siegel oder deren Abdrücke auf Ton zu Gesicht bekam'.

35. M.V. Fox, *The Song of Songs and the Ancient Egyptian Love Songs* (Wisconsin: University of Wisconsin Press, 1985), p. 169. It would be more precise to say that the seal impression 'was like a signature' (cf. the comments of Sarna on Gen. 38, mentioned above). Pope and Keel take more or less the same line as Fox, but then interpret the function of the seal as that of an amulet to protect against death. According to M.H. Pope, *Song of Songs: A New Translation with Introduction and Commentary* (AB, 7C; Garden City, NY: Doubleday, 1977), pp. 666-67, 'the following lines which emphasize Love's power over against that of Death suggest that there may be a blending of the functions of the signet with the memento and the phylactery'. Similarly, Keel bases his interpretation of the seal on the reason for the request to be made like a seal given in the lines, 'for love is strong as death, jealousy is cruel as the grave. Its flashes are flashes of fire, a most vehement flame'. The love of the beloved is a seal amulet, which overcomes death (*Blicke*, pp. 118-19; *Das Hohelied* [ZBAT, 18; Zürich: Theologische Verlag, 1986], pp. 247-51). The love and passion of the beloved protect against the destructive powers of death ('Siegel und Siegeln', p. 91). Keel calls this interpretation more profound and more adequate than the one which interprets the imagery as indicating inseparability and preciousness. In my view, the view of Keel (and Pope) is not profound but far-fetched. It is based on a misunderstanding of the point of comparison. The flaw in the argument is exposed by R. Murphy, *Song of Songs* (Hermeneia; Philadelphia: Fortress Press, 1990), pp. 197, 'v 6 does not "emphasize Love's power over against that of Death" [Pope]. Love is compared to Death as regards strength, but is not presented as being locked in battle with Death. The point of the comparison is the quality of love in its relationship to the beloved; in this respect it is comparable to Death and its relationship to a human being. Both attain their objects'.

If only I were her little seal-ring [*ḥtm*],
   the keeper of her finger!
I would see her love
   each and every day,

   ...

   [while it would be I] who stole her heart.[36]

Before one concludes that this kind of imagery is only the stuff of romance, here are some other examples. In an Assyrian letter dated to the time of the Assyrian king Sargon II (722–705 BCE), the writer (whose name is lost because the beginning of the tablet has been broken away, but who has been identified by Parpola as the king himself) indicates his difference of opinion concerning the qualities of a certain man called Bel-nuri, whom he charges with slandering and for that reason has removed him from different posts to which he had appointed him:[37]

[This] Bel-nuri cannot be trusted in what he says...; yet you lifted him and put him around your neck like a seal [*at-ta-[m]a ta-at-ti-ši ki-i kunukka*(NA₄.KIŠIB) *ina li-ba-ni-ka tak-ta-ra-ar-šú*]. For this very reason I relieved him of his office as major-domo, removed him and let you settle him in his house in the centre of Arrapha.

...

That you like Bel-nuri and [have placed him around your neck] like this seal *ša a-na* ᵐ*Bēl*(EN)-*nu-ri ta-ra-a-mu-šu-u-ni ša ki-i kunukka* (NA₄.KIŠIB) *an-ni-i*]...

In a passage in Ben Sira, seal imagery is used in parallelism with the imagery of the apple of the eye; again, the imagery is used to evoke the idea of preciousness, in this case of the virtues of almsgiving and kindness:[38]

---

36. Cairo Love Songs, Group B: No. 21C. The passage can be found in, e.g., Fox, *Song of Songs*, pp. 38, 40. The *ḥtm* is also mentioned in Cairo Love Songs, Group A: Np. 20B (a girl; see Fox, *Song of Songs*, p. 31) and in a text called 'O. Gardiner 304 recto' (Ramses; see Fox, *Song of Songs*, p. 81). Fox translates the Egyptian word *ḥtm* as 'signet-ring'. A. Erman and H. Grapow (eds.), *Wörterbuch der Aegyptischen Sprache* (Berlin: Akademie-Verlag, 4th edn, 1982), s.v., give 'seal' as the original meaning, from which 'signet-ring' is a later development. The Egyptian language also has a word for 'signet-ring', *db'.t*, the same root as the Hebrew טבעת, but it is not used here.

37. S. Parpola (ed.), *The Correspondence of Sargon II*. I. *Letters from Assyria and the West* (SAA, 1; Helsinki: Helsinki University Press, 1987), pp. 14-15, no. 12 (ABL 1042); on the identification of the writer of this letter, see p. xxii.

38. Compare the comment of P.W. Skehan and A.A. Di Lella, *The Wisdom of*

A man's almsgiving is like a signet with the Lord [ἐλεημοσύνη ἀνδρὸς
ὡς σφραγὶς μετ' αὐτοῦ],
and he will keep a person's kindness like the apple of his eye (Ben Sira
17.22).

If we interpret the חותם in Jer. 22.24 in this way we are able to see the
imagery as internally consistent: the king is compared to a seal on the
hand of YHWH, symbol of high personal value, but he has lost his privileged position, and YHWH feels like throwing him away, as if he had
become an object of no personal value at all.

It may also explain the choice of the word חותם, even when the
referent is a signet ring. It could be, but this explanation is perhaps
somewhat speculative, that the meaning of טבעת, with its special focus
on the ring (which in fact was just one of the ways to carry a seal) rather
than on the stone (which was indispensable for the proper function of
making a seal impression and which could be carried in different ways,
for example on a cord around the neck or on the wrist), made the word
טבעת in a sense too specific and therefore less suitable for the imagery
indicating preciousness, the object of great value being the stone, not
the thing used for carrying it.

What McKane considered a possibly 'new piece of imagery' appears
to be a piece of imagery that was already in existence, and could be
used in a variety of contexts. This diversity of contexts in which the
seal imagery can be used suggests that kingship is not essential to the
use of this imagery. If the passage is interpreted in the way I propose,
then there is nothing specifically 'royal' about the seal imagery.[39]

Another phenomenon may support the case for the incidental nature
of the application of the seal imagery to the king. Let us take a closer
look at the syntax of the verse:

חי־אני נאם־יהוה
כי אם־יהיה כניהו בן־יהויקים מלך יהודה חותם על־יד ימיני
כי משם אתקנך

Ben Sira (AB, 39; New York: Doubleday, 1987), p. 283, 'like something very
precious (v. 22a; cf. 49.11; Jer. 22.24; Hag. 2.23)'.

39. If one agrees to read חותֶם תכנית for MT חותַם תכנית in Ezek. 28.12, as
scholars like Zimmerli (*Ezechiel*. I. *Ezechiel 1–24*. II. *Ezechiel 25–48* [BKAT, 13.1-
2; Neukirchen–Vluyn: Neukirchener Verlag, 1969], p. 672) and L.C. Allen (*Ezekiel
20–48*, p. 90) do on the basis of the early versions, one would have a second passage where seal imagery is used with regard to a king. The phrase as a whole, 'the
signet of perfection, full of wisdom and perfect in beauty', would fit well in an
interpretation where the imagery evokes the idea of beauty, not kingship.

The protasis introduced by כי אם can indicate either a real condition, or a hypothetical condition. Translations like RSV and NJPS interpret the protasis as hypothetical:

> though Coniah the son of Jehoiakim, king of Judah, were the signet ring on my right hand, yet I would tear you off (RSV).

> if you, O King Coniah, son of Jehoiakim, of Judah, were a signet on my right hand, I would tear you off even from there (NJPS).

Unfortunately, as I argue in the Excursus at the end of this Chapter, it is not possible to make a compelling case for either a real or a hypothetical condition. The syntactical construction can be interpreted in either way. If taken as a hypothetical condition, this would support the case for the incidental nature of this imagery.

To sum up the discussion of the meaning of חותם in Jer. 22.24: interpreting the חותם imagery as indicating (the reversal of the delegation of) authority is highly problematic, because the details of the picture are different from what one would have expected in such a case. There is an attractive alternative in which the חותם imagery is seen as pointing to great personal value. This may explain the use of the noun חותם rather than טבעת, even though the referent of חותם is a signet ring in this particular case. It seems best to choose 'seal' as translation equivalent, because this rendering does not narrow the options for interpretation as much as 'signet ring' would do.

### d. *The Use of the* חותם *Imagery in Haggai 2.23*
I now turn to the discussion of the interpretation of the use of the חותם imagery in Hag. 2.23. As one might expect after the discussion of Jer. 22.24 there is no agreement about what the חותם imagery in Hag. 2.23 conveys.

*Authority.* A great number of scholars interpret Hag. 2.23 as a picture of the giving of authority to Zerubbabel. The precise nature of this authority is interpreted in different ways. It is possible to distinguish three positions. Scholars argue that in Hag. 2.23 Zerubbabel is to be made either the representative of YHWH, or the new king who will restore the monarchy, or the new world ruler.[40] One sometimes finds words like

---

40. Some scholars combine two or more of these views. For example, in Beyse one finds phrases like the restoration of the Davidic monarchy, Zerubbabel as representative of YHWH, and world rule (*Serubbabel*, pp. 56-57).

messianic or Messiah used to describe Zerubbabel's role; this is the case with each of these three positions.[41]

(a) Ackroyd, who seems to avoid using words like 'king', 'kingship', or 'monarchy', sees Zerubbabel in Hag. 2.23 as 'a royal representative of God', but at the same time wants to play down the political nature of the oracle.[42] Other scholars[43] also find the idea of Zerubbabel as repre-

41. E. Hühn, *Die messianischen Weissagungen des israelitisch-jüdischen Volkes bis zu den Targumim historisch untersucht und erläutert* (Tübingen: J.C.B. Mohr, 1899), p. 61, 'Der Messias wird von Haggai hiernach nicht erst erwartet; er ist bereits da, er lebt mitten unter seinen Volksgenossen'; Marti, *Dodekapropheton*, p. 390, 'Dann beginnt das messianische Reich, die Herrschaft Israels, und Serubbabel wird König'; Nowack, *Propheten*, p. 322: Zerubbabel is called 'die Weltherrschaft des messianischen Königs der Zukunft aufzurichten'; Edelkoort, *Zacharia*, p. 74 'dat Haggaï in Zerubbabel den Messias heeft gezien' (Haggai has seen the Messiah in Zerubbabel); Horst, *Propheten*, p. 209, 'zweifellos "messianischen" Rang'; Elliger, *Propheten*, p. 97, 'in Serubbabel...weilt der Messias schon mitten unter dem Volke... Serubbabel wird als Messias, als Statthalter Gottes, das Land regieren...so soll Serubbabel die Leibhaft gewordene Herrschermacht Gottes, der Messias, sein'; Chary, *Aggée, Zacharie*, pp. 33-34, 'un personnage messianique'; Rudolph, *Haggai, Sacharja*, p. 54, 'er ist der Messias, auch wenn der Name nicht ausdrücklich genannt wird'; Mason, *Haggai, Zechariah*, p. 25, 'Haggai saw Zerubbabel as a messianic figure and therefore envisaged political independence for the community in the new age'; Amsler, *Aggée; Zacharie 1–8*, pp. 39-40; P.C. Craigie, *The Twelve Prophets*, II (DSB; Edinburgh: St Andrews Press; Philadelphia: Westminster Press, 1985), p. 152: Haggai 'expected Zerubbabel to be the messianic prince'; Van der Woude, *Haggai–Maleachi*, pp. 73-76; J. Hausmann, *Israels Rest: Studien zum Selbstverständnis der nachexilichen Gemeinde* (BWANT, 124 [7/4]; Stuttgart: Kohlhammer, 1987), p. 42; G. Fohrer, *Erzähler und Propheten im Alten Testament: Geschichte der israelitischen und frühjüdischen Literatur* (Heidelberg: Quelle & Meyer, 1988), p. 156. According to Van Hoonacker, *Prophètes*, p. 575, Zerubbabel receives the honours due to the messianic king, but not 'à titre personnel', but as representing the dynasty.

42. Ackroyd, *Exile*, pp. 164-66. L.L. Grabbe, *Judaism from Cyrus to Hadrian*. I. *The Persian and Greek Periods* (Minneapolis: Fortress Press, 1992), p. 78, also seems to avoid using language of kingship, he goes no further than saying that the ring 'signifies royal authority' and that the 'reference to kingship is implicit rather than explicit'.

43. Driver, *Prophets*, pp. 168-69: Zerubbabel's position 'will remain secure, and Yahweh will constitute him His trusted representative' (both protection and authority); Horst, *Propheten*, p. 209; Mowinckel, *He that Cometh*, p. 160, 'Zerubbabel ben Shealtiel, a signet on God's hand, one who will execute and put into effect on earth the decrees of Yahweh'; cf. Koch, *Profeten*, II, p. 167, 'Dann wird Serubbabel der Siegelring an der göttlichen Hand sein, mit der der Erde der frieden-

sentative here, but do not qualify it as royal. For example Jagersma, 'Presumably this signet ring is regarded as a sign that Zerubbabel is appearing as head of the people and acting as God's representative'.[44]

(b) A number of scholars interpret the oracle as announcing that Zerubbabel will be king.[45] Japhet expresses this interpretation in a way which is representative for this view:[46]

> Haggai does not explain, however, for what Zerubbabel was chosen. From what is described in the prophecy—the overthrow of the kingdoms of the nations as the first stage in the choosing of Zerubbabel—we may conclude that Haggai sees Zerubbabel as a king, whose kingdom is made possible by a change in the political structure... [F]rom now on, since Zerubbabel has been chosen as a 'signet', he will be 'sitting on the throne of David and ruling again in Judah'. All this, however, is only hinted at in the prophecy of Haggai and not stated explicitly.

stiftende Wille Gottes aufgeprägt wird' (ET *Prophets*, II, p. 163, 'the ring which God will use to stamp his will to peace into the very earth itself'); Petersen, *Haggai and Zechariah*, pp. 104-106, 'earthly representative, equivalent to a king in significance'; Wolff, *Haggai*, p. 85 'Der Gehorsame wird der Bevollmächtigte'; R. Albertz, *Religionsgeschichte Israels in alttestamentlichter Zeit*. II. *Vom Exil bis zu den Makkabäern* (Grundrisse zum Alten Testament; ATD Ergänzungsreihe 8.2; Göttingen: Vandenhoeck & Ruprecht, 1992), p. 481, '...so daß Serubbabel sein Amt als "Siegelring", d.h. Mandatar Jahwes auf Erden ganz im Sinne der älteren Königstheologie antreten könnte' (ET *A History of Israelite Religion in the Old Testament Period*. II. *From the Exile to the Maccabees* [London: SCM Press, 1994], p. 452, 'Zerubbabel could enter into his office as a "signet ring", i.e. the one mandated by Yahweh on earth').

44. H. Jagersma, *Geschiedenis van Israël in het oudtestamentische tijdvak* (Kampen: Kok, 1979), p. 277, 'Deze zegelring moet vermoedelijk gezien worden als een teken, dat Zerubbabel als hoofd van het volk optreedt en handelt als Gods vertegenwoordiger'. (ET *A History of Israel in the Old Testament Period* [London: SCM Press, 1983], p. 199.)

45. Marti, *Dodekapropheton*, p. 390; Seybold, 'Königserwartung', pp. 71-73; Bickerman, 'Marge', p. 24 (reprinted in *Studies*, p. 332); Japhet, 'Zerubbabel', pp. 77-78; Van der Woude, *Haggai–Maleachi*, pp. 70, 73-74; Craigie, *Prophets*, pp. 152-53: Haggai 'affirms the restoration of the line of David'; Hanson, 'Messiahs and Messianic Figures in Proto-Apocalypticism', in Charlesworth (ed.), *Messiah*, pp. 67-75 (69); E.E. Platt, 'Ancient Israelite Jewelry', *ABD*, III, pp. 823-34 (830); Laato, *Josiah*, p. 226; Roberts, 'Messianic Expectations', p. 49; Ahlström, *History*, p. 820; Albertz, *Religionsgeschichte*, II, p. 481 [ET *Religion*, p. 452]; Redditt, *Haggai, Zechariah*, p. 32.

46. Japhet, 'Zerubbabel', pp. 77-78.

(c) Phrases like 'universal and eschatological ruler' and 'world ruler'[47] are used by Clines:[48] 'the book of Haggai ends with the announcement that Zerubbabel is to be appointed world ruler'.

*Value*. Others interpret the imagery of the signet ring in v. 23 as a picture of high personal value resulting in special care.[49] Interestingly, this is the view one finds in all major dictionaries. BDB interprets the use of חותם in Hag. 2.23 as an image for 'a precious article'. GB takes the use of חותם in Hag. 2.23 as 'an image of something which one does not let go'.[50] *LH* explains it, 'as something valuable, which one does not allow to be taken away' (*ut res cara, quam quis sibi eripi non sinit*). *HALAT* writes about the use of חותם in Jer. 22.24 and Hag. 2.23, 'a person as a seal ח (= closely connected)'.[51]

47. Sellin's position seems also to suggest world rule: Zerubbabel will be the vizier of God in the world of nations, the only king, God's representative on earth (E. Sellin, *Das Zwölfprophetenbuch* [KAT, 12; Leipzig: Deichert; Erlangen: Scholl, 1922], p. 416; cf. Beyse, *Serubbabel*, p. 57, 'ein Weltreich').

48. 'Haggai's Temple', p. 78.

49. Sometimes scholars interpret Hag. 2.23 as indicating the special relationship between YHWH and Zerubbabel, without specifying the nature of the relationship with words like 'care' or 'protection'. E.g., B.J. Oosterhoff, 'De schriftprofeten', in A.S. van der Woude (ed.), *Bijbels handboek*. IIa. *Het Oude Testament* (Kampen: Kok, 1982), pp. 362-427 (420), 'Als alle koningstronen en rijken ineenstorten, zal Jahwe Zerubbabel aandoen als een zegelring. Dit wijst op een bijzondere relatie. In tegenstelling met zijn voorvader Jojakin (Jer. 22.24) zal Zerubbabel tot heil van zijn volk zijn'. (ET Oosterhoff, 'The Prophets', in A.S. van der Woude (ed.), *The World of the Old Testament* (Bible Handbook, 2; Grand Rapids: Eerdmans, 1989), pp. 226-70 (266), 'All power and all the kingdoms of the nations will be destroyed, but Zerubbabel will stand in a special relationship to God, and thus he will be a blessing to the people'. In my view, 'special relationship' seems to be expressed in 'I have chosen you'. The focus of the seal imagery is care/protection as a *result* of this special relationship. It seems that the Targum also interprets the words along the lines of special relationship, when it translates: ואשׁוינך כגלף דעזקא על יד 'I will make you as the engraving of a signet ring upon the hand'. Whatever one thinks about the adequacy of this as a translation of the Hebrew, it seems clear that it is based on an interpretation of the imagery as indicating value, rather than authority.

50. 'Bildl[ich] f[ür] das was man nicht losläßt'. *HAH*, the 'new' GB, does not provide an explanation, it only gives 'bildl[ich] i. Vergleich: (wie) ein Siegel Jer. 22,24... Hag. 2,23. Cant 8,6'.

51. 'e. Mensch als ח (= eng verbunden)'. Along the same lines is the view of Moscati, 'Sigilli', pp. 314-38 (319), who finds in Hag. 2.23 the same simile as in Jeremiah, indicating special value as of something dear and precious. A note at

In more recent commentaries this view does not have many adherents. But in some of the older commentaries[52] the חותם imagery is
interpreted in this way. According to Köhler, the *tertium comparationis*
in the use of this imagery is the most intimate, inseparable communion
between a signet ring and its owner. On the day when he will destroy
the power of the nations, YHWH will bring Zerubbabel into a position
in which he will be like a signet ring: Zerubbabel will be inseparably
connected with YHWH, as a signet ring is inseparably connected with
its owner. Zerubbabel will not be thrown away and destroyed like the
kingdoms of the nations, just as someone does not remove his signet
ring or throw it away.[53] Lagrange writes that a seal is a precious object
which one guards with care (referring to Jer. 22.24). The imagery of the
seal indicates that in the great overthrow of the world Zerubbabel will
be preserved.[54] According to Junker, the oracle states that even on the
occasion of the collapse of the whole world Zerubbabel has nothing to
fear: YHWH will protect him as carefully as someone protects his signet

Hag. 2.23 in the margin of NJPS reads, 'I.e., bring you close to me; contrast Jer. 22,
24-30'.

52. See Hitzig, *Propheten*, p. 332 'nicht: [ich] *lege dich wie einen Siegelring an*
(vgl. Jer. 22, 24), sondern: halte dich so werth und hüte dich so sorgfältig wie
meinen Siegelring vgl. Hoh. L. 8, 6'; André, *Aggée*, p. 357, 'il le fera sien (je te
mettra [au doigt]) et le gardera lui seul comme on garde avec un soin jaloux, sans le
quitter, un objet aussi précieux qu'un sceau'. F. Giesebrecht, *Das Buch Jeremia*
(HKAT, 3.2; Göttingen: Vandenhoeck & Ruprecht, 1907), p. 125, writes on Jer.
22.24, 'Der Siegelring Bild für ein Kleinod, das man in Ehren und fest hält, cf. Hag.
2₂₃ Cnt 8₆'.

53. Köhler, *Sacharja*, pp. 113-14. Later on in his discussion (p. 115), Köhler
states that the messianic hope is now focused on the person of Zerubbabel as the
descendant of David, but this does not seem to imply the Authority View in any
sense.

54. Lagrange, 'Prophéties', p. 69, 'Dans le grand bouleversement du monde,
Zorobabel sera donc préservé'. Lagrange rejects a messianic interpretation of this
passage ('Il y a loin de là à lui supposer un rôle messianique actif'), and makes
some interesting remarks about messianic interpretations of this passage: he seems
somewhat surprised over the phenomenon that a number of scholars who usually
are less eager to find messianism anywhere (in the Old Testament), state of this
passage that Haggai points to Zerubbabel as the future messianic king ('Plusieurs
critiques, d'ordinaire moins prompts à mettre du messianisme partout, déclarent
qu'ici Aggé désigne Zorobabel comme le roi messianique de l'avenir. C'est du
moins mettre dans un jour très cru une pensée que l'auteur a volontairement
voilée').

ring. The reason for this special protection is the fact that God had chosen him.[55] Or, in the words of Barnes:[56] 'Haggai promises complete safety'.

Other biblical scholars interpret the imagery of the seal as picturing closeness of relationship or great value, but in the end go for an overall interpretation of the oracle along the lines of delegated authority. So, Van der Woude writes about the seal that it was 'a symbol of a precious personal possession and object of special care', but then continues to interpret the whole of the phrase 'I will make you like a seal' as indicating the elevation of Zerubbabel to be the representative of YHWH.[57]

*Hag. 2.23 and Jer. 22.24*. This is the place to take another look at the חותם oracle in Jer. 22.24. The precise nature of the relationship between the oracles in Hag. 2.23 and Jer. 22.24 is not immediately clear. While some leave the nature of the relationship between the two oracles somewhat vague,[58] others state that the oracle in Haggai reverses the one in Jer. 22.24.[59] If the oracle in Jeremiah implies removal from office, then the reversal of that oracle would imply institution in the office of kingship.

I do not want to disagree with finding a connection between the two oracles, though I would be somewhat cautious about whether one can say that Haggai was consciously reversing the Jeremiah oracle. Whether this was the case or not depends partly on how widely the חותם imagery was used. The examples which I have discussed suggest that this may have been wider than is usually thought. For the sake of the argument, I will suppose that Haggai indeed meant to reverse the oracle of Jer.

55. Junker, *Propheten*, p. 107.

56. W.E. Barnes, *Haggai; Zechariah and Malachi: With Notes and Introduction* (CBSC; Cambridge: Cambridge University Press, 1934), p. 20.

57. *Haggai–Maleachi*, pp. 73-74, 'een symbool van kostbaar persoonlijk bezit en een voorwerp van bijzondere zorg'. Compare Driver, *Prophets*, p. 169, 'Yahweh will make him his signet-ring, inseparable from Himself, and the symbol of His authority'; and see also Van Hoonacker, *Prophètes*, p. 575; Amsler, *Aggée; Zacharie 1–8*, pp. 39-40; Oosterhoff, 'Prophets', p. 266; De Jonge, 'Messiah', p. 781, 'Zerubbabel will be the Lord's "signet ring" (cf. Jer. 22.24); that is, he will be protected by God whose representative he is'.

58. E.g. Reventlow, *Haggai, Sacharja*, p. 30, who calls the oracle in Jer. 22.24 '[e]ine vergleichbare Aussage'.

59. Baldwin, *Haggai, Zechariah*, p. 54; Meyers and Meyers, *Haggai, Zechariah*, p. 69.

22.24. Would that not corroborate the authority interpretation of the חותם imagery in Hag. 2.23? In my view this is not the case.

As I have mentioned in my discussion of Jer. 23.5 (in Chapter 3), the context in which that oracle and also the seal oracle of Jer. 22.24 is found is a collection of oracles dealing with kingship (Jer. 21.1–23.8). I have argued that kingship is not essential to the seal imagery, since the imagery is found in a variety of contexts. But if kingship is the main theme of the collection in which the oracle is found, is it not somewhat strained to interpret the imagery in a way which may create the impression of downplaying the royal associations which many find in the use of the seal imagery? In my view, this depends on whether in such a context where kingship is the main theme every single oracle needs to address the point of kingship specifically. I would suggest that this is not necessarily the case.

It is not difficult to find evidence to support this suggestion: I can point to the next oracle (v. 28) with the unwanted pot imagery, imagery which does not have any royal associations whatsoever,[60] and for which no one would claim such associations. If this imagery does not deal with the issue of kingship as such then there is no need to *a priori* assume that the seal imagery deals with it. One should study the terminology and the details of the imagery to find out whether any particular imagery addresses the issue.

As I have argued above, both the terminology and the details of the seal imagery point in a different direction: the חותם imagery conveys the notion of Coniah losing the special value which YHWH might have accredited to him. If the חותם imagery is used to convey the notion of a fall from grace, and the subject of that fall from grace is a king, what does this imply for his position as king? Does the fall from grace imply something like removal from office? Most scholars would say so on the basis of the passage as a whole, and I would agree. But I would want to question the assumption that the חותם imagery in v. 24 as such implies a removal from office. A similar question can be asked with respect to the imagery of the 'despised, broken pot' in v. 28. In both cases the notion of kingship is not essential to the imagery used, that is, both kinds of imagery can be used for persons in different positions or offices, not exclusively for kings.

Furthermore, a fall from grace does not necessarily imply an immedi-

---

60. The same imagery is used of a nation, Moab, in Jer. 48.38.

ate removal from office, as can be seen in the case of King Saul: after
his fall from grace he is not immediately removed from his office, and
is respected as YHWH's anointed by David who has already been
anointed as his successor. I would say that it is only on the basis of the
verses in between (Jer. 22.25-27) which describe the fate of Coniah as
being given into the hands of his enemies and being hurled into another
country that we can safely conclude that Coniah will no longer be king,
but note that even in these verses this is not stated explicitly.

In Hag. 2.23 חותם imagery similar to that in Jer. 22.24 is used. In this
case also, the notion of kingship is not a feature of the imagery itself, so
that the use of the imagery as such does not decide the issue of whether
this oracle announces that Zerubbabel will be king. One has to look to
other elements in the context to answer the question whether the restoration of kingship is at stake in this oracle. Even if the oracle in Hag. 2.23
reverses the one in Jer. 22.24, as such this is not enough to resolve that
question.

Whatever the precise nature of the relationship between Hag. 2.23
and Jer. 22.24,[61] one difference between the two passages should not be
overlooked. In contrast to Jer. 22.24, there is nothing in Hag. 2.23 to
indicate the exact position of the חותם, and so the translation 'signet
ring' (RSV) is question-begging, and even 'signet' (NJPS) prejudges the
interpretation of the verse because it creates a possibly misguided association. The only word which does not say more than the Hebrew allows
is 'seal'.

The delegated authority view suffers from the same problem as does
the authority interpretation of Jer. 22.24. The details do not match.
Scholars have to treat the details of the imagery of the signet ring in a
very superficial way.[62] What happens in the case of delegated authority
is that A gives his signet ring to B. What one finds in Hag. 2.23 is rather
different: A *makes* B *like* a seal, resulting in B becoming (like) a seal,
or being treated like one. If delegated authority were the point of the
imagery, one would have expected the oracle to go something like this:

---

61. Most scholars find in the oracle in Hag. 2.23 a deliberate reversal of the
message of Jer. 22.24.

62. And thus are able to write things like 'the symbolic, if not actual, placing of
a royal ring upon the finger of Zerubbabel' (S.J. De Vries, *From Old Revelation to
New: A Tradition-Historical and Redaction-Critical Study of Temporal Transitions
in Prophetic Prediction* (Grand Rapids: Eerdmans, 1995), p. 214.

Hag. 2.23 MT                          *delegated authority

| | |
|---|---|
| ביום ההוא | ביום ההוא |
| נאם־יהוה צבאות | נאם־יהוה צבאות |
| אקחך זרבבל בן־שאלתיאל עבדי | אסור את־טבעתי מעל ידי |
| נאם־יהוה | ונתתיה לך זרבבל בן־שאלתיאל עבדי |
| ושמתיך כחותם | נאם־יהוה |
| כי־בך בחרתי | כי־בך בחרתי |
| נאם יהוה צבאות | נאם יהוה צבאות |

| | |
|---|---|
| On that day, | On that day, |
| says the LORD of hosts, | says the LORD of hosts, |
| I will take you, | I will take my signet ring |
| O Zerubbabel my servant, | from my hand |
| the son of Shealtiel, | and give it to you, |
| says the LORD, | O Zerubbabel my servant, |
| and make you like a seal; | the son of Shealtiel, |
| for I have chosen you, | says the LORD; |
| says the LORD of hosts. | for I have chosen you, |
| | says the LORD of hosts |

The difference is too substantial to let the delegated authority interpretation go unchallenged, both as a complete interpretation of the oracle, and as one element in a combination with an interpretation of the use of חותם as indicating personal value.

There is another factor which might be seen as supporting the interpretation of the חותם imagery as indicating personal value, and that is the presence of the preposition כ in the phrase שים כחותם, which suggests that שים here is not used in the sense of 'to appoint someone (as)...',[63] but to introduce a simile. Zerubbabel will be treated like a חותם, in a way similar to the woman in Song 8.6 who asks the man to treat her as a חותם (exactly the same phrase with the same preposition: שימני כחותם).

## 5. Politics and Rule in the Context of the Oracle

To sum up the argument so far: the two words used to describe Zerubbabel's position at the moment of receiving the oracle, עבד and בחר,

---

63. Contra, e.g., E.H. Merrill, *An Exegetical Commentary: Haggai, Zechariah, Malachi* (Chicago: Moody Press, 1994), p. 56. Clines also speaks about 'Zerubbabel's appointment' ('Haggai's Temple', p. 78). In the case of 'appointing' one would have expected that the verb would be complemented by either a direct object, or a phrase with the preposition ל (occasionally כ).

allow for a royal interpretation, but it would be wrong to say that they require it. The first word used to describe what will happen to him, לקח, may just indicate 'take because of a special relationship', or 'for protection as a component in that special relationship'; it would be wrong to say that it requires an interpretation along the lines of selection for mission or service. An interpretation of the חותם imagery as indicating kingship is problematic, and should be abandoned in order to adopt an interpretation of the imagery as indicating preciousness and protection.

These considerations taken together make a non-royal interpretation of the oracle a serious option. Pomykala reaches a somewhat similar conclusion:[64]

> All in all, Haggai's language in v. 23, although sometimes associated with David, is, on the one hand, not typically applied to succeeding davidic kings, and on the other, used quite widely to designate all kinds of divine agents. If one considers how Haggai's language would have differed if Zerubbabel had clearly not been of davidic stock, it is evident that his present terminology would be equally suitable. In other words, there is nothing exclusively davidic about it.

I now want to address the question whether it is not somewhat unduly minimalistic to propose a non-royal interpretation when there are several words and phrases present which in other contexts clearly have royal overtones? Would not the accumulation of such language suggest that the issue of kingship is at stake in this particular oracle in Hag. 2.20-23? One could sharpen the question by focusing on the mentioning in the preceding verses of the overthrow of present political (and

---

64. Pomykala, *Dynasty Tradition*, p. 49. R. Mason, 'The Messiah in the Postexilic Old Testament Literature', in Day (ed.), *King*, pp. 338-64 (341-42), admits that 'All the terms used could have royal connotations but, equally, none necessarily need be so interpreted' and continues, 'while Hag. 2.23 may imply special royal status now being, or shortly to be reinstated, it may carry a more general connotation of God's remembrance of and affection for Zerubbabel and the people he represents'. He calls the conclusion of Meyers and Meyers (*Haggai, Zechariah*, p. 70), that 'Haggai uses no language that refers directly to Zerubbabel as king', a 'perfectly possible and legitimate reading of Hag. 2, 23'. However, what in my view is a failure to deal properly with the lexical problems of the usual interpretation of the חותם imagery eventually leads him to conclude that 'the balance of probability (it is no more) seems to me to tilt towards a belief that Haggai thought, that when Yahweh begins his universal reign in the completed temple, Zerubbabel will succeed to royal status'.

military) structures: does that not suggest a new political structure with
a new role for Zerubbabel?

One of the scholars to argue along these lines is Japhet. She states
that 'Haggai does not explain, however, for what Zerubbabel was
chosen'. But the context makes things clear: 'From what is described in
the prophecy—the overthrow of the kingdoms of the nations as the first
stage in the choosing of Zerubbabel—we may conclude that Haggai
sees Zerubbabel as a king, whose kingdom is made possible by a
change in the political structure'.[65]

That there is a dramatic change of the political map is beyond dispute:

> I am about to shake the heavens and the earth, and to overthrow the
> throne of kingdoms; I am about to destroy the strength of the kingdoms
> of the nations, and overthrow the chariots and their riders; and the horses
> and their riders shall go down, every one by the sword of his fellow
> (Hag. 2.21-22).

Language of theophany and holy war is employed to describe a divine
intervention which will result in a mutual destruction of political and
military forces. Zerubbabel, the governor of Yehud, is one constituent
on the present political map. What will happen to him? That is the
question which the oracle in v. 23 is meant to answer.

But does a change of the political map always imply a change of
position for a particular constituent of that map, in this case the recipient of the favour of God? There are other passages in the Old Testament where one finds a similar notion of the overthrow of nations as an
exercise of God's sovereignty, for example, Ps. 2.8-9 and Isa. 45.1:

> Ask of me, and I will make the nations your heritage, and the ends of the
> earth your possession. You shall break them with a rod of iron, and dash
> them in pieces like a potter's vessel (Ps. 2.8-9; cf. Ps. 110.1, 5).

> Thus says the LORD to his anointed, to Cyrus, whose right hand I have
> grasped, to subdue nations before him and ungird the loins of kings, to
> open doors before him that gates may not be closed... (Isa. 45.1).

Here the beneficiary of such an intervention is called the anointed of
YHWH (see Ps. 2.2 and Isa. 45.1). In both passages one finds a person

---

65. Japhet, 'Zerubbabel', pp. 77-78. Similarly, Roberts on Hag. 2.23 ('Messianic Expectations', p. 49), 'Given the context of God's promise to overturn the
kingdoms, such an oracle clearly implied the elevation of Zerubbabel to the Davidic
throne of his ancestors'.

already in a position of autonomous rule given by God. But note that here this authority is not a result of God's intervention comprising the submission of nations. It is just the other way around: the person spoken to has first received a position of authority and subsequently is promised the submission of (the) nations. No mention is made of a change in position or office resulting from this submission.

The main differences between these passages and Hag. 2.20-23 are the following: in the Haggai passage one does not find a statement about Zerubbabel being YHWH's anointed, or about his autonomous rule (given by God), present or future, and there is no explicit promise that God will make the nations submit to his chosen one. One reads only about a mutual destruction of political and military forces masterminded by God. On the basis of these observations, I think it is safe to conclude that there is no reason to assume that a divine intervention which does not mention autonomous rule or submission of the nations to Zerubbabel (Hag. 2) would necessarily imply a change of his position.

Only when the context gives reason to develop the idea of a change of position should one be prepared to take that line. And so we are back at v. 23. I have argued above that words like לקח, עבד and בחר, do not require an interpretation supporting such an approach, and that an interpretation of the חותם imagery as signifying kingship or being God's representative, and thus a change in position, is difficult to maintain.

In my view the use of the חותם imagery interpreted along the lines which I have argued above is an important factor which makes the balance of probability tilt towards an understanding in which kingship is not the key issue. There may be another factor: the absence of any explicitly royal language in the oracle. One does not find the name of David mentioned, for example as a forefather of Zerubbabel (or elsewhere in Haggai [or in Zechariah]!), nor does one find a phrase like '(the) throne (of David)', nor does one find a word from the root מלך. Such words or phrases would unambiguously have pointed towards kingship as a crucial issue in the oracle.

For some, this absence of royal language is only an indication of the caution of the prophet not to cause concern for the Persian authorities.[66]

---

66. According to Van der Woude, *Haggai–Maleachi*, p. 74, royal language is avoided. According to Coggins, *Haggai, Zechariah, Malachi*, p. 36, there is 'no direct suggestion that Zerubbabel will have "royal" or "messianic" status of a precisely defined kind: the people were under the rule of a Persian king'.

This line of interpretation is difficult to prove: we have to assume that Haggai entertained such royal aspirations concerning Zerubbabel, but there is no possible evidence for this assumption apart from the passage under discussion.[67] It seems better not to beg the question but to conclude on the basis of both the contents of the passage as a whole and the absence of royal language that one should be cautious in reading royal expectations into the passage.

## 6. *Conclusion*

It is now the moment to draw all the lines together. In the final oracle addressed to Zerubbabel, the prophet Haggai announces a divine intervention which will change the political (and military) map in a definitive way. One of the constituents on that map is singled out for special treatment: Zerubbabel, the governor of Yehud. Though some of the language of the oracle may in other contexts carry royal overtones this seems not to be the case in this context, and the חותם imagery is more naturally understood to evoke the concept of value and protection rather than the idea of kingship or representation.

The message of the oracle concerning Zerubbabel in Hag. 2.23 as a whole would then be as follows. YHWH reminds Zerubbabel that he has chosen him to be his servant, and this choice is the ground for YHWH's intervention to protect Zerubbabel in an impending cosmic upheaval with political ramifications. Zerubbabel does not need to fear or worry whether he will survive. As YHWH's chosen servant, YHWH will single him out and protect him, so that he will not suffer the same fate as other political powers of the day. When I apply the categories of 'royal' and 'royalist' as I defined them in Chapter 4 (*royal*: 'pertaining to a king, his dignity or office'; and *royalist*: 'supporting a king or a king's rights'), then the Zerubbabel oracle in Hag. 2.20-23 is neither royal nor royalist.

The idea of 'care' or 'protection', but expressed in less artistic and more straightforward language, is also found in an oracle of the prophet Joel which is in some ways similar to Hag. 2.23 and its context (note the theme of cosmic upheaval [רעשׁ G],[68] also found in Hag. 2.21). In Joel the promise is addressed to the people of Israel as a whole:

67. Compare Lagrange, 'Prophéties', p. 69, 'Il nous est surtout impossible de savoir quelle conception Aggée se faisait du Messie'.
68. The hiphil of the same root is used in Hag. 2.21.

And the LORD roars from Zion, and utters his voice from Jerusalem, and
the heavens and the earth shake. But the LORD is a refuge to his people,
a stronghold to the people of Israel (Joel 3.16).

Finally, did Haggai expect Zerubbabel to become king? The prophet
would have had many ways in which to give us a hint that he wanted to
be understood as announcing that Zerubbabel would soon be king. The
absence of any reference to the Davidic line from which Zerubbabel
came, and the failure to use words like מלך or משל, these are all factors
which point in a different direction. If one takes the imagery and the
terminology of שים כחותם seriously, the answer to the question
whether Haggai expected Zerubbabel to be king must surely be
something like this: most likely not.[69]

69. In his recent article, Sérandour reaches a similar conclusion, though he
considers Hag. 2.20-23 as a secondary addition ('Construction', pp. 17-18), 'Le
passage ne saurait donc être entendu comme l'écho d'une tentative de restauration
monarchique, malgré l'opinion unanime des commentateurs modernes'. If Hag.
2.20-23 does not announce kingship for Zerubbabel, and neither does Zechariah,
then there remains no evidence for the view of Bianchi and others (see Chapter 1,
section entitled 'Survey') that Zerubbabel was actually the last king of Judah,
sponsored by the Persian government.

### Excursus: Real and Hypothetical Conditions

In a conditional clause the condition can be either real, expressing an actual state of affairs, or hypothetical, expressing a hypothetical state of affairs. A real condition is usually introduced by אִם, or כִּי, an hypothetical condition is usually introduced by לוּ, occasionally אִם.[70] In Jer. 22.24 the protasis is introduced by אִם, and the verbal form in the protasis is Imperfect; the apodosis is introduced by כִּי, and the verbal form in the apodosis is Imperfect. From this it is clear that the condition clause in Jer. 22.24 can certainly be a real condition.

But what about an hypothetical condition: is that a possibility as well, or is there a way to simply eliminate that option? The only way to establish this as a viable option is to see whether Jeremiah ever introduces a hypothetical condition protasis with אִם. If there are no such cases, then the likelihood that there is one in Jer. 22.24 would be small. On the other hand, if there are such cases, then the possibility that the condition in Jer. 22.24 is hypothetical cannot be excluded.

The following passages from Jeremiah are a selection of cases where an hypothetical or hypothetical condition is introduced with אִם (I have selected examples in which the verbal form of the protasis is Imperfect, as in Jer. 22.24):

> Though [כִּי אִם] you wash [Imperfect] yourself with lye and use much soap, the stain of your guilt is still before me (Jer. 2.22).

> Though [אִם] Moses and Samuel stood before me, yet [asyndetic] my heart would not turn [אֵין; no verbal form] toward this people (Jer. 15.1).

> 'If [אִם] this fixed order departs from before me, says the LORD, then [גַּם] shall the descendants of Israel cease [Imperfect] from being a nation before me for ever'. Thus says the LORD: 'If [אִם] the heavens above can be measured, and the foundations of the earth below can be explored, then [גַּם] I will cast off [Imperfect] all the descendants of Israel for all that they have done, says the LORD' (Jer. 31.36-37).

These examples show that from the perspective of syntax, it is possible to interpret the condition clause in Jer. 22.24 as an hypothetical condition. It seems difficult to settle beyond any dispute which of the two is the more plausible interpretation: a real or an hypothetical condition.

---

70. Waltke and O'Connor, *Syntax*, §38.2; Joüon and Muraoka, *Grammar*, §§167-68.

The presence of כִּי preceding אִם does not provide any help in making a choice between the two options. In Jeremiah כִּי אִם is used both to introduce real conditions (7.5; 22.4; 26.15) and hypothetical conditions (2.22; 37.10), so the issue cannot be settled on the basis of the presence of כִּי אִם.

In the discussion in this Excursus so far I have assumed (with most scholars) that there is a conditional clause in Jer. 22.24. Recently, Holladay and McKane have challenged this assumption and proposed an alternative interpretation.[71] McKane translates, 'By my life, says Yahweh, Coniah, son of Jehoiakim, king of Judah, shall no longer be a signet ring on my right hand. I will pull you off from my finger (O Coniah)!'[72] Holladay translates, 'As I live, oracle of Yahweh, I swear Coniah son of Jehoiakim, king of Judah, shall never be the signet-ring on my right hand. Yes, from there I would pull you off!' [73]

According to these scholars the כִּי אִם clause introduces the oath statement, which should be interpreted as a negative statement. The next כִּי clause is not part of the oath as such. Now the usual way to express a negative statement in an oath is with אִם, while a positive statement is introduced by כִּי.[74] כִּי אִם introduces a positive statement[75] after נִשְׁבַּע in Jer. 51.14:

> The LORD of hosts has sworn by himself: Surely I will fill you with men, as many as locusts, and they shall raise the shout of victory over you. (Jer. 51.14).

After 'as X lives', כִּי אִם introduces a positive oath statement in:

> And David said, 'As the LORD lives, [כִּי אִם] the LORD will smite him; or his day shall come to die; or he shall go down into battle and perish' (1 Sam. 26.10).

> Gehazi, the servant of Elisha the man of God, said, 'See, my master has spared this Naaman the Syrian, in not accepting from his hand what he brought. As the LORD lives, I will run after him, and get something from him' (2 Kgs 5.20).

---

71. Independent of each other, it seems: both commentaries were published in 1986.
72. McKane, *Jeremiah*, p. 540.
73. Holladay, *Jeremiah*, p. 604.
74. Joüon and Muraoka, *Grammar*, §166b-d.
75. Joüon and Muraoka, *Grammar*, §164c, 165c.e.

However, McKane is able to list two passages where the כִּי אִם construction is found for a negative statement (the second one is also mentioned by Holladay):

> For as surely as the LORD the God of Israel lives, who has restrained me from hurting you, unless you had made haste and come to meet me, truly [כִּי אִם] by morning there had not been left to Nabal so much as one male (1 Sam. 25.34).

> [B]ut David swore, saying, 'God do so to me and more also, if [כִּי אִם] I taste bread or anything else till the sun goes down!' (2 Sam. 3.35).

Therefore, the proposal as such is possible, and the possibility of the presence of 'a rare variant' (McKane) of a usual grammatical construction cannot be excluded *a priori*.[76] However, the reason given for the rejection of the usual interpretation is flawed. McKane does not indicate why the usual interpretation should be abandoned. He simply states:[77]

> A new departure is necessary and כִּי אִם should be construed as a rare variant of the אִם of the oath, coming as it does after חַי אָנִי נְאֻם יְהֹוָה.

Holladay gives two reasons for his alternative solution. The first one is alright: Jer. 26.15 is not a parallel to 22.24. There is a כִּי preceding אִם in 26.15, but the כִּי should be linked with יָדֹעַ ('know that').

> Only know for certain that if [כִּי אִם] you put me to death, [כִּי] you will bring innocent blood upon yourselves and upon this city and its inhabitants, for in truth the LORD sent me to you to speak all these words in your ears (Jer. 26.15).

The second reason is more problematic. Holladay states,

> There are no parallels for 'as I live' followed by protasis and apodosis in the twenty-one other instances of 'as I live' in the OT...[78]

This statement may be true as it stands.[79] However, the suggestion

---

76. Of course, the difference between the two passages from 1–2 Sam. and Jer. 22.24 is that after the כִּי אִם clause in these two passages there follows no clause introduced by כִּי, which makes the interpretation of the verse as containing a conditional clause with protasis and apodosis possible. In the two Samuel examples there is no such alternative interpretation available, and therefore on the basis of the context we have to adopt a negative statement interpretation.

77. McKane, *Jeremiah*, p. 541.

78. Holladay, *Jeremiah*, p. 605.

79. One may question Holladay's easy dismissal of three cases where the 'as I live' phrase is sandwiched between protasis and apodosis, in Ezek. 14.16, 18, 20.

which this statement creates is potentially misleading, because it limits the search to 'as I live' clauses, without any reason. If one broadens the search to include any 'as X lives' oath formulas, one indeed finds examples of חי followed by protasis and apodosis.

> For as the LORD lives who saves Israel, though [כי אם] it be [no verbal form] in Jonathan my son, [כי] he shall surely die [Imperfect + infinitive absolute] (1 Sam. 14.39).

> But Ittai answered the king, 'As the LORD lives, and as my lord the king lives, wherever [כי אם] my lord the king shall be [relative clause במקום אשר יהיה], whether for death or for life, [כי] there also will your servant be [Imperfect]' (2 Sam. 15.21).

What makes these examples the more interesting is that they share the sequence ...כי...כי אם...X חי with Jer. 22.24. The presence of the first כי in Jer. 22.24 could be explained on the basis of a remark in Joüon and Muraoka, *Grammar*, in a paragraph on oath and curse clauses: 'אם and especially כי are sometimes repeated' (§165i). An example of this is the sequence כי...כי יען after an oath formula:

> By myself I have sworn, says the LORD, because [כי יען] you have done this, and have not withheld your son, your only son, [כי] I will indeed bless you, and I will multiply... (Gen. 22.16-17).

Therefore, the usual interpretation, an oath containing a protasis and apodosis (an interpretation found in the early versions) is not unparalleled, and since it makes good sense there is no need to abandon it.

---

E.g. v. 18: 'though these three men were in it, as I live, says the Lord GOD, they would deliver neither sons nor daughters, but they alone would be delivered'. The protasis is introduced by ו in v. 18 and in v. 20, there is nothing to introduce the protasis in v. 16; the apodosis has asyndetic לא in v. 18, אם in vv. 16, 20. Holladay, *Jeremiah*, p. 605, states, 'Ezek. 14.18 is perhaps the closest, but the clauses are expressed differently there'. It may be true that 'the clauses are expressed differently', but that is not the point. What we are looking for is the combination 'as I live' + conditional clause with protasis–apodosis (what is the reason for limiting the search to 'as I live' *followed* by conditional clause with protasis–apodosis?), and as such the three passages in Ezek. 14 count.

Chapter 8

CONCLUSIONS

## 1. *Conclusions*

### a. *Zemah a Messianic Figure (Zechariah)*

This book set out to resolve the issue of the identity of the coming ruler called צמח (Zemah) in the צמח oracles in Zechariah 3 and 6. A semantic analysis of the noun צמח appeared to be crucial. In contrast to the nearly universal interpretation of צמח as 'sprout' or 'branch', the best supported meaning of the word is 'vegetation, greenery, growth'. The difference in meaning between צמח and נצר/חטר in Isa. 11.1 suggests that this passage does not provide a direct background for the understanding of the צמח oracles in Zechariah 3 and 6. An immediate background for the interpretation of these passages is found in Jer. 23.5, where the צמח imagery conveys the notion of discontinuity of historical means which then calls for a divine intervention.

The coming ruler called Zemah (Zech. 3.8 and 6.12) has usually been identified with Zerubbabel, the governor of Yehud (the ZZ view). Phrases like the one stating that Zemah 'shall sit and rule upon his throne' (Zech. 6.13) would then indicate that a restoration of the monarchy was expected to be imminent, with Zerubbabel as the new king. A number of factors make this view implausible. These include (a) the crowning of Joshua rather than Zerubbabel, (b) the use of the name Zemah rather than Zerubbabel, (c) the discontinuity conveyed by the name Zemah, and (d) the consistent future reference of the coming of Zemah. None of these elements can be done justice within the framework of an interpretation which identifies Zemah with Zerubbabel.

The alternative interpretation which finds in Zemah a future figure (FF view) has much more to be said for it. It makes good sense of the factors which the ZZ view had difficulties to explain. The temple which Zemah will rebuild must then be interpreted as either a future temple, or an expansion of the present one. If Zemah is a future figure who will build the temple and rule, then the צמח oracles can be called messianic in the sense described in Chapter 1: expectations focusing on a future royal figure sent by God who will bring salvation to God's people and the world and establish a kingdom characterized by features like peace and justice.

Proposals have been made to consider part of the oracles in the vision reports in Zechariah 1–6 (including the two צמח oracles) as secondary, and date them to a period before the visions. In this way some of the obstacles to the identification of Zemah with Zerubbabel could possibly be removed. On closer examination these proposals appear to be based on dubious grounds, and the recent trend to abandon such proposals is commendable.

### b. *Zerubbabel a Seal (Haggai)*

Whereas the ZZ view and the FF view disagree over the identification of Zemah in Zechariah 3 and 6, they see eye to eye concerning the interpretation of the final oracle of Haggai, where YHWH says to Zerubbabel (Hag. 2.23, my translation): 'I will take you, O Zerubbabel my servant, the son of Shealtiel, says the LORD, and make you like a seal; for I have chosen you, says the LORD of hosts'. Both views understand this oracle to indicate an imminent restoration of the monarchy. For the ZZ view, this interpretation implies that the views of Zechariah and Haggai on this issue were more or less similar. The FF view finds a difference between expectations in Zechariah which delegated the issue of kingship to the future, and expectations in Haggai which raised hopes for an immediate restoration of the monarchy.

Concerning the interpretation of the final oracle of Haggai 2, I take issue with the interpretation shared by both the ZZ and the FF view. The royal connotations of words like לקח, עבד and בחר have been seriously overstated. As is also the case in Jer. 22.24-26, both the terminology (חותם) and the details of the picture in Hag. 2.23 are wrong for a kingship interpretation of the seal imagery to work. One has to conclude that either both prophets confused the imagery, or that the imagery was not meant to convey the idea of kingship.

Seal imagery (in which 'seal' is to be distinguished from 'signet' [טבעת]) is used in the Old Testament and in the ancient Near East in various contexts to evoke the idea of special care or protection for a person who has a high personal value for someone. The usage of this imagery in a variety of contexts suggests that kingship is not essential to the image. YHWH's promise to Zerubbabel should therefore be inter-

preted as comprising special protection for God's chosen servant at a
time of substantial changes in the political landscape. This interpretation leaves no room to call Haggai's final oracle royal or messianic. In
the absence of other oracles dealing with the theme of kingship in Haggai, one has to conclude that we cannot tell what Haggai's expectations
concerning the restoration monarchy or messianism were.

### c. *Emergence of the Priesthood as a Political Power*

Different priests figure within the צמח oracles and in the passages in
which these oracles are embedded. Priests are the addressees of both
oracles, and they function as 'men of portent': the presence of the
priesthood is made a guarantee for the fulfilment of the promise of the
coming ruler. The portent character of the priesthood is symbolised by
setting a crown on the head of the high priest (Zech. 6.11).

The high priest is given (3.7) a certain responsibility over the temple
area (either jurisdiction, or government and administration). This is a
prerogative that formerly belonged to the king. Loyal performance of
the high priest will be rewarded by a new relationship with persons who
function as a bridge between heavenly council and earth, possibly
prophets. The second צמח oracle mentions a priest by the throne of the
coming ruler. His position is rather vague, but his role is possibly that
of a counsellor to the ruler. There is no evidence here for a joint rule of
the coming ruler and the priest.

In the introductory Chapter I have stated that the view which dates an
emergence of the priesthood as a political power (hierocracy) to the
Persian period runs into problems for historical reasons: the written evidence in the books Ezra and Nehemiah supported by archaeological evidence in bullae and seals make it possible to reconstruct the presence of
governors in Yehud from the beginning of the period of Persian rule
through to the end.

This historical case can now be complemented by an exegetical
argument. In my discussion of passages like Zech. 3.7, 4.14 and 6.13, I
have argued that the passages which were said to reflect a rise of the
political powers of the high priest in fact provide little support for such
a view. On the basis of Zech. 3.7 it can reasonably be argued that the
high priest takes over prerogatives which once belonged to the king, but
his new authority is at the same time limited: it only comprehends jurisdiction or government and administration of the temple and the temple
area. Zech. 6.13 envisages a priest beside the throne of the royal figure,

but there is no evidence for a joint rule: the best that can be said about the role of the priest is that he serves as a counsellor to the royal figure. This scenario is far removed from the idea of political power shared by a royal figure and a priest.

#### d. *Diarchy*

Perhaps the most surprising outcome of my study (at least to me) is that the evidence adduced to support the almost universally held idea of a diarchy has been found seriously wanting. Not only is there no evidence for this in Zech. 6.13, but the other passage which has been interpreted in such a way as to support the notion of diarchy (4.14) has been shown most likely to refer not to human leaders on earth, but to heavenly beings in the council of YHWH.

#### e. *The Perspective of History*

If my interpretation of these oracles in both Haggai and Zechariah is correct, then it becomes more difficult to read these prophets as announcing the restoration of the monarchy in the immediate future, let alone as promoting something like a revolt against the Persian empire. This conclusion would tie in well with the warning which Briant in his study of the Persian empire sounds concerning the situation in Yehud in the time of Haggai and Zechariah:

> People have often supposed that troubles would have emerged in the same way in Judah, in connection with the Babylonian revolts. However, the prophetic texts appealed to in support of this should be taken with caution: one could question whether the Judeans, 15 years after a difficult and painful return, would have disposed over the strength and the energy needed for seriously considering the restoration of the ancient monarchy for the benefit of Zerubbabel.[1]

---

1. Briant, *Empire Perse*, p. 128, 'On a parfois supposé que des troubles se sont également produits en Juda, en liaison avec les révoltes babyloniennes. Mais les textes prophétiques amenés à l'appui doivent être pris avec précaution: on peut douter que les Judéens, une quinzaine d'après un retour difficile et heurté, aient disposé des forces et de l'énergie nécessaires pour envisager sérieusement la restauration de l'ancienne royauté au profit de Zerubabel'. The background to this remark is the revolt against Darius in Egypt in the year 521 BCE. Others put it even more strongly; Siebeneck comments that the miserable conditions of Jerusalem make 'it unbelievable that Ag and Za proclaim Zorobabel as the Messias and ascribe to him future universal domination' ('Messianism', pp. 312-28 [327] [abbreviations original]; cf. M.-J. Lagrange, 'Prophéties', pp. 67-83 [72]).

# BIBLIOGRAPHY

Achtemeier, Elizabeth, *Nahum–Malachi* (Interpretation; Atlanta: John Knox Press, 1986).

Ackroyd, Peter R., 'Two Old Testament Historical Problems of the Early Persian Period', *JNES* 17 (1958), pp. 13-27.

—'Zechariah', in Matthew Black and H.H. Rowley (eds.), *Peake's Commentary on the Bible* (London: Nelson, 1962), pp. 646-55.

—*Exile and Restoration: A Study of Hebrew Thought of the Sixth Century BC* (London: SCM Press, 1968).

—*Israel under Babylon and Persia* (Oxford: Oxford University Press, 1970).

—'Archaeology, Politics and Religion in the Persian Period', *IR* 39 (1982), pp. 5-24 (reprinted in Ackroyd, *Chronicler*, pp. 86-111).

—'Historical Problems of the Early Achaemenian Period', *Orient* 20 (1984), pp. 1-15 (reprinted in Ackroyd, *Chronicler*, pp. 141-55).

—*Studies in the Religious Tradition of the Old Testament* (London: SCM Press, 1987).

—*The Chronicler in his Age* (JSOTSup, 101; Sheffield: JSOT Press, 1991).

Aharoni, Yohanan, *Arad Inscriptions* (Judean Desert Series; Jerusalem: The Bialik Institute and The Israel Exploration Society, 1975) (Hebrew); ET *Arad Inscriptions* (Jerusalem: The Israel Exploration Society, 1981).

Ahlström, Gösta W., *The History of Ancient Palestine from the Palaeolithic Period to Alexander's Conquest* (JSOTSup, 146; Sheffield: JSOT Press, 1993).

Aitken, Kenneth T., *The Aqhat Narrative: A Study in the Narrative Structure and Composition of an Ugaritic Tale* (JSSM, 13; Manchester: University of Manchester Press, 1990).

Albertz, Rainer, *Religionsgeschichte Israels in alttestamentlichter Zeit. II. Vom Exil bis zu den Makkabäern* (Grundrisse zum Alten Testament; ATD Ergänzungsreihe; 8.2; Göttingen: Vandenhoeck & Ruprecht, 1992); ET *A History of Israelite Religion in the Old Testament Period. II. From the Exile to the Maccabees* (London: SCM Press, 1994).

Allen, Leslie C., *Ezekiel 20–48* (WBC, 29; Waco, TX: Word Books, 1990).

—*Psalms 101–150* (WBC, 21; Waco, TX: Word Books, 1990).

Alt, Albrecht, 'Die Rolle Samarias bei der Entstehung des Judentums', in Alt, Baumgärtel et al., *Festschrift Procksch*, pp. 5-28 (reprinted in Albrecht Alt, *Kleine Schriften zur Geschichte des Volkes Israel*, II (Munich: Beck, 1953), pp. 316-37.

Alt, Albrecht, Friedrich Baumgärtel et al. (eds.), *Festschrift Otto Procksch zum 60. Geburtstag* (Leipzig: Deichert and Hinrichs, 1934).

Amsler, Samuel, 'צמח', *THAT*, II, cols. 563-66.

—'La parole visionnaire des prophètes', *VT* 31 (1981), pp. 359-63.

—*Aggée; Zacharie 1–8* (CAT, 11c; Geneva: Labor et Fides, 2nd edn, 1988).

—'Des visions de Zacharie à l'apocalypse d'Esaïe 24–27', in Vermeylen (ed.), *Isaiah*, pp. 263-73.

André, Tony, *Le prophète Aggée: Introduction critique et commentaire* (Paris: Fischbacher, 1895).

Arnold, B.T., 'The Use of Aramaic in the Hebrew Bible: Another Look at Bilingualism in Ezra and Daniel', *JNSL* 22.2 (1996), pp. 1-16.

Avigad, Nahman, *Bullae and Seals From a Post-exilic Judean Archive* (Qedem, 4; Jerusalem: Hebrew University, 1976).

—'The Contribution of Hebrew Seals to an Understanding of Israelite Religion and Society', in Miller, Hanson and McBride (eds.), *Ancient Israelite Religion*, pp. 195-208.

—'Hebrew Seals and Sealings and their Significance for Biblical Research', in Emerton (ed.), *Congress Volume Jerusalem 1986*, pp. 7-16.

—*Corpus of West Semitic Stamp Seals* (revised and completed by Benjamin Sass; Jerusalem: Hebrew University, 1997).

Balcer, Jack Martin, *Herodotus and Bisitun: Problems in Ancient Persian Historiography* (Historia Einzelschriften, 49; Stuttgart: Steiner, 1987).

Baldwin, Joyce G., '*Ṣemaḥ* as a Technical Term in the Prophets', *VT* 14 (1964), pp. 93-97.

—*Haggai, Zechariah, Malachi* (TOTC; London: Tyndale Press, 1972).

Bandstra, Barry L., 'Word Order and Emphasis in Biblical Hebrew Narrative: Syntactic Observations on Genesis 22 from a Discourse Perspective', in Bodine (ed.), *Linguistics*, pp. 109-23.

Barker, Margaret, 'The Two Figures in Zechariah', *HeyJ* 18 (1977), pp. 38-46.

Barnes, W. Emery, *Haggai, Zechariah and Malachi: With Notes and Introduction* (CBSC; Cambridge: Cambridge University Press, 1934).

Barr, James, *The Semantics of Biblical Language* (Oxford: Oxford University Press, 1961).

—*Comparative Philology and the Text of the Old Testament* (Oxford: Clarendon Press, 1968).

Barton, John, 'The Messiah in Old Testament Theology', in Day (ed.), *King*, pp. 365-79.

Barth, Hermann, *Die Jesaja-Worte in der Josiazeit: Israel und Assur als Thema einer produktiven Neuinterpretation der Jesajaüberlieferung* (WMANT, 48; Neukirchen–Vluyn: Neukirchener Verlag, 1977).

Bauer, Lutz, *Zeit des zweiten Tempels—Zeit der Gerechtigkeit: Zur sozio-ökonomischen Konzeption im Haggai–Sacharja–Maleachi-Korpus* (BEATAJ, 31; Frankfurt: Peter Lang, 1991).

Becker, Joachim, *Messiaserwartung im Alten Testament* (SBS, 83; Stuttgart: Verlag Katholisches Bibelwerk, 1977); ET *Messianic Expectation in the Old Testament* (Edinburgh: T. & T. Clark, 1980).

Bedford, Peter Ross, 'Discerning the Time: Haggai, Zechariah and the "Delay" in the Rebuilding of the Temple', in Holloway and Handy (eds.), *Pitcher*, pp. 71-94.

Bentzen, A., 'Quelques remarques sur le mouvement messianique parmi les juifs aux environs de l'an 520 avant Jésus-Christ', *RHPR* 10 (1930), pp. 493-503.

Bergen, Robert D. (ed.), *Biblical Hebrew and Discourse Linguistics* (Winona Lake, IN: Eisenbrauns, 1994).

Berger, P., 'Mémoire sur une inscription phénicienne de Narnaka dans l'île de Chypre', *RA* 3 (1895), pp. 69-88.

—'[Communication in] "Livres Offerts"', in *idem*, *Comptes rendus des séances de l'Académie des inscriptions et belles lettres* (1904), pp. 721-22.

Berquist, Jon L., _Judaism in Persia's Shadow: A Social and Historical Approach_ (Minneapolis: Fortress Press, 1995).

Beuken, Willem André Maria, _Haggai–Sacharja 1–8: Studien zur Überlieferungsgeschichte der frühnachexilischen Prophetie_ (SSN, 10; Assen: Van Gorcum, 1967).

Beyer, Bryan E., 'Zerubbabel', _ABD_, VI, pp. 1084-86.

Beyer, Klaus, _Die aramäischen Texte vom Toten Meer samt den Inschriften aus Palästina, dem Testament Levis aus der Kairoer Genisa, der Fastenrolle und den alten talmudischen Zitaten: Ergänzungsband_ (Göttingen: Vandenhoeck & Ruprecht, 1994).

Beyse, Karl-Martin, _Serubbabel und die Königserwartungen der Propheten Haggai und Sacharja: Eine historische und traditionsgeschichtliche Untersuchung_ (AT 1.48; Stuttgart: Calwer Verlag, 1972).

—'שׁתל', in _ThWAT_, VIII, cols. 535-37.

Bianchi, Francesco, 'Le rôle de Zorobabel et de la dynastie davidique en Judée du VIe siècle au IIe siècle av. J.-C.', _Trans_ 7 (1994), pp. 153-65.

Bič, Miloč, _Das Buch Sacharja_ (Berlin: Evangelische Verlagsanstalt, 1962).

Bickerman, Elias J., 'En marge de l'écriture. I. Le comput des annés de règne des Achéménides; II. La seconde année de Darius', _RB_ 88 (1981), pp. 19-28 (reprinted in Elias J. Bickerman, _Studies in Jewish and Christian History_, III [AGJU, 9; Leiden: E.J. Brill, 1986], pp. 327-36).

Bodine, Walter R. (ed.), _Linguistics and Biblical Hebrew_ (Winona Lake, IN: Eisenbrauns, 1992).

Boehmer, Julius, 'Was bedeutet der goldene Leuchter Sach. 4, 2?', _BZ_ 24 (1938–39), pp. 360-64.

Bordreuil, P., 'Sceaux inscrits des pays du Levant', _DBSup_, LXVI, cols. 86-212.

Borger, Riekele, _Die Inschriften Asarhaddons Königs von Assyrien_ (AfO, 9; Graz: E. Weidner, 1956).

—'Die Chronologie des Darius-Denkmals am Behistun-Felsen', _NAWG_. I. _Philologisch-historische Klasse_, 3 (1982), pp. 105-31.

Borger, Rykle, and Walther Hinz, 'Die Behistun-Inschrift Darius' der Grossen', _TUAT_, I/4 (1984), pp. 419-50.

Borowski, Oded, _Agriculture in Iron Age Israel_ (Winona Lake, IN: Eisenbrauns, 1987).

Botterweck, G.J., and V. Hamp, 'דין', _ThWAT_, II, cols. 200-207.

Brenner, Athalya, _Colour Terms in the Old Testament_ (JSOTSup, 21; Sheffield: JSOT Press 1982).

Briant, Pierre, _Histoire de l'empire perse: De Cyrus à Alexandre_ (Paris: Fayard, 1996).

Briend, J., 'L'édit de Cyrus et sa valeur historique', _Trans_ 11 (1996), pp. 33-44.

Brownlee, William Hugh, _Ezekiel 1–19_ (WBC, 28; Waco, TX: Word Books, 1986).

Butterworth, M., _Structure and the Book of Zechariah_ (JSOTSup, 130; Sheffield: JSOT Press, 1992).

Buzy, Denis, 'Les symboles de Zacharie', _RB_ 15 (1918), pp. 136-91.

Cantineau, J., _Le Nabatéen_. I. _Notions générales: Ecriture grammaire_ (Paris: Librairie Ernest Leroux, 1930).

—_Le Nabatéen_. II. _Choix de textes: Lexique_ (Paris: Librairie Ernest Leroux, 1932).

Caquot, André, 'La littérature ugaritique', _DBSup_, IX, cols. 1361-417.

Carroll, Robert P., _When Prophecy Failed_ (London: SCM Press, 1979).

—'So What Do we _Know_ about the Temple? The Temple in the Prophets', in Eskenazi and Richards (eds.), _Second Temple_, pp. 34-51.

Carter, Charles E., 'The Province of Yehud in the Post-exilic Period', in Eskenazi and Richards (eds.), *Second Temple*, pp. 106-45.

Cazelles, Henri, *Le Messie de la Bible: Christologie de l'Ancien Testament* (Collection 'Jésus et Jésus-Christ', 7; Paris: Desclée de Brouwer, 1978).

Ceresko, Anthony R., *Job 29–31 in the Light of Northwest Semitic* (BibOr, 36; Rome: Biblical Institute Press, 1980).

Charlesworth, James H. (ed.), *The Messiah: Developments in Earliest Judaism and Christianity* (Minneapolis: Fortress Press, 1992).

Chary, T., *Aggée, Zacharie, Malachie* (SB; Paris: J. Gabalda, 1969).

Childs, Brevard S., *Old Testament Theology in a Canonical Context* (London: SCM Press 1985).

Claassen, W. (ed.), *Text and Context: Old Testament and Semitic Studies for F.C. Fensham* (JSOTSup, 48; Sheffield: JSOT Press, 1988).

Clark, David J., 'Vision and Oracle in Zechariah 1–6', in Bergen (ed.), *Biblical Hebrew*, pp. 529-60.

Clements, Ronald Ernest, *God and Temple* (Oxford: Basil Blackwell, 1965).

—*Isaiah 1–39* (NCB; Grand Rapids: Eerdmans, 1980).

—*Jeremiah* (Interpretation; Atlanta: John Knox Press 1988).

Clermont-Ganneau, C., 'La nouvelle inscription phénicienne du temple d'Echmoun à Sidon', *RAO* 6 (1905), pp. 162-67.

Clines, David J.A., 'X, X *ben* Y, *ben* Y: Personal names in Hebrew Narrative Style', *VT* 22 (1972), pp. 266-87.

—'Haggai's Temple, Constructed, Deconstructed and Reconstructed', in Eskenazi and Richards (eds.), *Second Temple*, pp. 60-87.

Coggins, Richard, *Haggai, Zechariah, Malachi* (OTG; Sheffield: JSOT Press, 1987).

Coggins, Richard, Anthony Phillips and Michael Knibb (eds.), *Israel's Prophetic Tradition: Essays in Honour of Peter S. Ackroyd* (Cambridge: Cambridge University Press, 1982).

Coogan, Michael D., J. Cheryl Exum and Lawrence E. Stager (eds.), *Scripture and Other Artifacts: Essays on the Bible and Archaeology in Honor of Philip J. King* (Louisville, KY: Westminster/John Knox Press, 1994).

Cook, F.C. (ed.), *The Holy Bible According to the Authorized Version (A.D. 1611): With an Explanatory and Critical Commentary and a Revision of the Translation, by Bishops and Other Clergy of the Anglican Church.* VI. *Ezekiel–Daniel–The Minor Prophets* (London: John Murray, 1876).

Cook, J.M., *The Persian Empire* (London: Dent & Sons, 1983).

Cook, Stephen L., *Prophecy and Apocalypticism: The Postexilic Social Setting* (Minneapolis: Fortress Press, 1995).

Cooke, Gerald, 'The Sons of (the) God(s)', *ZAW* 76 (1964), pp. 22-47.

Cox, Claude E. (ed.), *VII Congress of the International Organization for Septuagint and Cognate Studies Leuven 1989* (SBLSCS, 31; Atlanta: Scholars Press, 1991).

Craig, Kenneth M., Jr, 'Interrogatives in Haggai–Zechariah: A Literary Thread?', in Watts and House (eds.), *Forming Prophetic Literature*, pp. 236-38.

Craigie, Peter C., *Psalms 1–50* (WBC, 19; Waco, TX: Word Books, 1983).

—*The Twelve Prophets*, II (DSB; Edinburgh: St Andrews Press; Philadelphia: Westminster Press, 1985).

Craigie, Peter C., Page H. Kelley and Joel F. Drinkard, Jr, *Jeremiah 1–25* (WBC, 26; Waco, TX: Word Books, 1991).

Cross, Frank Moore, 'The Council of Yahweh in Second Isaiah', *JNES* 12 (1953), pp. 274-77.

—'A Phoenician Inscription from Idalion: Some Old and New Texts Relating to Child Sacrifice', in Coogan, Exum and Stager (eds.), *Artifacts*, pp. 93-107.

Crowley, Terry, *An Introduction to Historical Linguistics* (Oxford: Oxford University Press, 2nd edn, 1992).

Dahood, M., *Psalms*. I. *1–50: Introduction, Translation, and Notes* (AB, 16; Garden City, NY: Doubleday, 1966).

Dalman, Gustav, *Arbeit und Sitte in Palästina*. IV. *Brot, Öl und Wein* (Gütersloh: C. Bertelsmann, 1935).

Dambrine, Liliane, 'L'image de la croissance dans la foi d'Israël: Etude de la racine צמח et de ses dérivés' (Mémoire de l'Institut des Sciences bibliques de l'Université de Lausanne; 1971).

Dandamaev, Muhammad A., and Vladimir G. Lukonin (eds.), *The Culture and Social Institutions of Ancient Iran* (Cambridge: Cambridge University Press, 1989).

Dandamaev, Muhammad A., *A Political History of the Achaemenid Empire* (Leiden: E.J. Brill, 1989).

Dassmann, Ernst, and Günter Stemberger (eds.), *Der Messias* (JBTh, 8; Neukirchen–Vluyn: Neukirchener Verlag, 1993).

Davies, Philip R. (ed.), *Second Temple Studies*. I. *Persian Period* (JSOTSup, 117; Sheffield: JSOT Press, 1991).

Davis, John D., 'The Reclothing and Coronation of Joshua: Zechariah iii and vi', *PTR* 18 (1920), pp. 256-68.

Day, John, *Psalms* (OTG; Sheffield: JSOT Press, 1990).

Day, John (ed.), *King and Messiah in Israel and the Ancient Near East: Proceedings of the Oxford Old Testament Seminar* (JSOTSup, 270; Sheffield: Sheffield Academic Press, 1998).

De Boer, P.A.H., *De voorbede in het Oude Testament* (OTS, 3; Leiden: E.J. Brill, 1943).

—'The Counsellor', in Noth and Thomas (eds.), *Wisdom*, pp. 42-71.

De Jonge, Marinus, 'Messiah', *ABD*, IV, pp. 777-88.

De Moor, Johannes C., *An Anthology of Religious Texts from Ugarit* (Nisaba: Religious Texts Translation Series, 16; Leiden: E.J. Brill, 1987).

De Moor, Johannes C., and Klaas Spronk, *A Cuneiform Anthology of Religious Texts from Ugarit: Autographed Texts and Glossaries* (SSS NS, 6; Leiden: E.J. Brill, 1987).

De Vries, Simon J., *From Old Revelation to New: A Tradition-Historical and Redaction-Critical Study of Temporal Transitions in Prophetic Prediction* (Grand Rapids: Eerdmans, 1995).

Demsky, Aaron, 'The Temple Steward Josiah ben Zephaniah', *IEJ* 31 (1981), pp. 100-102.

Dijkstra, Meindert, and Johannes C. De Moor, 'Problematical Passages in the Legend of Aqhâtu', *UF* 7 (1975), pp. 171-215.

Dillard, Ray, *2 Chronicles* (WBC, 15; Waco, TX: Word Books, 1987).

Dommershausen, Werner, 'Der "Spross" als Messias-Vorstellung bei Jeremia und Sacharja', *TQ* 148 (1968), pp. 321-41.

Drake, W., 'Zechariah', in Cook (ed.), *Holy Bible*.

Driver, S.R., *The Book of the Prophet Jeremiah* (London: Hodder & Stoughton, 1906).

—*The Minor Prophets: Nahum, Habakkuk, Zephaniah, Haggai, Zechariah, Malachi* (CB, Edinburgh: Jack, 1906).

—*The Book of Exodus* (CBSC; Cambridge: Cambridge University Press, 1911).

Duguid, Iain M., *Ezekiel and the Leaders of Israel* (VTSup, 56; Leiden; E.J. Brill, 1994).

Duhm, Bernhard, *Das Buch Jeremia* (KHAT, 11; Tübingen: J.C.B. Mohr, 1901).

—'Anmerkungen zu den Zwölf Propheten. VII. Buch Sacharja I. (Kapitel 1–8)', *ZAW* 31 (1911), pp. 161-75.

Edelkoort, A.H., *De profeet Zacharia: Een uitlegkundige studie* (Baarn: Bosch & Keuning, 1945).

Eichrodt, W., 'Vom Symbol zum Typos: Ein Beitrag zur Sacharja-Exegese', *TZ* 13 (1957), pp. 509-22.

Eissfeldt, Otto, *Einleitung in das Alte Testament unter Einschluss der Apokryphen und Pseudepigraphen sowie der apokryphen- und pseudepigraphenartigen Qumran-Schriften: Entstehungsgeschichte des Alten Testaments* (Neue theologische Grundrisse; Tübingen: J.C.B. Mohr, 3rd edn, 1964); ET *The Old Testament: An Introduction, Including the Apocrypha and Pseudepigrapha, and Also the Works of Similar Type from Qumran. The History of the Formation of the Old Testament* (Oxford: Basil Blackwell, 1965).

Eitan, Israel, 'Some Philological Observations in Daniel', *HUCA* 14 (1939), pp. 13-22.

Elayi, J., *Sidon, cité autonome de l'empire perse* (Paris: Editions Idéaphane, 1989).

Elayi, Josette, and Jean Sapin, *Nouveaux regards sur la Transeuphratène* (Turnhout: Brepols, 1991); ET *Beyond the River: New Perspectives on Transeuphratene* (trans. J. Edward Crowley; JSOTSup, 250; Sheffield: Sheffield Academic Press, 1998).

Elliger, K., *Die Propheten Nahum, Habakuk, Zephanja, Haggai, Sacharja, Maleachi* (ATD, 25.2; Göttingen: Vandenhoeck & Ruprecht, 6th edn, 1967).

Emerton, J.A. (ed.), *Congress Volume Göttingen 1977* (VTSup, 29; Leiden: E.J. Brill, 1978).

—*Congress Volume Jerusalem 1986* (VTSup, 40; Leiden: E.J. Brill, 1988).

Eph'al, I., 'Syria-Palestine under Achaemenid Rule', CAH, IV, pp. 139-64.

Erman, Adolf, and Hermann Grapow (eds.), *Wörterbuch der Aegyptischen Sprache* (Berlin: Akademie Verlag, 4th edn, 1982).

Eskenazi, Tamara Cohn, and Kent H. Richards (eds.), *Second Temple Studies. II. Temple Community in the Persian Period* (JSOTSup, 175; Sheffield: JSOT Press, 1994).

Ewald, Heinrich, *Die jüngsten Propheten des alten Bundes mit den Büchern Barukh und Daniel* (Göttingen: Vandenhoeck & Ruprecht, 2nd edn, 1868.

Fishbane, Michael, *Biblical Interpretation in Ancient Israel* (Oxford: Clarendon Press, 1985).

Floyd, Michael H., 'The Nature of the Narrative and the Evidence of Redaction in Haggai', *VT* 45 (1995), pp. 470-90.

—'Cosmos and History in Zechariah's View of the Restoration (Zechariah 1:7-6:15)', in Sun, Eades, *et al.* (eds.), *Problems in Biblical Theology*, pp. 125-44.

Fohrer, Georg, *Die symbolische Handlungen der Propheten* (ATANT, 54; Zürich: Zwingli-Verlag, 1968).

—*Erzähler und Propheten im Alten Testament: Geschichte der israelitischen und frühjüdischen Literatur* (Heidelberg: Quelle & Meyer, 1988).

Fox, Michael V., *The Song of Songs and the Ancient Egyptian Love Songs* (Wisconsin: University of Wisconsin Press, 1985).

Frye, Richard N., *The History of Ancient Iran* (HA, 3.7; Munich: Beck, 1984).

Furcha, E. (ed.), *Spirit within Structure* (Festschrift George Johnston; Pittsburgh: Pickwick, 1983).

Galling, Kurt, 'Serubbabel und die Wiederaufbau des Tempels in Jerusalem', in Kuschke (ed.), *Verbannung*, pp. 67-96.

—*Studien zur Geschichte Israels im persischen Zeitalter* (Tübingen: J.C.B. Mohr, 1964).

Garbini, Giovanni, 'Hebrew Literature in the Persian Period', in Eskenazi and Richards (eds.), *Second Temple*, pp. 180-88.

Gibson, John C.L., *Textbook of Syrian Semitic Inscriptions*. II. *Aramaic Inscriptions Including Inscriptions in the Dialect of Zenjirli* (Oxford: Clarendon Press, 1975).

—*Textbook of Syrian Semitic Inscriptions*. III. *Phoenician Inscriptions Including Inscriptions in the Mixed Dialect of Arshlan Tash* (Oxford: Clarendon Press, 1982).

Gibson, McGuire, and Robert D. Biggs (eds.), *Seals and Sealing in the Ancient Near East* (Bibliotheca Mesopotamica, 6; Malibu, CA: Undena, 1977).

Giesebrecht, F., *Das Buch Jeremia* (HKAT, 3.2; Göttingen: Vandenhoeck & Ruprecht, 1907).

Goldingay, John, *Daniel* (WBC, 30; Dallas: Word Books, 1987).

Gordon, Cyrus H., *Ugaritic Manual: Newly Revised Grammar. Texts in Transliteration. Cuneiform Selections. Paradigms–Glossary–Indices* (AnOr, 35; Roma: Pontificio Istituto Biblico, 1955).

Gordon, Robert P., 'Nahum–Malachi', in *The Targum of the Minor Prophets* (translated, with a critical introduction, apparatus, and notes by Kevin J. Cathcart and Robert P. Gordon; The Aramaic Bible, 14; Edinburgh: T. & T. Clark, 1989).

Gorelick, Leonard, and Elizabeth Williams-Forte (eds.), *Ancient Seals and the Bible* (OPNE, 2.1; Malibu, CA: Undena, 1983).

Grabbe, Lester L., 'Reconstructing History from the Book of Ezra', in Davies (ed.), *Second Temple Studies*, I, pp. 98-106.

—*Judaism from Cyrus to Hadrian*. I. *The Persian and Greek Periods* (Minneapolis: Fortress Press, 1992).

Gray, John, *The Legacy of Canaan: The Ras Shamra Texts and their Relevance to the Old Testament* (VTSup, 5; Leiden: E.J. Brill, 2nd edn, 1969).

Greenberg, Moshe, *Ezekiel 1–20* (AB, 22; New York: Doubleday, 1983).

Greenfield, J.C., and B. Porten (eds.), *The Bisitun Inscription of Darius the Great: Aramaic Version* (text, translation and commentary; Corpus Inscriptionum Iranicarum; Part 1, Inscriptions of Ancient Iran; V. The Aramaic Versions of the Achaemenian Inscriptions, etc.; Texts 1; London: Lund Humphries, 1982).

Greenfield, Jonas C., 'Lexicographical Notes ii. IX The Root צמח', *HUCA* 30 (1959), pp. 141-51.

Gressmann, Hugo, *Der Messias* (Göttingen: Vandenhoeck & Ruprecht, 1929).

Groß, Walter, *Die Pendens-Konstruktion im biblischen Hebräisch* (Studien zum althebräischen Satz, 1; ATSAT, 27; Erzabtei St. Ottilien: EOS Verlag, 1987).

Grossberg, Daniel, 'The Dual Glow/Grow Motif', *Bib* 67 (1986), pp. 547-54.

Haag, H., 'בן', *ThWAT*, I, pp. 670-82.

Haeussermann, Friedrich, *Wortempfang und Symbol in der alttestamentlichen Prophetie* (BZAW, 58; Giessen: Alfred Töpelmann, 1932).

Hallo, William W., 'Seals Lost and Found', in Gibson and Biggs (eds.), *Seals and Sealing*, pp. 55-60.

—' "As the Seal upon Thine Arm": Glyptic Metaphors in the Biblical World', in Gorelick and Williams-Forte (eds.), *Ancients Seals*, pp. 7-17.

Hallo, William W., and K. Lawson Younger, Jr (eds.), *The Context of Scripture: Canonical Compositions, Monumental Inscriptions, and Archival Documents from the Biblical*

*World.* I. *Canonical Compositions from the Biblical World* (Leiden: E.J. Brill, 1997).

Halpern, Baruch, 'The Ritual Background of Zechariah's Temple Song', *CBQ* 40 (1978), pp. 167-90.

Hamerton-Kelly, R.G., 'The Temple and the Origins of Jewish Apocalyptic', *VT* 20 (1970), pp. 1-15.

Hammershaimb, E., *Some Aspects of Old Testament Prophecy from Isaiah to Malachi* (Teologiske Skrifter, 4; Copenhagen: Rosenkilde of Bagger, 1966).

Hammerschmidt, Ernst, 'Königsideologie im spätantiken Judentum', *ZDMG* 113 (1963), pp. 493-11.

Hanhart, Robert, *Dodekapropheton.* VII.1 *Sacharja 1–8* (BKAT, 14/7.1; Neukirchen–Vluyn: Neukirchener Verlag, 1998).

Hanson, Paul D., *The Dawn of Apocalyptic: The Historical and Sociological Roots of Jewish Apocalyptic Eschatology* (Philadelphia: Fortress Press, 1975).

—*The People Called: The Growth of Community in the Bible* (San Francisco: Harper & Row, 1986).

—'Messiahs and Messianic Figures in Proto-Apocalypticism', in Charlesworth (ed.), *Messiah*, pp. 67-75.

Harrelson, Walter, 'The Trial of the High Priest Joshua: Zechariah 3', *Eretz Israel* 16 (H.M. Orlinksy Volume, 1982), pp. 116*-24*.

Harris, Zellig S., *A Grammar of the Phoenician Language* (AOS, 8; New Haven: American Oriental Society, 1936).

Hausmann, Jutta, *Israels Rest: Studien zum Selbstverständnis der nachexilichen Gemeinde* (BWANT, 124 [7/4]; Stuttgart: Kohlhammer, 1987).

Hawkins, J.D., 'The Neo-Hittite States in Syria and Anatolia', in CAH, III/I$^2$ (1982), pp. 372-41.

Hayes, John H., and J. Maxwell Miller (eds.), *Israelite and Judaean History* (OTL; London: SCM Press, 1977).

Healey, John F., *The Nabataean Tomb Inscriptions of Mada'in Salih* (edited with introduction, translation and commentary; JSSSup, 1; Oxford: Oxford University Press, 1993).

—'Lexical Loans in Early Syriac: A Comparison with Nabataean Aramaic', *SEL* 12 (1995), pp. 75-84.

Heerma van Vos, M.S.H.G., Ph.H.J. Houwink ten Cate and N.A. van Uchelen (eds.), *Travels in the World of the Old Testament: Studies Presented to Prof. M.A. Beek* (Assen: Van Gorcum, 1974).

Hinz, Walther, 'Kambyses', *RLA*, V, pp. 328-30.

Hitzig, Ferdinand, *Die zwölf kleinen Propheten erklärt* (KEHAT; Leipzig: Hirzel, 1881).

Hoglund, Kenneth G., *Achaemenid Imperial Administration in Syria-Palestine and the Missions of Ezra and Nehemia* (SBLDS, 125; Atlanta: Scholars Press, 1992).

Holladay, William L., *Jeremiah 1: A Commentary on the Book of the Prophet Jeremiah Chapters 1–25* (Hermeneia; Philadelphia: Fortress Press, 1986).

Holloway, Steven W., and Lowell K. Handy (eds.), *The Pitcher is Broken: Memorial Essays for Gösta W. Ahlström* (JSOTSup, 190; Sheffield: Sheffield Academic Press).

Holwerda, B., '...*Begonnen hebbende van Mozes...*' (Terneuzen: Littooij, 1953).

Honeyman, A.M., 'Observations on a Phoenician Inscription of Ptolemaic Date', *JEA* 26 (1940), pp. 57-67.

Horst, Friedrich, *Die zwölf kleinen Propheten: Nahum bis Maleachi* (HAT, 14; Tübingen: J.C.B. Mohr [Paul Siebeck], 1964).

Howard, David M., *The Structure of Psalms 93–100* (BJS, 5; Winona Lake, IN: Eisenbrauns, 1997).

Hug, Volker, *Altaramäische Grammatik der Texte des 7. und 6. Jh.s v. Chr* (HSAO, 4; Heidelberg: Heidelberger Orientverlag, 1993).

Hughes, Jeremy, *Secrets of the Times: Myth and History in Biblical Chronology* (JSOTSup, 66; Sheffield: JSOT Press, 1990).

Hühn, Eugen, *Die messianischen Weissagungen des israelitisch-jüdischen Volkes bis zu den Targumim historisch Untersucht und Erläutert* (Tübingen: J.C.B. Mohr, 1899).

Ishida, Tomoo, *The Royal Dynasties in Ancient Israel: A Study on the Formation and Development of Royal-Dynastic Ideology* (BZAW, 142; Berlin: W. de Gruyter, 1977).

Jacob, E., *Esaïe 1–12* (CAT, 8a; Geneva: Labor et Fides, 1987).

Jacquet, Louis, *Les Psaumes et le coeur de l'homme: Etude textuelle, littéraire et doctrinale. Introduction et premier livre du Psautier. Psaumes 1 à 41* (Gembloux: Duculot, 1975).

Jagersma, H., *Geschiedenis van Israël in het oudtestamentische tijdvak* (Kampen: Kok, 1979); ET *A History of Israel in the Old Testament Period* (London: SCM Press, 1983).

Japhet, Sara, 'Sheshbazzar and Zerubbabel: Against the Background of the Historical and Religious Tendencies of Ezra–Nehemiah', *ZAW* 94 (1982), pp. 66-98.

—'The Temple in the Restoration Period: Reality and Ideology', *USQR* 34 (1991), pp. 195-51.

—*I and II Chronicles: A Commentary* (OTL; London: SCM Press, 1993).

—'Composition and Chronology in the Book of Ezra–Nehemia', in Eskenazi and Richards (eds.), *Second Temple*, pp. 189-216.

Jastrow, M., *A Dictionary of the Targumim, the Talmud Babli and Yerushalmi, and the Midrashic Literature. With an Index of Scriptural Quotations* (London: New York: Putnam's Sons, 1903).

Jepsen, A., 'Kleine Beiträge zum Zwölfprophetenbuch III', *ZAW* 61 (1945/48), pp. 95-14.

Jeremias, Chr., *Die Nachtgesichte des Sacharja: Untersuchungen zu ihrer Stellung im Zusammenhang der Visionsberichte im Alten Testament und zu ihrem Bildmaterial* (FRLANT, 117; Göttingen: Vandenhoeck & Ruprecht, 1977).

Jones, Douglas Rawlinson, *Jeremiah: Based on the Revised Standard Version* (NCB; London: Marshall Pickering; Grand Rapids: Eerdmans, 1992).

Joüon, Paul, and Takamitsu Muraoka, *A Grammar of Biblical Hebrew* (SB, 14; Rome: Pontificio Istituto Biblico, 1991).

Junker, H., *Die zwölf kleinen Propheten*, II (HSAT, 8; Bonn: Peter Hanstein Verlagsbuchhandlung, 1938).

Kaiser, Otto (ed.), *Lebendige Forschung im Alten Testament* (ZAW 100 supplement; Berlin: W. de Gruyter, 1988).

Kaltner, John, *The Use of Arabic in Biblical Hebrew Lexicography* (CBQMS, 28; Washington: Catholic Biblical Association, 1996).

Keel, Othmar, *Jahwe-Visionen und Siegelkunst* (SBS, 84/85; Stuttgart: Verlag Katholisches Bibelwerk, 1977).

—*Deine Blicke sind tauben: Zur Metaphorik des hohen Liedes* (SBS, 114-15; Stuttgart: Verlag Katholisches Bibelwerk, 1984.

—*Das Hohelied* (ZBAT, 18; Zürich: Theologische Verlag, 1986).

—'Bildträger aus Palästina/Israel und die besondere Bedeutung der Miniaturkunst', in Keel and Schroer, *Stempelsiegeln*, pp. 7-45.

—review of *Ancient Seals*, edited by Gorelick and Williams-Forte, in *JAOS* 106 (1983), pp. 307-11.

—'Siegel und Siegeln in der Bibel', in Keel and Uehlinger (eds.), *Altorientalische Miniaturkunst*, pp. 87-92.

Keel, Othmar, and Silvia Schroer, *Studien zu den Stempelsiegeln aus Palästina/Israel*, I (OBO, 67; Freiburg: Universitätsverlag; Göttingen: Vandenhoeck & Ruprecht, 1985).

Keel, Othmar and Christoph Uehlinger (eds.), *Altorientalische Miniaturkunst: Die ältesten visuellen Massenkommunikationsmittel. Ein Blick in die Sammlungen des Biblischen Instituts der Universität Freiburg Schweiz* (Mainz: Philipp von Zabern, 1990).

Keil, Carl Friedrich, *Die zwölf kleinen Propheten* (Leipzig: Dörflin und Franke, 3rd edn, 1888).

Kellermann, D., 'עטר', *ThWAT*, VI, cols. 21-31.

Kellermann, Ulrich, *Messias und Gesetz: Grundlinien einer alttestamentlichen Heilserwartung. Eine traditionsgeschichtliche Einführung* (Neukirchen–Vluyn: Neukirchener Verlag, 1971).

Kent, Roland G., *Old Persian: Grammar, Texts, Lexicon* (AOS, 33; New Haven: American Oriental Society, 1953).

Kessler, John A., 'The Second Year of Darius and the Prophet Haggai', *Trans* 5 (1992), pp. 63-86.

Khairy, Nabil I., 'An Analytical Study of the Nabataean Monumental Inscriptions at *Medā'in Ṣāleḥ*', *ZDPV* 96 (1980), pp. 163-68.

Khan, G., *Studies in Semitic Syntax* (LOS, 38; Oxford: Oxford University Press, 1988).

King, Philip J., *Jeremiah: An Archaeological Companion* (Louisville, KY: Westminster/ John Knox Press, 1993).

Kleven, Terence, 'The Use of *ṣnr* in Ugaritic and 2 Samuel V 8: Hebrew Usage and Comparative Philology', *VT* 44 (1994), pp. 195-204.

Kline, Meredith G., 'The Structure of the Book of Zechariah', *JETS* 34 (1991), pp. 179-93.

Knibb, Michael A., 'The Exile in the Literature of the Intertestamental Period', *HeyJ* 17 (1976), pp. 253-72.

Koch, Klaus, *Die Profeten. II. Babylonisch-persische Zeit* (UT, 281; Stuttgart: W. Kohlhammer, 1980); ET *The Prophets. II. The Babylonian and Persian Periods* (London: SCM Press, 1983).

Köhler, A., *Der Weissagungen Sacharjas erste Hälfte, Cap. 1–8* (Die Nachexilischen Propheten Erklärt, 2; Leipzig: Deichert, 1861).

Köhler, Ludwig, 'Eine archaistische Wortgruppe', *ZAW* 46 (1928), pp. 218-20.

König, Friedrich Eduard, *Historisch-kritisches Lehrgebäude der hebräischen Sprache: Erste Hälfte: Lehre von der Schrift, der Aussprache, dem Pronomen und dem Verbum* (Leipzig: J.C. Hinrichs, 1881).

—*Historisch-kritisches Lehrgebäude der hebräischen Sprache*, III (Leipzig: J.C. Hinrichs, 1897).

Koole, J.L., *Haggai* (COT; Kampen: Kok, 1967).

Krašovec, J., *La justice (ṣdq) de Dieu dans la Bible Hébraïque et l'interprétation juive et chrétienne* (OBO, 76; Freiburg: Universitätsverlag; Göttingen: Vandenhoeck & Ruprecht, 1988).

Kraus, Hans-Joachim, *Psalmen. I. Psalmen 1–59; II. Teilband: Psalmen 60–150* (BKAT, 15.1-2; Neukirchen–Vluyn: Neukirchener Verlag, 5th edn, 1978).

Kuhrt, Amélie, 'The Cyrus Cylinder and Achaemenid Imperial Policy', *JSOT* 25 (1983), pp. 83-97.

—'Babylonia from Cyrus to Xerxes', CAH, IV, pp. 112-38.

—*The Ancient Near East. c. 3000–330 BC* (Routledge History of the Ancient World; London: Routledge, 1995).

Kuschke, A. (ed.), *Verbannung und Heimkehr: Beiträge zur Geschichte und Theologie Israels im 6. und 5. Jahrhundert v. Chr.* (Festschrift W. Rudolph; Tübingen: J.C.B. Mohr, 1961).

Kutscher, Eduard Yechezkel, 'מהלכים ואחיותיה', *Leš* 26 (1960–61), pp. 93-96 (Hebrew).

—*Hebrew and Aramaic Studies* (Jerusalem: Magnes Press, 1977).

Laato, Antti, *Josiah and David Redivivus: The Historical Josiah and the Messianic Expectations of Exilic and Postexilic Times* (ConBOT, 33; Stockholm: Almqvist & Wiksell, 1992).

Laetsch, Theodore, *The Minor Prophets* (Concordia Classic Commentary Series; St Louis: Concordia Publishing House, 1956).

Lagrange, M.-J., 'Notes sur les prophéties messianiques des derniers prophètes', *RB* NS 3 (1906), pp. 67-83.

Laperrousaz, Ernest-Marie, 'Le régime théocratique juif a-t-il commencé à l'époque perse, ou seulement à l'époque hellénistique?', *Semitica* 32 (1982), pp. 93-96.

—'Jérusalem à l'époque perse (étendue et statut)', *Trans* 1 (1989), pp. 55-65.

Laperrousaz, Ernest-Marie, and André Lemaire (eds.), *La Palestine à l'époque perse* (Paris: Cerf, 1994).

LaSor, William Sanford, David Allan Hubbard and Frederic Wm. Bush, *Old Testament Survey: The Message, Form, and Background of the Old Testament* (Grand Rapids: Eerdmans, 1982).

Lemaire, A., 'L'epigraphie paléo-hébraïque et la Bible', in Emerton (ed.), *Congress Volume Göttingen 1977*, pp. 165-76.

—'Populations et territoires de la Palestine à l'époque perse', *Trans* 3 (1990), pp. 31-73.

—'Histoire et administration de la Palestine à l'époque perse', in Laperrousaz and Lemaire (eds.), *Palestine*, pp. 11-53.

—'Zorobabel et la Judé à la lumière de l'épigraphie (fin du VIe s. av. J.-C.)', *RB* 103 (1996), pp. 48-57.

Lescow, T., 'Sacharja 1–8: Verkündigung und Komposition', *BN* 68 (1992), pp. 75-99.

Lettinga, Jan P., 'Het "gezeten-zijn" van koning en rechter', *De Reformatie* 32 (1956–57), p. 360.

Lidzbarski, Mark, *Ephemeris für semitische Epigraphik: Zweiter Band 1903–1907* (Giessen: Alfred Töpelmann, 1908).

—*Ephemeris für semitische Epigraphik: Dritter Band 1909–1915* (Giessen: Alfred Töpelmann, 1915).

Liedke, Gerhard, *Gestalt und Bezeichnung alttestamentlicher Rechtssätze: Eine formgeschichtlich-terminologische Studie* (WMANT, 39; Neukirchen–Vluyn: Neukirchener Verlag, 1971).

Lipiński, Edward, 'Recherches sur le livre de Zacharie', *VT* 20 (1970), pp. 25-55.

—'Recherches ugaritiques', *Syria* 50 (1973), pp. 35-51.

—'Géographie linguistique de la Transeuphratène à l'époque achéménide', *Trans* 3 (1990), pp. 95-107.

Liwak, Rüdiger, and Siegfried Wagner (eds.), *Prophetie und geschichtliche Wirklichkeit im alten Israel: Festschrift für Siegfried Herrmann zum 65. Geburtstag* (Stuttgart: W. Kohlhammer, 1991).

Loewenstamm, Samuel E., *Comparative Studies in Biblical and Ancient Oriental Literatures* (AOAT, 204; Kevelaer: Verlag Butzon & Bercker; Neukirchen–Vluyn: Neukirchener Verlag, 1980).

Löw, Immanuel, *Die Flora der Juden. IV. Zusammenfassung, Nachträge, Berichtigungen, Indizes, Abkürzungen* (Hildesheim: Georg Olms, 1967).

Long, Burke O., 'Reports of Visions Among the Prophets', *JBL* 95 (1976), pp. 353-65.

Loretz, Oswald, *Die Königspsalmen: Die altorientalisch-kanaanäische Königstradition in jüdischer Sicht. I. Ps 20, 21, 72, 101 und 144* (Mit einem Beitrag von I. Kottsieper zu Papyrus Amherst; Ugaritisch-Biblische Literatur, 6; Münster: Ugarit-Verlag, 1988).

Lundgreen, Friedrich, *Die Benützung der Pflanzenwelt in der alttestamentlichen Religion* (Giessen: Alfred Töpelmann, 1908).

Lust, J., 'Messianism and Greek Jeremiah', in Cox (ed.), *VII Congress*, pp. 87-122.

Lyons, John, *Introduction to Theoretical Linguistics* (Cambridge: Cambridge University Press, 1968).

—*Semantics* (Cambridge: Cambridge University Press, 1977).

Maag, Victor, *Text, Wortschatz und Begriffswelt des Buches Amos* (Leiden: E.J. Brill, 1951).

Madsen, Iver K., 'Zur Erklärung der evangelischen Parabeln', *TSK* 104 (1932), pp. 311-36.

Malamat, Abraham, 'The Secret Council and Prophetic Involvement in Mari and Israel', in Liwak and Wagner (eds.), *Prophetie*, pp. 231-36.

Margalit, Baruch, *The Ugaritic Poem of AQHT: Text, Translation, Commentary* (BZAW, 182; Berlin: W. de Gruyter, 1989).

Marinkovic, Peter, 'What Does Zechariah 1–8 Tell us about the Second Temple?', in Eskenazi and Richards (eds.), *Second Temple Studies*, pp. 88-103.

Marti, Karl, *Das Dodekapropheton* (KHAT, 13; Tübingen: J.C.B. Mohr, 1904).

Mason, Rex, *The Books of Haggai, Zechariah and Malachi* (CBC; Cambridge: Cambridge University Press, 1977).

—'The Purpose of the "Editorial Framework" of the Book of Haggai', *VT* 27 (1977), pp. 413-21.

—'The Prophets of the Restoration', in Coggins, Phillips and Knibb (eds.), *Prophetic Tradition*, pp. 137-54.

—*Preaching the Tradition: Homily and Hermeneutics after the Exile Based on the 'Addresses' in Chronicles, the Speeches in the Books of Ezra and Nehemiah and the Postexilic Prophetic Books* (Cambridge: Cambridge University Press, 1990).

—'The Messiah in the Postexilic Old Testament Literature', in Day (ed.), *King*, pp. 338-64.

Mastin, B.A., 'A Note on Zechariah vi 13', *VT* 26 (1976), pp. 113-16.

May, Herbert Gordon, 'A Key to the Interpretation of Zechariah's Visions', *JBL* 57 (1938), pp. 173-84.

McConville, Gordon, *Old Testament* (Teach Yourself Books—World Faiths; London: Hodder & Stoughton, 1996).

McEvenue, S.E., 'The Political Structure in Judah from Cyrus to Nehemiah', *CBQ* 43 (1981), pp. 353-64.

McKane, William, *Jeremiah 1–25* (ICC; Edinburgh: T. & T. Clark, 1986).

Merrill, Eugene H., *An Exegetical Commentary: Haggai, Zechariah, Malachi* (Chicago: Moody Press, 1994).

Meyer, Rudolf, *Hebräische Grammatik* (4 vols.; Berlin: W. de Gruyter, 1966–72).

Meyers, Carol L., and Eric M. Meyers, *Haggai, Zechariah 1–8* (AB, 25B; Garden City, NY: Doubleday, 1987).

Miller, Patrick D., Paul D. Hanson and S. Dean McBride (eds.), *Ancient Israelite Religion* (Philadelphia: Fortress Press, 1987).

Miller, J. Maxwell, and John H. Hayes, *A History of Ancient Israel and Judah* (London: SCM Press, 1986).

Mitchell, Hinckley G., *A Critical and Exegetical Commentary on Haggai and Zechariah* (ICC; Edinburgh: T. & T. Clark, 1912).

Moberly, R.W.L., *The Old Testament of the Old Testament: Patriarchal Narratives and Mosaic Yahwism* (Overtures to Biblical Theology; Philadelphia: Fortress Press, 1992).

Möhlenbrink, Kurt, 'Der Leuchter im fünften Nachtgesicht des Propheten Sacharja', *ZDPV* 52 (1929), pp. 267-86.

Moscati, Sabatino, 'I sigilli nell'Antico Testamento studio esegetico-filologico', *Bib* 30 (1949), pp. 314-38.

Mosis, Rudolf, *Untersuchungen zur Theologie des chronistischen Geschichtswerkes* (FTS, 92; Freiburg: Herder, 1973).

Mowinckel, S., *He that Cometh* (trans. G.W. Anderson; Oxford: Basil Blackwell, 1956).

—*Psalmenstudien. III. Kultprophetie und prophetische Psalmen* (Amsterdam: Schippers, 1966).

Mullen, E. Theodore, Jr, *The Divine Council in Canaanite and Early Hebrew Literature* (HSM, 24; Chico, CA: Scholars Press, 1980).

Muraoka, Takamitsu, *Emphatic Words and Structures in Biblical Hebrew* (Jerusalem: Magnes Press; Leiden: E.J. Brill, 1985).

Murmela, Risto, *Prophets in Dialogue: Inner-Biblical Allusions in Zech 1–8 and 9–14* (Åbo: Åbo Akademi University, 1996).

Murphy, Roland, *Song of Songs* (Hermeneia; Philadelphia: Fortress Press, 1990).

Nelson, Richard D., *Raising up a Faithful Priest: Community and Priesthood in Biblical Theology* (Louisville, KY: Westminster/John Knox Press, 1993).

Neusner, J., William Scott Green and Ernest S. Frerichs (eds.), *Judaisms and their Messiahs at the Turn of the Christian Era* (Cambridge, 1987).

Newsom, Carol A., 'Angels', *ABD*, I, pp. 248-53.

Niditch, Susan, *The Symbolic Vision in Biblical Tradition* (HSM, 30; Chico, CA: Scholars Press, 1980).

Nielsen, Kirsten, *There Is Hope for a Tree: The Tree as Metaphor in Isaiah* (JSOTSup, 65; Sheffield: JSOT Press, 1989).

Noth, Martin and D. Winton Thomas (eds.), *Wisdom in Israel and in the Ancient Near East* (VTSup, 3; Leiden: E.J. Brill, 1955).

Nowack, W., *Die Kleinen Propheten* (HKAT, 3.4; Göttingen: Vandenhoeck & Ruprecht, 3rd edn, 1922).

O'Connor, M., 'The Arabic Loanwords in Nabatean Aramaic', *JNES* 45.3 (1986), pp. 213-29.

Olmo Lete, Gregorio del, 'Los nombres "divinos" de los reyes de Ugarit', *AUOr* 5 (1987), pp. 39-69 (reprinted in Gregorio del Olmo Lete, *La religión Cananea: Según la litúrgia de Ugarit. Estudio textual* [AuOrSup, 3; Barcelona: Editorial AUSA, 1992], pp. 116-26).

Olmstead, A.T., *History of the Persian Empire* (Chicago: University of Chicago Press, 1959).

Oosterhoff, B.J., 'De schriftprofeten', in Van der Woude (ed.), *Oude Testament*, pp. 362-427; ET 'The Prophets', in Van der Woude (ed.), *Old Testament*, pp. 226-70.

Otzen, Benedikt, 'חתם', *ThWAT*, III, cols. 282-88.

Parker, Simon B., 'Appeals for Military Intervention: Stories from Zinjirli and the Bible', *BA* 59 (1996), pp. 213-24.

Parpola, Simo (ed.), *The Correspondence of Sargon II. I. Letters from Assyria and the West* (SAA, 1; Helsinki: Helsinki University Press, 1987).

Perowne, T.T., *Haggai and Zechariah* (CBSC; Cambridge: Cambridge University Press, 1888).

Petersen, David L., *Haggai and Zechariah 1–8* (OTL; London: SCM Press, 1984).

Petit, Thierry, 'L'evolution sémantique des termes Hébreux et Araméens *PḤH* et *SGN* et Accadiens *PĀḤATU* et *ŠAKNU*', *JBL* 107 (1988), pp. 53-67.

Petitjean, Albert, *Les oracles du Proto-Zacharie: Un programme du restoration pour la communauté juive après l'exil* (Paris: Gabalda; Louvain: Editions Imprimerie Orientaliste, 1969).

Platt, Elizabeth E., 'Ancient Israelite Jewelry', *ABD*, III, pp. 823-34.

Polzin, Robert, *Samuel and the Deuteronomist: A Literary Study of the Deuteronomistic History. II. 1 Samuel* (Indiana Studies in Biblical Literature; Bloomington: Indiana University Press, 1989).

Pomykala, Kenneth E., *The Davidic Dynasty Tradition in Early Judaism: Its History and Significance for Messianism* (SBLEJL, 7; Atlanta: Scholars Press, 1995).

Pope, Marvin H., *Song of Songs: A New Translation with Introduction and Commentary* (AB, 7C; Garden City, NY: Doubleday, 1977).

Redditt, Paul L., 'Zerubbabel, Joshua, and the Night Visions of Zechariah', *CBQ* 54 (1992), pp. 249-59.

—'Nehemiah's First Mission and the Date of Zechariah 9–14', *CBQ* 56 (1994), pp. 664-78.

—*Haggai, Zechariah, Malachi* (NCB; London: Marshall Pickering; Grand Rapids: Eerdmans, 1995).

Rendsburg, Gary A.,'Regional Dialects', in Bodine (ed.), *Linguistics*, pp. 65-88.

—*Linguistic Evidence for the Northern Origin of Selected Psalms* (SBLMS, 43; Atlanta: Scholars Press, 1990).

Reventlow, Henning Graf, *Die Propheten Haggai, Sacharja und Maleachi* (ATD, 25.2; Göttingen: Vandenhoeck & Ruprecht, rev. edn, 1993).

Ridderbos, J., *De kleine Profeten. III. Haggai, Zacharia, Maleachi* (Kampen: Kok, 3rd edn, 1968).

Rignell, L., *Die Nachtgesichte des Sacharja* (Lund: C.W.K. Gleerup, 1950).

Ringgren, Helmer, 'יצהר', *ThWAT*, III, cols. 825-26.

—'עמד', *ThWAT*, VI, cols. 194-204.

—'צמח', *ThWAT*, VI, cols. 1068-72.

—'שמן', *ThWAT*, VIII, cols. 251-55.

Roberts, J.J.M., 'The Old Testament's Contribution to Messianic Expectations', in Charlesworth (ed.), *Messiah*, pp. 39-51.

Rogerson, J.W., and J.W. McKay, *Psalms 1–50* (CBC; Cambridge: Cambridge University Press, 1977).

Rokay, Zoltán, 'Vom Stadttor zu den Vorhöfen. Ps 82—Sach 1–8 (ein Vergleich)', *ZKT* 116 (1994), pp. 457-63.

Rooke, D.W., 'The Role and Development of the High Priesthood with Particular Reference to the Postexilic Period' (DPhil thesis; Oxford University, 1996).

Rose, Wolter H., 'The meaning of *ṣdq* in North-West Semitic', forthcoming.

Rosenthal, Franz, *A Grammar of Biblical Aramaic* (Porta Linguarum Orientalium, 5; Wiesbaden: Otto Harrassowitz, 1983).

Rost, Leonhard, 'Bemerkungen zu Sacharja 4', *ZAW* 63 (1951), pp. 216-21 (reprinted in Leonhard Rost, *Das kleine Credo und andere Studien zum Alten Testament* [Heidelberg: Quelle & Meyer, 1965]).

Rothstein, J.W., *Die Nachtgesichte des Sacharja: Studien zur Sacharjaprophetie und zur jüdischen Geschichte im ersten nachexilischen Jahrhundert* (BWANT, 8; Leipzig: J.C. Hinrichs, 1910).

Rudolph, Wilhelm, *Chronikbücher* (HAT, 21; Tübingen: J.C.B. Mohr [Paul Siebeck], 1955).

—*Hosea* (KAT, 13.1; Gütersloh: Gerd Mohn, 1966).

—*Jeremia* (HAT, 12; Tübingen: J.C.B. Mohr [Paul Siebeck], 3rd edn, 1968).

—*Haggai, Sacharja 1–8, Sacharja 9–14, Maleachi* (KAT, 13.4; Gütersloh: Gerd Mohn, 1976).

Rüthy, Albert Emil, *Die Pflanze und ihre Teile im biblisch-hebräischen Sprachgebrauch* (Bern: Francke, 1942).

Runnals, D.R., 'The King as Temple Builder', in Furcha (ed.), *Spirit*, pp. 15-37.

Sader, Hélène S., *Les états araméens de Syrie depuis leur fondation jusqu'à leur transformation en provinces assyriennes* (BTS, 36; Wiesbaden: Franz Steiner Verlag, 1987).

Sæbø, Magne, 'Zum Verhältnis von "Messianismus" und "Eschatologie" im Alten Testament: Ein Versuch terminologischer und sachlicher Klärung', in Dassmann and Stemberger (eds.), *Messias*, pp. 25-56.

Sarna, Nahum M., *The JPS Torah Commentary: Genesis. The Traditional Hebrew Text with the New JPS Translation* (Philadelphia: Jewish Publication Society of America, 1989).

Satterthwaite, Philip E., Richard S. Hess and Gordon J. Wenham (eds.), *The Lord's Anointed: Interpretation of Old Testament Messianic Texts* (Tyndale House Studies; Carlisle: Paternoster Press; Grand Rapids: Baker, 1995).

Schmid, Hans Heinrich, *Gerechtigkeit als Weltordnung: Hintergrund und Geschichte des alttestamentlichen Gerechtigkeitsbegriffes* (BHT, 40; Tübingen: J.C.B. Mohr, 1968).

Schmidt, Werner H., 'Der Ohnmacht des Messias: Zur Überlieferungsgeschichte der messianischen Weissagungen im Alten Testament', in Struppe (ed.), *Messiasbild*, pp. 67-88.

Schöttler, Heinz-Günther, *Gott inmitten seines Volkes: Die Neuordnung des Gottesvolkes nach Sacharja 1–6* (TTS, 43; Trier: Paulinus Verlag, 1987).

Schottroff, Willy, 'Zur Sozialgeschichte Israels in der Perserzeit', *VuF* 27 (1982), pp. 46-68.

Schroer, Silvia, *In Israel gab es Bilder: Nachrichten von darstellender Kunst im Alten Testament* (OBO, 74; Freiburg: Universitätsverlag; Göttingen: Vandenhoeck & Ruprecht, 1987).

Segert, Stanislav, *A Grammar of Phoenician and Punic* (Munich: Beck, 1976).

Sellin, Ernst, *Das Zwölfprophetenbuch* (KAT, 12; Leipzig: Deichert; Erlangen: Scholl, 1922).

Selman, Martin J., 'Messianic Mysteries', in Satterthwaite, Hess and Wenham (eds.), *The Lord's Anointed*, pp. 281-302.

Sérandour, A., 'Les récits bibliques de la construction du second temple: leurs enjeux', *Trans* 11 (1996), pp. 9-32.

Seybold, Klaus, 'Die Königserwartung bei den Propheten Haggai und Sacharja', *Judaica* 28 (1972), pp. 69-78 (reprinted in Struppe [ed.], *Messiasbild*, pp. 243-52).

—*Bilder zum Tempelbau: Die Visionen des Propheten Sacharja* (SBS, 70; Stuttgart: KBW Verlag, 1974).

Shiloh, Yigal, and David Tarler, 'Bullae from the City of David: A Hoard of Seal Impressions from the Israelite Period', *BA* 49 (1986), pp. 197-209.

Siebeneck, R., 'The Messianism of Aggeus and Proto-Zacharias', *CBQ* 19 (1957), pp. 312-28.

Sinclair, Lawrence A., 'Redaction of Zechariah 1-8', *BibRes* 20 (1975), pp. 36-47.

Skehan, Patrick W., and Alexander A. Di Lella, *The Wisdom of Ben Sira* (AB, 39; New York: Doubleday, 1987).

Skinner, J., *The Book of the Prophet Isaiah Chapters I-XXXIX* (CBC; Cambridge: University Press, 1915).

Smith, Morton, *Palestinian Parties and Politics that Shaped the Old Testament* (London: SCM Press, 2nd edn, 1987).

Smith, Ralph L., *Micah-Malachi* (WBC, 32; Waco, TX: Word Books, 1984).

Soggin, J. Alberto, *Introduction to the Old Testament: From its Origins to the Closing of the Alexandrian Canon* (London: SCM Press, 3rd edn, 1989).

—*An Introduction to the History of Israel and Judah* (London: SCM Press, 1993).

Sokoloff, Michael, *A Dictionary of Jewish Palestinian Aramaic of the Byzantine Period* (Dictionaries of Talmud, Midrash and Targum, 2; Ramat Gan: Bar Ilan University Press, 1990).

Speiser, E.A., *Genesis* (AB, 1; Garden City, NY: Doubleday, 1964).

Spieckermann, Hermann, *Heilsgegenwart: Eine Theologie der Psalmen* (FRLANT, 148; Göttingen: Vandenhoeck & Ruprecht, 1989).

Spiegelberg, W., *Die demotischen Denkmaler 30601-31166. I. Die demotischen Inschriften* (Catalogue general des antiquites egyptiennes du Musee du Caire. Nos. 30601-31166; Leipzig, 1904).

Spina, Frank Anthony, 'Eli's Seat: The Transition from Priest to Prophet in 1 Samuel 1-4', *JSOT* 62 (1994), pp. 67-75.

Stacey, W.D., *Prophetic Drama in the Old Testament* (London: Epworth Press, 1990).

Stern, E., *Material Culture of the Land of the Bible in the Persian Period 538-332 B.C.* (Warminster: Aris & Phillips; Jerusalem: Israel Exploration Society, 1982).

Strack, Hermann L., and Paul Billerbeck, *Kommentar zum Neuen Testament aus Talmud und Midrasch. III. Die Briefe des Neuen Testaments und die Offenbarung Johannis* (Munich: Beck, 1926).

Strack, Hermann L., *Grammatik des Biblisch-Aramäischen, mit den nach Handschriften berichtigten Texten und einem Wörterbuch* (Clavis Linguarum Semiticarum, 4; Munich: Beck, 6th edn, 1921).

Strand, Kenneth A., 'The Two Olive Trees of Zechariah 4 and Revelation 11', *AUSS* 20 (1982), pp. 257-61.

Struppe, Ursula (ed.), *Studien zum Messiasbild im Alten Testament* (SBA, 6; Stuttgart: Verlag Katholisches Bibelwerk, 1989), pp. 243-52.

Sun, Henry T.C., and Keith L. Eades *et al.* (eds.), *Problems in Biblical Theology: Essays in Honor of Rolf Knierim* (Grand Rapids: Eerdmans, 1997).

Swetnam, James, 'Some Observations on the Background of צדיק in Jeremias 23,5a', *Bib* 46 (1965), pp. 29-40.

Thiele, Edwin R., *The Mysterious Numbers of the Hebrew Kings* (Chicago: University of Chicago Press, 3rd edn, 1985).

Thompson, J.A., *Jeremiah* (NICOT; Grand Rapids: Eerdmans, 1980).

Tigay, Jeffrey H., *The JPS Torah Commentary: Deuteronomy* דברים. *The Traditional Hebrew Text with the New JPS Translation* (Philadelphia: Jewish Publication Society of America, 1996).

Tigchelaar, E.J.C. , 'L'ange qui parlait à Zacharie, est-il un personnage apocalyptique?', *EstBíb* 45 (1987), pp. 347-60.

—*Prophets of Old and the Day of the End: Zechariah, the Book of Watchers and Apocalyptic* (OTS, 35; Leiden: E.J. Brill, 1996).

Tollington, Janet E., *Tradition and Innovation in Haggai and Zechariah 1–8* (JSOTSup, 150; Sheffield: JSOT Press, 1993).

Tomback, Richard S., *A Comparative Semitic Lexicon of the Phoenician and Punic Languages* (SBLDS, 32; Missoula, MT: Scholars Press, 1974).

Torrey, Charles C., 'Two Letters from Professor Porter in regard to the Bod'aštart stones in Beirut', *JAOS* 25 (1904), pp. 324-31.

Touzard, J., 'L'âme juive au temps de Perses', *RB* 35 (1926), pp. 174-205.

Tropper, Josef, *Die Inschriften von Zincirli* (ALASP, 6; Münster: Ugarit-Verlag, 1993).

Ulrich, Eugene, and James VanderKam (eds.), *The Community of the Renewed Covenant: The Notre Dame Symposium on the Dead Sea Scrolls* (CJAS, 10; Notre Dame: University of Notre Dame Press, 1994).

VanderKam, James C., 'Joshua the High Priest and the Interpretation of Zechariah 3', *CBQ* 53 (1991), pp. 553-70.

—'Messianism in the Scrolls', in Ulrich and VanderKam (eds.), *Notre Dame Symposium*, pp. 211-34.

Van der Spek, R.J., 'Cyrus de Pers in Assyrisch perspectief', *TG* 96 (1983), pp. 1-27.

Van der Woude, Adam Simon, 'Die beiden Söhne des Öls (Sach 4:14): Messianische Gestalten?', in Heerma van Vos, Houwink ten Cate and Van Uchelen (eds.), *Travels*, pp. 262-68.

—*Haggai–Maleachi* (POT; Nijkerk: Callenbach, 1982).

—*Zacharia* (POT; Nijkerk: Callenbach, 1984).

—'Serubbabel und die messianischen Erwartungen des Propheten Sacharja', in Kaiser (ed.), *Lebendige Forschung*, pp. 138-56.

—'Zion as Primeval Stone in Zechariah 3 and 4', in Claassen (ed.), *Text and Context*, pp. 237-48.

Van der Woude, Adam Simon (ed.), *Bijbels handboek. IIa. Het Oude Testament* (Kampen: Kok, 1982); ET *The World of the Old Testament* (Bible Handbook, 2; Grand Rapids: Eerdmans, 1989).

Van Hoonacker, A., *Les Douze Petits Prophètes traduits et commentés* (EBib; Paris: Gabalda, 1908).

Von Voigtlander, Elizabeth N., *The Bisitun Inscription of Darius the Great: Babylonian Version* (Corpus Inscriptionum Iranicarum; Part I, Inscriptions of Ancient Iran; II. The Babylonian Versions of the Achaemenian Inscriptions; Texts 1; London: Lund Humphries, 1978).

Vermeylen, J. (ed.), *The Book of Isaiah—Le livre d'Isaïe. Les oracles et leurs relectures: Unité et complexité de l'ouvrage* (BETL, 81; Leuven: University Press and Uitgeverij Peeters, 1989).

Von Rad, Gerhard, *Das Erste Buch Mose* (ATD, 2-4; Göttingen: Vandenhoeck & Ruprecht, 5th edn, 1958); ET *Genesis: A Commentary* (OTL; London: SCM Press, 1972).

Wagner, S., 'בנה', *ThWAT*, I, cols. 689-706.

Wallis, G., 'Erwägungen zu Sach 6, 9-15', in *Congress Volume Uppsala 1971* (VTSup, 22; Leiden: E.J. Brill, 1972), pp. 232-37.

Waltke, B., and O'Connor, M., *An Introduction to Biblical Hebrew Syntax* (Winona Lake, IN: Eisenbrauns, 1990).

Wanke, Gunther, *Jeremia. I. Jeremia 1,1–25,14* (ZBAT, 20.1; Zürich: Theologische Verlag, 1995).

Ward, James M., *Thus Says the Lord: The Message of the Prophets* (Nashville: Abingdon Press, 1991).

Waterman, Leroy, 'The Camouflaged Purge of the Three Messianic Conspirators', *JNES* 13 (1954), pp. 73-78.

Watts, James W., and Paul R. House (eds.), *Forming Prophetic Literature: Essays on Isaiah and the Twelve in Honor of John D.W. Watts* (JSOTSup, 235; Sheffield: JSOT Press, 1996).

Weippert, Helga, 'Siegel mit Mondsichelstandarten aus Palästina', *BN* 5 (1978), pp. 43-58.

Weiser, Artur, *Die Psalmen: Übersetzt und erklärt* (ATD, 14; Göttingen: Vandenhoeck & Ruprecht, 1950); ET *The Psalms: A Commentary* (OTL; London: SCM Press, 1962).

—*Das Buch Jeremia* (ATD, 20/21; Göttingen: Vandenhoeck & Ruprecht, 1981).

Welch, Adam C., 'Zechariah's Vision of the Lampstand', *ExTim* 29 (1917–18), pp. 239-40.

Wellhausen, J., *Die kleinen Propheten übersetzt und erklärt* (Berlin: Reimer, 3rd edn, 1898).

Welten, P., 'Siegel und Stempel', *BRL²*, pp. 299-307.

Wenham, Gordon, *Genesis 16–50* (WBC, 2; Dallas: Word Books, 1994).

Westermann, Claus, *Genesis. III. Teilband Genesis 37–50* (BKAT, 1.3; Neukirchen–Vluyn: Neukirchener Verlag, 1982); ET *Genesis 37–50: A Commentary* (Minneapolis: Augsburg, 1986).

Widengren, Georges, 'The Persian Period', in Hayes and Miller (eds.), *History*, pp. 489-538.

Wildberger, Hans, *Jesaja 1–12* (BKAT, 10.1; Neukirchen–Vluyn: Neukirchener Verlag, 1972); ET *Isaiah 1–12: A Commentary* (Minneapolis: Fortress Press, 1991).

Williamson, H.G.M., 'Eschatology in Chronicles', *TynBul* 28 (1977), pp. 115-54.

—*1 and 2 Chronicles* (NCB; Grand Rapids: Eerdmans; London: Marshall, Morgan & Scott, 1982).

—*Ezra, Nehemiah* (WBC, 16; Waco, TX: Word Books, 1985).

—'The Governors of Judah under the Persians', *TynBul* 39 (1988), pp. 59-82.

—'Ezra and Nehemiah in the Light of the Texts from Persepolis', *BBR* 1 (1991), pp. 41-61.

—'Persian Administration', *ABD*, V, pp. 81-86.

—'Messianic Texts in Isaiah 1–39', in Day (ed.), *King and Messiah*, pp. 238-70.

Wolff, H.W., *Hosea* (BKAT, 14.1; Neukirchen–Vluyn: Neukirchener Verlag, 2nd edn, 1965).

—*Dodekapropheton. VI. Haggai* (BKAT, 14.6; Neukirchen–Vluyn: Neukirchener Verlag, 1986).

Wright, N.T., *Christian Origins and the Question of God*. I. *The New Testament and the People of God* (London: SPCK; Minneapolis: Fortress Press, 1992).

—*Christian Origins and the Question of God*. II. *Jesus and the Victory of God* (London: SPCK, 1996).

Younger, K. Lawson, Jr, 'The Phoenician Inscription of Azatiwada: An Integrated Reading', *JSS* 43 (1998), pp. 11-47.

Zaharopoulos, Dimitri Z., *Theodore of Mopsuestia on the Bible: A Study of his Old Testament Exegesis* (Theological Inquiries; New York: Paulist Press, 1989).

Zimmerli, W., *Ezechiel*. I. *Ezechiel 1–24*. II. *Teilband: Ezechiel 25–48* (BKAT, 13.1-2; Neukirchen–Vluyn: Neukirchener Verlag, 1969).

# INDEXES

## INDEX OF REFERENCES

### BIBLE

OTHER ANCIENT REFERENCES

# JOURNAL FOR THE STUDY OF THE OLD TESTAMENT
## SUPPLEMENT SERIES